Contours of English and English Language Studies

Edited by

MICHAEL ADAMS

ANNE CURZAN

Ann Arbor
UNIVERSITY OF MICHIGAN PRESS

Published in the United States of America
The University of Michigan Press
Manufactured in the United States of America

∞ Printed on acid-free paper

ISBN-13: 978-0-472-03466-6

2014 2013 2012 2011 4 3 2 1

CONTENTS

INTRODUCTION
MICHAEL ADAMS AND ANNE CURZAN 1

PART I. AMERICAN DIALECTS 11

1. Michigander Talk: God's Own English 17
DENNIS R. PRESTON

2. The African American English Canon in Sociolinguistics 34
WALT WOLFRAM

3. The Beholder's Eye: Using Self-Organizing Maps to Understand American Dialects 53
WILLIAM A. KRETZSCHMAR, JR.

Response:
4. To Continue Moving Forward in English Language and Linguistics Research in the Twenty-First Century 71
SONJA J. LANEHART

PART II. HISTORY OF THE ENGLISH LANGUAGE 82

5. Benjamin Smart and Michael Faraday: The Principles and Practices of "Talking Proper" in Nineteenth-Century England 87
LYNDA MUGGLESTONE

6. The Etymology of the Word *Wife* 108
ANATOLY LIBERMAN

7. English into Asia: From Singaporean Ubiquity to Chinese Learners' Features 135
EDGAR W. SCHNEIDER

Response:
8. History of the English Language in the English Department: Past and Present 157
COLETTE MOORE

PART III. ENGLISH LEXICOGRAPHY 168

9. New Suckers from the Old Root 173
JOAN HOUSTON HALL

10. How Quotation Paragraphs in Historical Dictionaries Work: *The Oxford English Dictionary* 191
JESSE SHEIDLOWER

11. The Core or the Periphery? The Lack of a *Dictionary of Irish English on Historical Principles* 213
MICHAEL B. MONTGOMERY

Response:
12. Embracing the Digital Siren: Collaborative Lexicography in the Twenty-First Century 237
MARSHA L. DUTTON

PART IV. ENGLISH LANGUAGE STUDIES AND EDUCATION 249

13. African American Language and Education: How Far Have We Come? 254
GENEVA SMITHERMAN AND MINNIE QUARTEY-ANNAN

14. Language and Education: The More Things Change 278
DENNIS BARON

15. Written Language in Use: An Essay on Returning Language to Writing Studies 298
AMY J. DEVITT

Response:
16. Watch the Language: Scholarship, Teaching, and Change 315
SUSANMARIE HARRINGTON

REFERENCES 325

CONTRIBUTORS 363

INDEX 368

INTRODUCTION

Today, most people think of language study as the business of linguistics departments, and many linguists are happy to promote the association; in fact, however, a considerable proportion of scholarship about the English language comes out of English departments. In Europe, linguists are often housed in English departments, and, because of graduate programs focused on English Language Studies, as well as undergraduate language tracks, some American university English departments also include members trained at least partly in linguistics, but who may write from disciplinary traditions and for disciplinary purposes often distinct from those of linguists. This interdisciplinary enterprise leads to a productive synthesis of research aims and methods and teaching interests among scholars in the field of English Language Studies.

Contours of English assesses the state of English Language Studies, a thriving discipline located primarily in English departments and English curricula, at the beginning of the twenty-first century. Chapter by chapter, it is a book about aspects of English — aspects which, in their own right, will fascinate readers of various disciplines, not only English and linguistics, but also American culture, history, sociology, education, and information sciences. Section by section and as a whole, the book considers ways in which the study of English language intersects with other concerns of the English curriculum (i.e., teaching and research in Anglophone literature and culture) as well as related public discourses and policy interventions. Language is very often a site where school meets world. For all of its range, though, *Contours of English* characterizes English Language Studies only partially; it is a discipline so commodious and various as to defy full description in a single book.

During the second half of the twentieth century, the contours of scholarship about the English language were redrawn dramatically. Partly this was due to the more or less simultaneous rise in the 1950s of two, sophisticated, competitive approaches to understanding language, namely sociolinguistics and Chomskyan theory (see Joseph 2002, 62–67). However, this dichotomy is somewhat of a caricature of linguistics. Many approaches to language have managed to thrive alongside generative grammar and sociolinguistics without quite achieving their prominence: Roman Jakobson's poetics, Michael Halliday's functionalism, semiotics and semiology, and corpus linguistics, Kenneth L. Pike's tagmemics, and Anna Wierzbicka's semantic primes and cross-cultural pragmatics are only a few significant exceptions from the too usual binary opposition of sociolinguistics and generative grammar.

English Language Studies has drawn from all of these frameworks while maintaining interests in philology, in particular the history of the language and the language of texts, which, through the power of computers, can be investigated more thoroughly and systematically than ever before. The rise of corpus linguistics, enabled by heavily tagged digital texts and increasingly flexible search protocols, has profoundly affected the study of language structure and style (including metrics, at one extreme, and epistolary discourse, at the other); it has also facilitated lexicography, a primary philological practice, whether adjunct to a particular text or generalized in a historical dictionary, like the *Oxford English Dictionary*.

When we were conceiving this book, it occurred to us that our purpose was embodied by a practitioner of English Language Studies we know, a mentor to both of us, and to scores of others committed professionally to the discipline, namely, Richard W. Bailey, the Fred Newton Scott Collegiate Professor of English Language and Literature emeritus at the University of Michigan. Most who work in English Language Studies have a particular interest, an expertise expressed in a subdiscipline: they are sociolinguists, or historians, or lexicographers, or they specialize in stylistics or English language pedagogy or some other subject. Bailey, on the other hand, from completion of his doctorate to the present day, has managed to contribute significantly to nearly every aspect of English Language Studies. Many who have written chapters of this book also work across subdisciplinary boundaries, but few have been as versatile or as central to defining simultaneously the breadth and focus of the field. Thus, we have taken Richard W. Bailey's career as a vehicle for describing the contours of English Language Studies across the second half of the twentieth century and into the twenty-first: it proves an invaluable guide to where we have been and where we are going.

Though not given much to Universal Grammar, or any other "lightbulb linguistics" (Adams and Bailey 2009, 357–359), Bailey has practiced nearly every discipline that might be considered sociolinguistics (see Preston 2004, 140–141), while idiosyncratically pushing disciplinary boundaries. He started in stylistics. His dissertation contrasted *The Public and Private Styles of the Earl of Chesterfield* (1965). From 1967–1969, he contributed annual bibliographies of stylistics to the new journal *Style* and served as a bibliographer interested in English Language Studies for the *MLA Bibliography*. From the outset, he was dedicated to sharing what he learned, a personal characteristic that has, we believe, become a disciplinary characteristic, partly because of his example. He edited, with Delores M. Burton, *English Stylistics: A Bibliography* (1968), as well as *An Annotated Bibliography of Statistical Stylistics* (1968) and the collection, *Statistics and Style* (1969), both with Lubomír Doležel. The 1960s weren't the end of Bailey's interest in stylistics (for instance, he published "The Future of Computational Stylistics" [1979] and "Determining Authorship in Ancient Greek" [1980a] considerably later, and, broadly, style is an issue in his books on the history of English), but they do comprise his focused attention to it.

It is worth pausing here to consider a remarkable characteristic of Bailey's work: he was, from the earliest possible days, alive to the value of new technology to the study of English language and literature and a leader in computer applications in English Language Studies. His bibliography with Doležel included a section on "Stylistics and the Computer" (1969, 80–87). Subsequently, he co-edited *The Computer and Literary Studies* (1973) and also edited *Computing in the Humanities* (1982). When, in the late 1960s, the Early Modern English Dictionary project was re-established, after a quarter century in cold storage, Bailey reinvigorated the project with statistical and automated methods, which resulted in *Michigan Early Modern English Materials* (1975). Though the Early Modern English Dictionary remains incomplete (in fact, barely started), Bailey's work significantly influenced other dictionary projects, including the *Dictionary of the Older Scottish Tongue* and the *Dictionary of American Regional English*, but especially the *Dictionary of Old English* (see Adams 2009, 2010). With Anne Curzan (Bailey and Curzan 1997), he was quick to engage in application of corpus linguistics to historical texts, and, as one of the editors of *A London Provisioner's Chronicle, 1550–1563, by Henry Machyn* (Bailey, Miller, and Moore 2006), he was among the first to prepare a hypertext edition of an Early Modern work interesting to historical sociolinguists.

Bailey's engagement with automation began long before scholars could search corpora or texts online via a personal computer—when Bailey began such work, no one had a personal computer. The revolution in English Language Studies that Richard W. Bailey led was not merely a matter of access to facts, not merely a technocratic triumph. As he wrote at the beginning of *Computing in the Humanities* (1982, 1), "Even a brief and incomplete survey of this volume suggests that the motives inspiring humanists to use a computer are by no means new, however innovative and revolutionary the machinery might be; they continue to strive for efficient use of labor, care, economy, and precision," the sorts of things towards which projects in English Language Studies, like big dictionaries, strive. But Bailey's perspective was not narrowly technical: early work on automation in language and literature, he wrote, was "conceived in the hope of multiplying the power of human imagination" (1982, 1). That is, Bailey was visioning and revisioning the role of the humanities and, within them, the role of English Language Studies. *Contours of English* is designed to extend this project of Bailey's into the new century—the computational influence is evident in the contributions by William A. Kretzschmar, Jr., Joan Hall, Jesse Sheidlower, Marsha Dutton, and Dennis Baron.

Once he had started work on the Dictionary of Early Modern English, Bailey was unable to shake the lure of lexicography. He supplemented his work on *Michigan Early Modern English Materials* (1975) with *Early Modern English: Additions and Antedatings to the Record of English Vocabulary* (1978), and, at the same time, helped to form the Dictionary Society of North America, of whose journal, *Dictionaries*, he was the first editor (1979–1989; see Bailey 2004, 161–163). He edited the foundational *Dictionaries of English: Prospects for the Record of Our Language* (1987b) and wrote a mass of material on lexicography, among other things, in *The Oxford Companion to the English Language* (1992), of which he was also associate editor. Year by year he has written articles on the history of English lexicography (1980b, 1985, 1986, 1987a, 1990a, 1996a, 2000a, 2000b), most recently the chapter on regional and national dictionaries in the *Oxford History of English Lexicography* (2009).

Dialects have been at issue in English Language Studies from the earliest times, whether measured from the earliest period studied (Toon 1983) or the earliest period of their study, for instance, in the nineteenth-century philological reconstruction of English. Bailey began with the immediate rather than the historical, in *Varieties of Present-Day English* (1973b), which he edited with Jay L. Robinson; and he expanded from America and the United Kingdom to the colonial reflexes of English in *English as a World Language* (1982), edited with Manfred Görlach. Bailey has pursued his trademark linguistic and cultural/historical research on varieties of English within the United States and around the world: Canadian English (1991), Scots (1991), English in Sri Lanka (1998), Japan (1997), China (1990b), and South Asia (1996c). These studies serve as context for another of Bailey's major articles, "American English Abroad" (2001), a chapter of *English in North America,* volume six of the Cambridge History of the English Language. He recently completed *Speaking American,* a book whose title and approach reflect Alexis de Toqueville's *Democracy in America.* It provides eight historical case studies, by half-century, that provide glimpses into how, for example, English was shaped in Boston from 1650–1700, New Orleans from 1800–1850, and Los Angeles from 1950–2000.

By the 1990s, Bailey had turned squarely to the history of English, publishing *Images of English: A Cultural History of the Language* (1991a) and *Nineteenth-Century English* (1996b), books that reflect his continuing interest in structure, style, and variation, as well as with words. In a way, these works turn Bailey's earlier approaches inside out: history had always been a background issue in his investigation of styles and dialects, though it was much more prominent in his lexicographical writing, not only because he has worked on English of early periods, but also because he is a historian of historical lexicography. Recently, he has written in a historical mode, but structure, variation, style, and the rest of his interests are all still part of the picture: Bailey's work affirms their mutual implications. He does not hesitate to take the long view, as in "A Thousand Years of the History of English" (2002b), but the historical landscape is made up of individuals like Henry Machyn, the London "provisioner," and Edward H. Rulloff, the criminal linguist whose "sinister life and celebrated death" are the subjects of *Rogue Scholar* (2003b).

Bailey has developed particularly the study of "Ideologies, Attitudes, and Perceptions" (2003a) and questioned traditional assumptions about what is at the center and what at the periphery of English (2007a). He has always focused on the real English of real speakers, whose experience of language is defined by change and so is inevitably historical: "Individuals change their languages throughout their lifetimes; adjusting to differing audiences makes our language different nearly every day from childhood to old age" (2000c, 385). As a result, understanding the history of English or any language is no easy matter: "the place to begin is not in the stolid center but at the vibrant edges of language—among the bilingual, the flouters of convention, the daring, the young—not at the middle of the road, where all the traffic flows, but on the verge, where the boundaries form and shift" (2000, 386). Bailey's history of English isn't what you'll find in textbooks, that is, until the textbooks finally catch up to Bailey and others, particularly in sociolinguistics, who investigate English on similar principles.

Bailey is indefatigably curious and certainly values knowledge for its own sake, but he also works hard to apply what he knows in the public interest. Besides being a distinguished university professor, he has also served for decades as a Trustee of Washtenaw Community College, where the library is named for him. His concern for speakers' control over their language has led to books like *Literacy for Life: The Demand for Reading and Writing* (1983), which he edited with Robin Melanie Fosheim; it also led him to testify in the Ann Arbor Black English case (see Bailey 1980c, 1981a, 1981b, and 1983). A principal justification for English Language Studies is to learn about the language from its speakers and then turn that knowledge to the benefit of those speakers, not only in greater understanding of their own social and linguistic behavior but also in more directly political and economic ways, as proposed in William Labov's Principle of Debt Incurred (1982, 172) and Walt Wolfram's Principle of Linguistic Gratuity (1993, 227). Such interventions have been distinctive features of Bailey's approach to English from his undergraduate days to the present day (Adams and Bailey 2009).

Recently, Bailey collaborated with Dennis E. Baron (who contributes to this volume) and Jeffrey P. Kaplan on an amicus brief in the Supreme Court case *District of Columbia v. Heller* (2008), a case about the District's authority to limit gun ownership rights on the basis of the Second Amendment of the Constitution. "The question, then," they advised, "is what does the specific language used in the Amendment mean? Meaning comes from the words of a text and, importantly, *how* they are used …"; they conclude, "the unmistakably military language used in the Second Amendment makes clear that what is protected is the right of the people to serve in a well regulated militia and keep arms for such service" (Baron, Bailey, and Kaplan 2009, 10), thus arguing that the Supreme Court reverse the ruling of the District of Columbia Court of Appeals. The majority of the Court disagreed with their conclusions, however, and Justice Antonin Scalia, writing the opinion for that majority, famously (at least among linguists) criticized the amicus brief on points of grammar: "A purposive qualifying phrase that contradicts the word or phrase it modifies is unknown this side of the looking glass … (except, apparently in some courses on Linguistics)" (2009, 13).

Supreme Court justices, like African American youth in Ann Arbor, Michigan, and Oakland, California, are entitled to their own discourse. And Justice Scalia's tart observation does not alter the scholar's motive to learn and then do good things with that knowledge, a motive the professor and the justice share. Bailey's career as scholar and teacher is characterized by openness, to new methods and conceptions of the discipline, of course, but also to hearing all voices raised on a given subject (Adams and Bailey 2009). In his scholarship, he quotes opinions and illustrates attitudes frequently and extensively, so that his argument is often partly an anthology of what others knew or thought they knew, know or think they know. Similarly, though he has certainly written his share of books and articles, he as frequently has collaborated and has chosen to edit an unusual number of collections and textbooks that focus and make accessible in one place the voices of many rather than the perspective of one or two.

Contours of English is offered in that collaborative spirit. The book is organized into four parts representing four particularly active and interesting fields central to English Language Studies, the discipline Richard W. Bailey has nurtured and developed so significantly. It would have been wonderful to assemble a book that mapped all aspects of the field, as represented in Bailey's career, but obviously that could not be accomplished in a single volume. The four parts in this book include American Dialects, the History of English, English Lexicography, and English and Education. Each part is structured neither miscellaneously nor as a debate, but rather as an unfolding disciplinary conversation, and includes three chapters by leading scholars in the relevant subfield marked by different perspectives, methods, and material, as well as a response to those chapters by one of Bailey's students. Part I, American Dialects, includes chapters by Walt Wolfram (North Carolina State University), Dennis R. Preston (Oklahoma State University), and William A. Kretzschmar, Jr. (University of Georgia), with a response by Sonja A. Lanehart (University of Texas, San Antonio); Part II, History of the English Language, includes chapters by Lynda Mugglestone (University of Oxford), Edgar Schneider (University of Regenstein), and Anatoly Liberman (University of Minnesota), with a response by Colette V. Moore (University of Washington); Part III, English Lexicography, includes chapters by Joan Houston Hall (*Dictionary of American Regional English*), Jesse Sheidlower (*Oxford English Dictionary*), and Michael B. Montgomery (University of South Carolina), with a response by Marsha Dutton (Ohio University); and Part IV, English Language and Education, contains chapters by Amy Devitt (University of Kansas), Dennis E. Baron (University of Illinois, Urbana-Champaign), and Geneva Smitherman and Minnie Quartey-Annan (Michigan State University), with a response by Susanmarie Harrington (University of Vermont).

The responses are significant essays in themselves, not formulaic end-pieces to the sections; they point toward the future of English Language Studies, bearing the chapters in mind. Generally, they discuss how the contributions perpetuate, extend, question, and dissent from a given subfield's traditions, assumptions, and disciplinary foundations. They engage questions about the limitations in current aims and methods that the contributions suggest as well as the research opportunities that emerge when we consider the state of current scholarship. The response essays contribute to the map of English Language Studies today by linking explicitly the contours implicit in a part's chapters and in the part taken as a whole; one might think of the chapters as "areas" and the part introductions, supplied by the editors, and responses as the "lines" that together with the areas configure the field.

All of the essays, chapters, and responses offer something new: experts in the subfields represented and scholars of English Language Studies will find them significant additions to the literature. But we have not prepared this book exclusively for experts. The authors have chosen to write about important topics and have written about them as accessibly as possible. We hope that several audiences will find the book interesting and useful, especially advanced undergraduate and graduate students, those who will reconfigure the discipline in decades to come; our colleagues in English departments, who may not have much experience of linguistics; and any in the public at large or in professions for which knowledge about English language and English Language Studies is important. All speakers of English have something at stake in the knowledge of English collected in this book and, following Richard W. Bailey's lead, we invite them all to learn from it and enjoy it. Study of the English language in all of its variety, contemporary and historical, has never been more exciting. "What a wonderful time to care about language!" Bailey (2000c, 386) has exclaimed. The editors and authors of this volume dedicated to that paragon of English Language Studies wholeheartedly share his enthusiasm.

We are indebted to many people for their help and support as this book has taken shape. We thank all the contributing authors, who have generously shared their research to make this book happen and have been admirably understanding about every logistical detail. We are grateful to the two anonymous reviewers for their valuable feedback on the full manuscript, and Laura Aull for her help with editing the book. And we feel fortunate to have had Kelly Sippell as our editor at the University of Michigan Press. The University of Michigan Press has published several of Richard W. Bailey's books, and we could not be more pleased that the Press is also publishing this volume in his honor.

MICHAEL ADAMS AND ANNE CURZAN

PART I

American Dialects

Introduction

Many speakers of English from around the world believe that some standard variety of the language (Standard American English, Standard British English) is historically, structurally, and expressively superior to all other dialects. But as Walt Wolfram (1991, 2) puts it, "Languages are invariably manifested through their dialects, and to speak a language is to speak some dialect of that language." All English speakers speak one or more dialects of English (a "home" dialect and a standard dialect, for instance), and dialects are all there is. So, dialectology, and the study of variation more broadly, is a core component of English Language Studies. Even if one prefers some standard English to other dialects, it's indisputable that the history, structure, and social value of that standard can only be understood fully in the context of English as it is actually spoken.

As early as Chaucer (in *The Reeve's Tale*), we have records of dialect consciousness and self-consciousness. Once a standard variety of British English developed in the fifteenth and sixteenth centuries—an invention for written communication, not everyday speech—many among the literate elevated the standard among dialects and began to criticize and marginalize the dialects people actually spoke. Criticism, however, wasn't inevitable: Richard Carew (1555–1620), an Early Modern proponent of the status of English among other European languages, was, according to Richard W. Bailey (1991a: 44), "the first on record to regard the diversity of English dialects as one of the ornaments of the language." However, for the past two centuries if not longer, those who have stigmatized non-standard English have had a more powerful public voice and wider audience than those who have celebrated the diversity of spoken English.

In the eighteenth and nineteenth centuries, standard English was implicated in various social and political tensions: country vs. city, craft vs. industry, county vs. nation, nation vs. empire, tradition vs. innovation, this last not quite what the twenty-first century expects, where tradition supported home dialect and innovation the educational technologies poised to erase non-standard English. The standard dialect became an instrument of social and economic mobility just when, for other reasons, new opportunities to move opened up. As the standard was associated with status, non-standard dialects were degraded socially, but they continued to thrive nonetheless. In the United States and elsewhere, the conflict between standard and non-standard plays out in everyday language attitudes, in educational expectations and classroom interaction, as well as sometimes in the media, for example after the "Ebonics Controversy" in 1996–1997.

Historically, scholarly interest in dialectology was fueled not by questions of prestige, effective pedagogy, and other social matters, but by the importance of dialects to the structural history of languages, as pursued by Rasmus Rask, Franz Bopp, Jacob and Wilhelm Grimm, and others in the early nineteenth century. Dialectology thus became a state of the art discipline, alongside and mingled with historical comparative philology and historical lexicography. Georg Wenker's early research on German dialects (*c*1870) led by example to Jules Guilléron and Edmond Edmont's *Atlas Linguistique de la France* (1902–1910) and further influenced A. J. Ellis' five-volume *On Early English Pronunciation* (1869–1889) and Joseph Wright's six-volume *English Dialect Dictionary* (1898–1905). J. A. H. Murray's *The Dialect of the Southern Counties of Scotland* (1873) was part of his intellectual equipment as chief editor of the *New English Dictionary* (now known as the *Oxford English Dictionary*); his experience as a speaker of non-standard English, as well as his scholarly interests in Scots and the Borders dialect, led him to draw dialect into the *OED* as historically essential rather than as a curiosity. Once dialectology was well established, twentieth-century scholars could refine its aims and methods, as they did in projects like the Linguistic Atlas of the United States and Canada, organized by Hans Kurath and now led by William

A. Kretzschmar, Jr.; the *Dictionary of American Regional English*, organized and first edited by F. G. Cassidy and currently led by Joan Houston Hall, who contributes to the section on lexicography; and the *Atlas of North American English* (2005), edited by William Labov, Sharon Ash, and Charles Boberg.

By the twentieth century, the importance of dialects in American English and dialectology to English Language Studies was clear, if not yet assumed. As George Hempl (1904, xxxvii–xxxviii), once professor of English at the University of Michigan, explained in his Presidential Address to the Modern Language Association (1903):

> No fact in linguistics is better established than the fact of the instability of speech. But it is not only constantly changing, it changes more rapidly in some places and in some classes of society than in others, and it changes differently in different places and different classes of society. . . . [I]t remains true that not only is there no one established usage—there can not be any . . . If we had to deal with a very small area and with people living practically the same life, we might have a certain uniformity of speech usage. But when we consider the conditions under which language life normally goes on, we see that speech can not be uniform even in restricted areas. And when a language, like the English, extends over the face of the globe and is spoken in all climes, its differentiation into varieties is a matter of course.

Hempl's philosophizing about the study of English implied practical consequences, however, and he concluded (1904, xlvii), though the warning is still not generally observed, "No teacher is warranted in trying to get his pupils to speak the English of another part of the English-speaking world." While this obviously means that Americans shouldn't be taught to speak like BBC newsreaders, it may just as well mean that African American children in Los Angeles should not be forced to speak like white New Englanders. Language, manifest only in dialect, is a matter of experience, of living among people in the world. So, Hempl (1904, lii) suggested, "To understand the nature of language he [the teacher and scholar] must study it not only from books, but as a living phenomenon. He must listen to the speech around him and compare it with that of those from a distance; in other words, he must make a study of the various forms of English and strive to discover the causes of their diversities and their historical relations to one another." Principles such as this formed the purpose and guided the work of the American Dialect Society, founded in 1889 by Hempl, among others, and active in promoting dialect study and English Language studies generally to this day.

In 1903, Hempl was not speaking speculatively but from experience in the field: he conducted the first North American dialect survey on the basis of a questionnaire he circulated in 1894 (see Bailey 1992), marking out the distribution of *greasy* v. *greazy*, for instance (Hempl 1896b), and *stovepipes* v. *funnels* (Hempl 1902). According to Bailey, Hempl had an insatiable interest in gathering dialect information: "As late as 1905," Bailey (1992, 319) writes, "on the eve of his departure from Michigan, he circulated penny postcards containing questions like "26 ½ c. Do they call the leaves around an ear of Indiana *corn husks, shucks,* or *corn-trash*? Do they call the spike on which the kernels grow a *corn-cob* or a *corn-husk*? Do they use the word *pone*? If so, what does it mean?" Hempl's work seemed primitive to later American dialectologists working on the nineteenth-century European model, especially those organized and trained by Hans Kurath under the aegis of the Linguistic Atlas Project, but "pioneering" might be a more appropriate label than "primitive" (see Bailey 1992, 310–314).

Linguistic geography is still a useful technology for understanding some things about dialects, but maps are inadequate descriptions of dialectal features: one can map only a few features at a time, in two dimensions, and the features are necessarily regional rather than social, even though linguists long ago noticed that dialect "covers" social as well as regional spaces. John E. Joseph (2002, 122–125) attributes this insight to Raven I. McDavid, Kurath's successor and Kretzschmar's predecessor on the Linguistic Atlas Project, though we have seen that Hempl anticipated McDavid, at least in general terms.

But linguistic geography has severe limitations: it is more or less impossible to imagine a map that would allow us to distinguish and contrast dialect characteristics simultaneously over geographical space, social context, and time—that is, a map that could account for the interaction of these factors in everyday speech, the real speech of real people.

This impossible map suggests something of the challenges dialectology confronts in the twenty-first century. Now, add another dimension to the impossible map: speakers' perceptions of dialects—that is, data about what people think about the language they speak. The linguist most responsible for defining and practicing this subfield of sociolinguistics, Dennis Preston, who contributes to this section, famously distributes maps to speakers in a range of formal and informal venues to gauge their perception of dialects. Preston's and others' findings provide important clues about why non-standard dialects flourish side by side with the supposed standard variety.

Even if we were able to map all data of all dialects and perceptions of dialect into the same multidimensional matrix, we nonetheless would have to admit the map's limitations, for, as James W. Marchand (1973, 122) has observed, "Most temporal and geographical divisions of language are ideal types and are not amenable to treatment as definable categories." William A. Kretzschmar, Jr., elaborates on this observation, laying out conceptual problems attending dialect and dialectology in his contribution to this section. And in his contribution, Walt Wolfram argues that we are tempted to idealize types of social variation, yet dialect is a moving target of systematic investigation:

> Even as some traditional American dialects recede, new ones appear, reflecting the changing dynamics of American demography and social structure. But the present contours are deeply embedded in the historical origins of American English, and future developments will no doubt take their cues from the present dialect profile. Dialects mark the regional and cultural cartography of America as much as any cultural artifact, and there is no reason to expect that they will surrender their emblematic role in American life in the future. (Wolfram and Ward 2006, 6)

As all of the contributions to this section, including Sonja Lanehart's response, make clear, dialect study and English Language Studies generally are on the edge of an era of shifting assumptions and new approaches. Dialects other than the standard variety, so often located on the periphery of English (or any other language), are actually at the center (see Bailey 2002b). And although dialectology is not the origin of historical lexicography or English language pedagogy, it is fundamental to both, as Joan Hall, Michael Montgomery, Dennis Baron, and Geneva Smitherman and Minnie Quartey-Annan prove in their contributions to this volume. As a result, American dialectology seems a fitting place to start our account of the challenges that English Language Studies face as the discipline passes from the last century into the new one.

1

Michigander Talk: God's Own English

DENNIS R. PRESTON
Oklahoma State University

In 1973 Richard W. Bailey confessed:

> The elite suburb of Detroit in which I grew up thrived on a certain smugness about its place in American life. My eleventh-grade class, I recall, was told of its good fortune because—unlike others—no one in the room spoke a "dialect." The teacher's celebration of our language was, after all, what we knew already from years of perfunctory attention to usage exercises. We would nearly always fill the blank with the "correct" verb form or pronoun from our own speech habits and could therefore ignore the general principle to which others would have to appeal in such circumstances. The rule and exercises, we believed, were designed to aid the unfortunate "dialect" speaker in altering his [sic] speech to make it conform to our own. (1973b, 385–86, quotation marks in the original)

Unlike many Michigan speakers, however, Bailey (1973b, 386) soon had an insightful experience.

> Later on, in a New England college, I was shocked out of this pharisaical complacency by being told that I would have to accept the ministrations of a speech correctionist if I wanted to pass a course in public speaking. My "Midwestern" dialect, the teacher said, would distract listeners from what I had to say. (quotation marks in the original)

Research done years after Bailey's high school days has confirmed his account of Michigander language beliefs, but not just for residents of the elite Detroit suburb he called his boyhood home.

Although I had begun a program of research on the perception of dialects in Hawai'i in 1980, the academic merry-go-round brought me to Michigan in 1983, and I soon learned the local myth of the correctness or normalcy of Michigan English. In what follows, my small attempt to help celebrate Bailey's career (and his long-lost adolescent linguistic security), I report on a number of approaches to teasing out the regard for local language among Michiganders and, necessarily, their regard for other varieties as well, for the concepts "normal" and "correct" would be empty without their foils. Although I have reported elsewhere on the details of perceptions of language and language variety, including those from southeastern Michigan (e.g., Preston 1996), I hope here to take a more comprehensive look at Michigan data and to update some findings from the 1980s. I hope that readers who care little about Michigan will nevertheless find in this survey methods of collection, representation, and interpretation that might serve them well in the investigation of areas they personally deem more interesting or even in consideration of the role of language attitudes in public and educational settings.

I begin this survey by attending to the most global and general accounts investigated in a perceptual approach and proceed to varieties of research that try to elicit responses to specific elements, particularly those of a phonological nature.

The first technique I used in what has come to be known as *perceptual dialectology* was one in which respondents were asked to outline, on a blank map of some territory, where they believe language differences exist and to label the kind of speech those areas supported. This outlining of distinct areas by laypersons was borrowed from the practice of cultural geographers known as *mental mapping* (e.g., Gould and White

1974). When Michiganders carry out such a task on a map of the entire U.S., results like Figures 1 through 4 emerge.

Although my entire collection of Michigan hand-drawn maps shows considerable diversity in the details, the four shown here are by no means idiosyncratic. They all, as many of the others do, show the local regard for Michigan as the homeland, in some cases the unique one, of *normal* and *correct* American English. They also point to Michiganders' lack of respect for the English in other areas—Nevadans' speech reflects their *snobbishness* (due to *money*), California has speech that is perhaps too relaxed (*beech talk* [sic] or *valley girl*); Texans have a *dralw* [sic] and Southerners a *draw* [sic]; Southerners and Appalachians have a *hillbilly accent*; New Yorkers speak *slang*, and nearby New Jerseyites *Draw Words Out*; Western farmers are *slow*, and even these labels are not as insultingly direct as some others I could have shown: one notes that the entire southeast is *Southern: the worst English in American* [sic] and that in New Jersey they *Twist words in mouth*.

These hand-drawn maps suggested, however, more than a little naïveté on my part. I had hoped, as a dialectologist, to compare and contrast where nonlinguists and dialectologists believed dialect boundaries to be. I had failed to foresee that, although dialectologists plot speech differences exclusively on the basis of linguistic features, laypersons might bring concerns other than actual linguistic ones into play. These maps suggest that pre-(and pro-)scription may be playing a very important role in where boundaries are drawn and that the judgments about variety might be based on regional caricatures that were not always directly connected to speech differences.

I was not just naïve about laypersons' views of language variety; I also overlooked the principal findings of the research program known as the *social psychology of language* (or, more simply, *language attitude* study). I should have assumed from the very beginning that laypersons' perceptions of regional language variety would not be simple reflections of their correlations of linguistic features and geographical space, and, as Figures 1 through 4 show, they very clearly were not. Regional identification seemed to rely to a great extent on where respondents believed "correct" or "good" English was spoken and, perhaps secondarily, on where they believed "likeable" or "friendly" speech (or persons) could

FIGURE 1. A Hand-Drawn Map of U.S. Speech Regions by an 18-Year-Old African American Female Michigan College Student

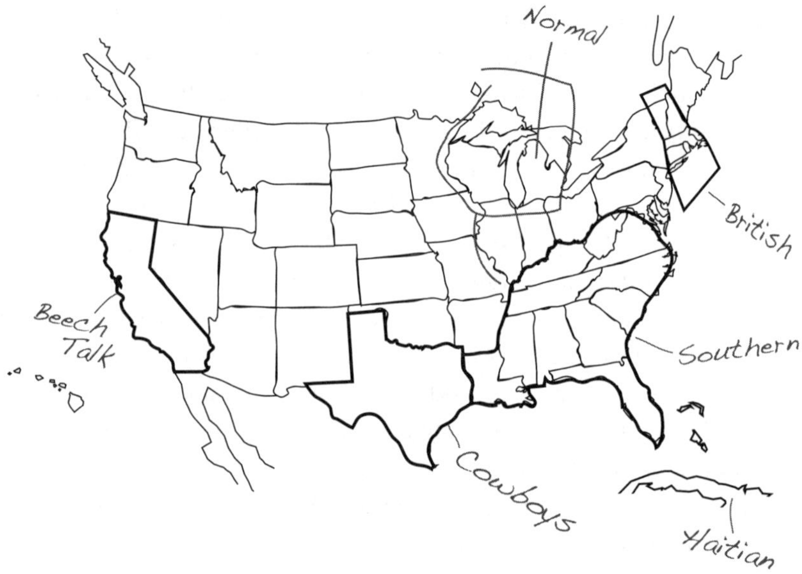

FIGURE 2. A Hand-Drawn Map of U.S. Speech Regions by a 19-Year-Old European American Female Michigan College Student

FIGURE 3. A Hand-Drawn Map of U.S. Speech Regions by a 19-Year-Old European American Male Michigan College Student

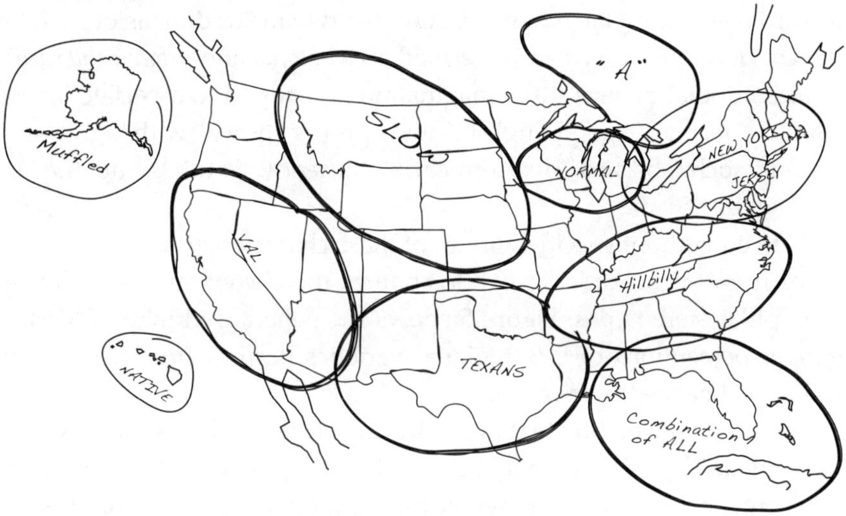

FIGURE 4. A Hand-Drawn Map of U.S. Speech Regions by an 18-Year-Old European American Female Michigan College Student

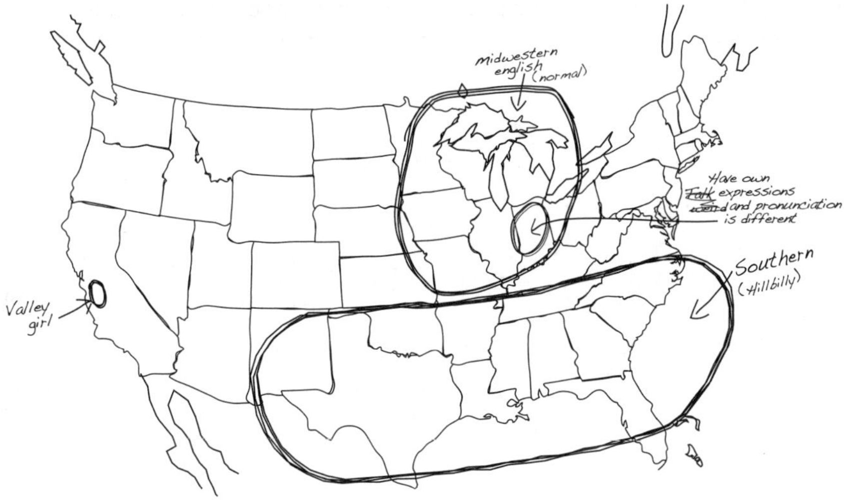

be found. That was hardly a surprising finding since it was the conclusion of years of work by students of attitude. Ryan, Giles, and Sebastian (1982, 8) put it succinctly: "With regard to the structure of attitudes toward contrasting language varieties, the two major dimensions along which views can vary can be termed *social status* and *group solidarity*" (italics mine). I believe little imagination is required to associate labels such as "normal," "good English," and "proper speech" with higher status and such labels as "down-to-earth," "friendly," and "sympathetic" with solidarity.

Even without specific pursuit of these characteristics, hand-drawn maps from Michiganders serve to confirm this dichotomy by referring to popular stereotypes. Figure 5 shows the generalized map of Michigander perceptions of U.S. regional varieties derived from nearly 150 individual hand-drawn maps.

Some confirmation that the caricature of status plays a primary role in regional identification may be found in the numbers of respondents who drew certain areas, shown at the right-hand side of Figure 5. The most striking figure is that, of the 147 respondents who completed this task, 138 (0.94) outlined a U.S. South (Area 1 in Figure 5). This is even more striking when compared with the second most frequently outlined

FIGURE 5. A Generalized Map of U.S. Regional Varieties, Computer-Derived from the Hand-Drawn Maps of 147 Southeastern Michiganders (Preston 1996:305)

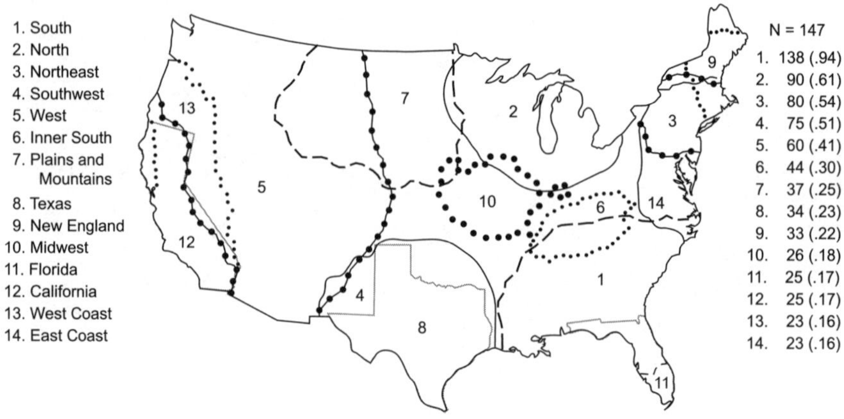

region, the respondents' own, a "Great Lakes North" (Area 2 in Figure 5), drawn by only 90 (0.61) persons. The New York City area (Area 3 in Figure 5) came in third with 80 persons (0.54) outlining it. The role of status seems clearly indicated by salience here; the South and New York City are the centers of "bad English" in the U.S., and the Great Lakes North (with Michigan at its core) is the home of "good English." The "good" and "bad" areas were outlined most frequently.

What continuing evidence do we have that the South and New York City are less well-regarded varieties of U. S. English? There is very recent evidence indeed. In a 2007 interview, the American Republican political pollster Frank Luntz was asked about the attractiveness of presidential hopeful Mitt Romney, a former governor of Massachusetts but the son of a Michigan family (in fact, the son of former Michigan governor and industrialist, George Romney). Here's what Luntz had to say:

> Let's start with his visual appeal. You put his photograph up against all the other potential candidates, and people say that he looks the most presidential; he looks charismatic, and then when the people hear him speak, they appreciate his tone—his uh lack of any kind of accent. He comes from the Midwest, and so you don't hear anything of New York or the South in him. (BBC Radio 4 "Today")

It would seem then that in 2007 the same areas are being singled out for distinctiveness as those drawn by the Michigander respondents in the mid 1980s. Except for the labels on the maps, however, how can we be sure that we are dealing with what the social psychologists of language call "status"? Perhaps the many Michiganders who identified local speech as "normal" have solidarity rather than status in mind. To make sure of the status interpretation, I borrowed another technique from cultural geographers, one in which pre-established areas are rated for some characteristic (e.g., desirability of residence, Gould and White 1974). In this task, I asked Michiganders to rate the fifty U.S. states, New York City, and Washington, D.C. on a scale of "correctness" (a more lay-friendly term for "status") and "pleasantness" ("solidarity"). The results for correctness are shown in Figure 6.

Figure 6 clearly shows that Michiganders consider themselves uniquely at the top of the heap. Michigan is the only area given a rating in the 8.00 range, confirming that Bailey's 1950s experience lasted at least into the 1980s and that Michiganders of lower status backgrounds than his were equally convinced, since the sample for this map included relatively equal numbers of respondents from lower working, working, lower middle, and middle classes, and statistical tests revealed no differences between them (Preston 1996). This map also confirms their low regard, at least for "correctness," for New York City and the South. Most of the U.S. South scores in the "4.00" range (Alabama in the "3.00" range); New York City and nearby New Jersey are the only areas outside the South that are rated in the "4.00" range.

Will Michiganders' language attitudes look the same twenty years later? Surely more than two decades of greater media exposure to regional varieties, particularly their use by obviously well-educated speakers, and perhaps some growing sense that severely downgrading the speech of others might not be the nicest thing one could do will have ameliorated these harsh views. Figure 7 shows the results of this same "correctness" task, this time given to Michigan residents who were undergraduate students at a large public university in Michigan.

This map shows that prejudice against the South and perception of Michigan as the site where the most correct English is spoken have not changed in twenty years. In fact, Figure 7 shows a harsher ranking for many areas. In the '85–87 data, only Alabama earned a 3.00; in the '06–07 data, the zone of 3.00 for southern incorrectness has been extended to Kentucky, Tennessee, Mississippi, Arkansas, Louisiana, and Texas, and the lower scores for Virginia, South Carolina, and Oklahoma are doubtless indicative of this trend. It is not just the South, however, that suffers in this score-lowering trend. In the '85–87 data, Michiganders allow nine areas a 7.00 rating, one almost as high as the home favorite (Washington, Colorado, Minnesota, Wisconsin, Illinois, Ohio, Pennsylvania, Connecticut, and Washington, DC). In the '06-07 data, this list is cut to four: Washington, Ohio, Connecticut, and Washington, DC. The most obvious pruning has been of neighbors. The plains and mountain West was rated the same as the West coast in the '85–87 task (6.00); it has now been demoted to 5.00. The only amelioration is of New York City and New Jersey; both earned 4.00 scores in the '85–87 study, and both improved to 5.00 in '06–07. The negative media portrayal of New York City speech is still common, however, and one might possibly suggest that the harshness of the earlier treatment was somewhat ameliorated

FIGURE 6. Southeastern Michigander Ratings for the 52 States, New York City, and Washington, DC, for Language "Correctness," Where 1 = "Least Correct" and 10 = "Most Correct" (Preston 1996:312; Data Collected 1985–87)

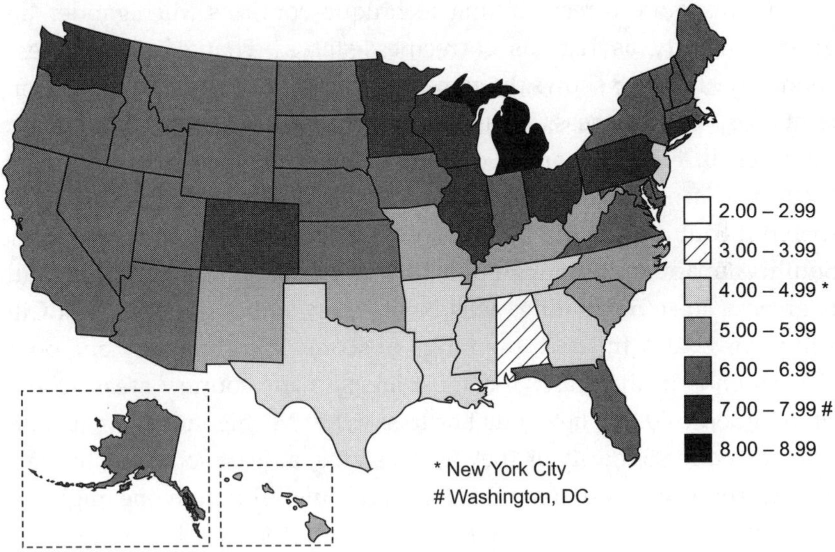

FIGURE 7. Michigan University Student Ratings for the 52 States, New York City, and Washington, DC, for Language "Correctness," Where 1 = "Least Correct" and 10 = "Most Correct" (Data Collected 2006–07)

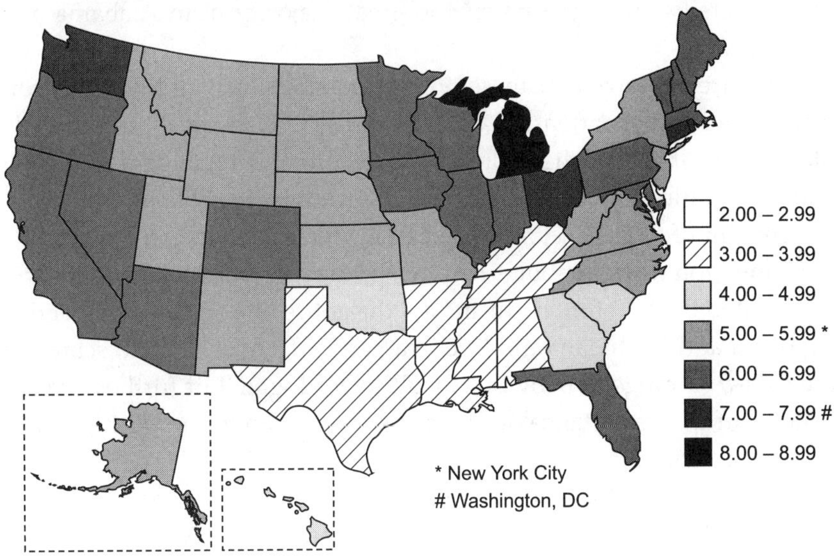

by the sympathy extended to New Yorkers after the 9/11 World Trade Center attack, although it is strange to find this weakening here with regard to correctness; one might have expected it to be more noticeable in measures of solidarity.

If this more direct ranking technique confirms Michigander linguistic security as regards correctness-status, what of pleasantness-solidarity? Figure 8 shows the same task carried out by the same respondents for "pleasantness." This is a very different representation from that seen in Figures 6 and 7. First, and perhaps most important here, Michigan is no longer uniquely correct and allows four other areas to join it (but only at the 7.00 level). Similarly, it is not as harsh on the South; Alabama improves from a 3.00 to a 4.00, and most of the South is given a so-so 5.00 rating, as is New Jersey, although New York City still earns a 4.00. In short, the range of scores is curtailed by one point at both ends of the scale, and most areas of the country areas score a pretty good 6.00. I believe it is fair to say that Michiganders are just not as invested in solidarity as they are in status, at least so far as language is concerned, and perhaps this is a general rule. Although one might not be particularly invested in *either* (apparently the case in Oregon, e.g., Hartley 1999), one apparently may not be heavily invested in *both*. To make that point more strongly, I will depart from Michigan data briefly to give an example of an area more certainly invested in solidarity. Figure 9 shows the "pleasantness" task as carried out by a sample of Southern university undergraduates, the great majority from Alabama and Georgia.

Figure 9 shows that these Southerners outdo even Michigan correctness with their attention to pleasantness. Alabama is as uniquely pleasant for them as Michigan was correct for Michiganders, and their harshness ratings for some Northern speech hits a very low point in the assignment of a mean score in the 2.00–2.99 range for New Jersey. I will not show you the map, but when this group of Auburn University students rated the U.S. for "correctness," the entire line of states connecting Alabama and Michigan (and Michigan and Alabama as well) scored in the 5.00–5.99 range, an obvious insult to Michigan, but further proof, I believe, of the importance of the status dimension to the Michiganders and the solidarity one to the Southerners. One might even speculate that the preferences on these two dimensions might relate to social practices other than language; Southerners, for example, are known for "hospital-

FIGURE 8. Southeastern Michigander Ratings for the 52 States, New York City, and Washington, DC, for Language "Pleasantness," Where 1 = "Least Pleasant" and 10 = "Most Pleasant" (Preston 1996:316; Data Collected 1985–87)

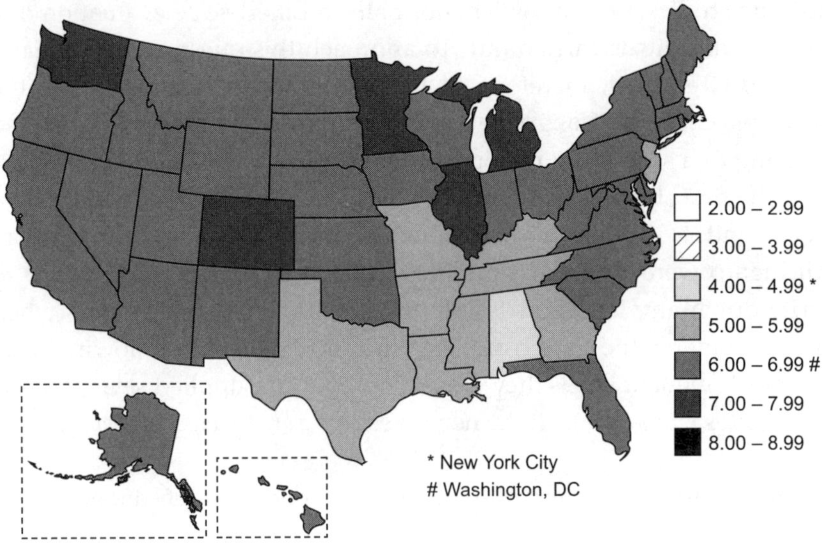

FIGURE 9. Southern University Undergraduate Ratings for the 52 States, New York City, and Washington, DC, for Language "Pleasantness," Where 1 = "Least Pleasant" and 10 = "Most Pleasant" (Preston 1996:317)

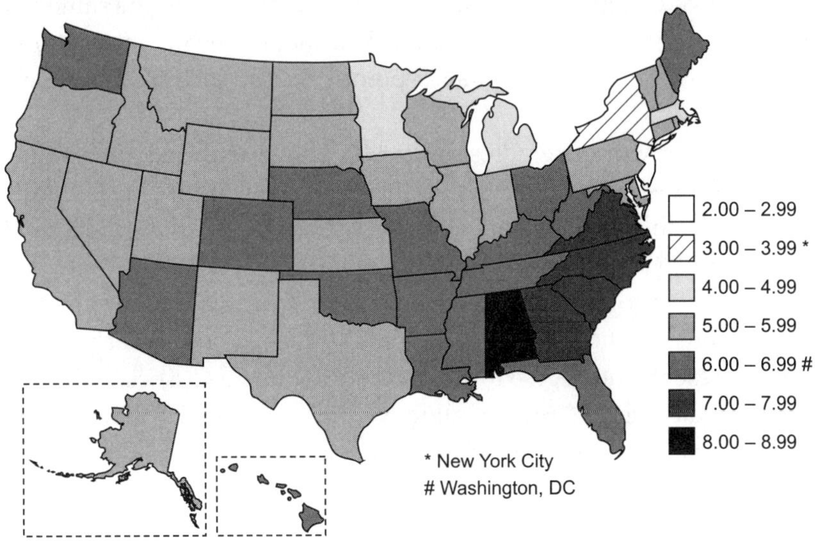

ity," and northerners, especially urban ones, are caricatured as brusque and cold, but we are moving away from language in such speculation.

One might reasonably argue that in asking for ratings of "correctness" and "pleasantness" I have caricatured the methods of language attitude studies, ones in which, normally, a Likert-scale evaluation of a number of traits is carried out. To approach this question with greater finesse, I returned, therefore, to the time-honored procedures of the social psychology of language (e.g., Shuy and Fasold 1973) but persisted in using as a stimulus a regional identification rather than a voice sample. The first step in such work is to derive the labels from local respondents, and, to accomplish this, undergraduate students (again all from Michigan) were shown a simplified version of Figure 5 and asked to write down any labels or descriptions that entered their minds when they considered the speech of these various regions. The following were the most frequent labels they offered (although I supplied several of the "opposites," including all the negatives of *nasal*, *drawl*, and *twang*):[1]

slow — fast	formal — casual	educated — uneducated
smart — dumb	polite — rude	snobbish — down-to-earth
nasal — not nasal	normal — abnormal	friendly — unfriendly
drawl — no drawl	twang — no twang	bad English — good English

I then showed another set of similar respondents (N=85) the same map I had used to elicit these labels and asked them to evaluate each of the regions shown in Figure 5 on a six-point scale for each of these twelve traits.

In earlier work (e.g., Preston 1999b), I have analyzed the results of this task for respondent reaction to the North and South (Areas 2 and 1, respectively, in Figure 5); here I add New York City (Area 3 in Figure 5) for a fuller consideration of Michigander characterizations of these three areas. Table 1 shows the means scores of those attributes for which the ratings were significantly different for all three regions. In each case the score represents the degree to which the respondents associate the attribute with the region (1=not at all to 6=very strongly). I will not outline the statistical details here except to note that all 12 attributes differed (in

TABLE 1. Attributes Rated Significantly Different for All Three Regions

Attribute/Region	South	North	New York City
Normal	3.22	4.94	3.73
Good English	2.86	4.41	3.56
No Twang	2.96	5.07	4.12
Friendly	4.58	4.00	2.47

an Anova test) at the level p=0.000002 or less and that the differences reported in these tables are the results of Tukey post-hoc comparisons.

For the first three of these (Normal, Good English, No Twang), the North is rated highest and the South lowest with New York City in a middle position. These are factors one would associate with the high linguistic security the previously outlined work suggests. On the last factor, "Friendly," however, the South scores better than even the North, and New York City scores considerably worse. What we see here is that the category "Pleasant," used in the state-ranking task (Figure 8), was perhaps too gross or not the home-grown terminology needed to elicit from Michiganders this preference for the friendly quality of Southern voices. Table 2 shows those attributes that were not significantly different for the North and New York City but were for the South.

Northerners share with New Yorkers the traits of "Fast," "Smart," and "No Drawl." Although none is as explicit as "Good English," "No

TABLE 2. Attributes Rated Significantly Different for the South but the Same for the North and New York City

Attribute/Region	South	North	New York City
Fast	2.42	4.12	4.21
Smart	3.04	4.53	4.19
No Drawl	2.22	5.11	4.81
Casual	4.66	3.53	3.38

Drawl" is presumably a trait Michiganders think well of and there is little doubt that "Smart" is positive. The South comes out ahead of both other areas in the rating for "Casual," presumably another local term that adds to the weight of the "Friendly" ranking of Table 1. Table 3 shows those attributes that single out New York City as different.

It is hardly surprising that New York City rates low for "polite": New Yorker rudeness is a common stereotype, and it is perhaps also not too surprising to find that a low rating for "Down to Earth" accompanies it. In these two features, the North raters align themselves with the South on affective dimensions. Speakers of New York City English, however, will be surprised to find that "Midwesterners" refer to them as "Nasal," since "Nasal" is a common caricature in New York City of Midwestern speakers. Table 4 shows the one attribute that isolates the North—"Educated." This continues to identify the North as the area most status-based in its evaluation, at least by these Michigan raters.

This exercise, making use of the cognitive map uncovered in the hand-drawn map task and local labels for speech varieties, begins to show a somewhat more complex picture of Michigander attitudes. Although it confirms their high opinion of their language along prestige dimensions, it also reveals a chink in the armor of Michigan linguistic

TABLE 3. Attributes Rated Significantly Different for New York City but the Same for the North and the South

Attribute/Region	South	North	New York City
Polite	4.20	4.00	2.34
Down to Earth	4.54	4.19	2.55
Not Nasal	4.09	3.94	3.02

TABLE 4. Attribute Rated Significantly Different for the North but the Same for New York City and the South

Attribute/Region	South	North	New York City
Education	3.46	4.33	3.54

security as regards certain dimensions. The South is friendlier and more casual than the North and equally "Down to Earth" and "Polite." Is there any way to tease out Michigander insecurity on the prestige dimension?

In Labov (1966) a method for calculating linguistic insecurity was introduced in which respondents were given alternative pronunciations of a word and asked to say which was correct and whether they personally used what they considered to be the correct form. If the respondent says a form is correct and he or she uses it, they are given a score of "0"; if they say a form is correct but they use another, they are given a "1." He goes on to suggest that the following score ranges be given these designations: 0=No linguistic insecurity, 1–2=Mild linguistic insecurity, 3–7=Moderate linguistic insecurity, 8–13=Heavy linguistic insecurity.

A similar test of 22 items was given to 121 undergraduate students at a large public university in Michigan. The following are three examples of the items given.

catch	A rhymes with "batch" B rhymes with "fetch"
diapers	A has three syllables — die - uh - purrs B has two syllables — die - purrs
often	A is pronounced without a "t" B is pronounced with a "t"

I will not investigate the results for individual items, but I will compare the Michigan scores with those reported by Labov for New York City (Tables 5 and 6).

The highest percentage of Labov's New York City respondents have no linguistic insecurity, and, when combined with those who show mild linguistic insecurity, they account for 63 percent of the respondents. Nearly half of the Michiganders studied had moderate linguistic insecurity and only 44.63 percent had no or mild linguistic insecurity, making Michiganders more linguistically insecure than Labov's New Yorkers.

Unlikely as these results may seem to Michiganders, I believe this little insecurity test reveals one eventual byproduct of the linguistic security seen in most of the other tests presented here that attempted to get at Michigander regard for the prestige factor of their own speech.

TABLE 5. ILI ("Index of Linguistic Insecurity") Scores for New York City Respondents (Labov 1966:334)

ILI Score	Lower Working	Upper Working	Lower Middle	Upper Middle	Total
0	44%	50%	16%	20%	36%
1–2	25%	21%	16%	70%	27%
3–7	12%	25%	58%	10%	29%
8–13	19%	04%	10%	00%	08%
N=	16	28	19	10	73

That regard in general would appear to make any investigation of items in particular even more sensitive to self-doubt. Although I do not have social status measures for my respondents, notice that Labov's most secure speakers are working class. This suggests to me that linguistic insecurity is promoted among those for whom linguistic correctness is an important concern, and all the language attitude work done in Michigan suggests that Michiganders of every social class have this concern. It should be no surprise, therefore, that their insecurity may emerge when they are tested on specific items with regard to their individual behavior. Of course, they may doubt themselves, but I suspect that they will not doubt Michigan.

TABLE 6. ILI ("Index of Linguistic Insecurity") Scores for Michigan Respondents

ILI Score	Total
0	28.10%
1–2	16.53%
3–7	49.59%
8–13	5.78%
N=	121

I believe these various approaches to Michigan attitudes towards varieties show us that just as respondents do not always speak the same way (we are all in possession of different repertoires), they also do not always have the same regard for language varieties. It would be surprising, in fact, if different contexts, different modes of presentation, different contents did not influence the way we regard language varieties just as such facts influence our choices in speaking.

What a stroke of luck for the profession that Richard W. Bailey, as a young man, was put face to face with the abominable idea that his Michigander talk was not the cat's meow of American English after all. It surely was an event that helped lead him to a career in which the respect for language varieties and the desire to instill that respect in others has been a prominent part. I am delighted to be able to offer this little piece of linguistic Michigania to help celebrate his career.

NOTE

1. I have no independent evidence that *drawl*, *twang*, and *nasal* are, in fact, pejorative and not simply descriptive. I am depending exclusively on my folk knowledge and on more extended comments on such labels from numerous interviews with folk respondents (e.g., Niedzielski and Preston 2000).

2

The African American English Canon in Sociolinguistics

WALT WOLFRAM
North Carolina State University

Introduction*

Sociolinguists have obviously performed a valuable service in establishing the linguistic integrity of African American English (AAE) and in describing its linguistic patterning and sociolinguistic status. At the same time, the tradition of study has led to a set of accepted precepts or axioms related to the sociolinguistic status of AAE. Though some of these foundational axioms may seem to be reasonable conclusions based on the research literature of AAE, there are also instances in which precedence and tradition have preempted empirical reality. I have argued elsewhere (Wolfram 2007) that sociolinguists have, in fact, unwittingly participated in the creation of a type of sociolinguistic folklore about the nature of AAE and its variation in time and place. Here, I set forth some of the central assumptions of AAE description that have evolved over almost a half-century of focused study. I examine some of the primary premises that now govern the study of and description of AAE in an attempt to distinguish empirically supported conclusions from reasonable but questionable assumptions about its nature.

The thoughtful study of AAE is of particular relevance for English language studies and the broader discipline of English. Those who study English are often bestowed special status and authority in presenting and interpreting the English language in education and in the public sector. Thus, it is essential for specialists to have an authentic understanding of the nature of AAE, its use in American society, its historical development, and its practical social and educational consequences. Furthermore, many English majors assume responsibility for teaching language in schools with linguistically diverse populations so that a genuine understanding of and appreciation for AAE has widespread implications for English language education.

The Uniformity of AAE

One of the conclusions that emerged from the first wave of AAE descriptive studies in sociolinguistics (e.g., Labov, Cohen, Robins, and Lewis 1968; Wolfram 1969; Legum, Pfaff, Tinnie, and Nichols 1971; Fasold and Wolfram 1970; Labov 1972) was the observation that a common set of structural features represents the vernacular speech of African Americans. Descriptions of morphosyntactic traits such as invariant *be* with a 'habitual' denotation (e.g., *They always be playing*), the absence of copula and auxiliary *be* (e.g., *She nice; she playing ball*), verbal *-s* (e.g., *She play_ ball*), possessive *-s* (e.g., *The man_ hat*), and plural *-s* absence (e.g., *Three dog_*) were well-documented in the vernacular speech of African Americans in the urban areas such as New York City (Labov et al. 1968; Labov 1972), Detroit (Wolfram 1969), Los Angeles (Legum et al. 1971), and Washington, DC (Fasold 1972), as were phonological features such as syllable-coda prevocalic consonant cluster reduction (e.g., *Wes' Africa*), labialization of non-initial interdental fricatives (e.g., *baf* for *bath*), and postvocalic *r*-lessness (e.g., *fea'* for *fear*). As William Labov (1972, xiii), arguably the most influential voice on the study of AAE for more than four decades, put it:

> By the "black English vernacular" we mean the relatively uniform dialect spoken by the majority of black young in most parts of the United States today, especially in the inner city areas of New York, Boston, Detroit, Philadelphia, Washington, Cleveland, Chicago, St. Louis, San Francisco, Los Angeles, and other urban centers. It is also spoken in most rural areas and used in the casual, intimate speech of many adults.

The explicit claim on the structural homogeneity of AAE rapidly became an assumed sociolinguistic position that has been perpetuated in most sociolinguistic texts since that time (e.g., Bailey and Robinson 1973b; Burling 1973; Wolfram and Fasold 1974; Rickford 1999; Green 2002; Wolfram and Schilling-Estes 2006).

Though structural features of AAE certainly appear to be shared among different communities of African Americans, there is, at the same time, considerable variability in the use of these features. For example, consider the relative incidence of third person singular *-s* absence, one of the traditionally recognized core vernacular structures of AAE, from a sample of regional settings in rural North Carolina. In Figure 1, summary statistics for *-s* absence are given for five different communities: two of them (Beech Bottom, Texana) are located in the Appalachian Mountain Range of Western North Carolina, two are on the Outer Banks (Roanoke, Hyde County) along the coast, and one is in the Coastal Plain (Princeville) region of North Carolina. The figures include third person singular *-s* absence for three different age groups of speakers in each community. Figures for Princeville are from D'Andrea (2005a), for Hyde County from Wolfram and Thomas (2002), from Roanoke Island from Carpenter (2004, 2005), from Beech Bottom from Mallinson and Wolfram (2002), and figures for Texana from Childs and Mallinson (2004) and Mallinson (2006).

Figure 1 shows that third person singular *-s* absence is highly variable in different communities and that it is quite sensitive to generational differences as well. For example, it is relatively rare—and receding—in the Appalachian African American communities but quite common in the Coastal Plain community of Princeville, with the Outer Banks com-

FIGURE 1. Comparison of *-s* Absence in Regionally Situated Communities in North Carolina

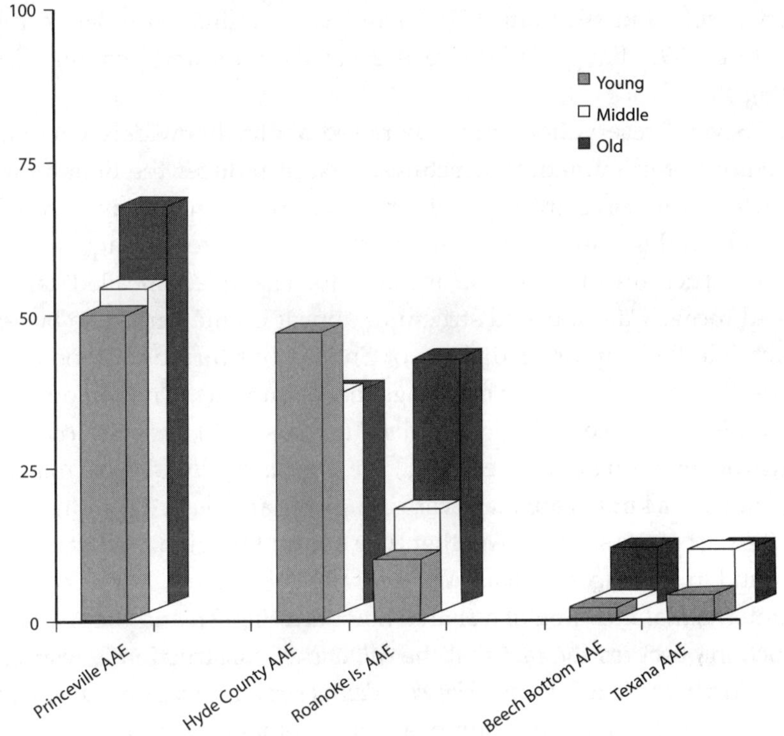

munities in between. Similar variability across these communities has been found for other "core" AAE structures such as copula absence, prevocalic cluster reduction, and postvocalic *r*-lessness (Wolfram and Carpenter 2006), suggesting that features commonly included in the inventory of AAE structures are not nearly as stable and uniform as is often assumed in traditional presentations of AAE.

The Centrality of Morphosyntax

It is commonly assumed that the vernacular core of AAE comprises an array of distinctive morphosyntactic structures that set it apart from cohort European American vernacular varieties. Most sociolinguists can readily cite the ordained list of features—habitual *be,* inflectional

-*s* absence, remote stressed *béen,* existential *they* or *it,* negative concord, *ain't,* and so forth. For four decades now, these structures have routinely been cited as foundational linguistic structures of AAE (e.g., Labov et al. 1968; Fasold and Wolfram 1970; Labov 1972; Burling 1973; Baugh 1983; Rickford 1999; Baugh 2001; Green 2002; Wolfram and Schilling-Estes 2006).

Several reservations must be raised about this widely circulated inventory of grammatical structures. First, it reduces the definition of AAE to an exclusive inventory of structures. Researchers may be content to settle on this transparent, canonized list of features and ignore more subtle structures of AAE that include, for example, so-called camouflaged forms. Camouflaged structures appear on the surface to be very much like those in other dialects of English but turn out, upon closer inspection, to have uses or meanings that are unique. One camouflaged structure is the case of 'indignant *come*' (Spears 1982), in which *come* in a construction with an *-ing* verb (e.g., *She come acting like she was real mad)* functions as a kind of auxiliary verb indicating annoyance or indignation on the part of the speaker. Another type of camouflaging (Wolfram 1995) is found in sentences such as *Walt call(s) himself dancing.* In this case, the counterfactual meaning of a shared Standard English and the AAE construction obscures the fact that the *call oneself* construction is restricted to noun phrase (e.g., *He calls himself a dancer*) or adjective phrase (e.g., *He calls himself athletic*) verbal complements in other dialects of English. In AAE, this construction extends to verb + *-ing* complements, thus setting it apart from other varieties. In this instance, a surface semantic similarity camouflages a syntactic difference, whereas the case of indignant *come* results from a surface syntactic similarity that obscures a semantic distinction.

It should be noted further that the reduction of AAE to a list of grammatical structures ignores the integrated, structural system in favor of an independent list of features. Syntacticians such as Green (2004) and Terry (2004), for example, describe AAE in terms of its overall system of tense and aspect, objecting to its definition as an unrelated list of structural traits. Is the definitional core of AAE primarily a subset of independent morphosyntactic structures or is it an overall linguistic system that encompasses the full range of language organization?

Research on perceptual cues (Graff, Labov, and Harris 1986; Thomas 2002; Thomas and Reaser 2004; Torbert 2004) suggests that ethnic identification is not nearly as sensitive to morphosyntactic structures as it is to phonetic cues that include vowel production and prosody, thus questioning the primacy of grammar in the definition of AAE. Still other studies show the relevance of other levels of language organization that range from discourse strategies (Smitherman 1977; Morgan 2002) to lexical choice (Smitherman 2000a; Childs and Mallinson 2006) in defining AAE, further challenging the centrality of morphosyntactic structures as the linguistic base of AAE. More importantly, the myopic focus on structural morphosyntactic detail has sometimes marginalized the essential role of discourse, conversational style, lexicon, and even narrative and poetics. As a number of language scholars have now pointed out (e.g., Smitherman 1977; Morgan 2001, 2002; Lanehart 2002), the definition of AAE extends far beyond a set of grammatical patterns, though of course such patterns are a part of its definition.

The Regional Context of AAE

Despite the concession early in the study of AAE that "there are no doubt regional differences not yet charted" (Labov 1972, xiv), many assume that regionality in AAE is invariably trumped by its supraregional linguistic core. In reality, regionality played a significant role in the earlier development of varieties of AAE and it continues to play a significant sociolinguistic role. In part, the impression that AAE is supraregional was created by the early focus on AAE in transplant, urban areas in the North though historically AAE was, of course, rooted in the rural South. Recent investigations of small, rural North Carolina African American communities in different regional contexts (Wolfram and Thomas 2002; Wolfram 2003; Mallinson and Wolfram 2002; Childs and Mallinson 2004; Mallinson 2006; Carpenter 2004, 2005; D'Andrea 2005a and 2005b; Rowe 2005) support the claim that AAE can, in fact, be highly regionalized. Consider, for example, in Figure 2 the case of postvocalic *r*-lessness in several regionally situated contexts in rural North Carolina. For the sake of comparison, figures for *r*-lessness are given for two cohort European

American communities, one in Appalachia and one on the Outer Banks of North Carolina. As with Figure 1, figures are given for three different age groups so that change in apparent time can be considered in the assessment of regional accommodation.[1]

The different regional communities of African Americans manifest *r*-lessness at very different frequency levels. The two Appalachian communities have little *r*-lessness, much like their cohort European American community. Furthermore, *r*-lessness seems to be a relatively stable pattern in the Appalachian communities, showing little change across the different generational groups. The patterning of *r*-lessness in communities in Eastern North Carolina shows more variability in time and

FIGURE 2. Comparison of *r*-lessness in Regionally Situated Communities in North Carolina

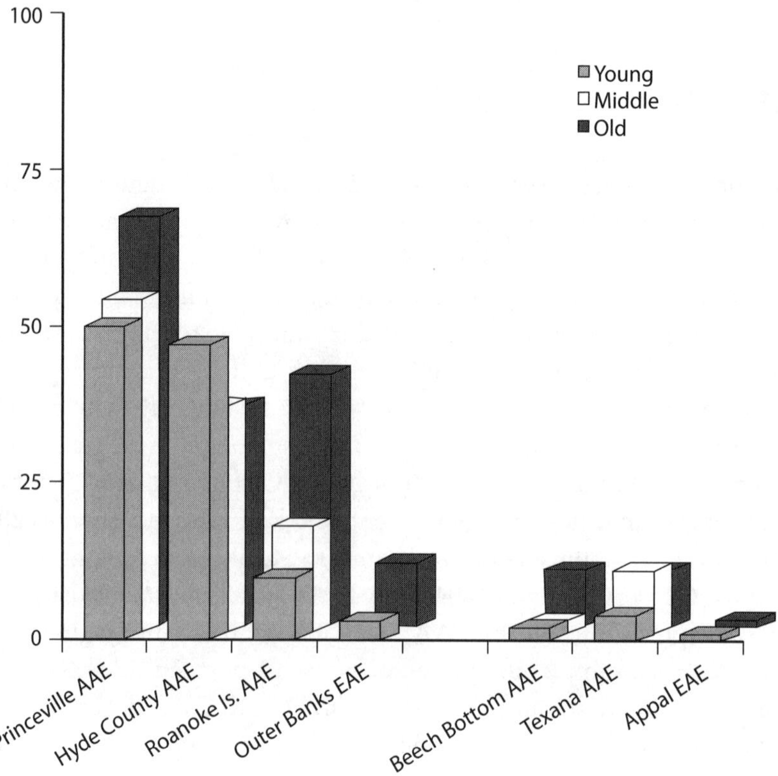

place. Princeville, situated in a region of the South that was historically *r*-less, shows the highest incidence of *r*-lessness while Hyde County and Roanoke Island, situated in the traditionally *r*-full dialect region of the Outer Banks of North Carolina (Wolfram and Thomas 2002), show more community-based and generational variation.

There are several types of regional variables that need to be recognized in AAE. First, there are traits that result from the accommodation of overarching, regional cohort varieties of English. These may range from accommodation to local vowel systems to the adoption of regional morphosyntactic patterns. For example, Wolfram and Thomas (2002) show that older African American residents of coastal North Carolina adopted the regional traits of past tense *be* leveling based on polarity (e.g., *She was there, She weren't there*) whereas Mallinson and Wolfram (2002) and Childs and Mallinson (2004) show that African Americans in Appalachian communities may accommodate the regional dialect pattern of third person plural -*s* marking (e.g., *The dogs barks*).[2] There is also regional variability in terms of the core features of AAE, as we saw in the patterning of third person singular -*s* absence presented in Figure 1. And then there are cases where shared AAE features and regional features may converge, as in the case of *r*-lessness. The role of regionality in AAE is summarized by Green (2002, 1), who observes:

> . . . there are regional differences that will distinguish varieties of AAE spoken in the United States. For example, although speakers of AAE in Louisiana and Texas use very similar syntactic patterns, their vowel systems may differ. Speakers of AAE in areas in Pennsylvania also share similar syntactic patterns with speakers in Louisiana and Texas; however, speakers in areas in Pennsylvania are not likely to share some of the patterns that the Louisiana and Texas speakers share with other speakers of southern regions.

Though some linguists (e.g., Spears 1999; Green 2002; Weldon 2004) explicitly recognize the regional, temporal, and social heterogeneity of AAE, the regional dimension is too often ignored or trivialized. In effect AAE continues to be treated as if it were a trans-regional, unitary dialect.

To some extent, sociolinguists may have fallen prey to the biracial socialization of American society that leads to overgeneralization and the illusion of ethnic homogeneity. As Bonfiglio notes (2002, 62–63), "The illusion of homogeneity is largely a function of secondary revision that glosses over differences and constructs a linear metanarrative…there is something in the popular consciousness that desires to see a unity of geography, ethnicity, and language." The supraregional assumption in AAE description is also at odds with relatively common observations by many African Americans (Wolfram 2007) about its regional distribution. Unfortunately, in the process of constructing sociolinguistic precepts with respect to AAE, sociolinguists have apparently also developed a socialized immunity that disregards community voice with respect to the social and regional distribution of AAE.

The Basilectal Base of AAE

Despite the social and regional diversity of AAE, sociolinguistic investigations have traditionally focused on the basilectal description of the variety.[3] The operational definition of AAE seems fixated on its most vernacular form. Furthermore, methodologies for sampling and conducting sociolinguistic interviews have centered on procedures for accessing the most basilectal version of AAE from the most vernacular speakers. The tradition of data collection and the descriptive precedent were established in studies of AAE launched in the 1960s (e.g., Labov et al. 1968; Labov 1972; Wolfram 1969; Legum et al. 1971; Fasold 1972), which highlighted structures that were most different from the standard variety of English. In fact, the traditional comparative base for most descriptive AAE accounts has always been, and continues to be, an idealized version of Standard English rather than localized norms within local speech communities.

The initial focus on vernacular AAE was not accidental, since there was a hypothesized link between AAE and significant social and educational problems that plagued its speakers, including poverty and racial disparity in school performance. Early studies of AAE such as Labov's landmark study in Harlem (Labov et al. 1968) and Shuy, Wolfram, and Riley's study of Detroit speech (1967) were, in fact, funded by the U.S.

Office of Education because of the concern for an apparent correlation between vernacular speech and low educational achievement. Early sociolinguistic studies often addressed critical educational issues such as literacy and educational achievement in urban areas in addition to their focus on dialect description (Baratz and Shuy 1969; Fasold and Shuy 1970; Labov 1972).

This early focus set the stage for the subsequent preoccupation with vernacular structures and basilectal versions of AAE, leading at times to a kind sociolinguistic nostalgia for the authentic vernacular speaker (Bucholtz 2003). Though some scholars (e.g., Spears 1999; Lanehart 2001, 2002; Weldon 2004) have urged sociolinguists to study acrolectal versions of AAE and a full range of social diversity within the African American community, descriptive attention still remains focused primarily on the vernacular variety despite the fact that identity, style, and politics intersect with the full range of AAE varieties in different African American communities. Furthermore, the full range of sociolinguistic variation affects the study of literature, rhetoric, and communication in English language studies.

The Urban Norm of AAE

Although contemporary AAE no doubt derived from the rural South, its twentieth century development as a sociocultural variety is strongly associated with its use in non-Southern urban contexts. Descriptive studies of AAE that helped launch the modern era of social dialectology concentrated on Northern metropolitan areas (Labov et al. 1968; Wolfram 1969; Legum et al. 1971; Mitchell-Kernan 1971; Fasold 1972; Labov 1972), and this urban focus has continued up to the present (Rickford 1992, 1999; Labov 1998; Baugh 2000). Though descriptive studies of rural Southern AAE now complement the urban focus (Wolfram 1974; G. Bailey 2001; Cukor-Avila 2001; Wolfram and Thomas 2002; Wolfram 2003), large metropolitan areas continue to be at the center of many of the linguistic, social, and educational concerns attendant on AAE. In the description of vernacular AAE, urban youth, particularly males, have received a primary—and probably disproportionate—amount of sociolinguistic attention.

There are several reasons for the preoccupation with urban AAE, ranging from personal and practical reasons to descriptive and theoretical interests. Most of the linguists who worked on AAE in the 1960s lived near Northern metropolitan areas, where the contrast between African American speech and varieties of surrounding European Americans was most salient. As noted above, AAE and significant social and educational problems in American society, including urban poverty and racial disparity in school performance, were apparently linked.

The focus on urban males seems related to the assumption that males most likely represent the most vernacular speech, a by-product of the preoccupation with the basilectal version of AAE discussed above. This is, however, a questionable assumption that needs to be considered more critically. There are, for example, instances where more vernacular speech patterns may be associated with females rather than males (Nichols 1983; Rickford 1999; Schilling-Estes 2002a). Furthermore, the critical age for vernacular speech remains an open question and cannot simply be assumed (Roberts et al. 2006; Van Hofwegen and Wolfram 2010); in fact, there has been a longstanding debate about the status of vernacular dialect in the life cycle of speakers. For example, Stewart (1967) maintained that vernacular speech is most prominent in childhood before speakers are exposed to the prescriptive norms of school, while Labov (1972) has maintained that vernacular speech is most prominent during adolescence when peers exert their strongest influence. In reality, until Van Hofwegen and Wolfram (2010) a longitudinal study had never been conducted that might address these alternative hypotheses on an empirical basis. Van Hofwegen and Wolfram (2010) show that several prominent trajectories characterized early language development, including a roller coaster and curvilinear trajectory in vernacular AAE use.

The significance of urban versions of vernacular AAE is also connected to the establishment of contemporary language norms related to African American youth culture. A new urban language ideology relies on, among other behaviors, the differential use of linguistic features. As Morgan (2001, 205) puts it: "Thus, urban African American life is not simply represented in relation to in-group inter-subjectivities, but through cultural symbols and sounds, especially linguistic symbols, which signify membership, role, and status." African American youth culture today certainly has a strong urban core, and many norms and models of behavior, including language, seem to radiate outward from these urban cultural hubs. Nonetheless, the urban base is just one segment of an African American population represented more expansively, both geographically and socially, in American society. Would we be satisfied to represent vernacular European American English by focusing on non-mainstream young males in a limited geographical context? In contemporary American society, there are representative African American populations in many suburban areas of the United States and current migratory trends are quite different from those of the Great Migration that brought many rural, Southern African Americans to Northern cities. One important demographic trend completely overlooked in current studies of AAE is back-migration, in which significant numbers of urban African Americans are moving back to both rural and urban regions of the South (Stack 1996).

Origin and Change in AAE

The origin of AAE has been in dispute for almost a half-century, fluctuating between extremes of an exclusive Anglican founder hypothesis to a foundational proto-creole hypothesis.[4] Though sociolinguists have certainly argued vehemently among themselves about the origin and trajectory of change in AAE, the dispute has typically been framed in terms of how AAE as a unitary variety may have come about and how it has changed over its history in North America. Given the dispute, it is somewhat ironic that sociolinguistics has now gone through several declared "consensus" positions regarding the development of AAE—from the Anglicist position of the 1950s, to the Creolist position of the 1970s, to the Neoanglicist divergence position of the 1990s. In fact, the professional desire for consensus opens the door to convenient but unjustified axioms that do not serve the best scholarly interests of AAE study.

Research on diverse, rural Southern communities again suggests that the common origin and change assumption in AAE is an unwarranted generalization (Wolfram and Carpenter 2006). In fact, empirical evidence reveals at least three different trajectories of change, one that supports the divergence hypothesis (see both Labov and Bailey in Fasold et al. 1987), one that supports the convergence hypothesis (Mallinson and Wolfram 2002), and one that shows a curvilinear trajectory including periods of convergence and divergence over time (Rickford in Fasold et al. 1987; Rickford 1999; Childs and Mallinson 2004; Carpenter 2004 and 2005). These studies show further that a number of historical, demographic, and social factors must be considered to explain different trajectories of change. Factors affecting change trajectories include the regional setting and the size of the community; macro and micro sociohistorical events; patterns of contact with adjacent European American communities and with external African American communities; intracommunity social divisions; and cultural values and ideologies. For example, the small Appalachian African American community in Beech Bottom is a receding community removed from other African American communities geographically and socially over the past half-century (Mallinson and Wolfram 2002). The few remaining members of the community self-report mixed ethnicity rather than African American identity, though older residents attended a segregated school established for African Americans in the area and were subjected to other kinds of institutional segregation (Mallinson 2004). Perhaps more importantly, residents show a value orientation that aligns with the surrounding European American culture. In this context, convergence seems quite understandable, and speakers are losing remnants of AAE as they fully accommodate the Appalachian English features of the European American dialect community.

In contrast, Hyde County, a long-term African American community of more than 2,000 people, was once highly insulated from outside influences (Wolfram and Thomas 2002). At present, younger community members indicate increasing social contact with external African American communities, and many reveal a kind of exocentric (i.e., community-external) value orientation that accommodates urban cultural norms. In this context, once-entrenched regional dialect features of the Outer Banks dialect based on almost three centuries of co-existence between African American and European American are rapidly receding, and linguistic features associated with contemporary urban AAE are intensifying. The reality of dialect change across time and place shows no single path in the change trajectories of AAE speakers, and a unilateral change assumption simply cannot be applied to variation in AAE.

The Social Distribution of AAE

Descriptions of vernacular AAE are often qualified by the observation that it is most commonly used by working-class speakers. Early in the study of AAE it was noted that "social status is the single most important variable correlating with linguistic differences" and that "linguistic differentiation correlates more consistently with differences on the education and occupation scales than with the residency scales" (Wolfram 1969, 214). There is a prevailing assumption among sociolinguists that AAE is not spoken by middle class African Americans so that there is a fairly straightforward social dichotomy in the use of vernacular AAE (Weldon 2004). Though there has been discussion of an idealized distinction between standard and vernacular AAE (e.g., Spears 1999; Weldon 2004) for some time, there has been surprisingly little empirical study of the social diversification of AAE within African American communities while there has been an inordinate preoccupation with its canonized set of vernacular linguistic structures.

The results of Weldon's (2004) study of language use by an accomplished group of nationally prominent African Americans is an important step in examining a more representative spectrum of language variation by African Americans across social strata and in different social settings. Weldon's study exposes spurious dichotomies such as the nominal distinction between standard and vernacular African American English; it also raises questions about the role of personal presentation and audience in public speeches, including the extent of stylistic shift, performative code-switching, and the persistence of vernacular variants in the speech of some prominent African Americans in more formal public settings with mainstream, public audiences.

Kendall and Wolfram (2009) departs from kinds of objective socioeconomic status indices traditionally applied in the few investigations of social stratification within AAE (Wolfram 1969). Instead, it focuses on a broadly defined linguistic marketplace in the Bourdieuian sense (1991), examining the speech of recognized African American community leaders and comparing their public speech at town meetings, during radio interviews, and at other public events with their speech during sociolinguistic interviews and in other informal interactional contexts. It also compares the speech of community leaders with the norms for their age and gender cohorts from the community. A comparison of the use of vernacular structures by two community leaders in rural North Carolina, one the Mayor of the oldest town established by blacks in the United States, Princeville, North Carolina, and one a County Commissioner from Roanoke Island, a longstanding Outer Banks black community surrounded by a European American population, shows both similarities and differences in their speech. Despite the similarities in social position and status—both female speakers have college degrees and post-baccalaureate education, and live in comparable types of residencies within the community—their use of vernacular forms differs dramatically. The Princeville Mayor uses vernacular forms predominantly while the Roanoke Island Commissioner generally avoids vernacular variants. Furthermore, the speech of these leaders does not necessarily conform to age and gender norms within their respective communities. The Princeville Mayor is among the most vernacular and the Roanoke Island Commissioner is among the least vernacular speakers in their respective communities. Part of the difference between them may be related to their local leadership roles and principal service constituencies. In Princeville, the Mayor's primary service community is centered on the local citizens of a predominantly black municipality. The historical values of Princeville are largely endocentric, and most of the public speaking still occurs within the local, largely autonomous community setting. In fact, it might be hypothesized that the mayor's vernacularity helps establish solidarity with local community members in Princeville. For sure, it does not exclude vernacular speakers from public office and community leadership roles.

By contrast, the Roanoke Island Commissioner's constituency is largely external to the local black community, a small community of about 150 residents surrounded by the predominantly European American community. The Commissioner, a pioneering leader in a dominant white social order for decades now, could not win any elected office without a significant white vote. By contrast, there is no white vote to speak of in Princeville. The use of vernacular forms by respective community leaders has more to do with differential contexts, community structures, and public constituencies than with traditional socio-economic indices such as education or residency. The investigation further indicates that a host of community, contextual, social, and personal factors has to be taken into account in understanding the use of vernacular AAE forms and in explaining the public and non-public speech of community leaders in the rural African American South—and everywhere for that matter. The relative autonomy of the community, the primary public service constituency, the different social affiliations and divisions within the community, personal background and history, and socialized demands in public presentation all seem to be factors in understanding the use of local vernacular and mainstream standard variants by such speakers. If nothing else, imagined dichotomies between middle-class and working-class speech and between standard and vernacular AAE speech must be reconsidered, along with unilateral explanations and simplistic assumptions about the social stratification of AAE within the community.

Style Shift and Code-Switching in AAE

AAE speakers, like speakers of all varieties of English, may show stylistic variation (Rickford and McNair-Knox 1994; Schilling-Estes 2002b). Discussions of style shifting among African Americans sometimes assume that they show greater stylistic versatility than speakers from other communities and that code-switching between an acrolectal and basilectal version of AAE is commonplace. Unfortunately, stylistic shifting and/or code-switching is a critically understudied phenomenon in AAE and these assumptions need empirical verification. As noted above, Kendall and Wolfram (2009) does not support the contention that speakers shift their use of vernacular forms significantly in public speeches vis-à-vis sociolinguistic interviews or casual conversation. Rather, community leaders appear to use a matrix AAE variety within a standard and vernacular continuum and selectively vary a subset of features in different speech situations.

Systematic study of 50 sixth grade African American students followed longitudinally since infancy (Roberts et al. 2006; Renn 2007) supports the contention that contextual dialect variation does not qualify as qualitative code-switching between distinctive linguistic systems. Data from experimentally controlled "formal" and "informal" styles in the interview with the children indicate that speakers use a broad range of vernacular features in informal situations and that they vary the relative incidence of a selective set of structures across contexts. Formal speech was defined operationally by mock (planned) speeches prepared by students and informal speech was defined by (unplanned) free talk, discussion, and a conversation with a peer during a snack period. The variables were extracted from dialect density measures (Craig and Washington 2006; Renn 2007) that included more than 30 traditional AAE phonological and morphological features. Figure 3, from Renn (2007, 53), shows the overall use of vernacular AAE features in formal and informal contexts (statistically significant at <.001) for the 50 sixth-graders in two contexts defined as formal and informal.

Renn's (2007) study shows a consistent overall shift in a cumulative index of features (Craig and Washington's [2006] Dialect Density Measure) and that almost twice as many different vernacular structures are used in contexts defined as informal. It also indicates that some of the diagnostic variables do not appear to participate significantly in the

FIGURE 3. Comparison of the Variety of AAE Features Used by Context

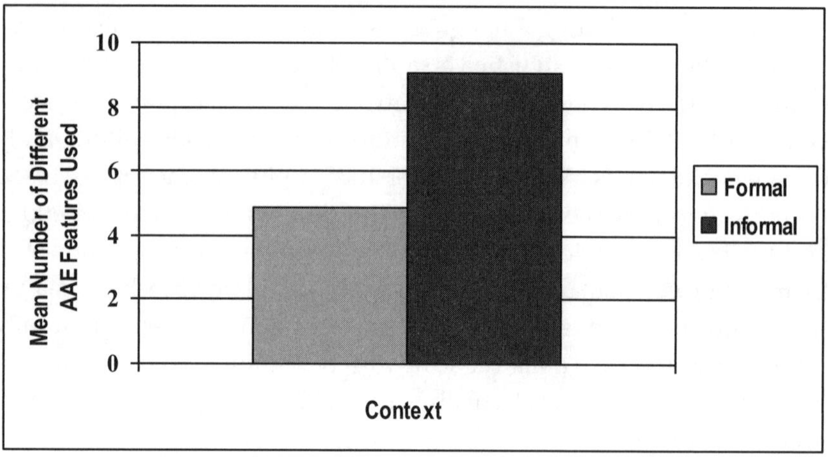

(from Renn 2007:53)

contextual shift. In a breakdown of individual features, the comparison of informal and formal contexts shows significant statistical differences for variables such as nasal fronting (e.g., *runnin'* for *running*) and copula absence (*She nice* for *She's nice*) but not for third person singular *-s* absence or multiple negation (e.g., *She didn't like nothin'*). Though it is possible that this might be an artifact of the limited potential for the occurrence of these structures in the speech samples, this outcome was certainly not predicted. It does, however, support the contention that stylistic dialect shifts are indeed selective and variable rather than discrete switches between disparate dialect codes. At the very least, studies such as Renn (2007) point to the need for detailed examination of stylistic shift in AAE that exposes unwarranted assumptions about stylistic variation.

Revising the Canon

In the preceding sections I have scrutinized some of the axioms that have evolved in the study of African American English. Notwithstanding the rich tradition of research on AAE, some of these tenets have developed more from precedent and tradition than from the critical examination of data. As Sally Johnson (2001, 606) aptly notes, "Linguists—like all other interested social actors—are 'ideological brokers' bidding for 'authoritative entextualization.'" In the early stages of the study of AAE, a kind of "strategic essentialism" (Bucholtz 2003) might have been understandable as a basis for combating the popular interpretation of language differences derived from the principle of linguistic subordination (Lippi-Green 1997), but sociolinguists need to be careful not to over-extend a harmonious authoritative voice. Part of coming of age in the study of AAE is the willingness to expand and revise our understanding of AAE in the process. The united stance that linguists took in controversial public debates about AAE may have lulled them into assuming that it was appropriate to speak in a common voice on matters related to its structure, distribution, and use. I personally find no need to strive for consensus positions related to the structural status of AAE and its variation in time and place.

Historical circumstance, professional enculturation, and academic exclusivity may have resulted in the unwitting acceptance of some questionable axioms about AAE, and it is now time to reconsider these "sociolinguistic facts." Convenient but unjustified sociolinguistic conclusions do not serve sociolinguists in the study of AAE any better than a misinformed understanding and folk theories of AAE serve the public at large. It is time to revise, to expand, and to move forward in understanding how AAE is distributed in the African American population and in American society. Notwithstanding the great contributions sociolinguists have made to the professional and public understanding of AAE, current assumptions, constructs, and explanations need to be examined more critically and the canon of AAE description revised accordingly.

NOTES

*Funding for research reported here was provided by NSF grants BCS-0236838, BCS-0544744, BCS-0542139, and BCS-0843865. I am indebted to Tyler Kendall, Christine Mallinson, Natalie Schilling-Estes, Susan Zeisel, Joanne Roberts, Michael Terry, and Jennifer Renn for insight and feedback. They saved me from myself—at times; I'm solely responsible for the other times.

1. The notion of "apparent time," as opposed to "real time," refers to an assumption that the central components of grammar and pronunciation in a person's speech will reflect the state of the language at the time they learned their language as a child. For example, a speaker born in 1950 would reflect the dialect of their community spoken as they were growing up, whereas a speaker born in 1980 would reflect of state of the language 30 years later. Based on the apparent time hypothesis, researchers often infer patterns of language change by looking at the speech of different generations of speakers at a single moment in time.
2. "Leveling based on polarity" refers to the exclusive use of *was* for affirmative sentences (e.g., *I was, you was,* etc.) and the use of *were(n't)* for negative sentences (e.g., *I weren't, you weren't,* etc.).
3. The term *basilect* refers to the variety of AAE that is most nonstandard or vernacular in its structure; *acrolect* refers to a more standard-like version of AAE.
4. The "Anglicist founder hypothesis" refers to the claim that AAE is derived almost exclusively from dialects found in the British Isles, whereas the "proto-creole hypothesis" refers to the position that it developed from an ancestral creole language. The "neo-Anglicist divergence hypothesis" refers to the position that AAE was once similar to Southern European American English but has been diverging over the last century. For an overview of the various positions on the origin and development of AAE, see Wolfram and Schilling-Estes (2006, Chapter 8).

3

The Beholder's Eye: Using Self-Organizing Maps to Understand American Dialects

WILLIAM A. KRETZSCHMAR, JR.
University of Georgia

"Beauty is in the eye of the beholder," though of great antiquity as an idea and often attributed to David Hume in the modern era, comes as a phrase from 1878, first appearing in a disremembered novel by a prolific but now unknown author, Margaret Wolfe Hungerford (sv, "The Phrase Finder," www.phrases.org.uk). A search of Google Scholar as of this writing shows that, while Hungerford may be forgotten, her phrase has been taken up no fewer than 1,490 times in academic publications, sometimes about mating behavior by animals or by people, but more often to mark the contrast between objective evidence and the perceptions that we draw from it. This essay makes 1,491, one more assertion of the importance of understanding relativism, or point of view, in modern "science."

One problem with the word *science* is that today it means too many things. The term has become attached to "the technical means of conducting experiments," what Aristotle in *Nicomachean Ethics* called *technē*, formerly translated as "art" in the phrase *arts and sciences*, as in the kind of knowledge that a shoemaker needs to produce shoes. The term *science* has traditionally been used to translate Aristotle's *epistēmē*, the other half of the phrase *arts and sciences*, which describes the way that we come to know something, either by induction from facts, such as the movement from particulars to species and genus, or by deduction from first principles. Induction and deduction may thus both be "scientific," although Aristotelian induction is today perhaps more often thought to describe the systematic empirical investigations of "science" than Platonic deduction. Thus the potential confusion of *technē* and *epistēmē*, because *technē* has become a common and important adjunct to the systematic empirical investigation of inductive science, and thus for some people may cross over from "art" to "science."

When it comes to dialects, it is particularly important to distinguish *technē* from *epistēmē*, so that we can distinguish the effect of the beholder's eye from qualities existing *in re*. As a case in point about contemporary relativism and "science," in a recent interview William Labov noted arguments that I have been making about the status of maps of American dialect areas, especially those created by Hans Kurath (Gordon 2006, 347):

> . . . the strength of American dialectology was always clear to me, and I was careful to point that out, that Kurath's work was the solid base to build on, particularly the distinction between North, Midland, and South that he established. I know some of his own students like Bill Kretzschmar have been rather critical and felt that there wasn't a scientific basis for the Kurath maps. But the *Atlas of North America*[*n English*] has found that, for example, the North/Midland line was a deep and important division in American language and society.

The key phrase here is "scientific basis": what we think we know about American dialect areas comes as much from perceptions of our language and culture as it does from rigorous analysis of the facts of how Americans produce their language (e.g., pronunciation, lexicon) in different places. To redirect Hume's statement, like beauty, dialect "is no quality in things themselves: it exists merely in the mind which contemplates them; and each mind contemplates a different" dialect (Hume 1757, 208–209). In this essay, I would like to show the results of an experiment that applies neural network analysis, in the form of Self-Organizing Maps (SOM), to some of the same data that Kurath used, to see whether this new "scientific" procedure (*technē* and induction) yields regions similar to Kurath's. The experiment cannot prove that Kurath and Labov are "wrong" in how they understand American dialect areas, but it will confirm that "science," in the sense of experimental technique and inductive analysis, is not the basis for Kurath's and Labov's understanding of American dialects.

In the articles to which Labov alluded (Kretzschmar 1992, 1996), I considered the foundational work of Hans Kurath, especially in its most famous incarnation, his general map of American dialect areas in the eastern states (Figure 1; Kurath 1949). This map is based on the interviews conducted for the *Linguistic Atlas of the Middle and South Atlantic States* (LAMSAS; see Kretzschmar, McDavid, Lerud, and Johnson 1993; and www.lap.uga.edu). *LAMSAS* covers the spoken American English of the region from New York State south to Georgia and northern Florida, from the eastern coastline as far west as the borders of Ohio and Kentucky. Along with the *Linguistic Atlas of New England* (Kurath et al. 1939, 1939–43), *LAMSAS* treats the primary settlement areas of the original colonies. *LAMSAS* today is a corpus of well over a million answers to questions, transcribed in fine phonetic notation, from interviews conducted with a questionnaire designed to reveal regional and social differences in everyday vocabulary and pronunciation, with some attention to verb forms and other word-level aspects of grammar. Field work was largely completed by 1949, with informants of middle-age through the oldest living generation. The significance of the *LAMSAS* corpus is thus historical: it describes aspects of American English among a consistent class of speakers for a particular region at a particular time. The principal findings from *LAMSAS* as Kurath saw them are treated in his *Word Geography* (1949), and in *Pronunciation of English in the Atlantic States* (1961) with Raven McDavid.

FIGURE 1. Kurath's Map of Dialect Areas in the Eastern States (Kurath 1949)

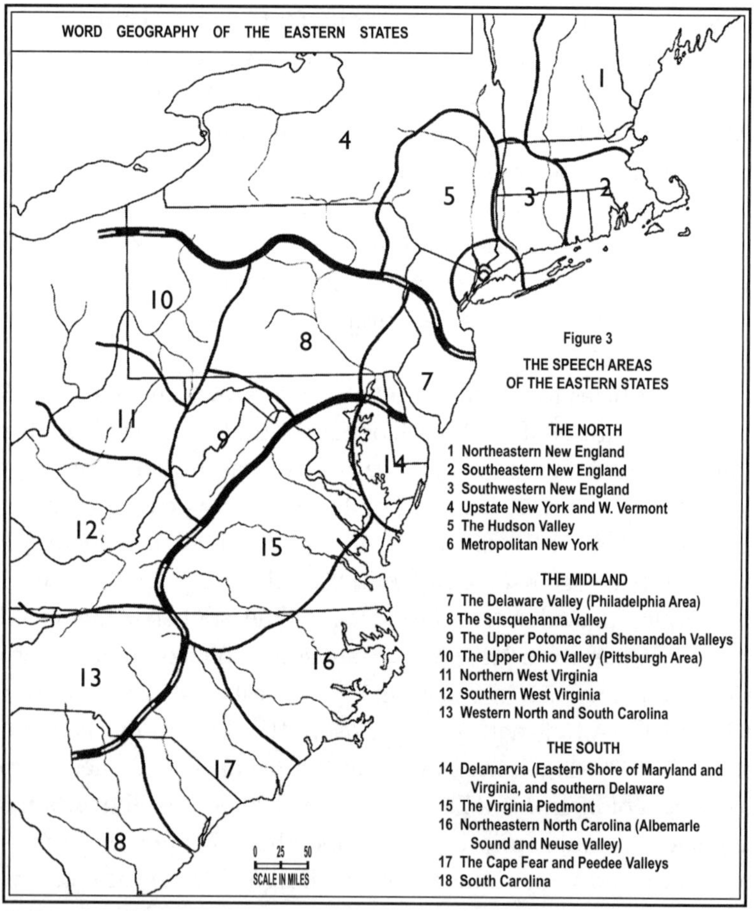

Used with permission.

In the 1992 article, I discussed the way that dialectologists had understood and created maps with their most basic traditional tool, the isogloss. With regard to where people say *pail* or *bucket* (as a name for the container in which one carries water from a well), Kurath did not draw a "limit of occurrence" (which is what an isogloss should nominally be) but instead used his judgment to create a generalization from the data at his disposal—he drew a line where he thought it should go (1992, 232). Still, as I noted, "Even though Kurath may have used the wrong tool (though in his defense it was a traditional one, and about the only one available besides draftsmen's shadings), his judgments on locating boundaries for *pail* and *bucket* appear to be accurate when checked with modern statistical modeling."[1] The point of the article was not to show that Kurath was wrong, but instead to demonstrate that Kurath's judgments about where isoglosses should be drawn make rough and informal use of differential frequency of occurrence of linguistic features, most likely guided by his intensive study of American history and culture (see Kretzschmar 1995). My more formal, "scientific" use of quantitative methods, *technē* and induction, did not falsify his judgment.

The second article Labov addressed (Kretzschmar 1996) considers this question of judgment versus inductive reasoning in more detail. Figure 2 shows a density-estimation map that estimates, with shadings of different intensity, how likely it was that the word *pail* would be elicited at any point in the LAMSAS survey area. Such maps show that, while there are occasions when the analyst can find an area of uniform use (as *pail* in the North in Figure 2), it is much more common for words to be used in scattered areas, clustered at differing frequencies. Starting with work by Dennis Preston (1989, 1997, 1999a) and Susan Tamasi (2003), I argued that American dialect areas, in particular the American South, are identified on the basis of perceptions more than by inductive reasoning from the evidence of speech production. These perceptions have had staying power over the years, from the original work of George Hempl (1896a, 1896b; see also Bailey 1992), carried forward by Kurath, and finally by the *Atlas of North American English* (Labov, Ash, and Boberg 2005; henceforth *ANAE*). In the end, Labov

> exercised his judgment—no doubt excellent judgment given his great experience—to draw his lines where he thought they ought to go, and we should decide to accept his map (or not to accept it) on that basis. It is no mark of disrespect for Hempl, Kurath, or Labov to note that their mapping methods are what they are, ultimately subjective interpretations of their evidence; it just permits us to consider their interpretive maps without misunderstanding. (Kretzschmar 2003, 137–138)

FIGURE 2. Density Estimation Map for the Word *Pail*

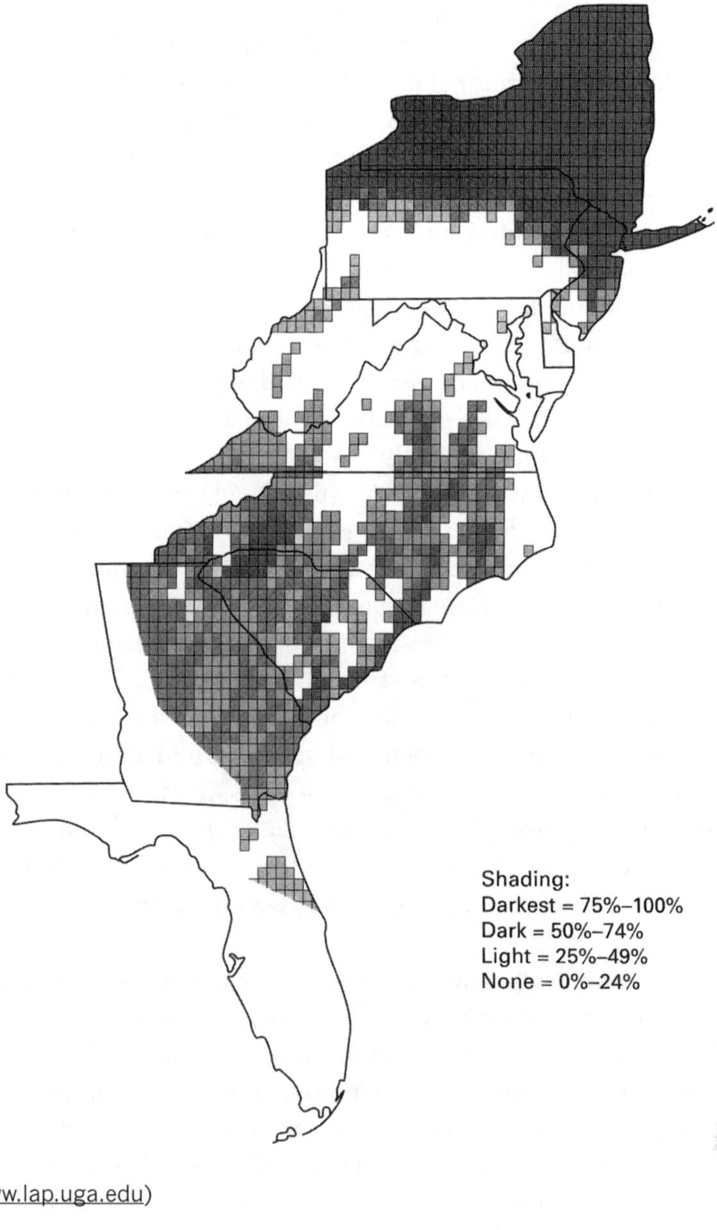

(see www.lap.uga.edu)

There is nothing wrong with believing Kurath or Labov, and indeed we ought to believe them because they have been among the best informed students of dialects of their times. In a recent review of *ANAE*, Richard W. Bailey (2007b, 298) writes:

> What is important for the purpose of this review . . . is to point out the uncanny similarity of outlook between Kurath and Labov. Kurath would certainly see *ANAE* as the culmination of his work, and he would celebrate Labov's accomplishment in setting out the structural patterns of American English phonology.

It is certainly true that Labov wrote in the same spirit as Kurath about dialect geography, but they did not use a technical discovery procedure that others can follow to get the same results given the same evidence.

When Labov said that my articles did not find a "scientific basis" for Kurath's dialect regions, he meant that I had shown Kurath's isoglosses not to be the product of induction from the linguistic facts. Labov may also have considered that my quantitative demonstrations employed a rigorous technical means of analysis (*technē* as "science") that Kurath lacked. Still, Labov did not concede that either Kurath's lines or his own were mistaken, because he felt that the dialect boundary represented a "deep and important division in American language and society," and one may well agree with them. Kurath and Labov have applied deductive reasoning to the picture of American dialects, but the appearance of building dialects from isoglosses should not be allowed to distract us from their actual practice of illustrating, always with a small number of selected features, the Dialects that they already believed to exist on perceptual and historical grounds" (Kretzschmar 2006, 406).

In their *epistēmē*, deductive analysts like Kurath and Labov make dialects into a first principle, then use evidence selectively to trace where the dialects might be. My inductive, "scientific" approach to American language variation is simply different from theirs, and my results do not describe traditional dialects (see Kretzschmar 2009). The *epistēmē* of inductive analysis does not assume that there are dialects, just tries to make what generalizations seem best to fit the data.

Having treated the major confounding terminological issues, I turn to the experiment announced at the beginning of the essay. One of the most prominent techniques now used to process large data sets is neural network analysis, in which the computer conducts an iterative process to compare possible associations in the data and, eventually, to identify relationships between data points given the evidence available at those points. The geographical application of neural network analysis is called Self-Organizing Maps (SOM; see Thill, Kretzschmar, Casas, and Yao [2008] for details of the algorithm described here). SOM is a purely inductive process, since it relies exclusively on associations in the data in order to group data points. One problem with SOM, in fact, is that any particular group of data points it selects may not be readily interpretable according to the received knowledge of the analyst. SOM is thus well-suited to test the dialect areas described by Kurath and Labov. If we use SOM to generate a large number of groups of data points (that is, the residential locations of *LAMSAS* speakers), how many of the groups *do* appear to match the traditional dialect areas? If we get the same result from a different approach, we can confirm that Kurath and Labov were on the right track.

For this experiment, I created six different semantic domains from the lexical evidence so far digitized for the *LAMSAS* project. Each domain contains between 22 and 32 separate variant words: day-wind (e.g., *fine day, threatening*), hearth (e.g., *andirons, mantel*), house-inside (e.g., *sitting room*), land-yard (e.g., *hog-pen, marsh*), rain (e.g., *cloudburst, sprinkle*), and time (e.g., *half past, sundown*). These rough semantic groups contain all of the available words; they were motivated by the accident of what data was available in digital form, not by any deliberate selection to influence the result of the experiment. For each of these domains, SOM chose the best 100 "nodes." A node is a particular pattern of the words from the domain, such that, for some group of speakers, each word in the domain tended to be present or tended to be absent with a specific weight determined by the iterative SOM process. For example, the "hearth" domain included twenty-two different response types from four LAMSAS questions:

cl08#3 andiron	cl08#4 mantelpieces
cl08#3 dog irons	cl08#4 fireboards
cl08#3 dogs	cl08#4 mantelboards
cl08#3 firedogs	cl08#4 mantels
cl08#3 fire-irons	cl08#4 mantelshelf
cl08#3 handirons	cl08#4 shelf
cl08#5 backlogs	cl08#6 kindling
cl08#5 back-stick	cl08#6 lighterd
cl08#5 chunk	cl08#6 lightwood
cl08#5 logs	cl08#6 pine
	cl08#6 pitch-pine
	cl08#6 rich-pine

Any given *LAMSAS* speaker will have a particular pattern of response types—the speaker will have used some of the words on the list and not used others. Thus, for a single speaker, a pattern would consist of something like "*andiron* yes, *dog irons* no . . . *lightwood* yes, *pine* no, *pitch-pine* no, *rich-pine* yes." Within a group of speakers, any of the words may have been used by all of the speakers, by some percentage of the speakers, or by none of the speakers. A possible node, then, consists of the pattern of weighted occurrence of the response types for some group of speakers, like ".4 *andiron*, .1 *dog irons* . . . .2 *lightwood*, 0 *pine*, 0 *pitch-pine*, .05 *rich-pine*." For a set of 22 items, each of which may be present or absent, there are 2^{22} (4,194,304) possible patterns for any single speaker; this figure rises by several orders of magnitude when percentage weights are allowed within a group of speakers. It rises by further orders of magnitude considering that groups of speakers may be of any size, up to all 1162 speakers. Out of billions of possibilities, the SOM algorithm will select the 100 best nodes.

Next, these nodes were themselves grouped into a given number of patterns according to their relative similarity. That is, some of the selected nodes differed in the values for just a few of the words in the domain, so could be grouped together. The analyst has to specify the number of patterns into which the 100 nodes for each domain should be grouped, and the SOM process creates that number of patterns by using the relative similarity of the nodes. Of course, each individual node has some number of speakers associated with it, so the patterns of nodes selected by SOM will also be associated with a particular set of speakers. For this experiment, I asked SOM to create solutions with three, six, and nine patterns for each domain, in order to observe different levels of scale within the data. The experiment thus yielded 108 different observations: six sets of three-pattern solutions (18), six sets of six-pattern solutions (36), and six sets of nine-pattern solutions (54). So far, all of this is fairly abstract. It becomes more concrete when we visualize the locations of the speakers in each abstract pattern created by SOM by making a map that highlights each of the speakers included in the nodes of the pattern (Figures 3 through 8). We can then compare the map from each pattern to Kurath's map of dialect areas, to see whether the SOM map recapitulates any of the dialect areas.

Among the eighteen maps from the three-pattern solutions, we do not find evidence for Kurath's major dialect areas. Five of the patterns show "relatively all" of the 1162 LAMSAS speakers, as in Figure 3.[2] Five of the patterns show "McDavid distributions," as in Figure 4, which come from a difference in field work practices by different field workers.[3] Four more of the three-pattern solution maps show general Midland and Southern distributions, as in Figure 5. The remaining four maps from the three-pattern solutions have scattered distributions of speakers, nothing that we can connect to a particular Kurath area or to any circumstance of the *LAMSAS* project.[4]

The 36 maps from the six-pattern solutions also fail to confirm Kurath's areas. Figure 6 recapitulates Kurath's Midland dialect area the best of all of the observations in the experiment. Of the remaining six-pattern maps, there are eight more cases of generally Southern or

FIGURE 3. SOM Map from *Day/Wind*, Three-Pattern Solution: All Speakers

FIGURE 4. SOM Map from *Day/Wind*, Three-Pattern Solution: McDavid Distribution

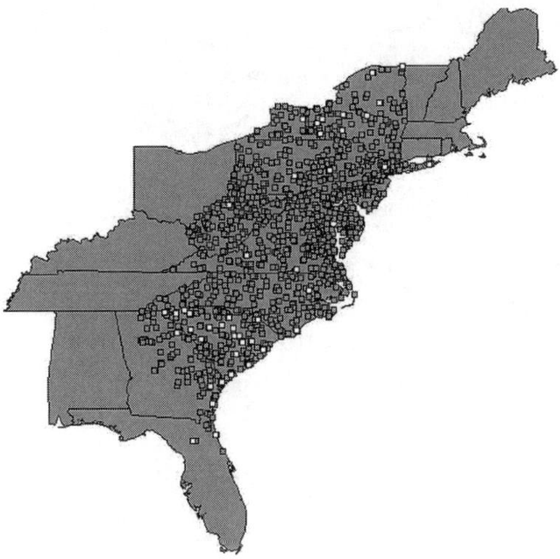

FIGURE 5. SOM Map from *Hearth*, Three-Pattern Solution: General Midland/Southern

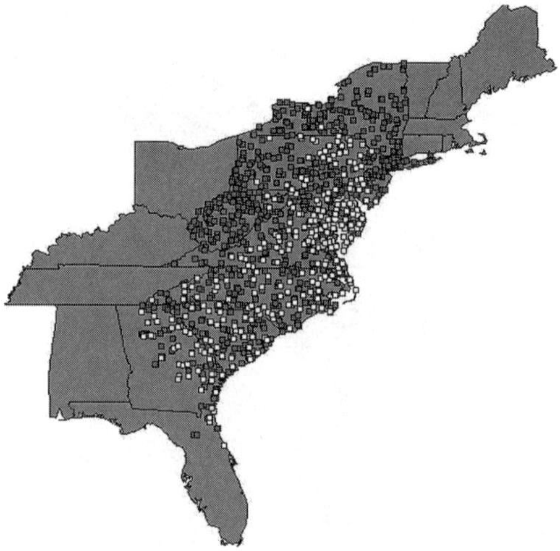

FIGURE 6. SOM Map from *Land/Yard*, Six-Pattern Solution: Midland

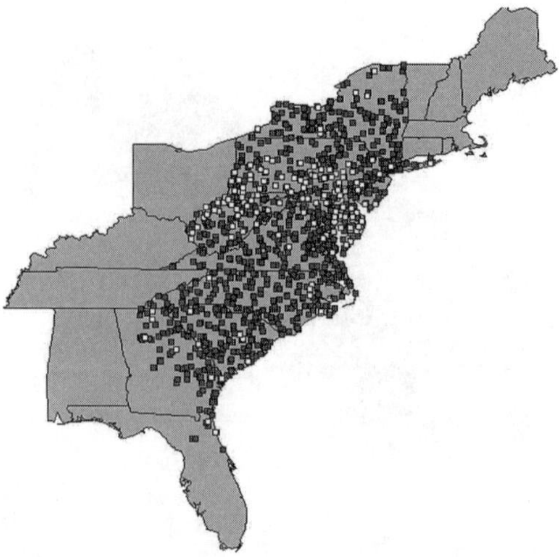

Midland/Southern distributions. There are six cases of McDavid distributions, including two cases of exclusive Georgia/South Carolina distributions that would be McDavid distributions without the evidence from Upstate New York. Only two maps have more than 600 of the 1162 *LAMSAS* speakers on them, so the greater number of patterns in the solution tends to limit the proportion of maps of "relatively all" speakers that we observe in the three-pattern solutions. Fifteen maps with scattered distributions cannot be connected to a Kurath area or to *LAMSAS*. Finally, two maps show what might be called "coastal" distributions that spanned more than one of Kurath's areas, and two maps include Kurath's Northern area, once combined with West Virginia and once combined with the Midland.

Finally, the nine-pattern solutions still do not show much recapitulation of Kurath's dialect areas. There are eleven more cases of McDavid distributions, two of which are exclusive to Georgia/South Carolina. Two more cases occur of distributions over 600 speakers. Twelve more maps have general Midland/Southern distributions. No fewer than twenty-one maps show scattered distributions, such as the one in Figure 7. This leaves eight maps with other kinds of distributions: two that focus on West Virginia, two that focus on Virginia, one more "coastal" pattern (as shown in Figure 8), one that focuses on Western North Carolina, and, finally, two more that include Kurath's North (one combined with West Virginia, and one combined with the South).

So, what do we learn from the experiment overall? When we tabulate the number of maps of each kind so far discussed, we find 40 cases of scattered distributions, 25 cases of general Midland/Southern distributions, 22 cases of McDavid distributions, 12 cases of "other" distributions, and 9 cases that show over 600 ("relatively all") speakers. The SOM algorithm did a far better job identifying Raven McDavid's field work practices than it did finding any of Kurath's particular areas. It did not usually distinguish the Midland from the Southern area (perhaps in 4 cases, including the map in Figure 6), but instead frequently found a general association of speakers from the Midland and South (25 cases). Kurath's North appeared only four times on the maps, always in association with another area.

FIGURE 7. SOM Map from *Rain*, Nine-Pattern Solution: Scattered

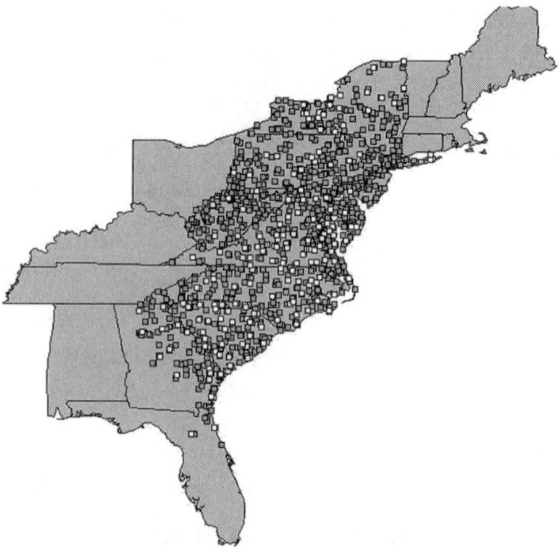

FIGURE 8. SOM Map from *Land/Yard*, Nine-Pattern Solution: Coastal

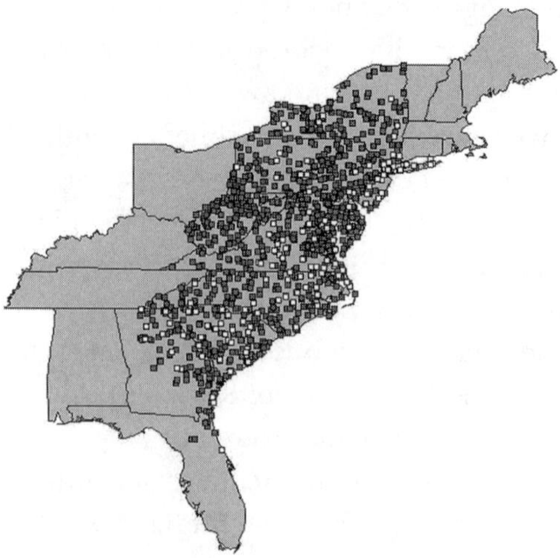

The clear finding from the SOM *technē* is that it cannot support Kurath's dialect areas. Induction by SOM from the language evidence never once supported Labov's belief that "the North/Midland line was a deep and important division in American language and society," because Northern patterns were always associated with another area. Highly selected linguistic data did a much better job of showing areas for Kurath and Labov—because it was highly selected by deduction to match areas that were already apparent to them from, as Labov might say, deep and important divisions in American society. Traditions of scholarship may also be involved. Since Labov generally recapitulated Kurath's dialect areas, which themselves generally recapitulated Hempl's dialect areas, and since inductive analysis does not validate the areas, then we are entitled to consider that the recapitulation may have come in part from knowledge of prior analysis by dialectologists who had understood the same divisions.

When we talk about American dialects, then, we are talking not about language in the first instance, not about any object observable *in re* from the evidence, but about our perceptions of American culture. In fact, we cannot use induction to develop dialect areas from the data, whether we use isoglosses, specific statistical tests, or advanced data mining tools like SOM. Regional patterns must first be conceived on perceptual or cognitive grounds, and only later furnished with selected language variation data to accompany our cultural judgments.[5] Kurath and Labov are still not wrong in their descriptions of American dialects, and neither do they lack a "scientific basis" for what they do. They have each applied deduction, a traditional component of *epistēmē*, in order to derive their maps. Richard W. Bailey is undoubtedly correct in his assertion (cited above) that Kurath and Labov were both committed to finding structural patterns in language; the only way that they could do so, in the absence of regional patterns derived by induction from language evidence, was to nominate regions in which they might deduce the structural patterns. Future work in this area should declare that it will apply inductive methods to evidence of language variation (and thus will not make generalizations about dialects), or should say that it will apply deductive methods that begin with perceptions of dialects (and thus will use evidence of language variation only selectively).

In talking about American dialects, we will do well to start not with the data from surveys, but with what Richard W. Bailey has written about as the "cultural history of the language." His work is replete with discussions of point of view, of the kind of relativism that determines the beholder's eye, for instance:

> Reading the English of the nineteenth century is not made difficult by problems of intelligibility. The danger of misreading lies rather in the apparent familiarity of the language, lulling modern readers into imagining that this English is much like our own, when it is not. (Bailey 1996b,vi)

The danger comes from easy acceptance of our unfiltered perceptions and unconsidered commonplaces. Bailey took up just this topic in *Images of English* (1991a, viii):

> I came to explore other beliefs about the language—ideas I had long accepted as unquestioned fact, even though they had nothing more than tradition to commend them. I soon discovered that most of our ideas about English have a long history. . . . While scientific theories may be made irrelevant through intellectual progress, more broadly cultural ideas [like language improvement and standardization] have greater endurance. Few of the claims about English described in this volume have been so thoroughly discredited that they no longer find adherents.

Moreover, commonplaces about language are not something endemic among the common people but easily avoided by the literati. Bailey included himself, as must we all, among those susceptible to belief in commonplace cultural notions. Yet, as Bailey reports, linguists ignore the danger of such cultural entanglements (1991a, viii–ix):

> Most linguists have held that notions of laypeople are worthless when it comes to language, and few of the ideas discussed in this book have been subject to rigorous analysis. Ideas about language—and the images used to express them—are usually held to have only the most distant connection to linguistic performance or to the directions of lan-

> guage change. Consequently, there is little reason to study them, and it is not hard for linguists to show that what speakers claim about their own language does not match the "facts."

Bailey himself, however, in the two books mentioned here as well as elsewhere in his large body of writings, has been the exceptional case: he has described with care and erudition the origins of our commonplaces about language, and the nature of cultural beliefs about language that condition the notions about language of both common people on the street and all but the most cautious among us in ivory towers. In this essay, I hope to have shown that Bailey's scare-quoted "facts" about language commonly cited by experts—among them the belief in regional dialects—can be less factual than perhaps we have believed. Confronted with such entanglements of culture, even after many such have been laid bare, we need clear notions of "science," of *technē* and *epistēmē*, of induction and deduction, to set against cultural commonplaces and to help us to separate the objective evidence of language in use from dialects in the beholder's eye.

NOTES

1. If I were writing this sentence today, I would say that the boundaries "appear to be plausible," not "accurate."
2. I defined "relatively all" as any set of more than 600 speakers associated with a node pattern, an arbitrary number but a consistent means of categorization. Sets with more than half of the speakers (600/1162) would overwhelm any of Kurath's geographical patterns.
3. Guy Lowman began as the principal interviewer for *LAMSAS* (see Kretzschmar, McDavid, Lerud, and Johnson 1993, Chapter 1), but he was killed in a car accident in 1941. Raven McDavid finished the remaining field work after World War II, just in Upstate New York, and in South Carolina, eastern Georgia, and northern Florida. Whenever we see a map like Figure 4, which shows speakers mainly in Upstate New York and in the Deep South, we can attribute the pattern to the way that McDavid conducted interviews.
4. "Scattered" does not mean that the speakers are evenly spread across the *LAMSAS* region, and does not mean that the speakers are randomly located (see Lee and Kretzschmar [1993] for definitions of spatial distributions); what I have called a scattered distribution is one in which speakers are spread across the survey region without any clear focal center in a particular area.

5. I offer a complete model for such perceptual and cognitive processing of language variation in Kretzschmar 2009. Suffice it to say here that perceptions of regional variation in American English are no more shared and coherent among groups of speakers than their production of language. While in the aggregate we do tend relatively to share notions of regional variation, individual speakers are unlikely to share perceptions in any detail owing to differences in the information and experience about who says what where that we as individuals may possess. Thus, if we want to talk about dialects as perceptual constructs, it is all the more important that we trust the perceptions of experts like Kurath and Labov, who have the best information and the greatest experience. For another interpretation of SOM results, which offers additional perspective on why the technique does not validate Kurath and Labov, and on how production data may be used in perception, see Kretzschmar 2008.

4

RESPONSE

To Continue Moving Forward in English Language and Linguistics Research in the Twenty-First Century

SONJA L. LANEHART
University of Texas at San Antonio

Introduction

Unlike Richard W. Bailey, whose experience of his own dialect is described in Dennis Preston's contribution to this section, I spent my early years hating my language (see Lanehart 2002). As an undergraduate I attended the University of Texas at Austin, which completely changed my attitudes and beliefs not only about my own language, African American Language (AAL), but about other varieties as well. I no longer thought of language differences as deficits to be pitied or remedied but simply as differences that represented our sociocultural and historical contexts. This experience helped me to integrate English language and linguistics (ELL)—the combination of English Language Studies (ELS) and the tools of linguistics—applying linguistic theories and methods to English language data in social and cultural contexts.

While ELL courses helped me to respect language variety and understand the science of language, especially phonetics and phonology, ELS helped me to appreciate the cultural richness, histories, and narratives that embody linguistic difference. So, while linguistics fueled my interest in how language works and how users' languages vary even though there is no hierarchy in the functionality of languages, ELS fueled my interest in why language works and how users make it their own in spite of the similarities and differences from one language to another.

The contributions made to this section by William Kretzschmar, Dennis Preston, and Walt Wolfram continue the traditions of American dialectology and ELL. Each provides methods and methodologies as well as epistemologies for contextualizing and interpreting data in American dialectology. Kretzschmar's use of mapping, Preston's use of folk dialectology, and Wolfram's critique of ELL through AAL research provide both the retrospective and forward-looking perspectives on American dialect research necessary for productive research in the twenty-first century.

In addition to responding to the chapters in this section, I want to address three future areas of ELL research: (1) the importance of scholars disclosing and understanding the impact of their subjectivities on their research and its outcomes; (2) the importance of sociocultural and historical contexts in ELL; and (3) the importance of multimethod research in ELL. All of these areas are well-fitted to ELL scholars in English departments in particular because of the importance that literary analysis, historical research, and multidisciplinary research have in the humanities, all of which serve to balance, supplement, and challenge the social scientific methodologies of linguistic inquiry into American dialect variation and change.

Subjectivities vs. Objectivity

Some people think of linguistics as "exotic": they speak language, but linguistics is beyond their experience. The first thing many non-linguists ask when they hear that I am a linguist is, "How many languages do you speak?" Once I admit that I am not a polyglot and that I study the English language, they respond, "I'd better watch what I say since English is my worst subject." The conversation has gone from the exotic to the excruciating. Though they may resist knowing much about language (in an academic sense, anyway), most non-linguists have opinions about it, and the follow-up question to me, as an African American, is usually, "What do you think about that Ebonics stuff?" as an entrée into discussing how Black people do not speak "good" or "proper" English. Surely linguists must be doing something to improve the situation since (my interlocutors believe) language variation is bad. In addition, since I am bidialectal, I also get, "You are so articulate" or "You don't sound like you're from Texas." They assume I agree with them, since I don't talk in the way they are defaming: "You overcame your deficient culture, so others can and must do it too, right?" is the subtext of their queries. These conversations capture a complete disconnect between how ELL *does* function and how laypeople believe it *should* function. Missing is an understanding of the relevance of sociocultural and historical contexts to the status of English dialects, while a belief that there is only one right way to speak and all other ways are bad is pervasive.

Because it is *just* English, every English speaker has an opinion about it regardless of the facts. As William Kretzschmar's contribution in this section shows, asymmetry of fact and opinion is not just an issue with non-linguists. Kretzschmar also suggests that our starting point in linguistic knowledge matters. I would add that our ideologies (i.e., our beliefs and attitudes about the world around us) matter as well as our epistemologies (i.e., how we come to know what we know), especially since what we believe does not always match what we know: for example, linguists know that no variety is better than another—all serve the purposes of the language users and fit their environment and culture; nonetheless, linguists sometimes hold pejorative beliefs about variation or particular varieties of English.

Despite the belief that science is objective, like all other human endeavors, it is quite subjective. Many find some comfort in the delusion that explaining physical phenomena is more "objective" than explaining human nature. Studying the English language is no less scientific because English is so banal, as opposed to something like quantum physics, though it is equally part of our everyday lives. All scholars should be forthcoming about their subjectivities and the impact they have on the questions they ask, how they research those questions, and how they interpret data, since all scholarship is inevitably tied to individuals and their ideologies and epistemologies, in turn influenced by sociocultural and historical contexts.

For example, my upbringing in a working class, predominantly African American community till I was twelve, before moving to a multiracial, middle-class neighborhood, had a profound impact on me. The conflict between the general lack of respect for AAL and its social significance and the everyday reality of being surrounded by language use in the African American community was disconcerting. I grew up deriding and ridiculing my native language because others did so—both in and outside of my community. I saw how much my parents wanted to "do better" in their language and looked to me to help them because I had access to a level of teaching and learning they never had. One day in fourth grade, when my favorite teacher spoke racially pejoratively to a fellow Black student, the reality of my Blackness and its inescapability hit me in the face; my tendency toward language prescriptiveness and self-loathing was strengthened for years to come.

African Americans and others whose varieties are perceived as inferior to the mainstream are expected to hate their language; that hatred should foster in them a desire to speak "better," as if speaking a variety not their own will somehow help them to be and think "better." So, as an ELL scholar and a Black person, I am expected by non-linguists to believe that those who speak the language I grew up with and others with similar histories need to be salvaged or, better still, transformed. Though I certainly was "transformed" during my childhood and young adulthood, it was at great sacrifice to my identity—a sacrifice I came to regret. I spent many years deconstructing and reinventing myself, and such rebirth has had a profound impact on my subjectivities. As Preston's contribution to this section shows, although we may have humbling beliefs about our own language varieties, there are sure to be many others who agree that we should.

It would be helpful to science, art, and the humanities if scholars would recognize that who we are is integrated with what we do (method), how we believe it should be done (methodology), and how we see or know it (epistemology). For example, as Walt Wolfram's contribution to this section notes, the historical data regarding the origins of

AAL lead scholars to quite different, even mutually exclusive, positions about those origins. Depending on one's methods, methodologies, and epistemologies related to Africans in the Americas, one is more willing to believe that AAL is a language or dialect; an African and British English creole or British English dialect; a (bad) variety of American English; etc. As such, the data one seeks and the ideologies one holds affect the interpretation of those data. It is no surprise that those who identify as Anglicists (i.e., those who hypothesize that the speech of African Americans essentially derived from British-based dialects) usually produce and interpret data that support their historical position about AAL, and those who identify as Creolists (i.e., those who hypothesize that the similarities between AAL and Caribbean creoles and the differences between AAL and British dialects is due to the existence of an earlier creole that has since decreolized) usually produce and interpret data that support their historical position about AAL.

Research on Samaná provides a useful case study. Dawn Hannah (1997) studied the same Samaná English community previously studied by Shana Poplack and Sali Tagliamonte (e.g., Tagliamonte and Poplack 1988; Poplack and Tagliamonte 1989; Poplack 2000), but she came up with different results about copula absence (e.g., "She not here" or "They gone"—the absence of any form of the verb *be*). Whereas Hannah's data align copula absence in Samaná English with Creolist suppositions about AAL, Poplack and Tagliamonte's data align with Anglicist suppositions. The differences may be attributed to the fact that Hannah (a Black woman who was married to one of the community's members and who was a graduate student working with John Rickford, a creolist) was viewed more as an insider in the community she was studying than Poplack and Tagliamonte (both white women whose research clearly positions them as Anglicists). Since we know that interviewer identity affects the data one gets in a community (see Cukor-Avila and Bailey 2001; Bailey and Tillery 1999; and Rickford and McNair-Knox 1994), it should be no surprise that the data obtained were different. The more one is like the participant one is researching, the more likely the data obtained is closer to the participant's vernacular. Combine interviewer identity differences with different methods, methodologies, epistemologies, and ideological presuppositions, and one can easily get different interpretations of data as well as different data.

The ideologies *and* knowledge of the researchers conducting a study are important and have to be taken into account. David Sutcliffe (2001) shows how ideologies create assumptions and how those assumptions not only can affect our interpretations of data but also the data collection process itself. For example, Sutcliffe attempts to make the case that AAL is related to tonal languages in Africa on the basis of ex-slave audio-recordings that are transcribed in G. Bailey, Maynor, and Cukor-Avila's *The Emergence of Black English* (1991). A focal point of this evidence lies in the use of the particle *duh* in the ex-slave recordings, which Sutcliffe sees as a tonal marker. He argues that many researchers either do not investigate this feature or do not see it in the data they collect because they are not looking for it and because they do not know enough about tone and tonal languages to recognize its importance if they hear it.

As these two examples demonstrate, ideology and knowledge shape the ways in which researchers understand their questions, data, and interpretations. This is an emerging perspective in American dialect research with little research to evoke yet, but it suggests the important connection between ELL and English departments: most English departments' immersion in feminist theory, cultural studies, narrative, etc., provides critical frameworks for ELL in terms of recognizing the researcher's subjectivities.

The Importance of Sociocultural and Historical Contexts

Richard W. Bailey's work captures the importance of sociocultural and historical contexts in ELL. It is no surprise that my first book, *Sociocultural and Historical Contexts of African American English* (2001), included those words in its title. Our language is part of who we are—past, present, and future—and that informs my conviction that sociocultural and historical contexts are vital to ELL.

When as an undergraduate student I finally transformed from self-loathing (at one point I wanted to be a speech pathologist so that I could "cure" all the "bad" English speakers, especially African Americans) into an admirer of language variation, I was pursuing Medieval Studies, in which I learned about the evolution of English from the Germanic dialects of a group without a single homeland, through several centuries to the present day. Because I undertook these studies at a university in the Southwest where linguistic ridicule was commonplace, I examined the socioculture and history of American English in order to understand the array of language attitudes all around me. As a senior in the Honors English Program, after having taken Medieval Studies courses as well as ELL courses, including Texas English and American English, I began to understand the relevance of who we are linguistically and where we have been to where we can go. Seeing the significance of history, society, and culture in medieval literature can make it easier to see that the same categories are at the foundation of the language we produce today and that social variation and change are reflected in language variety.

Dennis Preston's research in perceptual dialectology takes a multifocal view of Present Day English by asking people what they believe about their own language and also that of others. To this day, many language researchers are guilty of collecting linguistic data and then analyzing it by making assumptions about what the language users meant or believed or intended instead of asking them. We know that beliefs are not always reality—one's beliefs do not always match one's behavior—but one's beliefs about one's behavior are still important in understanding the complexity of language cognitively, psychologically, culturally, socially, and individually. Preston's work helps us to understand why Midwesterners and Northerners can hold complimentary beliefs (uninformed but sincere) about Southern speech as well as negative beliefs about one another's speech. Knowing the histories of these regions and communities along with current cultures and social workings helps to contextualize current beliefs and attitudes.

English departments bolster the viability of studying sociocultural and historical contexts of language more than linguistics departments because the former already have solid foundations in literary, historical, and critical analyses—such is not the case in linguistics research or linguistics departments. While linguistics departments are more concerned with theoretical issues about language use and production, ELS combines those theories with analysis of social, cultural, and historical contexts, both of speakers and their language. ELL scholars can thrive in English departments because, though they do not often share a connection to literature in content, they do share a connection in context. Literary scholars have to study literature in context, in order to understand how societies, histories, and cultures influenced its emergence and reception. The history of the language is, of course, reflected in those same literary texts.

The collaboration between ELL research (e.g., perceptual research, language attitudes and beliefs research, identity research) and the English department should foster the integration of sociocultural and historical contexts into future research. By doing so, we will have a better understanding of language, language variation, and applications of such knowledge for the betterment of humanity. In order to be able to utilize this knowledge and complex data, however, we need more tools of analysis.

Time for Multimethod Research

Because one's beliefs do not always match one's behavior and because humans are complex and curious and evolving, I believe the tools for processing the complex data required to *really* understand any language can be found in conducting multimethod research. Multimethod research can be defined as research that uses multiple quantitative research methods (e.g., survey, questionnaire, multivariate analysis, self-organizing maps), multiple qualitative research methods (e.g., portraiture, interview, observation, diaries), or a mix of both quantitative and qualitative research methods (Schutz, Chambless, and DeCuir 2004). Multimethod research is vital not just to ELL research, but also to most social science research. The questions to which we need answers are too complex for simply using a survey or questionnaire or phone interview. The complex interrelationships of the human condition, language, culture, and society demand more than a single method or methodology. English departments can be helpful in this endeavor because much research in English departments, including that in ELS, offers multiple qualitative methods, methodologies, and analyses. Since most ELS and linguistics scholars are trained in quantitative methods and methodologies, collaboration with liberal arts and education faculty can prove a win-win situation.

As we gather more and more complex data in response to ever more complex questions, inevitably, better research will be done through collaboration than in solitude.

Although I see some researchers incorporating more than one method in their work (e.g., Elaine Richardson, H. Samy Alim, and Walt Wolfram), not enough do. One possible reason for this slow transition is that most colleges and universities do not offer enough (if any) methods and methodology classes for students as part of their disciplinary training nor do they provide the opportunity for applying those methods and methodologies in a hands-on environment. The universities I have been involved with across the United States at best offered one course in sociolinguistic methods for both undergraduate and graduate students, and that course usually did not involve applying those methods in an actual study. Most important, qualitative methods and methodologies are largely underplayed in such courses and too many ELL programs. Simply teaching ELL students VARBRUL (variable rules analysis, a statistical analysis commonly used in sociolinguistic analysis to describe patterns of variation between alternative forms) or providing them with a reading on ethnography is not enough to make them the multimethod researchers our complex language questions require.

Two examples of best practices in multimethod language variation research are Patricia Cukor-Avila and Guy Bailey's research in Texas (1995, 2001) and H. Samy Alim's research in California and Pennsylvania (e.g., 2004, 2006). Bailey and Cukor-Avila have had a research site in Texas for 20 years. They have become part of the communities they have researched, so it is more than just a research site—it is a part of their lives. They have collected a variety of data including diaries, questionnaires, interviews (researcher-participant and participant-participant), social network data, contextual audio-taping, perceptual data, and ethnographic data. Alim has conducted similar multimethod research. Instead of researchers trying to guess what participants of their studies think or believe or do, these scholars actually ask the participants: the participants collect data as well as the researchers, and then researchers triangulate all of the data in order to "locate" linguistic knowledge in a cultural space, which only increases what we can know about the language. Such research has generated rich data about, in these cases, AAL and Southern White Vernacular Englishes. In particular, we have learned more about rural AAL from Bailey and Cukor-Avila and urban AAL and Hip Hop language and culture from Alim. It is encouraging for the future of ELL that the former researchers are senior scholars and latter relatively junior.

Multimethod research does not minimize quantitative inputs. Kretzschmar, for instance, has done an impressive job of including more quantitative research methods from other disciplines and refining them for American dialect research. His description and use of Self-organizing Maps in this section provides us with more effective ways of understanding and explaining dialects and language variation in combination with other quantitative and qualitative methods and methodologies. Kretzschmar has pushed the boundaries of dialectology before with (1) the Atlanta survey research he and I did by transforming the traditional dialectology interview of several hours into a one-hour interview that could yield similar data, (2) his Roswell study (a multimethod study that collected data from various community groups), and (3) his goal to make data available for study and use on the Internet (see http://us.english.uga.edu/).

Kretzschmar reminds us of Bailey's point in *Nineteenth-Century English* (1996b, vi), that

> Reading the English of the nineteenth century is not made difficult by problems of intelligibility. The danger of misreading lies rather in the apparent familiarity of the language, lulling modern readers into imagining that this English is much like our own, when it is not.

This is not only true for Medieval English to Present Day English, but also within Present Day English. English speakers see the word *nice* in Middle English and believe it has its current meaning when it actually means 'foolish, stupid.' Arthur Spears has proven the point for Present-Day English with his investigations of what has been called "camouflaged" language. In his studies of AAL, Spears has determined that there are usages in AAL that look similar to General American English (GAE) in structure and meaning, but they are not in reality (Spears 1982). For example, *call* or *come* in the sentences "She call herself dancing" and "She come in here talking like she had something," respectively, appear to be GAE words, but they have AAL meanings; listeners unfamiliar with AAL will misinterpret the sentences as though they were in GAE, much as many of us misread Old or Middle English texts.

We can easily be misled if we base our judgments and understanding of language on current methods and methodologies alone and decontextualize the information or data we collect from their socioculture and history or if we shortchange the data and analysis by not using more than one method or not starting with the complex research questions the real world demands. In addition, we also need to challenge our own ideologies and epistemologies in the process to be ever mindful of our own potential biases and shortcomings. I think more efforts are being made to mitigate researchers' blindspots now than at any point before, but we must continue to be vigilant and visible in our beliefs for future language variation research.

PART II

History of the English Language

Introduction

The history of technology and the history of the English language are intertwined. At perhaps the most obvious level, changes in writing technology have changed the transmission of the language: from a primarily oral culture, to the limited distribution of hand-copied manuscripts, to the much wider distribution of printed books, to the almost instantaneous worldwide circulation of electronic text. The more idiosyncratic copying practices of medieval scribes gave way to the more stable printed reproduction of texts, which now competes with the less stable world of hypertext. In the process, English speakers and writers have moved from the anonymity of most medieval manuscripts to the development of copyright laws—and now to the challenges to copyright law that blogging and "mash-ups" (splicing together two or more pre-existing pieces of music) pose. The population shifts caused by urbanization have affected the history of the language, as have the myriad ways that technologies—from ships to railroads to cars to planes to the Internet—have brought languages into contact with each other.

The field called "History of the English Language" (HEL) often has been interpreted narrowly, to focus exclusively on structural changes in English phonology, morphology, syntax, lexis, and semantics. At the transition from the twentieth to the twenty-first centuries, however, this tradition has been challenged and supplemented by new methodologies. The rise of historical sociolinguistics, for instance, encourages us to interpret "History of the English Language" as the history of English speakers, the ultimate agents of linguistic change. From this alternate point of view, the focus of scholarly inquiry expands and displaces what linguistic formalism used to put at the center. The language's history then encompasses the complex network of factors involved in linguistic change, including historical events, cultural contexts, social mores, and how and with whom English speakers communicated, both in speech and writing. Features of English observed at any point on the time-line are the effects of many simultaneous forces at work on the behavior of speakers who are so much more than speakers.

Richard W. Bailey has proposed that scholars in HEL need to consider seriously the ways in which centers and peripheries are defined in—and have defined—the field. Histories of English have often been the histories of standard varieties, as James Milroy's (1992) work has emphasized. Histories of English have often accepted the authority of the educated, putting these speakers at the center (Bailey 2002b). Britain and the United States tend to be centers, as the history of imperialism and social and economic power shape the linguistic narrative, moving to the periphery other nations with equally long or longer histories of English use (e.g., Scotland and Ireland) and nations where the number of native and non-native speakers of English are rapidly expanding, as Edgar Schneider's essay in this section demonstrates. Social network theory provides a critical insight: if we want to understand language change, we must look to peripheries as much if not more than to centers. We also need to remember that we, whoever we are, are probably at the periphery of someone else's center.

Historical sociolinguistics also brings together the oral and the written, as well as the synchronic and diachronic in History of English scholarship. For most of the history of the English language—English until the end of the nineteenth century—linguists must rely on extant written documents to reconstruct developments in the spoken language. As these documents diversify, with burgeoning literacy and printing in the fifteenth century, informal registers such as personal letters and diaries provide perhaps even better access to the colloquial spoken language. This range of documentation allows a fuller history of written English, which is, notwithstanding an emphasis on synchronic language systems throughout the last century, a central part of the history of the English language. William Labov's uniformitarian principle—the linguistic forces we observe operating today operated similarly in the past—helps scholars to interpret the variation witnessed in these written documents and productively brings the synchronic and diachronic into conversation. The current moment in time is as important a moment in the history of English as any moment in the past; while the structure of Modern English bears the imprint of earlier stages in the language's evolution, current variation often signals change in progress.

Under this broader definition, HEL studies intersects with two of the other subfields of English Language Studies distinguished in this volume. American dialectology, the study of past and present American dialects, draws attention away from idealized versions of English to those spoken by actual speakers of the language. In some ways, lexicography is obviously historical, as it attempts to determine the historical semantics of English (including etymologies); less obviously, synchronic lexicography, including that represented in commercial dictionaries like the Merriam-Webster and American Heritage dictionaries, also contributes to the study of the history of English, since an accurate record of word forms and meanings spoken and written now lends perspective to the overall historical picture.

In fact, the historical development of English lexicography and dialectology, as well as any other writing about language facts or attitudes, whether scholarly or popular, constitutes an important part of the history of the language and its speakers. All of these "language sciences," or ways of knowing about language, the History of English included, are mutually supporting and interdependent, and all of them, as well as the technologies on which they depend, have witnessed dramatic changes over the past few decades, as we have moved from index cards to computer files, as we have complemented human reading with computer scanning.

At this moment in the history of English, computers and the Internet are transforming not only the form of English texts and the ways in which interpersonal communication takes place, but also the study of the history of English. The extent to which computer technology is fundamentally affecting English morphosyntax or even English orthography beyond the register of text messages remains open to debate (see, for example, Baron 2008). But we know already that computers have dramatically changed the available methodologies for studying the history of English and, in conjunction with historical sociolinguistics, the scope of what we know about historical changes in English.

The development of historical corpora—systematically compiled databases of texts designed to be representative of historical periods (across registers, gender and class of authors, dialect, etc.), specific registers, specific varieties of English, etc.—have opened up entirely new possibilities for the linguistic questions that can be answered (see Curzan 2008; for a summary of available historical corpora, see Claridge 2009). With such corpora, histories of English can—and in fact should, in order to be considered adequately descriptive—fill in some of the details of how fundamental structural changes in English progressed, rather than simply providing the endpoints familiar from textbooks. Much of this change is difficult to detect, let alone to describe accurately, without the benefit of corpora. For example, we now have many more details about the rise of periphrastic *do*, from its distribution across different constructions (e.g., the development of its use in interrogatives [e.g., *do you see?*] versus in negative declaratives [e.g., *you do not see*]) to its variable use by speakers/writers of different genders and classes (based on material from the Corpus of Early English Correspondence). The auxiliary *do* variation that we see in the works of an author like Shakespeare becomes part of a much broader picture of the ongoing variation that characterized the progression of structural change in the language. Recently, corpus-based methodologies have been employed in historical pragmatics as well, a subfield that offers insights into the ways in which spoken interaction shapes the structure of a language and motivates changes in that structure.

The innovative work happening in corpus-based history of English studies should in no way overshadow the gains scholars are making in the more traditional enterprises of, for example, philology and historical phonology and syntax or with newer approaches such as social network theory, theories of language acquisition, or a focus on language ideology. As Anatoly Liberman demonstrates in his contribution to this section, there remain many etymological mysteries to be solved, for which meticulous comparative work is irreplaceable. Lynda Mugglestone's essay highlights the ways in which pervasive language ideologies that shaped attitudes about standards and correctness can be traced to the contributions of influential people at particular historical moments. History of English scholarship is exciting for its expansiveness, from the development of a word like *wife* or a construction like auxiliary *do* to the construction and influence of language attitudes that shape how English is spoken and spoken about, both informally and formally in places like the academy.

We may strive forever to meet Thomas Jefferson's challenge: "We want an elaborate history of the English language" (qtd. in Bailey 2002b, 466). To be elaborate, that history must encompass the many varieties of English that have always existed and the speakers of those varieties whose innovations, attitudes, and accomplishments shaped and continue to shape the vast bundle of varieties we call "the English language." In fact, it must do the nearly impossible, integrating linguistics, philology, and social and political history. As a highly synthetic discipline, the History of English challenges us, but also provides exciting opportunities to expand our knowledge, not only about the English language, but also about the cultures in which varieties of that language play central roles. In other words, the history of English is not exclusively a subject for historical linguists or professors of English, but for students of history, sociology, anthropology, and any other disciplines that study human behavior, past or present. To achieve Jefferson's "elaborate" history, historians of English, oriented from whatever scholarly perspective, must continually refine the "best practices" of past practice while they develop new methods in tandem with emerging technologies.

5

Benjamin Smart and Michael Faraday: The Principles and Practice of "Talking Proper" in Nineteenth-Century England

LYNDA MUGGLESTONE
University of Oxford

The nineteenth century has, in terms of writing the history of English, frequently seemed to exist in a territory remote from academic attention. Falling uncomfortably between the "normative" eighteenth century and a "modern English" that can appear irreconcilable with prototypical images of Victorian Britain, the language of this period has often found itself subject to a form of critical elision that occludes detailed engagement with the shifts of form and language attitude which can, in reality, be detected over its span. The image with which Richard W. Bailey opens his valuable *Nineteenth-Century English* is hence particularly apt. For Bailey, nineteenth-century English is to be memorably constructed as the unfortunate recipient—or victim—of "telescopic philology." It is in Dickens's *Bleak House*—and the "Telescopic Philanthropy" that heads Chapter IV—that, as Bailey points out, the analogical roots of this term are to be located. Within the novel itself, they are further epitomized in that shift of focus by which Mrs Jellyby's altruistic interests (and social concern) are displaced from her immediate location in a neglected household in nineteenth-century London onto the remote province of Borriboola-Gha in Africa (Dickens 1853, 25). For Bailey, the philological equivalent of this process of deflection is self-evident in conventional approaches to the history of English, and in that close scrutiny which is habitually accorded to the remoter past of language in preference to that which exists, at least temporally, in greater proximity. "Telescopic philology" thereby neatly encapsulates the paradox which is evident in the fact that, as Bailey (1996b, v) argues, "twelfth-century English has been more intensely studied than nineteenth-century English on the assumption that the conquest of England by speakers of Norman French produced revolutionary change, while the industrial revolution stimulated little change at all."

Bailey's own work has, of course, consummately served to re-orient the linguistic gaze, revealing the nineteenth century as a period of "unprecedented linguistic self-consciousness" with significant—and distinctive—shifts in language as social and cultural practice (Bailey 1996b, vi). This essay will explore one particular manifestation of this "unprecedented linguistic self-consciousness"—here by means of the (equally neglected) historical intersection of Michael Faraday, the largely self-educated son of a blacksmith who was to become one of the foremost scientists of the nineteenth century, and Benjamin Smart, one of its most prominent elocutionists. As Smart proclaimed in 1836, "I was born and bred in the west end of London; I appeared before the public five and twenty years ago, as soon as I became of age, in a 'Practical Grammar of English Pronunciation,' . . . from that time to the present I have been employed, seldom out of London, as a teacher of elocution in the first families of the kingdom, not excepting the family of the highest person." As he added, "during the same time, I have been engaged on frequent returning occasions as a lecturer on elocution at all the literary and scientific institutions of the metropolis" (xi, note). These include the Royal Institution where Faraday was Director of the Laboratory from

1825 and Fullerian Professor of Chemistry from 1833 (and where Smart was invited—by Faraday—to lecture on "The Audible Properties of Speech" in one of the celebrated Friday Evening Discourses in 1829).[1]

The history of nineteenth century elocution, and the reframing of language attitudes within notions of an emergent "received pronunciation"(RP), is itself one of the distinctive aspects of this period, one in which "talking proper"—especially in terms of the acquisition of an accent devoid of regional markers—was to be a major prescriptive commonplace (see Mugglestone 2007). Iterated in countless manuals of linguistic etiquette, as well as in schoolbooks and in works more expressly devoted to pronunciation, its reverberations equally informed popular novels, underpinning the contrastive social discourse of, say, Jo and Lady Dedlock in later chapters of Dickens' *Bleak House* or, perhaps more pertinently in this context, of Pip and Joe in *Great Expectations*.[2] Pip's social transformation from his own childhood in a blacksmith's family to a life in which he has conspicuously been "gentlefolked," as Jo the blacksmith remarks (Dickens 1861, ii, 125), can in this light reveal obvious parallels with Faraday's own life—and not least perhaps in the rise of an accompanying linguistic consciousness and a determined transformation in the styles of speech to be deployed (see further Mugglestone 2007, 200–201).

Faraday's exemplary status as a speaker and lecturer has become a commonplace of contemporary as well as later comment. He was an "outstanding lecturer" with "faultless delivery," writes Cantor (1991, 115, 117); "a scientific communicator of the first order" (James 1991–1999, i, pref.), a speaker whose "eloquence . . . compelled attention and insisted upon sympathy" as Jane Pollock affirmed (1870, 293). He was a "lecturer of the highest rank," stated his obituary in the *Times*; at the Royal Institution it was his gifts in this respect which made his "lectures attractive to crowded audiences in Albemarle-street for so many years, and which brought, Christmas after Christmas, troops of young people to attend his exposition of scientific processes and scientific discovery with as much zest as is usually displayed in following lighter amusements" ("The Late Professor Faraday" 1867).

Faraday's status as Smart's most famous protégé (and their lifelong connection after 1817) has, however, hitherto received little attention. Smart's entry in the *DNB* makes no mention of this fact while biographies of Faraday make cursory note of their friendship without exploring Smart's salience in Faraday's prowess as a lecturer, or his role in Faraday's determined self-fashioning (and continued self-monitoring) in terms of language. Nevertheless, in what is a unique resource in the context of elocution and instruction, Faraday's still extant Common Place Book records,[3] in almost 150 closely written pages, the information he gathered from attending Smart's London lectures on oratory in January 1818. The scale and detail of these notes alone provides a telling indicator of the value they held for the young Faraday. Still more telling perhaps, in terms of the enduring importance and influence of Smart, is the fact that over ten years later he was still being paid half a guinea per lecture to attend Faraday's own public performances of science at the Royal Institution "in order that he might inform him of any errors he might commit during the delivery of his lectures."[4]

In this context too therefore, a shift in the accustomed angle of focus may also bring valuable insights into individual language practice (and language attitudes) in the nineteenth century. Prescriptivism clearly demands an object as well as a subject; ideologies require participants as well as practitioners. In the long-term association of Faraday and Smart (and their shared interest in—and application of—elocution) we find a vivid illustration of both. As Bailey (1996b, vii) eloquently stresses, "our language is our most nuanced social gesture." In this particular instance, as we shall see, the precise nuances involved can illuminatingly be used to probe the complex motivations which underpin these mechanisms of reception and response, as well as the varied acts of linguistic (self-) transformation which can result.

Smart's work on oratory and elocution had its roots, in part, in classical theory, a fact noted by Faraday in the habitually neat script of his Common Place Book. A more immediate precedent, however, was located in the writers of the later eighteenth century, particularly Thomas Sheridan and John Walker (or "Elocution Walker" as the latter was known in a popular—and authoritative—sobriquet formed on the model of "Dictionary Johnson"; see Mugglestone 2007, 35). It was Sheridan, for example, who had sought to draw attention to the need for conscious reform in attitudes towards the arts of speech. "'No man can amend a fault of which he is not conscious," he had stressed; likewise "consciousness cannot exert itself, when barred up by habit or vanity"

(Sheridan 1762, 37). This emphasis on a normative consciousness of a "right" or, conversely, a "wrong" way to speak had certainly not been a prominent concern in earlier years. Isaac Watts—later to be another of Faraday's intellectual mentors—had been notably liberal on this head in 1721. "I do not suppose both these Ways of Pronunciation to be equally proper; but both are used, and that among Persons of education and learning in different Parts of the Nation," as Watts had written below a table setting out "Words Accented on Different Syllables, according to the Custom of the Speaker" (1721, 101–102, Note). Even Samuel Johnson, born in 1709, had ultimately rejected the possibility of phonemic constraint ("sounds are too volatile and subtile for legal restraints; to enchain syllables, and to lash the wind, are equally the undertakings of pride, unwilling to measure its desires by its strength" [Johnson 1755, C2[r]]). Only the recommended position of stress for entry-words is given in his *Dictionary*; no further delineation of sound is attempted. "A small intermixture of provincial peculiarities may, perhaps, have an agreeable effect, as the notes of different birds concur in the harmony of the grove, and please more than if they were all exactly alike" remained Johnson's professed view (Boswell 1934 (1799), 159), a position supported by his retention of his native Staffordshire tones, as well as the regional pride in his birthplace which his dictionary also affirms.[5]

Both Sheridan and Walker were, however, to encapsulate a marked shift in language attitudes in this respect, developing detailed notation systems for the transcription of "proper" pronunciation in their dictionaries of, respectively, 1780 and 1791. The title pages indicate the intended transformations at work. *A General Dictionary of the English Language. One Main Object of which, is, to establish a Plain and Permanent Standard of Pronunciation* proclaims Sheridan; *A Critical Pronouncing Dictionary and Expositor of the English Language* with *Rules to be Observed by the Natives of Scotland, Ireland, and London, for Avoiding their Respective Peculiarities,* as Walker states eleven years later. As in the prescriptive attention then being paid to matters of grammar or spelling, "consciousness" in this respect leads to a new-found intolerance of diversity, as well as an increased emphasis on the stated features of "standard" speech (and their socio-symbolic correlates). Both Sheridan and Walker directed specific attention, for example, to the remedial endeavours now deemed necessary for those whose speech revealed regional origins in

Scotland or Ireland. Johnson's Staffordshire was equally without merit. "Many provincials have grown old in the capital, without making any change in their original dialect," Sheridan (1762, 37) commented with distaste;[6] Johnson's language practice reflected the consciousness of an earlier age. Instead, for Sheridan, localized marking was deemed "a sign of disgrace" (its variation "ridiculous and embarrassing" for Walker) while assimilation to the "best speakers" of London was made a subject of explicit dictate. Johnson's biographer, James Boswell, accordingly shed his Scottish tones under Sheridan's direction and became a convert to the philosophy of language which Sheridan expressed ("You are My Socrates ... With unfeigned Joy to I thank Heaven for it," he told Sheridan [qtd. in Martin 2000, 81]); George Greville (the future Marquis of Buckingham), Alexander Wedderburn (who, like Boswell desired to lose his Scottish tones), and the actress Sarah Siddons, as well as the thousands who flocked to Sheridan's lectures over the years, benefited from similar instruction. Walker, as well a range of other writers, continued this emphasis on prescriptive—and proscriptive—exhortation, directing particular attention to the transgressive accents of the London poor, as well as to those suffering the disadvantage of other 'peculiarities' resulting from a location geographically removed from the capital, or one which was socially removed from its elite.

It was into this intellectual matrix that Smart placed his own work, capitalizing on the interest in elocution which was to be a prominent feature in work on language in the late eighteenth and early nineteenth centuries. Smart capitalized too on the language anxieties that, as Bailey (1996b, 71) has commented, were an inevitable result of this often stringent emphasis on images of linguistic deficit. The stratified linguistic landscape depicted in Smart's *Practical Grammar of English Pronunciation* of 1810 was, for instance, to engage in an uncompromising opposition of "ignorant" and "educated": "the cultivated speaker employs a definite number of sounds which he utters with precision, distinctness, and in their proper places; the vulgar speaker misapplies the sounds, mars, or alters them" (Smart 1810, 9). Articulation, as Smart stressed, was of more than words alone, participating instead in the communication of a host of supra-linguistic associations. Appeal is made to "well-bred speakers" as paradigms to be followed in the individual reform of articulation; the judgment of "polite ears" is appealed to in instances in which pronunciations may vary. As in Sheridan and Walker, the reader is impressed with the sense that remedial instruction is desirable for all "Persons with Provincial Habits, Defects and Impediments in Speech," a situation for which Smart is also, we are told, willing to provide private instruction.[7] Within his later work, Smart was to provide detailed "Principles of Remedy for Defects of Utterance." For "defects" originating in "Vulgar and Rustic, Provincial and Foreign Habits," elocution would, with dedicated practice and industry, undoubtedly provide a cure (Smart 1836, xl).

Smart's words serve to reinforce a dominant topos of the age, one which spans both eighteenth and nineteenth centuries. "The most forcible reasoning loses half its effect when disguised in the awkwardness of a provincial dress," as Sylvester Douglas (1991 [1779], 99) had written in 1779, likewise reflecting a consciousness of this hegemonic emphasis on the acquisition of one particular style of speech above other co-existing varieties. "It is EVERYBODY'S BUSINESS to speak; and if it is EVERYBODY'S BUSINESS to speak, it is worth EVERYBODY'S while to speak correctly," as Marcus Davis (1865, 18) later endorsed. The "educated" speaker, well-versed in knowledge of the requisite arts of speech, was in such ways to become a popular cultural touchstone, its legacies still evident of course in modern collocations such as an "educated voice," an "educated accent." Moreover, while Sheridan and Walker had stressed the desirability of assimilating regional modes of speech to "the best speakers of the metropolis," Smart's work can also be used to confirm a more significant shift within the history of pronunciation in the nineteenth century. The identification of RP as a non-localized and prestigious—if minority—form of speech (one devoid of those geographical markers early proscribed by Sheridan) is today usually credited to the phonetician Alexander Ellis ("In the present day we may ... recognise a received pronunciation all over the country, not widely differing in any particular locality, and admitting a certain degree of variety" [Ellis 1869–1889, i, 23]). However, it is this particular variety (and its needful acquisition) to which Smart was to devote much of his writing and lecturing career. As he wrote in 1836: "the common standard dialect is that in which all marks of a particular place of birth and remedy are lost, and nothing appears to indicate any other habits of intercourse than with the well-bred and well-informed, wherever they may be found" (xl). Possession of a localized accent could, conversely signal the converse. Even if "a person need not blush because he cannot help betraying he is a Scotchman or an Irishman," nevertheless "it may be an object of ambition to prove that his circle of intercourse has extended ... beyond his native place." This was still more imperative for those whose discourse signalled the cockney or provincial. As Smart added, "a man displaying either must have a large portion of natural talent or acquired science, who surmounts the prejudice it creates" (1836, xl).

A determined acquisition of science was, in a variety of ways of course, to be a salient characteristic of Michael Faraday throughout his life. An exemplary autodidact, he had, he records, received "little more than the rudiments of reading, writing, and arithmetic" at "a common day-school" located near the family's lodgings over a coach-house in London (Williams 1965, 8–9). Born in Newington Butts in 1791 (the year in which Walker's seminal *Critical Pronouncing Dictionary* was first published), Faraday's childhood was spent on the outskirts of London, in the area which forms the modern Elephant and Castle. Here he undoubtedly grew up, as Hamilton (2002, 2) states, bearing the accent of the streets. While his elder brother followed his father in becoming a blacksmith, Faraday was instead apprenticed in 1805 to Mr George Riebau, a bookseller and bookbinder in Blanchford Street. Like the young Samuel Johnson (who read assiduously among the contents of his father's bookshop), Faraday's application during his apprenticeship evidently extended to the contents as well as the construction of books. He read Jane Marcet's *Conversations on Chemistry*, Fanny Burney's *Evelina*, and a lengthy section of the *Encyclopaedia Britannica* dealing with electricity (among a range of other works). As Faraday wrote in 1810 (dedicating a bound volume of his scientific notes to Riebau), he had been "readily permit[ted] to examine those books in your possession that were in any way related to the subjects then occupying my attention" (qtd. Pearce Williams 1965, 10). Such subjects were—as Faraday's bound notes attest—already increasingly inclined to science.

In the practical application of self-help which this already reveals, it was Faraday's reading of Isaac Watts's *The Improvement of the Mind* in 1809 which proved of seminal importance. An inspirational treatise "made up of a Variety of Remarks and Directions for the Improvement of the Mind in useful Knowledge," Watts's *Improvement* was explicitly addressed to "Persons in Younger years" (Watts 1743, x). His stated hope that such readers "may find something here which may waken a latent Genius, and direct the Studies of a willing Mind" was to be remarkably prescient in Faraday's case. "May there not be Sir *Isaac Newtons* in every science?" Watts (1743, 16) demanded: "You should never despair . . . of finding out that which has never yet been found." As Riebau confirmed in a letter written in October or November 1813, Watts' *Improvement* was, for Faraday, to be a work which "was read and frequent took in his Pocket" (James *CMF*, i, 67). Faraday was moreover to be strikingly receptive to its exhortations. Watts's directives on the beneficial role of close observation, of reading, of commonplace books, on the "Advantages of verbal Instructions by publick or private lectures" (Watts 1743, 38), and of improvement in language were all followed, quite literally, to the letter. In Watts, one can, for example, trace the foundation of the later Faraday's interest in scientific instruction for children, and at least some of the impetus for the inception in 1826 of the Juvenile Lectures which would henceforth be delivered at the Royal Institution each Christmas ("In order to furnish the Mind with a rich Variety of Ideas, the *laudable curiosity of young people should be indulged and gratify'd* ... It is a very hopeful Sign in young Creatures, to see them curious in observing, and inquisitive in searching into the greatest Part of Things that occur ..." [Watts 1743, 53]). Watts's precepts on the wider intellectual value of observation would likewise be echoed by Faraday throughout his life. "Our sense-perceptions are wonderful. Even in the observant, but unreflective infant, they soon produce a result which looks like intuition, because of its perfection. Coming to the mind as so many data, they are stored up, and without our being conscious, are ever after used in like circumstances in forming our judgment," as he wrote in a lecture in 1854, the title of which—"Observations on Mental Education"—further confirms Watts's influential role (see Faraday 1991).[8]

Watts's comments on language were also the subject of Faraday's close attention. With reference to written style, for example, Watts made it clear that usage was qualitative, able to reveal both "blemishes" and "excellencies." Both were to be monitored by the reader bent on self-improvement. "Blemishes" were to be noted so that they might henceforth be avoided; observation of perceived "excellencies" was conversely to foster emulation and subsequent adoption. Spoken language was, for Watts, equally a matter for concern. While books—as "*dumb teachers*"—offered merely "silent and sedentary" instruction (Watts 1743, 38), lectures—and the direct presentation of information to ear as well as mind—were, he stressed, particularly potent in their effects:

> There is something *more sprightly, more delightful,* and *entertaining* in the living Discourse of a wise, a learned, and well-qualified Teacher . . . The very Turn of Voice, the good Pronunciation, and the polite and alluring Manner which some teachers have attained, will engage the Attention, keep the Soul fixed, and . . . convey and insinuate into the Mind, the Ideas of Things in a more lively and forcible way. (Watts 1743, 38)

Watts's exhortations on the rightful acquisition of knowledge by the zealous individual were met by a program of extensive reading and note-taking on Faraday's part. His attendance at Mr Tatum's lectures on scientific subjects (as well as his active membership of the City Philosophical Society with its own agendas for self-improvement) satisfied Watts's criteria for "living instruction." Watts's strictures on language also clearly fostered a disciplined response. "*Grammar* . . . teaches us to speak and pronounce, to spell and write with Propriety and Exactness, according to the Custom of those in every Nation who are . . . supposed to speak and write their own Language best," Watts (1743, 349) had stated. Faraday's conviction of his own "deficiency" in this respect likewise led to a determined programme of reform, carried out by means of his correspondence with Benjamin Abbott, a well-educated clerk he had met at the City Philosophical Society. As Faraday declared with appropriately scientific precision in a letter to Abbott in July 1812, "MF is deficient in certain points, that he wants to make up. Epistolary writing is one cure for these deficiencies, therefore, MF should practice Epistolary writing" (James *CMF*, i, 4: M. Faraday to B. Abbott, 12–13/ 7/ 1812). His aim was the amelioration of "the expression, the delivery, the composition a manner of connecting words." All are "points" on which "I want improving," Abbott was informed.

Faraday's comments reveal, of course, his own embedding within the prescriptive consciousness of the age, as well as his own responsiveness to the prescriptive desiderata to acquire "standard" rather than "non-standard forms." His regionally (and socially)-marked grammar in these early letters bears out his sense of conscious deficit. "I understand from my brother that you was in good health," he comments in the same letter to Abbott (James *CMF*, i, 7), displaying an infelicity of noun and verb which was the subject of explicit censure in contemporary grammatical writing. Describing his manuscript notes on the celebrated Humphry Davy's lectures (which Faraday had heard, courtesy of some free tickets to the Royal Institution in 1812), he confesses "there is in them errors that will not bear to be jested with" (James *CMF*, i, 9: M. Faraday to B. Abbott, 20/9/1812). Full stops, commas, and other marks of punctuation display a latitude markedly out of step with the prescriptive thrust of work by eighteenth-century grammarians such as Lindley Murray or Robert Lowth; incidental confusions—of *hear* and *here*, *principle* and *principal*—confirm the presence of still other areas of linguistic uncertainty ("Hear I am dear Sir on the third page of my paper . . ."; "I have thus dear Abbott detailed the principle facts that I am acquainted with . . ." [James *CMF*, i, 9: M. Faraday to B. Abbott 20/7/1812; James *CMF*, i, 26: M. Faraday to B. Abbott, 1/9/ 1812]). While the content of Faraday's letters ranges fluently over the discoveries of Davy and Lavoisier, or the chemical properties of various substances, grammar—famously defined by Lowth as "the art of speaking with propriety"—hence frequently operates at an entirely different level.

The components of Faraday's later written style triumphantly affirm the success of these attempts at linguistic amelioration (consider, for instance, the opening of a letter to Ada Lovelace on 24 October 1844: "Your letter ought to have been answered before but there are two circumstances which have caused delay, its high character and my want of health, for since I returned from a very forced journey to Durham I have been under the Doctor's hands: I am quickly recovering and now have the difficult pleasure of writing to you . . . the thanks which I owe you can only properly be acknowledged by an open & sincere reply and the absence of all conventional phrase"[James *CMF*, iii, 264–65]). Language in its spoken form, however, also occupied Faraday's attention. Watts's comments on the need to pay attention to the "good pronunciation" (or otherwise) of lecturers was, for instance, actively assimilated into Faraday's early assessment of Humphry Davy's skills in 1812: "He spoke in the most energetic and luminous manner of the Advancement of the Arts and Sciences ... during the whole of these observations his delivery was easy, his diction elegant, his tone good and his sentiments sublime."[9] Abbott's own delivery, in a lecture at the City Philosophical Society, was also the subject of explicit comment:

> Of the Lecture, its Character and Delivery, to you I shall say nothing but that all was excellent ... I was highly gratified with the order observed throughout the last Lecture when I perused it it was not so evident but it appeared in an eminent degree in the delivery and conferred upon it a degree of clearness & simplicity even beyond what I expected. (James *CMF*, i, 43: M. Faraday to B. Abbott, 7/12/1812)

As Faraday here confirmed, the oratorical skills of the speaker affected sense as well as sound, facilitating or impeding the communication of ideas. "There is . . . a great deal of Art necessary in the representation of matters to the Auditory," as Watts (1743, 350) had pointed out.

Lecturing—and the oral exposition of ideas—was to become a central topos of the letters exchanged between Faraday and Abbott. Even if, as Faraday admitted, "I have yet to learn" (James *CMF*, i, 55: M. Faraday to B. Abbott, 1/6/1813), it is clear that he was already directing explicit attention to the qualities which contributed to effective spoken communication. While these include "the utmost precision and clearness that language allows," as a letter to Abbott three days later confirms (James *CMF*, i, 58), as well as (again echoing Watts), the need to adjust style and content according to the addressee, it is, for Faraday, "good delivery" which is identified as "the most prominent requisite." As he stressed: "A Lecturer should endeavour by all means to obtain a facility of utterance and the power of cloathing his thoughts and ideas in language smooth and harmonious"(James *CMF*, i, 60: M. Faraday to B. Abbott, 11/ 6/1813). Three years later he was still occupied by the same considerations, writing to Abbott on 14 January 1816 to demand his "opinions of & observations on English composition—style—delivery—reading—oratory—grammar—pronunciation" (James *CMF*, i, 138; M. Faraday to B. Abbott, 14/1/1816).

By this point, moreover, Faraday was also three years into a determined program of remedial instruction with reference to his own mode of speech. A "mutual improvement plan" established in 1813 with Edward Magrath and other equally motivated individuals made the spoken language its prime focus. As Faraday explained, the remit of this plan was for all concerned "to read together; and to criticize, correct, and improve each other's pronunciation and construction of language" (qtd. in Gladstone 1872, 11–12). Further revealing a willing engagement with contemporary ideas of norm and deviation (and the resulting sensitization to notions of 'good' speech as advocated by both Sheridan and Smart), the plan was self-evidently also designed to aid in the conscious displacement of features deemed deleterious, as well as facilitating assimilation of the kind of articulatory confidence in the properties (and proprieties) of speech which had been commended in Smart's 1812 *Grammar of English Sounds* or in Walker's highly influential works.

Faraday's self-imposed apprenticeship in language was to be a lengthy one. Language had, of course, already in part proved the key to Faraday assuming a role at the Royal Institution; it was his bound notebooks—this time of Davy's lectures in 1812—which had been shown to Humphrey Davy (then Professor of Chemistry at the Royal Institution). When, as a result of his sight being injured in the course of an experiment, Davy had need of an amanuensis, it was Faraday's commendably clear script and precise written exposition (as well as his scientific enthusiasm) which came to mind. While this appointment was merely temporary, the opportunity to accompany Davy on a tour through Europe as his "Philosophical Assistant" followed (James 2004); by 1815, Faraday found himself no longer "bookseller and binder"[10] but a fully-fledged employee at the Royal Institution (the aims of which tallied precisely with his own committed interest in knowledge and its diffusion in all spheres of life).[11] He was lecturing to the City Philosophical Society (on the general properties of matter) in 1816, already starting to put to the test his assimilation of a different—and "improved"—style of speech (his first lecture—on electricity—had been delivered there in 1810). Sessions with Magrath on the plan outlined above continued; only in 1820 did his private instruction on this model cease. Even afterwards, Magrath's attention to Faraday's spoken delivery remained in evidence. As Margery Reid, Faraday's niece, recalled, Magrath would, for instance, attend Faraday's morning lectures during the 1830s "for the sole purpose of noting down for him any faults of delivery or defective pronunciation that could be detected. The list was always received with thanks; although his corrections were not uniformly adopted, he was encouraged to continue his remarks with perfect freedom" (Jones 1870, 115).[12]

As Faraday would argue in 1854, "education has for its first and last step *humility* . . . . It can commence only because of a conviction of deficiency"(1991 [1854], 485). While public commendation therefore attended the apparent ease and artless fluency of his later lectures at the Royal Institution, behind the scenes, as Faraday, Abbott, and Magrath were aware, an all too conscious art was at work, eliminating perceived 'deficiency' through stringent industry and self-improvement. "I must exert myself to attain their language, so as to join their world," as Faraday had commented on his first day in Paris with Sir Humphry and Lady Davy (qtd. in Hamilton 2002, 61). Formally directed to his observation of the French, it is a comment which nevertheless can be seen to underpin his unremitting industry in the arts of educated discourse as well as his personal translation between the radically different spheres of artisan and scholar.

Smart's connection with Faraday would participate in these same convictions of beneficial change and qualitative improvement. Faraday began attending Smart's lectures in 1817 and his letters in September of that year show that Smart's instruction already took precedence over a social meeting with Abbott. By January 1818, he was beginning a new course of eight lectures with Smart. Financially, attendance was no trivial matter. Smart's courses on elocution were prominently advertised on the first page of the *Times*,[13] and their cost—half a guinea—reflected the value of the knowledge he had to impart. For Faraday, who was then earning some 20 shillings a week, this represented a significant investment. It was, however, one which was deemed eminently worth it as the extent and detail of his subsequent notes confirm. Smart's stress on "theory" and "science," as well as the precision of his terminology and instructions, would clearly have proved congenial. His dictates on the modulation of the voice in relation to the specific requirements of a room gave careful consideration to issues which Faraday had already explored in his letters to Abbott (see, e.g., James *CMF*, i, 56: M. Faraday to B. Abbott, 1/6/1813). Smart's recommendation that the good lecturer should always look at the member of the audience who is nearest and speak as if talking directly to them—a precept also carefully noted down by Faraday—would later establish an important, and highly successful, aspect of his own lecturing style. In the Common Place Book Faraday inscribes too the need for "variety and harmony of inflection," especially since it "enables us to avoid that monotony in sound and manner which never fails to throw a dullness over the speaker" (Faraday CPB, 192).

For Smart, the art of speaking was always far more than the incidental deployment of the voice. As Faraday's notes record, Smart's lectures distinguished between *Mechanical Reading* ("which includes as distinct parts the command of the voice Pronunciation of Words Distinctness of Articulation Smoothness in the utterance of words when connected in sentences and a due preservation of the Rithmus both in Prose & Verse"), *Significant Reading* (in which sound, rhythm, and intonation unite to underscore the sense), *Impassioned Reading* ("those variations of voice look and manner that indicate the sensitive and impassioned state of mind"), and *Dramatic Reading* (that which is directed to performance of a particular character or role). Since, as Smart acknowledged to his audience in 1818, "I do not suppose that you want to be actors but speakers," (Faraday CPB, 184) it was the more general proprieties of speech—and the effective use of the voice in lecturing—which assumed prominence for much of the course. Smart stressed the salience of first principles—and the articulatory foundations of good speech. "We first have to consider the capacity and command of the voice its defects and the best means of removing them," Faraday diligently echoed in his notes, mindful perhaps of his own tendency to pronounce /r/ as /w/ (Faraday CPB, 192–93).[14] The consonance of this with Watts's earlier words could hardly have failed to escape his notice. Whereas Watts had considered pronunciation only in its most general terms, however, Smart was to engage in a precise anatomization of the nature of possible "defects" as well as the means for their "removal."

Smart was unequivocal in his endorsement of a normative approach to speech. Exhortatory verbs are common, again meticulously recorded in Faraday's hand. "Provincialities must be corrected by a dictionary for which purpose I would recommend Walker's," Faraday writes, inscribing too Smart's axiom "always pronounce words according to the best usage of the time" (Faraday CPB, 195). While Faraday's notes of Tatum's earlier lectures on science can register dissent as to what is stated, or introduce the possibility of other interpretations, no such departures are recorded here. "It is absolutely necessary," Faraday echoes, to study the principles of articulation; effective use of language "should be founded in a perfect knowledge of all the different simple sounds in our language as being the elements of all speaking sounds" (Faraday CPB, 196). Smart's caution that, without such knowledge, the speaker—especially in public discourse, "will immediately fall into error" is likewise noted on the following page.

Smart's exposition of the infelicities of particular sounds receives considerable attention. The rightful deployment of /h/—perhaps the foremost shibboleth in nineteenth-century speech—is given pride of place (Mugglestone 2007, 95–134). A negative marker of both cockney and provincial speech, this is, Smart states, the one sound in English which is "the most subject to a corrupt pronunciation and therefore requiring our early attention" (Faraday CPB, 199). In the Common Place Book, Faraday's attention remains fixed on /h/—and its absence—for almost a page of his closely-written text. He notes its "want where it ought to be used and the use where it is not required." He carefully sets out the eight words which were, with propriety, pronounced without /h-/ in the early nineteenth century (*hour, honour, hospital, humble, heir, hostler, honest, honesty*). He likewise transcribes Smart's directions for correcting individual fallibilities in this context ("The person should practice himself in lists of words beginning with H, then in mixed lists of words some beginning with H, and some with a vowel and lastly with the introduction of the words commencing with H mute") (Faraday CPB, 199). As before, Walker's dictionary is commended for the achievement of "correct use," its role as a reference model essential, Faraday notes, "for the attainment of facility in the pronunciation of words."

The acquisition of the recommended accent is methodically described. Systematic instructions given throughout the lectures set down practice exercises which will bring improvement in, for example, the articulation of *-ing* with a velar nasal /ŋ/ rather than merely as *-in* (a form of speech which, as in the novels of Dickens and others, would evolve into a ready stereotype of the uneducated speaker). Smart's second lecture presents a detailed account of consonants while the recommended articulation of vowels occupies Lecture 3, attended by Faraday on January 13, 1818. Smart's presentation of information on this head was, as Faraday's Common Place Book confirms, far more detailed than it was to be in his *Theory of Elocution* which was published in the following year. Moreover, Faraday was here clearly able to profit—as Watts had early indicated—by the particular advantages of "living instruction." While *The Theory of Elocution*, or Smart's earlier works on, say the *Grammar of English Sounds*, attempt to articulate the necessary vocal precision—and oratorical skills—by means of the printed page, Faraday had the benefit of Smart's own abilities as elocutionist incarnate. Moreover, as Faraday's notes attest, Smart did not merely lecture a passive audience but actively engaged with their queries on the pronunciation of particular words and sounds, discussing and elaborating on the substance of his lecture after its formal conclusion.

The experience—and thrust—of Smart's lectures was deliberately transformative. "As a teacher it is my duty to give you all the assistance my art can afford," he promised (Faraday CPB, 284). As in Watts, self-improvement is assumed to be the desired goal: "I have constantly supposed that you would endeavour to make these lectures useful by applying them to actual improvement at your homes . . . I have endeavoured to accommodate them to this use" (Faraday CPB, 318–19). The "steady attention" of his audience is directed to his *Grammar of English Sounds* as an additional guide in articulatory reform, not least in the exercises it provides for the continued application of the student in the forms of "good pronunciation" as adapted to "good speakers." While other parts of the lecture course deal with the art of oratory in ways which undoubtedly also influenced Faraday's own later practice as lecturer, it was the fundamental importance of articulation which Smart repeatedly impressed upon his audience. Such skills "are essential to form the finished speaker and are the first requisites to be obtained," he declared in his final lecture (his words once again noted down by Faraday) (Faraday CPB, 315–16). Faraday noted too Smart's insistence on "the confidence which is given by a consciousness that one knows the correct sounds to be uttered."

Confidence is, of course, the antidote to anxiety, to the sense of "deficiency" which Faraday early expressed in his letters to Abbott. Given the "burning desire for self-improvement" which Pearce Williams (1965, 43) describes, as well as Faraday's assiduous application in writing up the

146 pages of his lecture notes (which are carefully indexed for ease of later reference), one cannot doubt his receptivity to Smart's directives on deliberate reform of the voice—especially perhaps given the highly negative positioning of London accents (outside those of the elite) which appears in much contemporary prescriptive rhetoric. If Faraday had indeed once had the accent of the streets, its elimination was assured by the recommendations for improvement which Smart had here proffered in abundance, and which Faraday records in meticulous detail. As Faraday declared in a lecture he gave to the City Philosophical Society a few months later "man is an improving animal": "that man only is to be contemned and despised who is *not* in a state of transition."[15]

In later years, Faraday would unreservedly commend "the great service of [Smart's] instructions" which he had himself received (James *CMF,* iii, 659: M. Faraday to B. H. Smart, 16/12/1847). Smart too stressed Faraday's paradigmatic status in this respect. "No one can better judge my claims whether as to merit or defect," he wrote to Faraday (James *CMF*, iii, 7: B. H. Smart to M. Faraday, 10/2/1841); their early relationship as pupil and teacher, and later as celebrated scientist and humble elocutionist, is celebrated in the dedication to Smart's *Thought and Language* of 1855 ("To Michael Faraday Esq. . . . This Essay, though in a Department of Philosophy distinct from that in which his name Stands Illustrious, yet Being an Attempt to be Carried Out in the Inductive Spirit which his Example Eminently Recommends, is, with Vivid Recollections of early Friendship and Continued Kindness, Affectionately Inscribed"). For Faraday, the enduring value of elocution would be endorsed in private as well as public roles. As Watts had early stressed, the diligent pupil must in turn become a "disciple." Faraday duly instructs his niece on the models of standard speech and effective oral delivery that he had learned from Smart ("I well remember how unweariedly he would go over and over one sentence, and make me repeat it with the upward and downward inflections, till he was satisfied," as Margery Reid later recalled [qtd. in Hamilton 2002, 175]).

Nevertheless, as Bailey (1996b, vii) also reminds us, such simple oppositions of "standard" and "non-standard," or "good" and "bad," in matters of language, are rarely the end of the story. In the wider history of English, models that merely assume "metropolis and hinterland, capital and colony, standard language and dialect have little to offer except fragmentation and prejudice." Prejudice—the skewed and arbitrary valuing (and devaluing) of different aspects of human identity—is, of course, perceptible in Faraday's own history, whether in the "haughty and proud" Lady Davy's attempts to "debase" him—as servant rather than savant—on the European tour[16] or, in linguistic terms, in the cultural dyads which informed popular language attitudes on the perceived merits (or demerits) of particular varieties of speech. As in Smart's work, a qualitative divide was, in popular opinion, often to separate "good" and "bad" speech (and those who used these forms). "Language, both oral and written, is an exponent of the condition of the mind," the Reverend D. Williams firmly proclaimed, for instance, in 1850, "when mean and inappropriate if infers that the habits of life and the condition of the mind are equally mean and uncultivated."

Faraday's own religious faith (even if not that of the Reverend Williams) would have ensured his own indifference to any such assumptions about "habits of life."[17] As his biographers record, Faraday was entirely unconcerned by "social and fashionable frippery" (Cantor 1991, 111). He had, comments Tyndall (1870), "not a trace of worldly ambition." Neither the stated influence of accent on the social affections, nor its often extolled role as a signifier as social status, would have held appeal. Popular nineteenth-century constructions of "educatedness"—complete with its assumed linguistic correlates—were nevertheless of a different order. As in his early musings to Abbot on the nature of "good" delivery, language—both spoken and written—was, for Faraday, to be a vital tool in the exposition of ideas, able to facilitate—or impede—an audience's response. Faraday's determined acquisition of "standard" grammar—as in his later deployment of *you were* rather than *you was*—can, in this respect, be placed alongside his equally studied response to the prevalent tenets of standard speech and his acquisition of a largely "accentless" and thereby "educated" voice, complete with /h/ and /ɪŋ/ where they should "properly" be present. Faraday's aim, as he admitted, was to counter "illiterate" language with that which connoted—and conveyed—its converse ("His language being that of the most illiterate, [he] induced Mr. McGrath (the Secretary of the City Philosophical Society, and now of the Athenaeum Club) … to devote two hours every week to his instruction; and for seven years, did Faraday uninterruptedly receive them" [James *CMF*, ii, 246: 'Memorandum to Robert Peel', 31/3/1835]).

Nineteenth-century language attitudes that unreservedly depicted one form of language as reflective of education—as opposed to others which, however arbitrarily, connoted "ignorance"—seem therefore to have ensured Faraday's determined self-fashioning under the tutelage of Smart and Magrath (aided perhaps by an early encounter with the negative consequences of disfavoured forms of speech) (Faraday CPB, 192). In Smart's words, "acquired science" (here on a wide variety of levels), together with the "large portion of natural talent" which Smart also commends, were indeed to ensure that Faraday was remembered for his skills as a communicator of science, and as an "educated speaker" of the first order.

NOTES

1. The Friday Evening Discourses at the Royal Institution were founded by Faraday in 1826; he delivered 123 of these before 1862, attracting wide audiences (including members of the royal family) and considerable acclaim.
2. For a wider examination of the politics and problems of representing speech in the nineteenth-century novel, see Mugglestone (2007), Chapters 4–6.
3. See M. Faraday, "Lectures on Oratory by Mr B. H. Smart." IEE UK0108 SC MSS 002/1/4. Common Place Book 1816-46. Henceforth referred to as Faraday CPB.
4. F. A. J. L. James (ed.), *The Correspondence of Michael Faraday* (London: The Institution of Electrical Engineers, 1991-99), ii, 246: Memorandum to Robert Peel 31/3/1835. Henceforth referred to as *CMF*.
5. See, e.g., Johnson's entry for *lich*: "A dead carcase; whence lichwake, the time or act of watching by the dead; lichgate, the gate through which the dead are carried to the grave; Lichfield, the field of the dead, a city in Staffordshire, so named from martyred Christians. *Salve magna parens*."
6. *Dialect* here signifies speech as much as the regionalized forms of lexis or grammar (a usage in keeping with the definition given in Sheridan's 1780 *Dictionary*: "the sub-divisions of a language; style, manner of expression, language, speech").
7. See also the title page of Smart's *A Grammar of English Sounds or the First Step in Elocution* (1812). The swift appearance of this work, two years after the *Grammar* of 1810, is also some indication of demand as well as the "consciousness" urged by Sheridan in 1762.
8. The lecture was originally delivered before Prince Albert and the assembled members of the Royal Institution on May 6, 1854.
9. M. Faraday, MS of "Lectures by Sir H Davy" (1812), 363. Cited in Hamilton (2002), 30.
10. See M. Faraday to an unidentified aunt and uncle, 13 September 1813: "I was formerly a bookseller and binder, but am now turned philosopher." In James, *CMF* i, 66.

11. The Royal Institution was founded in 1799 for "diffusing the knowledge, and facilitating the general introduction, of useful mechanical inventions and improvements; and for teaching, by courses of philosophical lectures and experiments, the application of science to the common purposes of life." It received its Royal Charter in 1800.
12. Margery Reid's recollections of her uncle in the years 1830–40 are given in Bence Jones, ii, 112–115.
13. See e.g., *The Times* 12 August 1814, 1; *The Times*, 15 April 1815, 1.
14. Early evidence of this inability is attested in Hamilton, though the story of the educational correctives his "common day-school" attempted to provide for this perceived deficit might well be apocryphal. If true, however, it might well contribute to explaining Faraday's acute sensitization to voice and its needful "correction."
15. M. Faraday, "Observations on the Inertia of the Mind," 342. Originally delivered to the City Philosophical Society on 1 July 1818, the lecture is transcribed in full in Faraday's CPB, pp. 337-63.
16. See his letter to Abbott, 25 January 1815, in James, *CMF*, i, 117 . While the tour contributed to his continuing improvement by means of Humphry Davy's scientific instruction (see Faraday's letter to R. G. Abbott, 6 August 1814 in James, *CMF*, i, 80), Lady Davy clearly contributed to Faraday's consciousness of social difference, and the "polishing" which acquaintance which polite life should bring. As he confessed to Abbott), "when I left England unused as I was to high life & to politeness . . . I was little suited to come within the observation of one whose whole life consist of forms etiquette & manners . . . as I became more acquainted with the manners of the world and those things necessary in my station and understood better her true character I learned to despise her taunts . . . this kind of determined conduct added to a little polishing which the friction of the world had naturally produced in your friend made her restrain her spleen from its full course to a more moderate degree."
17. See Cantor (1991) for a full discussion of Faraday in the context of his faith.

6

The Etymology of the Word *Wife*

ANATOLY LIBERMAN
University of Minnesota

Introduction

Probably no other area of linguistics throws the contours of a language into such sharp relief as does etymology. In studying the origin of words, one deals with phonetics, morphology, semantics, style, and occasionally syntax, all of them in their synchronic and diachronic aspects. Besides, etymology is unthinkable without the broadest exposure to the wide world, for what are words unless we know the reality behind them? Words are born every day, and we wonder where they come from. Some of the latest neologisms are often as difficult to trace to their source as the oldest nouns and verbs.

Because etymology is harder than they expect, many (not only amateurs but also professionals) invent word histories that only "foul the trail" and take us further away from sought-for solutions. Some of the more industrious imagine "systems" of etymology that appeal to common sense (or at least to their sense) rather than subject themselves to the rigors of comparative linguistics. For example, in *Rogue Scholar:*

The Sinister Life and Celebrated Death of Edward H. Rulloff (2003b), Richard W. Bailey describes Rulloff's etymological "method," which "explained the relation between *awe* and *daunt* by saying that the latter was simply the former with some consonants attached to it and that *love* and *lust* were related to *voluptas* by the fact that all three words shared some of the same letters" (190). As will become clear, far-fetched etymologies are far from isolated to Rulloff or to these words.

The subject matter of this essay is the "protohistory" of English *wife* and its cognates. Many generations of etymologists have tried to reconstruct the circumstances in which this word arose. Which feminine quality underlies *wife*, from *wīf* 'woman'? Gone is the age of innocence when E[1] *girl* could be derived from Lat. *garrula* 'garrulous', for "girls are notorious chatterboxes." Unlike our predecessors, we need sound laws, grammatical transparency, and stylistic congruity. Why did *wife* emerge as a neuter? Was it a taboo word? Did the protoform have a suffix, or are we dealing with "a pure root"? As usual in works on etymology, before proposing a new solution (and I have one), it will be necessary to examine the older views on the subject. My earliest reference goes back to 1617; the latest is dated 2003. The plot is complex, and the witnesses are many. But an etymologist always writes thrillers. The solution comes as the denouement of a long goal-oriented search. My piece is not an exception.

The Problem

The Old English for *wife* was *wīf*, and it meant "woman," as it still does in the phrase *old wives' tale* and such compounds as *midwife, goodwife, housewife*, and *fisherwife* (a fisherman catches fish, while a fisherwife sells it: note the lack of parallelism). Already in Old English, *man(n)* "person" was appended to *wīf*, and *wīfmann*, by a series of sound changes, yielded *woman*. The only indubitable cognates of OE *wīf* are OFr/OS *wīf* and OHG *wîb* (G *Weib*), later often spelled *wîp*. (I will stick to the irritating convention and designate vowel length in three different ways: by means of a macron for Old English, a circumflex sign for Old/Middle High German and Old Saxon, and an acute for Old Icelandic.) ON *víf* may be a borrowing from Old English. It occurs only in poetry, and its reflexes in the modern Scandinavian languages are also poeticisms, a fact that seems to point to its antiquity, but in Old Icelandic, even words from the sphere of ancient religion are sometimes borrowings. Holthausen (1920) noted the Gothic proper name *Vivildis* (= OHG *Wîbhilt*) and reconstructed Go. **weif* (GEW[2]). Krogmann (1958–59, 13) gave this reconstruction full support, but it is hard to share his enthusiasm. In the extant Gothic texts, only *qens* 'wife' and *qino* 'woman' occur. If **weif* had existed, it would probably have turned up at least as an element of some compound. *Vivildis* may have been a borrowed name, or its bearer may have had German roots.

Wīf and its congeners have always meant "woman." A complete lack of semantic variation knocks the bottom out of etymological fantasies, and that is why it is so easy to refute all the existing hypotheses and so difficult to offer an acceptable solution. Words for "woman" come from many sources. Specific occupations (like guarding the hearth and making bread) and physiological functions (like childbearing and breastfeeding) often leave traces in agent nouns (from "guardian" or "bread maker" to "woman"), metonymies are common (cf. the history of *chaperon:* from "hood" to "protecting object/person"), and so are proper names (from *Molly* to "woman"). Languages abound in pejorative metaphors for "woman." Keller's collection of words from English dialects (?1938), about 600 of them, makes instructive reading. Here again *wīf* leaves nothing to an imaginative scholar, for, as far as we can judge, *wīf* and its cognates lacked emotional overtones from time immemorial. Despite such severe limitations, conjectures on the origin of *wīf* are numerous. A persuasive etymology of this word should, I believe, be simple, even obvious. And—the greatest riddle of all—it will have to explain why a stylistically neutral name for "woman" (probably not a metonymy of the *chaperon* type) was neuter. G *Weib*, Icel. *wíf*, and Sw. *viv* are still neuter nouns; only in Danish and Norwegian have sex and gender merged: in both of them, *viv* is feminine.

Earlier and Later Fanciful Derivations of *Wīf* and Its Cognates

The earliest attempts to discover the origin of *wīf* and its cognates revolve around mythological names and come from editions of medieval poems. Reportedly, the *Edda* constructed the nonexistent name

Vé-Freyja (*vé* 'sacred, sacral') and derived OI *wíf* from the first three letters of that compound.[3] The Middle High German poem *Frauenlob* (V, 104, 113, 114, 117) referred to the legendary King Wippeon: he was an incorrigible womanizer, chased those who were no longer "girls" but not yet maidens in full bloom, and enjoyed making them pregnant, as we are informed. "From him *wib* came." Our other authorities are dictionary makers. Modern researchers seldom open their works, because they do not expect to discover reasonable conjectures there, but the history of ideas is no less interesting than the solutions of etymological riddles. Also, outdated hypotheses die hard and tend to be reinvented in later scholarship. Helvigius (*Weib*)[4] traced G *Weib* to Gk Φοίβη ~ Lat. *Phoebe* and Gk φοιβάς 'Phoebe's priestess'. Minsheu cited Helvigius with evident approval. Wachter (*Weib*) did the same but considered the possibility of *Eva* being the etymon of *Weib*. He referred to Tacitus, who emphasized women's high status in Germanic society. Upton may have been the first to compare *wife* and Gk οἴφω 'copulate, sleep with a woman', which he glossed 'conjoin, unite together' (see Lemon, *wife*). Junius and Skinner found the Greek parallel plausible, but Skinner, being a sensible man, traced *wife* to E *swive*, the most popular predecessor of our *F*-word. However, he remarked that both the Greek and the English verb describe the man's rather than the woman's behavior during intercourse. (Pictet [1863, 169, note] also observed that if *wīf* were related to οἴφω, a suffix pointing to her passive role could have been expected.)

According to Terwen (*wijf*), Bilderdijk separated *w* from the rest of the word and identified *-ijf* with the word for "egg" (Du. *ooi*, G *Ei*, F *œuf*); the result came out as "woman" = "feeder." (In Bilderdijk 1822, *wijf*, he refers to "Aant. *gg*," but I was unable to find that note in the book.) Curiously, in Semerano (1994), *w-* is again pried loose from *-if*. In the volume called *Semitic Foundations* (or: *Bases*) *of the Indo-European Languages* (Semerano 1994, 708), *wīf* is compared with Aramaeic *'immā*, Hebrew *'em*, and Accadian *umma* 'mother.' Bilderdijk (1822) thought that he knew the origin of *-īf* (from "egg") and left *w-* in limbo. In Semerano's opinion, *w-* is a trace of a laryngeal, whereas *-if* did not bother him. Perhaps the two fanciful theories should be combined. Ode (1927, 97) thought that the root of *wīf* can be detected in Gk ιφ- 'strong' (< **weibh*). He discussed taboo in Indo-European, but it remains unclear how "woman" developed from "strength."

The first serious Indo-Europeanists pointed to several Sanskrit words resembling *wīf: vapus* 'body', *vap* 'sow, spread seeds', *vivah* 'marry', and others, some of which resembled Gk οἴφω and ὀπυίω 'marry' (Benfey I, 1839–42, 340–41; Diefenbach 1851:150; Holmboe, *vif*). Those putative cognates of *wīf* kept surfacing in dictionaries for years. Less promising was Skt *vāmā* 'woman', though even Wedgwood[5] (who hardly read Benfey and Diefenbach) did not reject outright the affinity between *woman* and E *womb*. Only Chambers (1867), otherwise a dictionary that showed exemplary restraint in matters etymological, repeated Wedgwood's suggestion (it was known that *woman* developed from *wīfman*, but the proximity of *woman* to *womb* with its mute *b* appeared to be too great a temptation to resist). Another dead end comparison was between OI *vif* and *fifla* 'deceive; seduce a woman' (*fífl* 'fool, simpleton'), which Holmoe cited along with Norw. dial. *viva* 'mate" (said about birds).

Semerano's work shows that not only in international relations but also in etymology the Middle Ages are hard to leave behind. Makovskii has offered hundreds of typically medieval etymologies. *Wife,* as he thinks, is related to *duo* 'split', that is, split from Adam's rib, and also E *weapon,* Gk οἴφω 'copulate', OHG *uoba* 'celebration' (in fact, *Übung* 'performance'), *Übel* 'evil', and Toch. A *wip* 'wet' (see a summary in Makovskii 1999 *wife; uoba* is in Makovskii 1989, 138).

Among the earliest untenable ideas on the origin of *wīf* the one connecting *wīf* and *weave* could have been mentioned, but it turned out to be so long-lived that it deserves a special rubric.

Wife as Weaver

OI *wíf* sounds like *vefa* 'weave', and the *Edda* (reportedly, as pointed out above) suggested their relatedness. The eddic etymology ("woman" = "weaver") was remembered in Scandinavia (Serenius, *wife,* note), and in Germany Wachter (*Weib*) knew and endorsed it, whereas Grimm (1835, 190, note) called it wrong. It is absent from Minsheu, Skinner, and Johnson, but Todd added it to Johnson's entry. Judging by Picton (1862–63, 50; 1863–64, 53), long after Todd, even after Grimm, some knowledgeable people in England did not question the validity of the *wife–weave* connection, and as late as 1882, Ogilvie (*wife*) found it necessary to say: "Often connected with *weave.*" (See also the passage from CD, pp. 125–126). Adelung (*Weib*), an immensely erudite linguist, called attempts to derive *Weib* from *weben* foolish (*albern*), and made an important observation that, since *wîb/wīf/víf* was a non-derived word, it could not be traced to a verb. This "foolishness" should have come to an end with the appearance of Wedgwood's dictionary (he saw no possibility of tracing *wīf* to *wefan*) and especially Skeat's, for Skeat pointed out that in Old English, the names of a male and a female weaver were *webbe* and *webbestre* respectively and that trying to interpret *wīf* as "weaver" cannot be contemplated. Yet not too long ago one could read the following: "Wife comes from OE. *wif* [sic], allied to *wefan;* weave; while the unmarried daughters spun the wool for their mother and thereby became 'spinsters'" (Noble 1984, 70).

The derivation of *wīf/wîb* from *wefan/weban* is impossible from the point of view of word formation (the roots of *wīf* and *wef-* look alike but the noun has no suffix) and of ablaut: in Germanic *ī* does not alternate with *e.* The weaver etymology was revived by Tavernier-Vereecken (1954, 99-100), who, while operating with Dutch forms, set up the proportion **lība* 'life' : *leven* 'live' = **wība-* (the unquestionable etymon of *wīfe/Weib/wijf* : **weban* (the etymon of *weave/weben/weven*). But her proportion is wrong, for the root vowel of the weak verb *leven* (OHG *lebên*) almost certainly goes back to **i*, the zero grade of *ī*, as in OE *līf* 'life', whereas **e* in the strong verb *weban* is old. Tavernier-Vereecken contented that **wība* meant 'weaver' and acquired its neuter gender under the influence of **lība* 'life' because the status of weavers was low. When and where was it low? Ten Kate (1723, 513) held the opposite view. Considering the importance of weaving (it was one of the most ancient of the fundamental arts), her idea lacks credence. Nor is it likely that such an early agent noun should have been neuter. Polomé (1961, 555) and DeVries (NEW, *wijf*) rejected Tavernier-Vereecken's reconstruction but discussed it with undue deference. Adelung said that *wîb* could not be a derivative of *weben* because, among other things, the noun is much older than the invention of weaving, and his argument occasionally turns up in later literature. However, the relative chronology of this type is beyond recovery: we do not know when **wība-* was coined.

Wīf and Go. *-waibjan*

Weave and *-waibjan*

An attempt has been made to connect *wīf* and OE *wefan* at the level of Proto-Indo-European roots, with reference to Go. *biwaibjan**[6] 'surround, encompass; clothe, wrap,' and its cognates: OE *wǣfen* 'clothe'/*bewǣfen* 'wrap,' and OHG *weibôn* 'sway, vacillate'/*ziweibjan* 'scatter.' (In English, *wafian* 'wave', v. and *wǣfre* 'unstable, unsteady' are related. *Waver* belongs here too, but it is a borrowing from Scandinavian. Another congener is *wobble* ~ *wabble,* a borrowing from Low German.) OI *veifa* designated waving (swinging, swaying) and was used to describe the movement of a ship, brandishing a sword, shaking a gown, pulling an oar, flopping the wings, and so forth. With regard to meaning, OE *wǣfen* and OHG *weibôn* align themselves better with OI *veifa* than with Go. *biwaibjan**. The same holds for Du. *weifelen* 'waver, vacillate, hesitate,' which was first recorded by Kiliaen (1599), with the glosses *zwefen* 'wander,' *onvast bewegen* 'move unsteadily,' *zwaaien* 'sway.' 'Clothe,' attested in Gothic, seems to be a specialized meaning of "surround," which, apparently, derives from a verb denoting waving and any kind of movement that does not follow a straight line (hence "move in a circle, surround"?).

The history of *weave/weben/weven* shows that this verb originally meant "move back and forth" (still so in Luther, and cf. E *weave from lane to lane*). "Swing, sway" and "move back and forth" are close. The root of *weave* was PIE **webh-*. Lat. *vibrāre,* with its *-b-*, can be a reflex of a root with **b* or **bh* or **p*. If, as is usually believed, Skt *vepáyati* 'set in agitated motion', the causative of *vépate* 'trembles, is agitated', belongs here, the Proto-Indo-European root of *(bi)waibjan** is **veyp-* (in Germanic, **p* > *f* by the First Consonant Shift and the voicing of **f* by Verner's Law).

Thus **webh-* (the root of *weave*) should be juxtaposed with **weib-*, **weibh-*, or **weip-*. All of them have reflexes in Germanic; hence the confusion in the early works dealing with *wīf:* Lat. *vibrāre*, Go. *(four) waipjan* 'muzzle, bind up' (along with OI *veipr* 'head covering', OE *wāpe* 'kerchief' and, in other grades of ablaut, OE *wīpian* 'wipe' and OHG *wīfen* 'swing, wind'), and Gmc* *wība-*, the etymon of *wife*, were lumped together with Sanskrit words having *-p-* in the middle, though Benfey and Diefenbach offered reasonable lists of correspondences. *Biwaibjan** will be the subject matter of the next section. Here we are mostly interested in whether **webh-* is compatible with **weibh, -b, -p.* Their kinship will be recognized only if we accept the idea of so-called enlargements and represent the roots as **we-bh* versus **we-ibh,* etc. For a long time, historical linguists have been assembling seemingly related words with the view to abstracting their ancient roots. One procedure enjoys special popularity, even though its weakness is an open secret. A single modern example will suffice to expose this weakness. E *nibble, nod, nag, nap* (understood as 'doze off and wake up'), *notch,* and *knock,* all of which, perhaps with the exception of *notch,* once began with *gn-, kn-, hn-* and have a vague unifying meaning 'push or move gently'. Their varying vowels can be represented as so many grades of ablaut. It would be absurd to set up the root **gni-, *gna-,* 'push gently,' etc., "enlarged" by *p, t, k, b, d, g,* and no one has proposed such an idea. However, this is exactly what is done in Indo-European reconstruction, as evidenced by Walde-Pokorny's great dictionary (WP) and Pokorny's later version of it (IEW). *Nod, knock, nap,* and the rest are indeed related; it is the nature of their relatedness that has to be explained. The same is true of the forms of Sanskrit, Greek, Latin, and other ancient languages. Schwenter (1927) endorsed the amputation of postvocalic consonants for etymological purposes, and Tavenier-Vereecken (1954, 100 and note 1), who referred to WP (II, 251; see also IEW, 1114), was of the same opinion. Obviously, the shorter the stump equated with the original root, the greater the number of words that will end up as related. It is more prudent to stay away from dismembering reconstructed roots unless enlargements can be identified with regular suffixes. The protoform of *weave* should be kept apart from the protoform of *-waibjan**. The Germanic **wība-* did not get her name because she was a weaver.

Only a few remarks are still needed here. Götze, Kluge's long-time collaborator and his successor as editor of *Etymologisches Wörterbuch der deutschen Sprache* (EWDS), naturally, dissociated *Weib* from *weben* (DW, *Weib,* etymological introduction), but ended his survey with an unexpected proposal, which he attributed to Karl von Bahder. No reference is given (personal communication?). According to Bahder-Götze, *wîb-* finds its explanation in MHG *weberen,* a synonym of MHG *weiben*

(< OHG *weibôn*) 'move back and forth; be actively engaged in something.' A quotation from Tacitus is again pressed into service, this time the one about Germanic men, who occupied themselves with hunting and war and left household duties and field work to women. **Wība* emerged as "a busy one." Coming at the end of a critical survey, this etymology reads like an anticlimax. *Weberen* was not recorded in Old High German. Götze may be right that this lack of attestation is fortuitous, but the greatest number of verbs like *weberen* seem to have been coined relatively late. *Weberen,* whenever it arose, is a frequentative counterpart of *weben* 'move back and forth.' Its *e* in the root is incompatible with *ī* (see above). "Woman" as "a busy one" is too vague to carry conviction. Finally, the two most important questions about the type of word formation that produced an agent noun from *weben* and the grammatical gender of the noun remain unanswered. Pedersen (1942, 253) was right in stating that Götze's etymology explains nothing.

Wīf and Go. *-waibjan** /OE *wǣfen*/OHG *weibôn*/OI *veifa*

The root *waib-* is such a perfect phonetic match for *wîb-/wīf-* that, regardless of the *wife* – *weave* imaginary connections, it held out some promise to those who studied the etymology of *wība-*. Adelung mistakenly translated *waibjan** as 'bind' and suggested that perhaps woman had been named "the bound one" because of her subservient position in society. Since the gloss 'bind' is wrong, his conclusion falls to the ground, but we will have to return to women's status later. Grimm (1831, 323) wondered why *Weib* is neuter and concluded that one should know more about the meaning of *vaibjan* (his spelling) to get an answer; he, as could be expected, glossed the verb correctly: Lat. *cingere.* In his examination of the Proto-Indo-European root **wip-*, Fick[3] (1874–1876, 305) concentrated on Lat. *vibrāre* and Skt *vep* and chose the meaning "tremble" as providing a clue to **wiba-*. To some of Fick's contemporaries his solution seemed tenable. For example, Skeat[1] (*wife*) wrote that "trembling" may have been an epithet of a bride, but admitted that "the real origin of the word remains obscure." He did not elaborate on what made the Germanic bride tremble and why the noun is neuter. (In Skeat[4], the root is given as **weip-*, the last statement is left unaltered, but the trembling part is gone.)

Kluge believed that the main semantic component of the root in question is "movement" and glossed **wība-* as 'inspired, inwardly excited by priests' *(begeistert, innerlich erregt von Priestern): vide* Tacitus, who reports that Germanic women were looked on as "sacred and prophetic" *(sanctum aliquid et providum).* This etymology appears in the first seven editions of EWDS. The entry is short (some space is devoted to separating **wība-* from οἴφω and to the fact that the non-occurrence of a cognate of *Weib* in Gothic cannot be accidental), and the neuter is again left without an explanation, unless "being excited" is taken for an abstract noun. With time, Kluge offered a new explanation (see below), and it became customary to characterize his initial idea as an echo of romantic notions in historical linguistics. The distance between an inspired prophetess and Bahder-Götze's stay-at-home doing chores is indeed considerable.

Dissatisfied with the existing explanations, Wiedemann (1902, 219) took his cue from OHG *weibôn* 'stagger, shake; move unsteadily' and glossed **wība-* as 'person with a swaying gait.' "To be excited," he pointed out, is a specifically Sanskrit meaning. Heyne (DWB, *Weib*) came up with a more realistic interpretation of *weibôn,* namely, "go from place to place"; **wiba-* turned out to be the name of someone who moved to her husband's family. However, *weibôn* describes vacillation, shifting, swaying, that is, moving there and back, not going away. As Van Wijk (FvW, *wijf*) put it, in this case one can let one's imagination go in several directions, without arriving at worthwhile results.

A new development in the uneasy relation between **wība-* and the cognates of *-waibjan** began with Falk and Torp (Fick[4], 412; FT and Torp, *viv* in both). The entry in FT was so influential that I will reproduce it almost in full (the text is identical in the Norwegian and the German edition; the translation is mine).

> The original meaning seems to be "veiling;" hence "veiled bride." In all likelihood, the word belongs with ON *vífaðr, vífinn* 'veiled', *veifa* 'bind, veil': see *veiv* ['clapper', among other things, a detailed analysis of OE *wǣfen,* OHG *weibôn,* and their cognates]. The veiling of the bride was customary among all Western Indo-Europeans: cf., for example, Lat. *nupta* 'bride'/*nūbere* 'veil oneself'. In the old countries of the

> North, the bride wore a head dressing (*brúðarlín*); cf. *ganga und líni/ripti* ['go under the veil', dictionaries cite only *setjask,* not *ganga und ripti*]. This corresponds to the later bridal veil. Married women wore a head scarf (ON *hǫfuðdúkr,* East Norse *hvífr*).

FT is one of the most outstanding achievements of Germanic philology, but the entry *viv* has nothing to recommend it. To begin with, ON (= OI) *veifa* did not mean "bind, veil" (see p. 116). Second, Lat. *nupta* is related to *nūbō, nupsi* 'marry' (cf. E *nubile* and *nuptial),* not to *obnubō, -nūbi* 'veil,' though the two verbs were already confused in antiquity (WH, *nūbō;* Krogmann 1958-1959, 137). Third, the information on OI *vífaðr* and *vífinn* is misleading. *Vífinn,* a derivative of *víf,* has been recorded only with the sense "amorous," while *vífaðr* is a hapax legamenon, the second element of the compound *svell-vífiðir* '?encompassed by ice' (pl.), an epithet applied to *Sólundir* (*Sólund* is the name of an island, often used in the plural, as here). Those "islands" may have been wrapped in, encompassed, or tossed (shaken) by ice. In any case, as support for veiling this form is useless. Finally, veiling was part of betrothal, rather than the marriage ceremony (WH, loc. cit.).

The authority of Falk and Torp, two great Old Norse scholars, was such that it did not occur to anybody to check *vífinn* and *vífaðr* in dictionaries, and both words have been copied dozens of times with FT's glosses. Only Krogmann (loc. cit.) pointed to the mistake, but even he did not say enough. BL's passing remark on the meaning of *vífinn* (*viv*) does not go far (the authors were not interested in destroying FT's etymology, for they could not think of a better one). *Wīf* and its cognates never meant "bride." The conclusion that an abstract neuter noun ("veiling") became the main name for "woman" is incredible. Yet this is still the explanation one most often finds in dictionaries of English, German, Dutch, and the Scandinavian languages. To add a note of levity to a serious disquisition, I will quote Eric Partridge's *Origins* (1958, 776):

> *Wife* derives, via ME *wif,* a wife, a woman, from OE *wīf,* orig[inally] a woman. . . . Sem[antically], the Gmc word for a woman app[arently] means either 'the vibrator' (OI) or 'the veiled one' (OGmc)—cf. ON *vīfinn,* veiled (adj), akin to ON *veifa,* to vibrate, to wave (as a veil does in the wind); the former notion is the more basic and, hist[orically], the more prob[able].

Woman, Her Clothes, and Genitals

Here the central characters will be OE *wīfman(n)* 'woman' and *wǣpnedmann* 'man'. Beside *wǣpnedmann,* its shortened form *wǣpmann* occurred. The first element of the compound is therefore not *wǣpen* 'weapon' but *wǣpned,* which alone means "man," a word also recorded as an adjective ("male"). The compounds *wǣpned-bearn* 'male child,' *-cild* (the same), *-cynn* 'male sex,' *wǣpnedhād* (the same and 'sexual power'), *-hand* 'male line,' *-healf* (the same), and *-wīfestre* 'hermaphrodite' leave no doubt on this score (cf. Krogmann 1958–59, 140).

Wǣpned is a substantivized past participle of *wǣpnan* 'arm' (v.). Two approaches to the pair of Old English words are possible. Either *wǣpned,* simplified to *wǣp(en),* means 'weapon'; then *wīf* in *wīfmann* perhaps designates some object typical of women's occupation or outward appearance (cf. the English expressions *spear side* versus *distaff ~ spindle side*) and OHG *swertmac* 'relative on the male side' versus *spindelmac;* Wachter (*Weib*) and Ten Kate (loc. cit.) cite slightly different forms. Or *wǣpen* means "penis" (a sense recorded in texts); then *wīf* is perhaps "vagina" or "womb." Both approaches have been tried.

Kluge, who once thought that **wība-* is related to OHG *weibon,* changed his mind, interpreted *wǣpned* in *wǣpnedmann* as "someone who has a penis," and concluded that *wīf* in *wīfmann* might also have "an obscene meaning" (1916, 182). Yet he said (Kluge 1918, 147) that he could not solve the problem to his satisfaction and only pointed to offensive names like G *alte Schachtel* ('old casket') for "woman." According to him, in such names, when containers are mentioned, they are euphemisms for "vulva." This seems to be an exaggeration, but, be that as it may, to make such an etymology convincing, Kluge needed a cognate of *wīf* that meant "vulva." He failed to find a single one. In the 8th and 9th editions of EWDS, *weibōn* is no longer mentioned, and the origin of *Weib* is called obscure. In the 10th edition, a reference to Kluge 1918 appears. It is repeated in the first posthumous (11th) edition and expunged from the 16th. In Mitzka's editions, Kluge's etymology is replaced by FT's, but with references to other scholars, a circumstance that irritated Krogmann (1958-59, 13).

More than eighty years after Kluge suggested that *wīf* probably had an "obscene" meaning, Schmidt and Strunk (1989) cited what they took for other "obscene" cognates of *wīf*, though they no longer needed or used Kluge's euphemism. The cognates they discovered are Toch. B *kwīpe* and Toch. A *kip* 'shame'. In one of the texts, Toch. B. *kwīpe-ike* 'shame place' means "penis," and the Toch. A ablative of *kip-kapśane** means "mother's shame body" (= "womb" or "vulva"). The proposed semantic development was "shame" > "place to be ashamed of" > *"genitals" > *"female genitals" > "woman." *Wīfmann* and *wǣpnedmann* emerged as "vulva person" and "penis person." According to Schmidt and Strunk (272), the protoform of the word designating "shame" (**ghʷeibho* or **ghᵘibho*) seems to have been neuter, whence the neuter of the noun in Germanic.

Seebold (EWDS[23–24], *Weib*) found this reconstruction rather improbable because the change from "shame" to "female genitals" is too specific and because he was reluctant to accept the change of **ghʷ-* to **w-* in any Germanic word. Winter (1998, 348-49) concentrated on the semantic aspect of the proposed reconstruction. He noted that in Tocharian only the change from "shame" to "place to be ashamed of" was reached; the next steps had to take place in Germanic. Schmidt and Strunk admitted that the Tocharian noun might be an *-s-* or an *-o-* stem, but, as Winter shows, the first option is to be preferred. If so, the Tocharian and the Germanic noun belong to different declensions. Moreover, there is no certainty that Toch. B *kw-* and Toch. A *k-* reflect PIE **w* preceded by a dorsal. However, he was ready "to acknowledge that the etymological connection proposed by Schmidt (and Schmidt and Strunk 1989) presents a possible way of breaking down the isolation of the Germanic word for 'woman'" (349). I am not aware of other comments on that proposal, except that S. Zimmer (1999, 151) characterized it as "a serious and important attempt to solve the riddle inherent in the Germanic lexemes" and censured Mallory and Adams (1997, 642, 648), who also thought of the "obscene" meaning of *wība-* but made no mention of Schmidt and Strunk's work.

The entire line of reasoning initiated by Kluge's remark strikes me as untenable. OE *wǣpen* has indeed been recorded with the sense "penis." This was a metaphor of the same type as *tool* 'penis' in Modern English. *Tool* 'instrument' and *tool* 'penis' exist in different spheres. If someone coined the word *tool man* (a person making or working with tools) on the analogy of *newspaper man, milkman, postman,* and *chairman,* who would have thought of *penis man*? Will even the most inveterate punster associate *tool basket* with *condom*? The main Old English word for "male" was *wǣpnedmann*, that is, "armed person." This circumstance makes the gloss "penis person" even less attractive. If we assume for the sake of argument that the Tocharian words and **wība-* are a good phonetic and morphological fit, it will still be almost unimaginable that the change from "place to be ashamed of" to "woman's genitals" and "woman" could have occurred in Germanic and left no trace in any language between Germanic and Tocharian, particularly because **wība-* is not a Germanic but only a West Germanic word. ON *víf* is more probably a borrowing, and Go. **weif* is fiction. A common parent of *kip* ~ *kwīpe* and **wība-* hardly existed. OI *karlmaðr* and *kvenmaðr* show that *maðr* 'person' could be added to stylistically neutral words for "man" and "woman" (see the end of the chapter).

Words for "sword" ("tool, weapon") and "sheath" understood as "penis" and "vagina" are near universal, and so is the change from "sheath; opening; slit" to "woman," but the examples cited in this connection invariably belong to the low style and slang. "Slit" is not "woman," but "whore," and *alte Schachtel* means "old hag," not "aged lady." This is also true of OI *sprund* (if its "vulgar" etymology is right; Lockwood 1991, 26–28, and see OI *skauð, skjóða,* and *sprund* in Fritzner) and the words Printz (1932) discusses. Some ancient words of this type have come down to us only as glosses, and the context in which they were used is unknown.

The other possibility of rescuing the original parallelism *wīfmann/wǣpnedmann* is to ascribe some specifically "feminine" meaning to *wīf.* Men wear weapons, whereas women wear –? The history of filling in this blank goes back to at least Wachter, who compared the Old English compounds for "man" and "woman" and even quoted the same line from Tacitus that caught Kluge's fancy (though he did not offer Kluge's etymology). Researchers moving from different directions arrived at similar conclusions. As early as 1855, it was suggested that E *girl* derives from OE *gyrla* 'dress'. More than a century later, this idea found new supporters (see the discussion in Liberman 2008, 98–99). The pair *girl–gyrla/girdle* and *girl – G Gehre* 'edge of a skirt; triangular piece' (akin to E *gore* 'triangular piece of cloth'; historically, 'triangular piece of land') led to a search for similar partners for **wība-*. Adelung and Grimm connected *Weib* with *-waibjan* decades before Kluge (see above). Schwenck (1834) thought that *wîb-* might be the root of the name for a kerchief, veil, or belt. Mueller shared his opinion, with reference to *girl–gyrla* (more cautiously in the second edition). If *-waibjan,* he reasoned, meant "turn, wind," *wîb* could perhaps be understood as "binding, combining." Although Richardson did not go beyond *wife – weaver,* he avoided the trap of identifying *wife* with *weaver:* his glosses of the Old English compounds were "weapon man" and "woofman." OI *veipa* 'woman's hood' (Thomson) looked like another promising cognate of *wife.* In the words of Wedgwood, "[it] was to be expected that the distinctive names of man and woman should be taken in the first instance from their physical characteristics." As we will see, this expectation proved wrong in both cases.

Holthausen must have read nearly all the works mentioned above but offered his idea as a novelty: **wība-,* he remarked (1920, 368), was a metonymy like G *Schürze* 'apron' (= 'woman'). This idea has less appeal than FT's, who did not identify **wība-* with a word for "veil" but spoke about veiling. By contrast, Pedersen (1942) tried to improve on FT's solution. He found the gloss "penis person" ridiculous and differed from FT on two points: according to him, *wīf-* was a concrete noun (not an abstraction like "veiling") and it denoted some article of a woman's, rather than a bride's, clothing. The rest followed the by now familiar path of the metonymy as in Holthausen 1920 and his predecessors. Lindquist (1943, 81-82) was especially pleased with that reconstruction. According to Pedersen, **wība-* went back to PIE **weip-* (then **p* > **f* > **b* by Verner's Law) or **weibh-.*

Krogmann (1958–59, 140–145; 1960, 74–76) had good things to say only about Holthausen's etymology and believed that he had discovered what part of women's apparel *wīf-* once designated. His gloss was "head cover of a married woman." He went to great lengths to show that women in different cultures wore their hair differently from unmarried ones, but this widely known fact did not need belaboring. The only piece of evidence for *wīf-* 'head cover of a married woman' Krogmann cited is the Old Frisian compound *wīfstrēwene,* a punishable crime. OFr *-strēwene,* derived from the root *streu-* (it is related to E *strew* and *straw,* with cognates in all the Old Germanic languages, including Go. *straujan* 'spread out', *gastraujan** 'cover', and *ufstraujan** 'spread beneath') does not occur in other texts. OFr *strēwa,* like its modern reflex *struie,* means "scatter, sow; sprinkle; spread." Go. *gastraujan**, with its perfective prefix, must have developed the sense "cover" from *"spread many layers over something" and is a good reminder of how unpredictable a word's meaning may be, even when the root is transparent. The recent etymological dictionary of Old Frisian (OFED) is not helpful: on p. 380, it follows Krogmann and glosses *wīfstrēwene* as "snatching a woman's kerchief" and on p. 440 as "snatching a woman" (the traditional interpretation). Most likely, neither gloss is right. This compound must have been a legal term for "exposing a woman (?attacking sexually)" with *wīf-* meaning "woman" not "kerchief." If East Norse *hvífr* 'woman's kerchief' (an alleged congener of *wīf;* so Krogmann) were related to *wīf-*, it would have preserved *h-* in Old English and Old High German, and if the first element of *wīfstrēwene* is the only extant cognate of *hvífr,* it has no bearing on the origin of **wība.* Thomson says that *wīf* was "[s]upposed to be G [= Swedish] *huif.*" He found the connection in Ihre. FT also mention *hvífr*, but not as a cognate of **wība-*. Forms like *(h)viv* 'kerchief' occur in Old Danish, Old Swedish, and modern dialects.

Wīf as a Remnant of a Longer Word or of a Disguised Compound

Bezzenberger (1907) suggested that G *Weibel,* the historical name for an inferior serviceman (glossed in Old High German as *praeco* 'messenger') had arisen from **voi[k]pó-* or perhaps **voi[k]poló-* (with **kp* simplified to *p*), whereas *wîb* is the continuation of **voi[k]pó-*. He cited Vedic *vič-páti* 'master of the house' and *vič-pátni* 'mistress of the house' as analogs and listed several more words of the same type. This etymology can be ruled out without further discussion: a word meaning "mistress of the house" would not have been coined as a neuter noun. It is therefore surprising that both ISEW (119) and ÁBM (*víf*) refer to Bezzenberger and say that *víf* "hardly" continues a compound like *vič-pátni.* To account for the neuter, Hirt (1909, 169) set up **veik-vom* 'what belongs to the house or clan/tribe'. This is a stillborn form supplied with a meaning that does not lead to "woman," and Hirt expunged it from the second (1921) edition of his book.

Finally, Szemerényi (1977, 79-82) followed in the footsteps of Bezzenberger and Pisani (1934) and asked what Germanic form could have corresponded to old Lithuanian *viespatni* 'woman' (the first element of all the words given above means "house, village, clan"; cf. Go *weihs* 'village', Gk (*F*)οικος 'house', Latvian *vīcus* 'village', and so forth; the second is a cognate of **potis* 'powerful'). He begins with PIE **wóiko-potnī*, proceeds to Gmc **wéike-potnī*, **weihefaþnyā-*, **weihebaðnyā-*, and **wīhibannyā,* which allegedly yielded WGmc **wīhibanna* and *wībanna.* "In this form *-anna* came to be felt as an independent word connected with (OHG) *ana* 'grandmother', and since the age, suggested thereby, mostly did not tally with the facts, it was cut off. Thus a new word *wīb* was created which on the analogy of *līb* 'body', became a neuter" (82). In note 302 on p. 80, Szemerényi rejected Tavernier-Vereecken's idea of *wīf* being related to **weban* 'weave', but, as can be seen, he appropriated her conclusion that **wīb* became neuter on the analogy of **līb*. Some short words (E *barn* and *lord,* for instance) are disguised compounds, but Szemerényi's convoluted etymology could have been taken seriously only if he had not been obliged to reconstruct the last two steps: the folk etymological interpretation of **wībanna* (which holds only for Old High German) and a last minute change of grammatical gender, from the feminine to the neuter, of a word meaning "woman."

Wīf and Lith. *vaĩk* 'child'

Lith. *vaĩk* 'child, offspring' figures prominently in the etymology of Proto-Slavic **čelověkъ* 'man,' for, despite many points of disagreement, it is customary to divide this word into two parts: *čelo-věkъ* 'clan's/tribe's offspring' (but see below). The meaning of the Proto-Indo-European root of *vaĩk* has been reconstructed as *"vitality." Hirt, who identified *wīf/wîb* with the root **veik'-*, must have believed that Lith. *vaĩk* is another reflex of that root, for he mentions *vaĩk* in his 1909 book and in his reworking of Weigand's dictionary (WHirt, *Weib*). Since Hirt's original idea found no support and Hirt himself abandoned it, *vaĩk* had not been mentioned in the entry *Weib* in etymological dictionaries until Seebold (EWDS[23–24]) resurrected the connection. He posited the root **weik^w-*, the etymon of both the Germanic and the Baltic noun. The suggestion that two simple (non-compounded) words designating "woman" and "child" go back to the same root is not appealing.

The Proposal

The State of Previous Scholarship

The origin of the word *wife* remains opaque, a fact recognized by most historical linguists and lexicographers. (W)Gmc **wība-* does not go back to a mythological name, to a word for "egg," or to the verb "weave"; it is not an agent noun. None of the Tocharian, Sanskrit, Greek, Latin, and Lithuanian nouns and verbs suggested as cognates of **wība-* seems to be related to it. **Wība-* cannot be understood as "someone excited" or "someone staying at home," whatever Tacitus had to say about Germanic women. The word is not traceable to a metonymy: from "clothes" to "weaver of those clothes" or from "womb/vulva" to "woman." Numerous attempts to connect **wība-* with *waibjan**, regardless of the sense chosen, have borne no fruit. No ancient compound developed into **wība.* The scholarly literature on the origin of *wife* and its cognates is vast (part of it has been mentioned above), but dictionaries refer to it unsystematically. The best surveys of opinions are about a century old. The one by Götze is a standard source of reference; the other, by Charles P. G. Scott (CD, *wife*), has been neglected and deserves being reproduced here:

> . . . not found in Goth[ic] and not traced outside of Teut[onic]; root unknown. It cannot be connected, as commonly thought, with *weave.* Some compare S[ans]k[rit] √*vip,* tremble, L[atin] *vibrare,* vibrate, quiver, OHG *weibōn,* waver, be inspired, be irresolute, and suppose that the word orig[inally] meant 'something inspired' (the Germans orig[inally] seeing in woman *sanctum aliquid et providum*), or that it orig[inally] meant 'trembling,' with ref[erence] to the timidity of a bride. Some connect it with Goth[ic] *waibjan,* wind, twine, in *bi-waibjan,* wind about, clothe, envelop, because of a woman's 'enveloping

> clothes,' or because she is the 'one who binds or unites herself.' These are all vagaries. The earlier Teut[onic] word, the one with other Indo-European cognates, is that represented by *queen, quean*. The neuter or inadequate significance of the word is prob[ably] indicated also by the formation in A[nglo]-S[axon] of the appar[ently] more distinctive word *wīfman*, whence ult[imately] E. *woman*.

Books on family relationships and kin terms in Germanic (Campbell 1905, 112–16; Ellert 1946, 53–62; Wittmann 1982, 110–14) have nothing new to say.

Approaches to the Neuter

Discrepancies between the grammatical gender of the word and the sex of its referent are common and have been the subject of numerous investigations. For instance, OI *svarri* 'noble lady' is masculine. **Wība-* is not the only neuter noun of its type: cf. OS *frīa* 'wife,' OIr *ben* 'woman,' and Gk φῆλυ 'woman' and 'womankind' (note both meanings.) The neuter was occasionally used to express contempt or abomination. The anthologized examples are OI *flagð* 'giantess, ogress,' Latin *mancipium* 'slave' and *scortum* 'hide, skin; profligate' (especially 'slut, whore'), Gk ἀνδράποδον 'slave' (especially 'enslaved prisoner of war'), and G *das Mensch*, n. 'slut' (as opposed to *der Mensch*, m. 'person, human being').

It has been said more than once that the neuter of **wība-* reflected women's inferior position in society. This view has to be rejected. Attitudes to women changed from epoch to epoch. In the oldest myths of the Indo-Europeans, female deities inspire even greater fear than the male ones. Warrior maidens of the Brünhild type are more than a match for male heroes; Grendel's mother is a tougher opponent than Grendel. The other stylistically "unmarked" words for "woman" in Germanic were feminine (except for OS *frīa* 'wife'). In dealing with *wīf, frīa, ben,* and φῆλυ, we should look for the reasons they ended up as neuters in the history of the words rather than social institutions. I am leaving out of account the neuters that are byproducts of morphology. Here G *Mädchen* and *Mädel*, diminutives of *Magd*, f. 'girl, maiden', are usually cited: both words are neuter because of the suffixes added to the root *Mäd-*.

A neuter like *wīf* might, in principle, develop semantically: the word may have meant something else and been neuter; later the meaning supposedly changed, but the grammatical gender remained (this was Grimm's hypothesis). As far as we can judge, **wība-* has always meant "woman" and in the earlier epoch had no disparaging overtones. The source of a neuter is sometimes an abstraction (of sorts). For example, Go. *qineins** 'belonging to a woman' (an adjective), 'female' (it glosses Gk φῆλυς) occurs as a noun glossing γυναικάρια, the accusative plural of the diminutive γυναικάριον (n.) 'woman' (derogatory; *foolish women* in the *Authorised Version*: 2TIII, 6). The Gothic form is also neuter. The important thing is the blurred line between "female" (adjective) and "female" (noun). **Wība-* (again to the best of our knowledge) did not have such a source.

A third, and perhaps the most common, process responsible for the rise of unexpected neuters is an exchange of forms between homonymous plurals and singulars. Since in Proto-Indo-European, the neuter plural had the same endings as the feminine singular, the two were often confused. In Germanic, the neuter plural is also quite often indistinguishable from the neuter singular (so in Old High German, Old Icelandic, and partly Old English), and the process of a collective noun yielding a homonymous name for an individual unfolds before us in full view. Only the plural *goð* ~ *guð* existed in the earlier Old Icelandic, and it was neuter: the gods were thought of as a mass. Presumably, the Germanic words for *troll* and *dwarf* were also coined as neuter plurals. A masculine noun for an individual god became necessary only after Christianization. A huge but loose collection of facts pertaining to this subject (with references) can be found in Royen (1929, 401–32, "Gender As Opposed to Sex," and 594–659, "The Collective and Plurality"). See also Schwink (2004) and an interesting discussion of OI *kind* (f.) 'kin,' OE *(ge)kynd* (n., f.) 'origin; species; offspring; genitalia', and G *Kind* (n.) 'child' in Meijerling (1985, 17–21), De Tollenaere (1987), and Meinecke (1987, 25–31, 115). In my view, the origin of **wība-* will be discovered if we try this third way: from the collective to the individual.

The Etymology

Help comes from the name of the Scandinavian goddess Sif. She is the wife of Thor (Þórr). Despite the paucity of information about her, the origin of her name is clear, because the common name *sifjar,* the plural of *Sif,* means "affinity (connection) by marriage." E *sib,* Lat. *suus* 'one's own', and ethnic names like *Suebi* are among its cognates (the material in Johannson [1893, 5-8] and Mezger [1948, 102] is not outdated, and see WP II, 456, IEW, 883; AEW, *Sif*). The protoform of *Sif/sif* is **sebhā-* (Gmc **sebjō-*; Gothic had *sibja** 'relationship' and, by extension, 'peace'). *Sebha- contains a pronominal root and the suffix */-bh/*. **Wībha-* appears to have had a similar origin: the suffix **-bh* (Gmc **-b*) was appended to the root of the personal pronoun *we*. The Proto-Germanic form of this pronoun was **wīs* (Go. *weis*), that is, **wī-s* (PIE**wei-s*). OE *wē* ~ *wĕ* is a reduced variant of **wīs*. In contradistinction to **wī-s* 'we', inclusive 'all of us' or exclusive 'those belonging only to us,' **wī-b-a* (*a* is an ending) must have meant approximately "group of people tracing their origin to the same woman." It must have sounded as *y'all* does to Americans. Unlike **wīb-*, **sib-* referred to a community bonded by marriage, not by blood. **Wība-*, as is usual with collective nouns, was neuter and, most probably, had two meanings from the start: in the plural it designated the people descended from the same woman, and in the singular, the progenitrix of such a clan. The barrier separating the collective noun ("matriarchal clan") and the name of an individual ("woman") was no more vexing than it is to us when the singular and the plural cannot be distinguished (*one sheep – many sheep, these people are – this people is*) or when we deal with the brass, the wind, and the wood (in an orchestra). Cf. also E youth /'young people' and 'a young person'.

My argument would not have been stronger (in fact, it would have been weaker) if OI *Sif* were also a neuter noun. The "sib" included people of various descent, whereas *wīb-* was coined as the name of a community whose members descended, or believed that they had descended, from the same woman. It was vital for this word to be applicable to the entire group and to a single female ancestor. The grammatical gender of *sib* did not contribute anything it its message. *Sib-* und *wīb-* share only the type of word formation: a pronominal root followed by the suffix **bh* (> **b*); see Ellis (1956, 169) on the "collective or typifying" role of **-bh*. The case of *sib-/wīb-* (a basic kin term formed from the root of a pronoun) may not be unique. Proto-Slavic **čelověkъ* 'man, person', mentioned above in connection with *-věkъ*, perhaps begins with a form of an indefinite pronoun ("some, someone"), the whole meaning approximately "a certain person," a vague analog of G *jemand* (so Martynov 1972, 187–88;

Trubachev, in ESSI IV, 50, was not ready to accept this derivation but had little to say against it).

With reference to an individual, the neologism **wība-*, a term of societal organization, entered into an opposition with **kʷeno-*, an ancient word denoting a woman in her function as child bearer. The absence of Go. **weif* shows that the Germanic-speakers in the East felt no need for such a term. It looks like a West Germanic innovation. This is an additional piece of evidence against the Scandinavians' possessing a special term for "clan tracing its origin to a certain woman." As suggested above, ON *wíf* is, most probably, a borrowing from Old English. It is up to historians and anthropologists to decide whether the existence of **wība-* in only one subgroup of Germanic testifies to some differences in the social organization of the oldest Germanic tribes.

Our texts preserved no traces of **wība-* as a collective plural (otherwise, my etymology would have been offered at least two centuries ago). Only the incongruous grammatical gender of that word is a relic of the meaning I reconstructed. The matriarchal term proved to be relatively short-lived. With time, *wīf/wîb* joined the other neuter nouns whose singular coincided with their plural. To make usage less ambiguous, *mann* 'person' was added to OE *wīf; wīfmann* could be only singular. That way out of the ambiguity was not fortunate: the addition of a masculine noun (*mann*) to a neuter one (*wīf*) for obtaining a compound meaning "woman, wife" cannot but strike one as a bizarre development. Characteristically, no analogs of *wīfmann* have been attested in Frisian, Dutch, or German. Equally important is the fact that in later Old English *wīfman(n)* could occur as a feminine noun. Cf. Dan. and Norw. *viv*, f. and such phrases as Lat. *mea Glycerium*, MHG *ein schœne* (rather than *schœneȝ*) *wîp* 'beautiful woman', and the title of Alfonse Daudet's book *Le petit chose* (F *chose* is feminine), cited by Sommer (1921, 7).

The rest is guesswork. I think that the emergence of *wīfmann* resulted in the coining of the artificial (and superfluous) compound *wǣpnedmann*. The parallelism was restored, but *wǣpned* 'man, male person' and *wīf* 'woman' came from different sources and had existed indefinitely long before *-man(n)* was affixed to them. In the absence of **wība-*, the Old Norse pair *karlmaðr* 'man' ~ *kvennmaðr* 'woman' looks unexpected. Could *karlmðr* have been a calque of a foreign word? The

German personal name *Karl(e)mann* appeared early and either referred to a free man from the start (like OE *ceorlman*) or was one of numerous tautological compounds (here "man-man") current in the older Indo-European languages and partly extant: cf. Go. *marisaiws* 'sea' ("sea-sea"), OE *mægencræft* 'great strength, might' ("strength-strength"), OHG *lintwurm* 'dragon' ("snake-snake"), and E dial. *lass-quean.* There was a time when this type of reinforcement was productive (Liberman 2007; 2008, 200); perhaps the first to mention such compounds was Skeat (see Skeat 1882, the end of the entry *akimbo*). Also, *Charlemagne* sounded like a pun on *Karlmann.* If *karlmaðr* was not modeled on *Karlmann,* it may have been a tribute to the vogue for tautology. *Kvennmaðr* would have been coined as a partner for *karlmaðr.* The order of events in English, as I suggested above, was reverse: first *wīfmann,* then *wǣpnedmann.*

The Germanic word for "man" was, in all probability, abstracted from **ga-man* 'circle of votaries of the god Mannus.' Both Go. *gaman* 'partnership; partner' and OI *man* (which lost **ga-*) 'slave' (the Scandinavian analog of the Greek ανδράποδον); 'all the servants in a house; girl, maid' were neuter nouns (discussion in Liberman 2008, 30, *man**). The concept of a group of people (like that of a group of gods) preceded the concept of an individual (*man*, m.). The history of the West Germanic word for "woman" ran along roughly similar lines: **wība-* *'clan descended from the same female ancestor' (n. pl., later indistinguishable from n. sg.) acquired or coexisted with the meaning "woman." The development of self-awareness from "a human being only as part of a collective body" to "a human being as a separate entity, an individual" is a process reflected most clearly in medieval and early modern literature. It is no wonder that language provides us with the same evidence.

If **wība* goes back to **wei-b(h)* 'we all' (specifically, 'we who trace our lineage to a certain progenitrix'), the value of the foregoing investigation is twofold. First, the origin of an especially obscure word has been discovered. Second, confidence is restored in future searches for native etymologies. When a word defies all explanations, it is tempting to relegate it to a substrate. *Wife* has not escaped this fate either (Kauffmann 1913, 67, the continuation of note 5 from p. 66; hesitatingly OFED, *wib*). Apparently, not "all those hard words" are so hard and not all good etymologies were discovered long ago.

NOTES

1. The following abbreviations are used in the text: dial.—dialectal, Dan.—Danish, Du.—Dutch, f.—feminine, E—English, F—French, G—German, Gk—Classical Greek, Gmc—Germanic, Go.—Gothic, IE—Indo-European, Lat.—Latin, Lith.—Lithuanian, m.—masculine, n.—neuter, Norw.—Norwegian, OE—Old English, OFr—Old Frisian, OGmc—Old Germanic, OHG—Old High German, ON—Old Norse, OS—Old Saxon, PIE—Proto-Indo-European, pl.—plural, sg.—singular, Skt—Sanskrit, Toch.—Tocharian, v.—verb, WGmc—West Germanic.
2. Most dictionaries are referred to as this one. See the abbreviations in the list following the Notes. No pages are given. The necessary information appears in the entries on the words under discussion (here, for example, under *Vivildis*). In dictionaries other than English, the word is always indicated, e.g. EWDS (*Weib*).
3. References to this etymology and the one discussed at the beginning of Section 3 (without giving the source) abound, but I could not find it in either Snorri's or the poetic *Edda.*
4. Some dictionaries are cited as here. What is said in Note 2 applies to them as well. See the authors' names in the list following the Notes.
5. If a dictionary ran into several editions and the edition is not specified in the text, it means that the same information appears in all of them.
6. An asterisk after a word means that this word has been attested but not in its "dictionary form" (the infinitive and the nominative).

Dictionaries Cited

WITH ABBREVIATIONS

ÁBM—Ásgeir Blöndal Magnússon, *Íslenzk orðasifjabók.* Orðabók Háskolans, 1989.

AEW—Jan de Vries, *Altnordisches etymologisches Wörterbuch.* Leiden: E. J. Brill. 3rd ed., 1974.

BL—Harald Bjorvand and Frederik O. Lindeman, *Våre arveord. Etymologisk ordbok.* Oslo: Novus Forlag, 2000.

CD—*The Century Dictionary: An Encyclopedic Dictionary of the English Language.* William D. Whitney, ed. New York: The Century Co., 1889-1911. Revised by Benjamin E. Smith, 1911.

Chambers—William Chambers, *Etymological Dictionary of the English Language.* James Donald, ed. London and Edinburgh: W. & R. Chambers, 1867.

DW—*Deutsches Wörterbuch von Jacob Grimm und Wilhelm Grimm.* Leipzig: S. Hirzel, 1854–1971.

DWB—Moritz Heyne, *Deutsches Wörterbuch.* Leipzig: S. Hirzel, 1890–95. 2nd ed., 1905–06.

ESSI—*Etimologicheskii slovar' slavianskikh iazykov. Praslavianskii leksicheskii fond.* O. N. Trubachev, ed. Moscow: Nauka, 1974–.

EWDS—Friedrich Kluge, *Etymologisches Wörterbuch der deutschen Sprache.* Straßburg: Karl J. Trübner. 1st and 2nd eds., 1883; 3rd ed., 1884 (unchanged); 4th ed., 1889; 5th ed., 1894; 6th ed., 1899; 7th ed., 1910; 8th ed.,1915; 9th ed.,1921; 10th ed., 1924; 11th ed., by Alfred Götze in collaboration with Wolfgang Krause, 1934; 12th–13th (1943) and 14th (1948) eds. (unchanged); 15th ed., by Alfred Götze with the assistance of Hans Krahe, completed by Alfred Schirmer, 1951; 16th ed. (unchanged), 1953; 17th ed., by Alfred Schirmer, revised by Walther Mitzka, 1957; 18th through 21st eds., by Walther Mitzka, 1960, 1963, 1967; 21st ed. (unchanged); 1975; 22nd, 23rd, and 24th eds., by Elmar Seebold, 1989, 1995, 2003. The post-1915 editions were published by Walter de Gruyter: Berlin, New York.

Fick—August Fick, *Vergleichendes Wörterbuch der indogermanischen Sprachen.* 3rd ed. Göttigen: Vandenhoek, 1874-76; 4th ed., Göttingen: Vandenhoeck, 1890-1909.

Fritzner—Johan Fritzner, *Ordbog over det Danske Sprog*…. 4th ed. Oslo, Bergen, Tromsø: Universitetsforlaget, 1972-73.

FT—Hjalmar Falk and Alf Torp, *Etymologisk ordbog over det norske og det danske sprog.* Kristiania: H. Aschehoug (W. Nygaard), 1903–06. The German edition: *Norwegisch-dänisches etymologisches Wörterbuch.* Heidelberg: Carl Winter, 1910–11.

FvW—Johannes Franck, *Etymologisch woordenboek der Nederlandsche taal.* 2nd ed., by N. van Wijk; Supplement by C. B. van Haeringen. Reprinted in one volume: 's-Gravenhage: Martinus Nijhoff, 1949.

GEW—Ferdinand Holthausen, *Gotisches etymologisches Wörterbuch....* Germanische Bibliothek I/8. Heidelberg: Carl Winter, 1934.

Helvigius—Andreæ Helvigius, *Origines dictionvm germanicarvm....* Hanoviœ: Impensis Conradi Eifridi.

Holmboe—Chr. A. Holmboe, *Det norske Sprogs væsentligste Ordforraad....* Wien: Det keiserlig-kongelige Hof- og Stats-Trykkerie, 1852.

IEW—Julius Pokorny, *Indogermanisches etymologisches Wörterbuch.* Bern and München: Francke, 1959.

Ihre—Johan Ihre, *Glossarium Suigothicum....* Upsaliæ: Typis Edmannianis.

ISEW—Alexander Jóhannesson, *Isländisches etymologisches Wörterbuch.* Bern: Francke, 1956.

Johnson—Samuel Johnson, *A Dictionary of the English Language.* London: Printed by W. Strahan for J. and P. Knapton, etc., 1755. 2nd ed., by H. J. Todd. London: Longman, etc., 1827.

Junius—Francisci Junii Francisci filii, *Etymologicum Anglicanum.* Edward Lye, ed. Oxonii: E Theatro Sheldoniano, 1741.

Kiliaen—Cornelius Kilianus, *Etymologicum teutonicæ linguæ....* Antverpiæ: Ex Officina Plantiniana, apud Joannem Moretum.

Lemon—George W. Lemon. 1783. *English Etymology.* London: G. Robinson.

Minsheu—John Minsheu, *Ductor in linguas. The Guide into the Tongues....* London: Published by the author, 1617.

NEW—Jan de Vries, *Nederlands etymologisch woordenboek.* Leiden: E. J. Brill, 1971.

OFED—Dirk Boutkan and Sjoerd M. Siebinga, *Old Frisian Etymological Dictionary.* Leiden Indo-European Etymological Dictionary Series 1. Leiden, Boston: Brill, 2005.

Ogilvie—*The Imperial Dictionary of the English Language.* John Ogilvie, ed. 2nd ed., by Charles Annandale, 1882.

Serenius—Jacob Serenius, *An English and Swedish Dictionary.* Harg and Stenbro: Per Mommer, 1757.

Skeat—Walter W. Skeat, *An Etymological Dictionary of the English Language.* Oxford: Clarendon Press, 1882. 2nd ed., 1884; 3rd ed., 1887, 4th ed., 1910.

Skinner—Stephen Skinner, *Etymologicon Linguæ Anglicanæ....* Londini: Typis T. Roycroft, 1671.

Ten Kate—Lambert ten Kate, *Aenleiding tot de kennisse van het verhevene deel der Nederdeuitsche Sprake....* Part 2. Amsterdam: Rudolf and Gerard Wetstein, 1723.

Terwen—L. Terwen, *Etymologisch Handwoordenboek der nederduitsche taal....* Gouda: G. B. van Goor, 1844.

Thomson—John Thomson, *Etymons of English Words.* Edinburgh: Oliver & Boyd, London: Longman, etc., 1826.

Todd, H. J. *See* Johnson.

Torp—Alf Torp, *Nynorsk etymologisk ordbok.* Kristiania: Aschehoug & Co. W. Nygaard, 1919.

Wachter—Johann Wachter, *Glossarium Germanicum....* Lipsiæ: Apud Joh. Frid. Gleditschii B. Filiam, 1737.

Wedgwood—Hensleigh Wedgwood, *A Dictionary of English Etymology....* London: Trübner & Co., 1859-65. 2nd ed., 1872; 3rd ed., 1878; 4th ed., 1888.

WH—Alois Walde, *Lateinisches etymologisches Wörterbuch.* 3rd ed., by Johann B. Hofmann. Heidelberg: Carl Winter, 1938-54.

WHirt—L. K. Weigand, *Deutschtes Wörterbuch.* 5th ed., by Herman Hirt. Gießen: Friedrich A. Töpelmann, 1909-1910.

WP—Alois Walde, *Vergleichendes Wörterbuch der indogermanischen Sprachen.* Julius Pokorny, ed. Berlin: Walter de Gruyter, 1927-1932.

7

English into Asia: From Singaporean Ubiquity to Chinese Learners' Features

EDGAR W. SCHNEIDER
University of Regensburg

Introduction

Globalization has been the predominant trend of late–twentieth century changes in the worlds of business, cultural exchange, and international travel and communication; it has also been the most visible, and perhaps the most influential, of all the changes that have shaped the recent "contours" of the English language. The continent on which this development has been most immediately visible is Asia. The history of English, at least for the last few centuries, has been a history of expansion, and the move of English into Asia, early steps of which were documented by Bailey (1997), represents but the latest step in this global process. So while what this chapter discusses may seem a little unusual in a section devoted to the history of English, it continues the history of English into the postmodern age.

Crystal (2004) regards the world's ongoing penetration by English as a major component of an ongoing "language revolution." In an earlier book (1997), he surveyed the process and its causes, arguing that English happened to be at the right places at the right times, as the language of the British Empire during colonial expansion, the language of the industrial revolution, and the language of the twentieth century's dominant and only remaining superpower. Not surprisingly, the process has attracted a lot of scholarly attention from various angles. Kachru's school (e.g., B. Kachru 1986, 1992) has emphasized the importance and independence of the "Outer Circle" countries, in which English is rooted and increasingly indigenized as a strong and highly important second language. Work by Görlach (e.g., 1991, 1995c) has emphasized the historical, sociolinguistic, and philological dimensions of the process. Useful documentation is provided by McArthur (1998, 2002); and by now the discipline has matured and brought forward textbooks (e.g., Mesthrie and Bhatt 2008; Schneider 2011), voluminous handbooks (Schneider et al. 2004; Kortmann et al. 2004; B. Kachru, Y. Kachru, and Nelson 2006), and a massive collection of pertinent scholarship (Bolton and B. Kachru 2006). Schneider (2007) presents a comprehensive and coherent perspective on globalization, surveying the evolutionary processes and present-day ecologies of English in a great many countries, including the United States, on all continents, arguing that the parameters of the global diffusion of English have been determined by constant relationships between colonizers and the colonized and resulting sociolinguistic constellations and identity assignments.

Language contact has played a special role in the history of the diffusion of English into Asia. Of course, Standard English itself is to a considerable extent the product of an unusually intense contact history, with traces of Latin, Scandinavian, French, and a wide range of European and also colonial contact languages showing primarily in its vocabulary. In a sense, English in Asia can be seen as continuing this rich contact tradition. It might be argued that this contact remains rather superficial, and restricted in its impact to a few more lexical borrowings from specific cultural domains, but such a view would not do justice to what is going on in Asia today. English is spreading vigorously everywhere, and the desire to acquire some competence and fluency in it, if only for the purpose of international interaction in the domains of business and technology, unites many countries on the continent. As it takes root in Asian countries, the language is developing indigenous forms; most notably, in Singapore, it is becoming the native language of many young people. It has been voiced loudly that "English Is an Asian Language"—such was the title of a series of pertinent conferences and the volumes resulting from them (Bautista 1997; Newbrook 1999; Halimah and Ng 2000), with the claim presented most pronouncedly by B. Kachru (1997, 2005) and his closest associates (Y. Kachru and Nelson 2006). Equally indicative is the establishment of a journal titled *Asian Englishes*, edited in Japan by Nobuyuki Honna and and a book series "Asian Englishes Today" by Hong Kong University Press, edited by Kingsley Bolton.

This chapter discusses aspects of the spread and indigenization of the English language in four Asian countries. First, I approach the topic by briefly comparing the histories and sociolinguistic usage conditions of English in three countries which represent radically different degrees of the intrusion of English in Asia, from approaching an endonormative, native-like status, as in Singapore, to representing a purely foreign language, as in Japan. Subsequently, I provide some empirical evidence of English as used by highly proficient speakers in China, interesting in this context, if only for the sheer number of learners there.

Degrees of Infiltration: Singapore—Hong Kong—Japan

The following brief surveys and comparisons are based on writings on these countries and on informal personal observations made in October 2006 and earlier. Space constraints force me to be brief here; more detailed discussions of the history and state of English in Singapore and Hong Kong, with further source references, are available in Schneider (2007, 153–161 and 133–139, respectively).

Singapore

Singapore's strategic location, on the southern tip of the Malay peninsula and along major trading routes, prompted Sir Stamford Raffles to found a colony there in 1819, which soon attracted large numbers of Chinese,

Indians, further Malays, and others who, together with the British colonizers, saw the opportunity of making a decent living in the prospering and rapidly growing colony. Since independence in 1963, the strong hold and successful policies of the country's ruling party have turned Singapore into South-East Asia's prototypical "tiger state," in which modernization, industrialization, and globalization have produced a young, extremely modern, highly successful and culturally hybrid nation, combining a western-style business orientation with traditional Asian values and lifestyles. A strong Singaporean identity, regardless of ethnic origins, has been constructed deliberately, and the English language has been an essential component in this nation-building process.

The new nation's policy of both maintaining standard forms of the major ethnic groups' Asian languages and developing English into a cross-ethnic tie was implemented in the educational system in the 1960s. Since then, every child has been educated in both English and an ethnic "mother tongue," which, however, being a standardized form, primarily Mandarin for the Chinese majority, frequently was not the children's or their parents' real home or ancestral language. English has thus grown tremendously in importance as both an inter- and intraethnic bond, the only language shared by almost everybody in the nation (even if proficiency levels are still tied to social class and education levels). Singaporean English has developed a number of characteristic features on all stylistic levels, primarily in pronunciation on the level of a local standard (see Wee 2004). Furthermore, the importance and vitality of English is proven by a deeply rooted local dialect known as "Singlish," a true identity-carrier cherished by local speakers, even against the government's opposition, which, in the interest of international intelligibility and business effectiveness, wishes to see it eradicated and replaced by Standard English (see Schneider 2007, 157–161). It is quite clear, however, that attempts at eradication have failed; for many Singaporeans their way of speaking English is a matter close to their hearts.

Singapore is on its way to becoming English-speaking to an unprecedented extent, more so than any other of Kachru's (1992) "Outer Circle" countries. According to recent census data about a quarter of all households have adopted English as a family language, while roughly a third of all children grow up speaking it as their first language, and these percentages are growing rapidly.

Hong Kong

In Hong Kong, English has played an important role since the first Opium War of the early 1840s, which turned Hong Kong Island into a crown colony. Britain's power base on the mouth of the Pearl River expanded with the lease of Kowloon in 1860 and of the New Territories, for 99 years, in 1898, and the population multiplied due to the city's importance in the trade with the East. Based on the 1984 Joint British-Sino Declaration, the 1997 "handover" terminated this status and returned Hong Kong to the People's Republic of China, with its status quo essentially guaranteed, however, as a "Special Administrative Region" for another fifty years. Similarly to Singapore, the Hong Kong of the later twentieth century has defined itself as a global city, an entrepreneurial powerhouse, a prime location of international commerce and service industries. Unlike Singapore, however, the relative ethnic homogeneity of the population, who are predominantly of Cantonese extraction, has prevented the need for and promotion of a twenty-first century lingua franca.

Hong Kong today is a classic ESL country. English is very important in business (both local and international), administration, and education. A substantial proportion of the population (but most likely still a minority) speak it, with estimates varying between about 30 and about 80 percent (with these figures presumably reflecting varying levels of proficiency), but, outside of a small proportion of expatriate native speakers, it is usually not a first or family language and not a language for social intimacy. Still, the demand for it is strong, as is witnessed by severe post–1997 resistance against the government's goal of turning many "English-medium" schools into "Chinese-medium."[1] Knowledge of English is typically associated with middle-class identity and a modern, international outlook on life. Young people, especially educated ones, enjoy mixing it with Cantonese in their daily informal interactions.

Japan

Bailey (1997) tells the "story of the penetration of English into Japan" (177), focusing upon the year 1853, with Perry's landfall and the forced opening of Japan to western influences, resulting in the Japanese mastery of "modern armaments, military tactics, and English" (178–79) in the next half-century. Since then, English has been appreciated and acquired as a gateway to western learning in Japan.

Interestingly enough, the label "Japanese English" exists and seems to be used without much hesitation (see Stanlaw 2004; Y. Kachru and Nelson 2006, 171–76; D'Angelo 2005) even if its justification seems doubtful, given that such a designation entails the existence of a stabilized, widely used, and distinctive variety, rather than a learners' interlanguage (Schneider 2007, 50). Of course, there is a lot of lexical borrowing, primarily from English into Japanese. According to Bailey (1997, 186), English is perceived "as an attractive vehicle for western culture," a fact reflected in the substantial number of loans: "12% of words in modern Japanese are of European origin, and of these 80% are from English." Many of these words are listed, illustrated, and categorized in Stanlaw (2004).

Undoubtedly, interest in English in Japan and the importance attributed to it in public discourse are great, as demonstrated, for instance, by the establishment of the world's first "College of World Englishes" at Chukyo University in Nagoya (see Sakai 2005).[2] In practice, however, this means very little. Even Stanlaw (2004), who argues for the recognition of "Japanese English," concedes that "many—if not most—Japanese claim little fluency in the language in spite of some six to ten years of schooling in it" (7).[3] While it is considered important to learn English, in practice the emphasis is not on communicative skills but on grammar and vocabulary.

Comparison of Singapore, Hong Kong, and Japan

These three countries broadly represent the three types of countries in which English plays a certain role (McArthur 1998, 42–46). Certainly, Singapore is not an ENL (English as a Native Language) country, but it is definitely moving from ESL to ENL status, and the proportion of speakers who grow up speaking English as their first language there is remarkable and increasing rapidly. Hong Kong is a classic case of an ESL country, in which English is essential for some public functions and for professional communication, and is commanded for these purposes by a substantial proportion of the population, but it does not function as a tool of social proximity. Japan, in contrast, represents the EFL (English as a Foreign Language) type, in which the language is recognized and taught for its international usefulness but has no noteworthy internal status.

Singapore is practically run in English, which there is the language of most formal political proceedings, of cross-cultural, international, and also some local informal interactions, and, above all, of the young. In Hong Kong, English is strong in political discourse, in business and the media, and among the educated. In Japan, English plays practically no role outside of educational and internationally oriented contexts.

These roles are reflected in the appearance and the usefulness of English in the public domain in the respective countries. In Singapore, the language is ubiquitous. Signs, posters and advertisements, unless targeted to a specific ethnic group, are mostly either only in English or in English plus the three other official languages (Malay, Mandarin, and Tamil), with these not infrequently printed aside and in a smaller font. Announcements in the MRT, the subway system, are mostly in English only, sometimes in all official languages. In most cases, a stranger who addresses a Singaporean passer-by in English will elicit answers, explanations, and complex verbal interactions in perfectly fluent English. A substantial proportion of conversations overheard in public, especially amongst younger speakers, are conducted in English. In contrast, in Hong Kong, English is heard in public in specific domains only, mostly involving interaction with non-locals. Posters and the like are either in Cantonese or bilingual; announcements in trains and the subway tend to be bilingual. For a visitor, asking locals a question in English may or may not be successful, depending on the interlocutor's education, age, and profession. Sales personnel in stores where a tourist may drop in are usually fluent in English, while shops which cater for the local population frequently have only some staff with a command of English. The success rate of communicating with locals in English is likely to be higher in central city locations than in the residential areas in the New Territories or on the outlying islands. I could not communicate with a shopkeeper in a bakery in Aberdeen but got a perfectly fluent response from a child in Sha Tin. On the other hand, in Japan a visitor is unlikely to encounter any naturally used English in public, and should not expect to be able to interact with locals in English. Not even taxi drivers or restaurant service staff can be expected to command any English. Bilingual explanations in Japanese and English are reserved for places tourists are likely to visit to but hardly found elsewhere; announcements in subways are mostly in Japanese only, and additionally in English at major intersections in big cities only (e.g., in Nagoya).

Japan is not the only country in Asia where even in the absence of a colonial history English is making deep inroads into the society (notwithstanding substantial limitations in practice); conditions of teaching and using English are also under discussion in other countries with westernized economies or strong tourism. Thailand exemplifies the last category; see Newbrook (1999) for discussions of the role of English in the country's language and education policy. The former category is most typically represented by South Korea, where the interest in English and the importance attributed to it are also great. The notion of "Korean English," including a short list of characteristic features, is proposed by Y. Kachru and Nelson (2006, 177–179). Remarkably, there is a community of Koreans who have deliberately chosen to reside in Singapore in order to improve their (and their children's) English (Lionel Wee, p.c. 12/2006). The number of fluent second-language speakers of English in India exceeds the number of native speakers in all "Inner Circle" countries. Agents in Indian call centers often undergo special accent training in order not to be identified as Indians by callers from the U.S. or Britain. And about the fastest-growing "market" for English in Asia, China, I have recently heard the bon mot (without having been able to trace or verify it) that today the number of learners of English there is higher than the number of native speakers of English in all other countries taken together.

Chinese Learners' English: A Feature Analysis

English in China

English has been spoken in China since the early seventeenth century. Its reduced form, Chinese Pidgin English, was extremely important in trade and intercultural contacts from the eighteenth through the early twentieth centuries (see Smith and Matthews 2005). The history of the language in China is excellently documented in two recent books: Bolton (2003), in addition to focusing strongly upon Hong Kong, thoroughly documents the "archeology" of Chinese English throughout its history; and Adamson (2004) shows that English education in China after World War II has always reflected current attitudes to the West and has been determined by the tension between conflicting needs, the retention of Chinese values but also the adoption of western technological advances. English was also perceived as carrying messages and attitudes unwelcome to the country's political leaders. However, at least since the Four Modernizations and Open Door policies of the 1970s and 1980s, the learning of English has been promoted by the ruling Communist Party as a vehicle for technology transfer, acquisition of western ideas, and diplomatic and intellectual interaction with the West.

Today, English is required for university entrance in China, and it is also a prerequisite for many attractive civil service posts (Adamson 2004, 169). The demand for the language is immense. It is symbolized and indicated best by the success of Li Yang's "Crazy English" campaign, a highly popular learning method of the late 1990s in which mass education (and acquisition of some rudimentary English) was supposedly achieved by loudly chanting English slogans (see Bolton 2003, 252–258; Adamson 2004, 169–170). The globalization of China's economy and the role of English as the door to improvement and wealth play major roles in the language's attraction, as did the importance, both symbolic and factual, of the Beijing Olympics in 2008. Adamson (2004) summarizes the situation as follows:

> At present the role and status of English in China is higher than ever in history as evidenced by its role as a key subject in the curriculum, with its growing use as a medium of instruction as many schools adopt a bilingual approach to education; and as a crucial determinant for university entrance and procuring well-paid jobs in the commercial sector. CCP [Chinese Communist Party] leaders value the contribution that English can make to the nation's modernization programme. (195)

> In many respects, this history of the English language curriculum in China is a history of China itself. The evolutionary process has moved from state-determined towards client-determined; from centralization towards decentralization; from closed systems towards pluralism. (208)

An Investigation of Chinese Learners' English: Background and Methodology

Given this situation, it seems obvious that we should study the acquisition process of Chinese learners of English in some detail, attending to frequent features and possible interference factors. Such investigation will identify areas of special difficulty to which then special attention should be devoted, so important guidelines for the teaching process can be expected as an outcome. Documentation and investigation of accommodation and alignment processes should provide important insights into principles of language contact and second language acquisition. One question is, of course, whether what we are describing here is sufficiently stabilized and homogeneous to be identified as "a variety of English," which could then be labeled "Chinese English" (cf. Schneider [2007, 50] for a discussion of whether there exists a "Hong Kong English" or just "English in Hong Kong").

Interestingly, much more has been written on general teaching strategies, language policy, and pedagogical theory than on what can be really observed in the classroom, i.e., which features characterize English as taught and used in China.[4] Y. Kachru and Nelson (2006, 167–171) actually use the label "Chinese English" and list some "characteristics," which in addition to a few loan words and discourse conventions includes one paragraph each listing features on the levels of phonology (conflation of tense and lax vowels, the replacement of the dental fricatives /θ/ and /ð/ by alveolar /s/ and /z/ and of labiodental /v/ by the continuant /w/, respectively, and stress shifts) and grammar (lack of articles, adverb marking, and third-singular verb endings, and avoidance of a few syntactically complex constructions). Deterding (2006) addresses pronunciation only.

A set of interesting features captured in interviews with six young Chinese speakers recorded at the Chinese University of Hong Kong on October 3, 2006, contributes modestly to such research. The informants were Master's students who participated in a sociolinguistics class and volunteered for the interviews.[5] Three of them were female and three male. They were in their early twenties and had studied English for more than ten years.[6] All come from southern and southeastern China, though from different provinces (one each from GuangDong, Shenzhen, Jiang-Su, Fujian, ZheJiang, and Hong Kong, with parental traces and an early childhood background also in Hunan in one case). Their native languages are predominantly Cantonese but also Putonghua and "Hangzhounese," presumably a Wu dialect as spoken in the city of Hangzhou. By the time of the interviews they had been at the Chinese University, and in most cases in Hong Kong, for only one month, so their English reflected their language education in mainland China (or, in one case, Hong Kong). Only one of them had ever been abroad, for an exchange year in Ireland. Given that admission to the Chinese University of Hong Kong is highly competitive, these students do not represent the vast majority of learners of English in China; rather, if anything, they represent the top echelons of proficiency provided by China's language education system.

The interviews themselves consisted of two parts. First, a free conversation of about ten minutes was held with each speaker on topics such as family background, study situation and goals, language education, and linguistic background. Obviously, in terms of style, this was not informal speech—an interview with a stranger in a university context never is; but the atmosphere was relaxed and casual, with some laughter in the conversations. Subsequently, each interviewee read the "North Wind and the Sun" passage which both the International Phonetic Association (1999, 39), the *Handbook of Varieties of English* (Schneider et al. 2004) and Deterding (2006) use as reference sample for speech and the sounds which the passage contains. Thus, it is possible in principle to compare two different styles in each speaker's performance: conversation and reading. The recordings were made directly into a notebook computer as mp3 files, using a high-quality microphone and the program "N°23 Recorder." The interviews were completely transcribed orthographically,[7] and select passages of interest in the conversations as well as the entire reading passages were also transcribed phonetically, using repetitive loop auditions in the audio software "CoolEdit 2000" to identify difficult portions.

Features of Chinese Learners' English

Here I document the most conspicuous features observed in these recordings. I look first at pronunciation and then at grammar, and list, describe, and exemplify phenomena observed in several speakers' idiolects, providing broad frequency assessments (in some cases including token frequencies as noted in my corpus, to give a general sense of the frequencies of features) but no detailed quantitative analyses. Interference phenomena or innovative features tend to appear in certain speech contexts only; thus, I pay special attention to the phonetic environments in which some phenomenon can be observed. I take Standard English forms (essentially those of British English Received Pronunciation, henceforth RP) as a terminological starting point for my descriptions. Obviously, some of the phenomena discussed here can be accounted for as transfer from Chinese, a problem discussed further below.

On the sound level, conspicuous processes involve resyllabification, the vocalization of nasals and liquids, and the deletion of consonants in word-final position or in clusters. In contrast, modifications of individual sounds are not common. In grammar, omissions of clause constituents or grammatical morphemes are most noteworthy. All of the features listed below occur variably—i.e., standard realizations are also heard.

(1) Vowel epenthesis, esp. after word-final consonants

It is not uncommon for a schwa to be appended after a word-final consonant. This is found fairly frequently (39 tokens overall) with three of the six speakers, and a fourth one shows it occasionally (twice, to be exact). In most cases schwa is attached to monosyllabic words, so that *grade* is pronounced [gredə], *but* becomes [bʌtə], and so on, e.g. in *child, wind, should, fold, last, most, you'd,* or *don't*. This feature combines easily with the deletion of a final consonant in a cluster, e.g., [dʒʌsə] *just*, [fɜːsə] *first*. Schwa epenthesis is also not uncommon in disyllabic words, both after a stressed second syllable (*except* [-tə], *attend* [-də]) and following an unstressed syllable (e.g., in *dialect, practice, language, English,* or, also after consonant cluster reduction, *almost* [-mosə]). There are also two attestations of the process in syllable-final and morpheme-final but word-medial position: [tʃaɪldəxʊdə] *childhood*, [pʰoʊstə-] in *postgraduates*. Finally, three speakers introduce epenthetic vowels to break up consonant clusters: one has [ɪŋgəlɪʃ] for *English*, one reads *blow* as [bɪləʊ], and the third (who shows no other epenthesis) pronounces *rhythm* as [-θəm].

(2) Vocalization of postvocalic /l/

As in many other varieties of English (including RP in certain contexts, like *half*) a postvocalic lateral, either word-final or in preconsonantal position, is vocalized, so the /l/ is not pronounced in words like *old* [oᵘd], *child* [tʃaɪdə], *school, will, almost, fold, call, small, still, functional,* etc. This is found in five of the six idiolects: quite commonly in two of them, repeatedly in one, and once each in two more; overall, there are 36 tokens. Vocalization of /l/ occurs also with suffixes following the /l/ (e.g., *enrolls* [-rəʊs], *rules*), syllable-finally but word-medially (e.g., in *fully, altogether* [ɔːtʊgedə]), and with syllabic, postconsonantal laterals (e.g., *people* [pʰɪpʰəw], *comfortable* [kʌmfətəbəw]). Sometimes a following consonant is also no longer articulated, so that *field* is pronounced [fɪə].

(3) Vocalization of nasals and replacive nasalization of pre-nasal vowels

Vocalization is common with postvocalic nasals, with examples provided by all speakers (42 tokens overall). In most but not all cases the previous vowel obtains a distinctly nasalized quality in compensation. Examples occur both word-finally (in *from* [frõ], *then* [ðɛ̃], *some, one, learn, Mandarin* [-rĩ]) and pre-consonantally (in *month, wind, kind,* etc.). All nasals are affected: bilabial (*some, times*), alveolar (*sun, then*), and velar (*young, working*) ones. As in the case of /l/, sometimes the deletion process affects both a nasal and another following consonant, so that *friend* becomes [frɛ̃].

(4) Velarization of the alveolar nasal in word-final / syllable-final position

Another process that may affect word-final nasals is velarization: the alveolar nasal is pulled back to a velar articulatory position, so we get [mɪŋ] for *mean,* [sʌŋ] for *sun,* or [bɪŋ] for *been;* in one instance this process affects even a bilabial nasal (*swim* is pronounced as [swɪŋ]). This is also found at the end of syllables in the middle of a word (twice in one idiolect: *confess* [kɒŋ'fæs], *contacts* [kʌŋtæts]) and together with the omission of another final consonant (so *don't* is [doŋ]). Interestingly, one speaker pronounces the preposition *in* consistently as [ɪŋ]. Apart from this high-frequency form, the phenomenon is not frequent (13 tokens) but certainly also not an idiosyncracy, since four different speakers provide tokens).

(5) Omission of single word-final consonants

Like (1)–(3), a strong tendency to delete a single dental stop, and occasionally also another single consonant, at the end of words affects syllable structure. This process most frequently affects voiceless /t/, sometimes also /d/, most commonly in high-frequency function words and verbs. Hence, the final consonant is not articulated in words like *not, that, at, but, get, what, right, cannot, about, thought, would,* and *applied;* and in one instance of *outside* the /t/ is left out in word-central but syllable-final position. This process operates also in a connection with a following *'s*, as in *it's, that's, what's, let's* (not included in the above count; *i(t')s* [ɪs] occurs very frequently). Other sounds which remain silent in this position are three tokens of /k/ in *like* and one instance each of a dental fricative (in *with*) and a labiodental fricative (in *have*). Final consonant omission seems a very general process with these Chinese speakers, found 57 times with all six speakers.

(6) Reduction of consonant clusters

In contrast with the previous process, which seems typical of some Asian Englishes but is much less common elsewhere, so-called "consonant cluster reduction" is found widely, especially in contact-induced varieties of English (Schreier 2005). My corpus contains 78 examples, from all six speakers. Most of these concern word-final clusters in which the last consonant, typically a stop and most frequently a dental stop, is omitted: *just* becomes *jus'*, *difficult* becomes *difficul'*, *wind* is realized as *win'*, etc. (further examples are *collec', almos', aroun', studen', amoun', mos', firs', atten', don', assistan'*). This works also before inflectional suffixes (as in *frien's*, or *wor's* from *words*). Occasionally in final two-consonant clusters not the last but the last but one disappears: *conta't, afterwar's*. A few examples of cluster reduction occur in the middle of words as well, always omitting a stop and leaving the alveolar fricative: *system* becomes *sys'em; mixing* is pronounced [mɪsɪŋ]; in *succeeded* or *successfully* we find [s] instead of [ks], and in *example* [z] replaces [gz]. Reduction in word-initial position seems idiosyncratic and contextually highly restricted: one speaker fails to pronounce the *-r-* in *pronunciation, produce*, and once in *probably*.

(7) Strong aspiration of voiceless stops

Voiceless stops, above all /t/, are followed by a strongly audible aspiration quite commonly (42 tokens, with four speakers). Unlike RP (where aspiration characterizes word-initial stops), this is heard in all positions (with raised *h* suggesting aspiration in the following examples): initially (in *t^{h}en, t^{h}own, t^{h}ime*), medially (in *att^{h}end, what^{h}ever*), finally (in *but^h, right^h, cloak^h, student^h, help^h*), and also several times in the same word (*p^{h}eop^{h}le, t^{h}aught^h*) and even in both stops of stop clusters (*worked* [-k^{h}t^h], *wrapped* [-p^{h}t^h]). Aspiration also combines with final schwa epenthesis (e.g. *not* [-t^{h}ə], *people* [-p^{h}ə]) and with consonant cluster reduction (*attempt* [-p^h]).

(8) Consonant devoicing, especially of word-final fricatives

It is a very strong tendency in the English of Chinese learners, found many times (I counted 93 tokens) with all six speakers, to pronounce certain voiced consonants, final fricatives in particular, without voicing. In the majority of instances this affects the inflectional suffix *-s* with verbs or nouns, which is voiceless in occurrences of, for example, the following words: *enrolls, has, seems, tries; Bachelor's, friends, girls, hours, journals, movies, questions, rules, schools, things, teachers, years*. The same process is common in high-frequency function words, so the final fricatives are frequently voiceless in *his, of, was, have, has, as, is*, and *because*. Sometimes this phenomenon also affects final fricatives of lexical items, which in Standard English end in a voiced consonant, so a final /-s/ can be heard in *overseas, Japanese, Chinese*, and *size*; *gave* may end in /-f/; and twice a final affricate is devoiced as well, in *large* [-tʃ]. One speaker in particular devoices also final dental stops and clusters, resulting in *allowed* with

[-t] and, in the reading passage, [ə'griːtʰ] for *agreed*, [kʊtʰ] for *could*, and [ə'blaɪtʃt] for *obliged*. In word-central position this is rare but also documented: *conclusion* has [-ʃ-], and *rhythm* has [-θ-].

(9) Avoidance of dental fricatives

As in many other World Englishes (Schneider 2004, 1123), there is a tendency to avoid dental fricatives, especially word-initially. There is some awareness of this feature, possibly generated by teaching practice, as there are a few instances of immediate self-correction: "something [-s-] something [-θ-]"; "father [-d-] uh, my father [-ð-]" (twice, precisely like this, in the same interview). Which of the two common replacement strategies (by a dental stop or an alveolar fricative) appears seems to vary idiosyncratically. Word-initially, i.e., in high-frequency function words including *the, this, then, though,* and *three*, two speakers have [d-] consistently; one has an occasional [d-] in addition to predominantly [ð-]; one has [s-] or, rarely, [z-], and [ð-] only sometimes in the reading passage; and the other two choose between all three types. Word-medially, the above examples document occasional (but apparently self-consciously used, and rare) replacements, also in *another* and *together*, where [-d-] is used by the same speaker who has it in *father*, and in *southeast* and *father*, where one speaker uses [-s-] and [-z-], respectively, in addition to [-ð-] in *mother*. Word-finally, where the word *north* in the reading passage allows a comparison across all speakers, two have [-s] consistently (one of them shows it also in *month* in the conversation); the others have [-θ].

(10) Open realizations of /e/

The only remarkable vowel feature, which was realized somewhat generally, in three idiolects (21 tokens), is a more open realization of /e/ as [ɛ] or even, mostly, [æ], in words like *then, when, tests, let's, lecture, attend, mention, confess,* or *friends*.

(11) Other pronunciation features

Further noteworthy pronunciation features occur but are idiosyncratic rather than characteristic of these speakers as a group. Stress shifts can be found, e.g., in *linguistics* ['lɪŋuɪstɪks], *England* [ɪŋ'lænd], and *competence* [kɔm'petəns] (with three different speakers), but not very frequently. Syllable-timing seems observable in the speech rhythm of multisyllabic words like *comfortable* or *secondary*. Replacement of the labiodental voiced fricative /v/ by the continuant [w], mentioned by Deterding (2006, 191) and Y. Kachru & Nelson (2006, 169), occurs only once in [prɔwɪns] *province*. One speaker consistently has initial [l-] in *North*, reflecting the "interchangeability of [l] and [n] in Hong Kong English" (Deterding 2006, 192). One speaker has [x] for /h/ in *he, his* and *how* (see Deterding 2006, 189–90). There are further interesting vowel replacements: confusion between corresponding short and long vowels, as in [ɪ] in *seems*, monophthongizations ([ɔ] in *home*) or diphthongizations, as with [eɪ] used consistently by one speaker for final /-i:/, e.g., in *degree*, and in the adverb suffix *-ly* (e.g. *warmly* [-leɪ].

(12) Omission or insertion of syntactic constituents

In grammar, there are fewer features and fewer tokens to be noted (which certainly also has to do with the restricted length and the relatively formal situation of the interviews). The most common phenomena are certain constituent omissions (for clarity, I explicitly indicate missing elements by inserting "∅"). In comparison with Standard English conventions, articles are sometimes left out (*have got ∅ English name; by ∅ English teacher; in ∅ English class; our school is ∅ only school that . . .*), even in the reading passage (*∅ North wind give – gave up*), but also sometimes inserted (*learn the English, in the primary school*). Three speakers show instances of deleted copulas: *I ∅ from Jiang-Su province; after I ∅ entering the . . .; actually I ∅ also from mainland China; it ∅ divided into . . . half*). In four of the interviews subjects are also sometimes omitted (as in *∅ Is a province; Here ∅ is very comfortable; here ∅ is more . . . people; ∅ Is near Shanghai; ∅ Is very difficult; for M.A. . . . ∅ is relatively easier; ∅ Is in German, right?; I grew up there until ∅ 15 years old*).

(13) Verb morphology

One speaker shows both a lack of the third-singular *-s* suffix (in *the course which have one year only; my father speak∅ . . .*) and its hypercorrect insertion (*we are belongs to . . .; they maybe . . . belongs to . . .*); another one has one instance of *it go∅*. What is much more common, however, is a lack of past tense marking on full verbs, both with regular verbs (*my parents move; we learn; he use; I stay; I study; I look*; 18 tokens,[8] five speakers; in all examples here the time reference is clearly to the past) and with irregular verbs, even in the reading passage (*I come here; he forget; I find; the sun shine*; 9 tokens, four speakers). The suffix *-ing* is missing twice, with different speakers, in progressive constructions (*I'm study . . . English; I'm not speak fluent Cantonese*), while another one provides a hypercorrect instance of it (*they're forced to speaking English*).

(14) Noun morphology

Four speakers occasionally omit the plural *-s*, also but not exclusively after numerals, e.g., in *student; four . . . district; many . . . band; a lot of campaign; those flowery shouting; two big part*, though all of them use it most of the time. Hypercorrect usage occurs in *peoples* and, self-corrected immediately, in *some datas, data*. Missing number concord may also involve a personal pronoun: *he will throw a lot of questions on us and we have to answer it*. The mass noun *research* is used like a count noun in *some researches* and *a research* (by different speakers).

Discussion

In general, these Chinese students speak English fluently and with standard-like, comprehensible accents (and an interesting mixture of British and American pronunciation features: rhoticity, /j/-usage in words like *new* or *students*, and vowel height in words like *staff* are highly variable). As always in speech, there are incomplete sentences, hesitation phenomena, and the like, but basically all of them present their arguments in complex syntax; only one of them produces constructions like *because of interesting* and repeatedly says *how to say . . . .*

One of my informants, having read Deterding (2006) for a course, wondered what such a description of features may be good for—a question valid for the present study as well. The answer should be obvious (in addition to the fact that for a linguist such an analysis should be of interest in its own right): a thorough description of the status quo is a prerequisite for applying remedying measures, for instance in language pedagogy (assuming an exonormative orientation, which clearly characterizes the present situation and the foreseeable future). Teachers of English in China and textbook authors need to know special areas of difficulty in order to develop convincing strategies for improvement. Studying the performance of such highly educated and basically fluent speakers is of interest because features which surface even in their speech can be taken to be strongly persistent and deeply rooted, and will therefore deserve special attention. Furthermore, in later stages of the development of World Englishes—certainly not in China for a long time to come—such feature descriptions form a necessary basis for strategies of language policy and the possibility of endonormative orientations (Schneider 2007): typically, at that point some countries consider adopting the accent of educated local speakers as a more realistic target of education, a step which presupposes the existence of a reliable description of such a future target variety.

Comparing the above findings with Deterding's (2006) enables us to get closer to a set of phenomena which are at the heart of and typical of Chinese learners' English. Deterding's speakers come from more rural backgrounds than my informants and, broadly, more from eastern and northeastern provinces, and they all speak Mandarin at home. Salient features which have surfaced strongly in that study as well are (1) schwa epenthesis after word-final plosives; (2) /l/ vocalization; (3) heavy vowel nasalization and loss of postvocalic nasals; (9) replacements of dental fricatives; and, listed in (11) above but found less regularly here, [x] for /h, /v/ replacement, and the confusion of /l/ and /n/.

Not surprisingly in a variety of English as a second language, many of the features observed here can be accounted for by transfer from the speakers' native tongues, though the range of mother tongues involved and of lects covered by the notion of "Chinese" requires us to be cautious here. Nevertheless, it seems clear that Chinese syllable structure rules explain some of the phonetic peculiarities noted above, and the analytic grammar of Chinese produces difficulties with inflectional morphemes in English.

While Cantonese allows final unreleased stops (Yip and Matthews 2000, 4), in Mandarin syllables can end only in a vowel or a nasal (or /r/; Duanmu 2000, 51, 77; Ross and Ma 2006, 3). The processes described above under (1) and (5) modify English words which end in a stop or fricative to be in line with this rule of Chinese. Feature (4), final nasal velarization, seems not motivated by transfer, as Chinese allows both /n/ and /ŋ/ word-finally, though no other consonants (Duanmu 2000, 58–59), a fact which, in turn, and in conjunction with tendencies in English itself, may support the disappearance of postvocalic /l/, described in (2). In line with (3), before a nasal coda Chinese vowels are nasalized, and "the rhyme may become a long nasalized vowel" (Duanmu 2000, 72–73). Aspirated voiceless stops stand in phonemic contrast with unaspirated stops in Mandarin and Cantonese (Duanmu 2000, 26; Yip and Matthews 2000, 1), which may explain their importance in Chinese English, as described in (7). Chinese has no voiced stops and fricatives and no dental fricatives (Duanmu 2000, 26, 49); viewed in that perspective, tendencies (8), consonant devoicing, and (9), dental fricative avoidance, cannot come as a surprise. The mid-front /e/ vowel is not a phoneme in Chinese but only a variant of a mid phoneme /ə/ (Duanmu 2000, 37); whether this may be reflected in its opening tendency as described in (10) remains open to investigation. The omission of subjects (in 12) is likely to be motivated by a tendency of both Mandarin and Cantonese to omit the subject if it is understood from the context (Ross and Ma 2006, 17; Yip and Matthews 2000, 18, 116). Also, Mandarin nouns "have a single, invariant form" and "do not reflect number" (Ross and Ma 2006, 22), which explains missing noun inflections as described in (14). In line with article inconsistencies in (12), Chinese noun phrases have specifiers, which are comparable to demonstratives, but no constituents directly corresponding to articles (Ross and Ma 2006, 39–55). Copula omission, reported above in (12), may reflect the fact that in Cantonese the verb *haih* 'to be' can be left out (Yip and Matthews 2000, 32).

Conclusion

The above analysis, admittedly based on limited evidence, identifies both some features widely spread among the informants and some phenomena with more restricted or even idiosyncratic distributions. Most of the forms and patterns noted can be accounted for as transfer phenomena from native Asian languages of the region, so at this point we are essentially dealing with learners' varieties in processes of second language acquisition rather than a newly emerging variety in itself.

Mollin (2007) has discussed and established criteria for a distinct variety status, and practically none of these—expansion in function, nativization of forms, and institutionalization of a norm—apply in the present case. Except for the impact of similarities in input features and constellations, a future focusing process as well as the expansion of usage ranges and the structural stabilization of English in China seem not very likely, and so I do not think that at this stage we are observing initial stages of an emerging variety. Hence, a label of "Chinese English," unless understood very loosely and non-technically, implies more homogeneity than is warranted, and I suppose Deterding (2006) is wise to just talk of English as used by speakers from China.

Generally, English has been spreading vigorously in Asia, arguably producing more speakers of the language (of various levels of proficiency) there than in the rest of the world taken together. However, some healthy skepticism also seems appropriate: currently, the standards of communicative ability vary highly and are frequently somewhat restricted. The movement of English into Asia has produced a wide range of different contexts as well as a number of linguistically highly interesting contact phenomena which are bound to determine the future shape of English in Asian countries. The penetration of English into these regions varies widely in depth and breadth, so Kachru's statement that "English is an Asian language," while acceptable in principle, requires some qualification. Still, as Bailey (1997) documented early in the process, the Asianization of English is robust and ongoing.

NOTES

1. Today, about 30 percent of all secondary schools are "English-medium"; in all others English is a compulsory subject on all grade levels. At the primary school level, government schools are Chinese-medium, with English taught as a subject from the beginning, while in some private schools English is the medium of instruction (A. Kirkpatrick, D. Li, p.c. July 2007).
2. The College was launched in 2002 and completed in 2005; it runs a Graduate School which emphasizes an international orientation for language educators.
3. English is a mandatory subject in Japanese Middle Schools and High Schools (Grades 7–12). English is also taught at a number of elementary schools, and it has been proposed to introduce it there on a broader scale, but this is controversial (J. D'Angelo, p.c. July 2007).

4. Obviously, this excludes Hong Kong, where due to the former colonial status the contact history and situation has been radically different from that of the mainland.
5. I am most grateful to Gavin Bei for having organized this session for me and to the students for having agreed to participate and for sharing some of their thoughts with me, and also for having generated such a pleasant atmosphere. I hope this paper will satisfy them and make it clear what such an activity may be good for.
6. Most of them, as they told me, started learning English at the beginning of secondary school, though some had had some schooling in English already in grades four or even three in primary school—a pattern which, they said, is more common nowadays.
7. I thank Bettina Hiel, Conny Treml, Brigitte Wesserle, and Christin Zwicknagl for having provided preliminary transcripts.
8. Of course, in the case of regular verbs such forms could also result from a phonological process, viz. final consonant cluster reduction.

8

RESPONSE

History of the English Language in the English Department: Past and Present

COLETTE MOORE
University of Washington

The study of the English language owes its present vigor to the past: both the English language of the past and the past of English studies. The history of the English language as a field is a product of both—it not only investigates early English language, but it is also an intellectual descendent of the earliest English study at universities. During the last two centuries, the history of the English language (HEL) has built upon its academic beginnings as philology. Current research continues to pursue philological ends, but it has also expanded its attention to the language of recent periods, expanded its geographic focus, expanded its attention to social variation, expanded its methodologies. The chapters in this section by Lynda Mugglestone, Edgar Schneider, and Anatoly Liberman exemplify the expansion of the field in the latter part of the twentieth century and beginning of the twenty-first. They show us the present richness of HEL studies and point to the changing contours of *the study of* the linguistic past as well as the changing contours of the linguistic past itself.

"History of the English language" and "English historical linguistics" are broadly interchangeable names for much current research in the field, but the first is—grammatically at least—the study of history, and the second the study of linguistics. The first term is the traditional description, so it gestures towards the field's background, while the second invokes connotations of "linguistics" as a social science. I will use the former term here to address the development of the field within English studies and English departments. Although the study of English language history predated the establishment of departments of English (cf. John Free's *An Essay Towards an History of the English Tongue* [1749]), it is valuable to examine its institutional development. Just as studying the language of the past helps us to understand the language of the present, so studying the development of the field of HEL within the boundaries of English departments helps us to understand the present state of the field of English language studies. Therefore, before looking at current developments, I would like first to consider the disciplinary past, especially the importance of philology to the development of English departments. This retrospective approach will show why investigations like those in this section must remain central to the future study of English.

The History of the History of the English Language

It is too easy at present for a U.S. undergraduate English major to regard History of the English Language as an unconnected class, with only a tangential relation to the broader curriculum of literary and cultural studies. It might come as something of a surprise to this hypothetical English major that the discipline of English in the contemporary university grew in large part out of philological roots, and that the history of the English language has played a central and even a defining role in departments of English studies from their inception.

Anglophone universities began to add dedicated chairs of English Language and Literature to their faculties only in 1828 (see also Eagleton

1996, 27). These professorships grew out of the teaching of rhetoric and found legitimacy in the tradition of philology. The first Professor of English Language and Literature, Thomas Dale, described in his inaugural lecture (1828) at the University of London (now University College, London) a plan for the critical study of English. The first step, he asserted, was to investigate: "I. THE HISTORY OF THE LANGUAGE, comprehending a view of its origin, formation, progress, and perfection" (Dale 1829, 16). This perceived centrality of the history of the language persisted in the nineteenth century, and the committee to appoint the ninth incumbent for this chair in 1865 still listed as the first priority for the position that "he ought to have made a systematic study of the Language, so as to be thoroughly conversant with its etymological structure, and the history of its formation through its successive stages" (Bacon 1998, 102).

The disputes over the appointment of the first English professor at Oxford in 1886–87 illustrate the utility of philology for overcoming nineteenth-century objections to English as an institutionalized discipline. The *Pall Mall Gazette* published a flurry of letters in 1886–87 expressing passionate opinions about the proposed Merton chair (see Bacon 1998, 236–276). Anxieties about the creation of dedicated English chairs centered on English as a field for exams: critics believed that English would be too easy a subject and, therefore, taken as an exam field by inferior students. Even some supporters of the study of English were afraid that the field would be labeled a "cram subject." The evaluation of English literature was also a source of uneasiness; it was widely believed that too much of the assessment would come down to personal taste. Objectors to the new field were not exclusively curmudgeons or conservatives: the radical William Morris complained that "the result would be merely vague talk about literature which would teach nothing" (Morris 1886, 27). Philology was the nineteenth-century solution; it ensured the discipline's integrity, from field of study to subject of examination. With philology to ground the discipline, departments of English grew in the nineteenth century: more and more professors were appointed to chairs of English language and literature.

From the very beginning, then, the discipline of English was built upon the history of the language, and the first practitioners of English as a discipline were scholars of the history of English. English departments in the U.S. were established on the same pattern: the first professor of English at Harvard was a philologist, Francis J. Child—appointed to professor (in a telling beginning for English department hiring practices) only after he received a competing offer from Johns Hopkins (Graff 1987, 66). In his memoir *And Gladly Teach* (1935), Bliss Perry, professor of English at Princeton and Harvard, writes: "The steel core of the English work at Harvard, then as now, was in the solid linguistic and historical courses covering the period from the earliest Anglo-Saxon writers to the decline of the Elizabethan drama" (Graff and Warner 1989, 141; see also Allen 1968, 4). Philology served in these early years as the anchor for English as a discipline and the organizing banner for all of the modern languages. The Modern Language Association was born in 1883 as a gathering of professors of the modern languages intellectually united under the flag of comparative philology in contradistinction to the study of Latin and Greek.

The academic ascent of modern language study and English in particular, though, should not be seen simply as the triumph of the local and vernacular over the classical and foreign, since philology was itself an import: most early English professors with doctorates earned them at German universities, and the publication venues for an English professor of the middle nineteenth century included *Anglia* and *Englische Studien*, journals of English philology published in Germany. We still find vestiges of the preeminence of philology in the titles of older American journals, the *Journal of English and Germanic Philology* (1899), *Modern Philology* (1903), *Philological Quarterly* (1922), few of which still examine philology, strictly speaking. Philology was the intellectual centerpiece of the discipline in the nineteenth century in a way that trickled down even to primary school; Ian Michael (1987, 358) has found, for instance, that by the mid–nineteenth century even school grammars typically contain a chapter on the history of the English language.

Proponents of the study of English literature, however, were not universally aligned with philology; some believed it obstructed institutional focus on English literature in its own right. Philology, once the authenticating backbone to the study of English literature, began to be treated as its impediment. Over the second half of the nineteenth-century, humanistic objections to philology motivated objections to the appointments of particular professors of English. A number of the *Pall Mall Gazette* letters after the appointment of A. S. Napier to the Merton chair complained that he was too much a student of language and insufficiently committed to literary study. The Merton professorship was conceived as a philological position, but many interested in literature objected to philology's dominance. Persistent resentment between camps was described in the mid–twentieth century valedictory address of a later successor to the Merton chair, J.R.R. Tolkien:

> Popular mythology seems to believe that *Lang* came from a cuckoo-egg laid in the nest, in which he takes up too much room and usurps the worms of the *Lit* chicken. Some believe that *Lit* was the cuckoo, bent on extruding her nest-fellow or sitting on him; and they have more support from the actual history of our School. But neither tale is well-founded (Tolkien 1983[1979], 230).

Tolkien testifies to a long-standing separation between two schools of *Lang* and *Lit*, though his own career shows how many scholars resisted such artificial divisions.

Over time, English began to justify its presence in the academy not by philological claims to intellectual rigor, but by the moral and spiritual value of literature. The history of the English language began to move toward the margins of the field, as philology became associated with the less humanistic (and thus allegedly less inspired) elements of English study (Court 1992, 85–118). The leader of the New Humanist group in the U. S., Irving Babbitt, described the state of English departments with phrases like "philological despotism" and "a literature ancient and modern controlled by a philological syndicate" (Graff and Warner 1989, 116 and 119). English departments began to legitimize their existence with the spiritual and nation-building capabilities of literature, as Woodrow Wilson (a professor before becoming U.S. president) wrote in the *Atlantic Monthly*:

> [T]here is no science of literature. Literature in its essence is mere spirit, and you must experience it rather than analyze it too formally. . . . If this free people to which we belong is to keep its fine spirit, its perfect temper amidst affairs, its high courage in the face of difficulties, its wise temperateness and wide-eyed hope, it must continue to drink deep and often from the old wells of English undefiled, quaff the keen tonic of its best ideals, keep its blood warm with all the great utterances of exalted purpose and pure principle of which its matchless literature is full (Wilson 1896, 26).

In the twentieth century, departments of English no longer needed philology to prove that they were sufficiently rigorous: the New Criticism promoted systematic evaluation of literature as aesthetic construction, not simply as a product of the language. HEL, once the signature approach of English departments, became one of many subfields. Meanwhile, HEL was developing and already incorporating concepts from the emerging discipline of linguistics.

The Present of the History of English Language

This history might suggest that developments in other branches of English studies progressed independently of change in language studies, but this is not the case. During the 180 years since the first professor of English was appointed, the study of English language history has evolved in tandem with broader shifts in departments of English. Although HEL has overlapped with and contributed to developing departments of linguistics, the history of the English language as a subject has traditionally been housed in English departments, and this has been generally a good fit. In the 1960s and 1970s, for example, when linguistics departments were inundated by generative approaches stemming from the work of Noam Chomsky, HEL scholars, who could not rely on the intuition of present-day speakers, continued to pursue questions empirically and functionally. Historical work (unless focused on the last century) can only use data provided by written texts of the past and thus differs fundamentally from much linguistic research that privileges spoken language.

Historians of English language have anticipated some of the shifting directions of research within English studies. Pursuing a broader range of non-literary genres as objects of study, for example, was characteristic of language work before it was more broadly characteristic of English department research. Language scholars have also led the way in the increasing focus upon global English and the residue of colonialism (see Gneuss 1996, 64–67), the focus upon sociocultural variables such as race, class, gender, and regional affiliation (see Gneuss 1996, 61–64), and scholarly engagement with computers in the humanities (Aitken, Bailey, and Hamilton-Smith 1973; Bailey 1982). Research approaches in the history of the English language have often preceded research in the field more broadly.

Historical study of English, in recent years, has seen both continuity and change: the ongoing pursuit of word history, linguistic relationships, and links between the external and internal histories of language, joined to an increased focus on geographic and social variation, and a broader range of tools, especially electronic corpora and databases. HEL research has always been interested in speakers and variation, of course, but recently this interest has become more explicit and institutionalized through, for example, the innovation of new subfields such as historical sociolinguistics and historical pragmatics. The three papers in this section embody several of the directions that historical study of English has taken.

Lynda Mugglestone's chapter exemplifies the increased attention to modern periods and the heightened importance of linguistic ideologies as a focus for analysis. As Richard W. Bailey put it, "ideas about English are as much a part of its history as the bare facts of sound, syntax, and vocabulary" (1996b, vii). Mugglestone turns to biographical and historical materials to uncover the relationship between the scientist Michael Faraday and the elocution master Benjamin Smart, who becomes for him the linguistic equivalent of a personal trainer. This case study demonstrates, in the nineteenth century what some sociolinguists have called "linguistic insecurity" and what might equally be called "linguistic self-improvement." Mugglestone's analysis of language practice and the influence of prescriptive norms complicates the notion of a simple opposition between "standard" and "non-standard" Englishes and presents a fuller cultural context for language variety in nineteenth-century British society. By examining shifting attitudes towards the language (or languages), Mugglestone, like other recent historians of English, enlarges the scope of the discipline from Dale's proposed study of the "origin, formation, progress and perfection" of English and fruitfully directs attention to ideological, cultural, and social roles of the language.

Nothing complicates Dale's prototype of philology more than the emergence and increased importance of world English. Edgar W. Schneider's article exemplifies the heightened focus on language change up to the present and the geographic decentering of the field. The frontiers of English research have spread with the frontiers of the English language, and it has been a dramatic journey for English from its humble roots to its current status as one of the dominant world languages. Present Day English does not merely center on London (or New York or Toronto or Edinburgh or Dublin or Sydney) but has many local foci all over the globe, and study of these has proceeded enthusiastically in the wake of Braj Kachru's *The Other Tongue* (1982) and Richard W. Bailey and Manfred Görlach's *English as a World Language* (1982). Calcutta, Jakarta, Hong Kong, Singapore, Beijing, Seoul, and others have become centers for English in the last century and influential to the language's development and future. Schneider's work examines the environment of language contact for English in three different cultural/linguistic environments in Asia—Singapore, Hong Kong, and Japan—and illustrates different modes of language contact in different national and colonial settings. Schneider reminds us that speakers can have a multiplex relationship with English: Asian English can present at once imperial residue and economic resource, and it can function at once as foreign import and homegrown self-improvement fad. Schneider shows us the range of methodologies HEL has appropriated: phonetics, language contact, sociolinguistics, and post-colonialism.

Anatoly Liberman's piece seems, at first glance, the most traditional of the three: pursuing an etymological argument through its cognates in other Indo-European languages. But Liberman's analysis is also a product of contemporary HEL methodology and concerns. The first half of Liberman's essay, for example, describes the history of theorizations of the etymology of *wife*. From derivations of *wife* as 'weaver' to 'busy one' to purported links with lexical items for clothing and genitals, Liberman's description demonstrates how etymology is a form of cultural narrative: the stories that we tell ourselves about our words and our world. Liberman's etymological history lays the groundwork for his own hypothesis, but it also explores the ideologies behind etymological thinking, an act of cultural/linguistic situating that was rarely part of nineteenth-century etymology. Liberman's own convincing explanation, drawn from analysis of the proto-Germanic roots, is that *wife* derives from a root *wība-, a term of social organization referring to the descent of a family group from a female forebear. This kind of matriarchal hypothesis is an etymological narrative that is, perhaps, more readily available in the wake of feminism than it was to earlier language historians. If our words are a product of the values of our age, we see, so are our word histories.

The study of the history of the English language has evolved in important ways in the nearly two centuries since the establishment of English departments. We not only study premodern English but extend our focus to language use and change up to the present day; we focus not on Britain alone but on English varieties all over the world; we examine linguistic aspects of the language, its sounds, words, and meaning, but we also investigate these in their broader cultural context—the ideas about language and the practices employed by speakers and writers. The chapters by Mugglestone, Schneider, and Liberman exemplify how incorporation of cultural and linguistic methods has shifted the questions that researchers pursue and the ways that we pursue them.

The Future of the History of the English Language?

The chapters in this section of the volume gesture toward future directions for historical English study. Questions that run through this section include: *What is the role of speaker attitudes in language change? How was language perceived as a ticket to success in the past and how is it today? How does the progress of words and their meanings follow the progress of the people who use them? How do the processes of language diffusion and language contact affect English? How does societal organization alter the meanings of other words, ideologies about usage, and the adoption of English?* These questions have driven historians of English for the last two centuries, and we see them approached again newly here. Surely, the future holds further development of classic topics for English language change with new methodologies and approaches. But how is this to be realized? How is it to be effected in the context of the English department?

Speaking about the departmental future of HEL is different for the United States than for continental Europe or the U.K. In settings where English is taught as a foreign language, HEL is given a boost by the broader framework of English Language Studies. Also, the field has not lost as much ground in Britain over the last century as it has in the U.S. By the late twentieth century, much of the influential work in HEL research was coming from Europe and from branches of linguistics, placing the U.S.in a position oddly similar to that it occupied in the nineteenth century, when much of our research rigor and methodology derived from Europe. Recent years, though, have seen an increased energy in historical English studies. In the inaugural U. S. conference, Studies in the History of the English Language (SHEL), Richard W. Bailey called for a "renewed philology" (2002b, 449). The energy and new directions in English language research (indeed, the very existence of the SHEL meetings) suggest our progress in attaining it. It remains, however, to build better bridges with English department research. New quantitative and linguistic methodologies, have led correspondingly to more technical research. Pursuit of specialized questions is certainly crucial, but it is important to keep at least some work accessible to all those interested in English. Works like Bailey's *Images of English* (1991a) and *Nineteenth-Century English* (1996b) show us how the stories of the linguistic past can engage a broad audience. Language history can and should continue to contribute helpfully to the larger humanistic projects of the discipline of English studies. Effective linking of English language history to departmental work in literary and cultural studies, writing instruction (including creative writing), and English education exemplifies the flexibility that HEL has shown over its history—and the kind of flexibility that it must continue to show. Historical study of the English language has shaped the contours of the discipline of English studies, and it should continue to do so.

Links between historical study of the English language and other important work in English departments deserve greater attention. Not only does HEL provide crucial tools for many of the important conversations in English studies, but it also provides glue for some of the divisions between subfields within the English department. Language study is the instrument for constructing and deciphering literary art, and it is the pursuit of the cultural, social, and national contexts that underlie it. Language study is also the interpretive tool for texts already written, and it is the instructional guide for writing new texts. Subfields within English departments grew out of shared philological roots, and so the history of language can, to some extent, link them together. F. D. Maurice's inaugural lecture as the first Professor of English Literature and History at King's College London (1840) presciently speaks to such separations:

> … I believe that the history of our words is a part of the history of our nation; that the knowledge of the changes which a word has undergone in different periods, may often (as has been remarked by a great man,) throw more light upon those periods than the history of a campaign. I am rather inclined to think that we shall find the study of words and constructions, the very link between literature and history, between the particular book we are reading and the age in which that book was written. (Maurice 1840, 279)

Maurice's explicitly political connection between the history of words and the history of nations, and between the literary work and its context, indicates that from the very outset, history of English language studies was central to the enduring concerns of literary and cultural studies. The inauguration of English departments, we see, can provide a helpful blueprint for our continuing development. Our future may well be found in our past.

PART III

English Lexicography

Introduction

English departments and dictionaries have a special relationship: student readers and writers habitually check dictionaries online and, like their professors, sharpen their scholarly arguments, and occasionally their own diction, on the whetstone of the *Oxford English Dictionary*. Though it no longer dominates English departments, philology—or the study of language in usually, but not exclusively, "literary" texts—still figures in the research and curriculum of most departments, and lexicography is an essential aspect of philology. Dictionaries serve many purposes, and among other things they are resources for reading seriously and writing thoughtfully. Many colleges and universities recommend a dictionary to their new students, if not require it for an introductory writing course; and some purchase a license to link the whole college or university to a suite of dictionaries.

Almost all literate speakers of English use dictionaries, and most see dictionaries as unproblematic, thinking in terms of The Dictionary, as though there were only one, or as though there were an ideal dictionary of which the ones we buy or consult are more or less successful versions. The reality is quite different. There are, in fact, many kinds of dictionary. They range from college dictionaries to really big or "unabridged" ones, like those produced by Merriam-Webster, the American Heritage Dictionaries, Oxford University Press, and other publishers. Then there are dictionaries compiled on historical principles like the *Oxford English Dictionary* or the *Dictionary of the Older Scottish Tongue*; and, in addition to these, scores of etymological dictionaries, bilingual dictionaries, learners' dictionaries, and even facetious dictionaries, like Ambrose Bierce's *The Devil's Dictionary* (1906).

Consider some structural differences among major dictionaries of current English. *The American Heritage Dictionary of the English Language, Fourth Edition* (2000), besides providing pronunciations, definitions, and brief etymologies, also traces modern words back to Indo-European roots; in addition, it includes usage notes, word history notes, and more. Merriam-Webster's *Webster's Third New International Dictionary of the English Language* (1961) is famous (or infamous, depending on the temperament of the user) for its single-sentence, stylistically clinical, semantically analytical definitions. *The New Oxford American Dictionary, Second Edition* (2005) does not present definitions chronologically from oldest to newest, but leads with "core meanings" and follows with extended ones.

Some dictionaries, the historical dictionaries, present considerable evidence of usage in quotation paragraphs; by contrast, commercial dictionaries, which do not share all of the purposes of historical dictionaries, differ from them in design and provide occasional illustrations of usage without elaboration. More or less all dictionaries are conceived by editors committed to treating a particular vocabulary according to principles and methods developed in the history of lexicography. Each dictionary's design reflects its editors' understanding of language history, linguistics, and the culture of which the dictionary is an artifact—indeed, sometimes, as in the cases of the *OED* and *Webster's Third*, a very significant artifact.

Perhaps surprisingly to some, many dictionaries are written to be read, written as much for the reader's pleasure as for bare-bones edification. Among readable dictionaries, the *Oxford English Dictionary* is clearly the best example. Richard W. Bailey, examining the *OED*'s reputation, writes that

> Naturally the first reviews were the most important ones, but, even after the dictionary was well established and making steady progress, editors of both popular and scholarly publications saw fit to tell the story again and again. In many ways, it was the same story year after

> year: a triumph of scholarship, a testimonial to the antiquity of the language, a tribute to the value of those who had written it. But if each word told its own story, each part of the dictionary told a new episode in the evolution of English and the sources of its expressiveness. It was thus a slightly different story each time, one that reviewers and readers loved to have told. (2000a, 253)

Reviewers and readers of the *OED* and readers of the reviews, as well, were all engaged in a literary pursuit: each word had its story, and part of that story was an anthology of its historical usage, and the dictionary as a whole was a sort of super-anthology of word stories. One can read it purposefully, as Ammon Shea illustrates in his account *Reading the OED: One Man, One Year, 21,730 Pages* (2008), or one can meander in it as time and energy allow.

The first English dictionary, Robert Cawdrey's *A Table Alphabeticall*, appeared in 1604. After four hundred years of lexicography, one would think we would have solved all of the "problems," that writing dictionaries would be routine. The chapters in this section suggest otherwise. In many cases, especially historical lexicography, the vocabulary to be treated in a dictionary requires a new approach. The *Dictionary of American Regional English* (*DARE*) is a historical dictionary, relying on printed texts and manuscripts for usage evidence and for determining the earliest known record of a word. But it also includes a large component of contemporary usage, collected by field workers from speakers across America in response to a questionnaire. *DARE* creatively synthesizes many types of evidence, from literature and documents, the questionnaire, linguistic atlas data, and other research in order, as Joan Houston Hall points out here, to compensate for limited evidence of use of many regional words.

At the other end of the spectrum, Jesse Sheidlower considers the challenge posed to the *Oxford English Dictionary* by exponentially increasing access to texts, digitized versions of old texts, as well as the new text types that continue to emerge in our suddenly digital world. Michael Montgomery speculates on the prospects for a "Dictionary of Irish English on Historical Principles," and the impediments he considers, matters of political and religious history, national identity, and interlinguistic relations, are not similarly central to conceiving a comprehensive historical dictionary like the *OED* or, indeed, most other historical dictionaries: the circumstances are more or less unique to the treatment of Irish English. Montgomery proves that it's not a foregone conclusion that there's a dictionary for every vocabulary.

One thing is certain: emerging technology and associated media will influence the future course of lexicography, as it has during the last several decades. Of course, technology introduces a continuous stream of new words, and new sites of speech (blogs, fanfiction, chatrooms, text messages) situated differently in literate culture from "traditional" ones (journalism, short stories, conversations, Post-it notes) prompt lexical innovation. Perhaps more important to lexicography than the new words, however, is the way that technology shapes lexicographical ambitions and techniques. As Richard W. Bailey (1973a, 293) once remarked, when the personal computer was merely a glint in IBM's eye, "the outcome of our research will be conditioned by the devices we use in its execution." Though lexicographers have rarely made much money, their dictionaries are often costly: automation is essential to controlling expense, of making lexical research widely available. Machines, Bailey (1973a, 296) wrote, "make it possible for us to pursue our uneconomic but amusing research into the English lexicon."

It isn't so "uneconomic" to make a dictionary nowadays. Lexicography no longer requires paper, printing presses, editors, marketing, sales, or distribution. You can make a dictionary to amuse yourself and hope that others passing along the information highway will stop for a while to amuse themselves, too. Internet dictionaries come in as many formats and styles as the traditional ones. On Wiktionary, proudly amateur contributors attempt to write definitions with as much authority as those compiled by professionals. Urban Dictionary entries list contributors' definitions and examples of words without synthesis. It's hard to tell just how many contributors are behind the compendious dictionary at SlangSite.com. It's also hard to tell which entries reflect bona fide language use and which are examples of what the site calls "lexifabricography," creating words to suit your purpose or for the pleasure of invention.

Sites like Grant Barrett's Doubletongued Dictionary and Mark Peters's Worldlustitude are examples of lexicography as an aesthetic practice: they don't attempt to collect all words but only those that appeal to the lexicographers as interesting for cultural, political, or aesthetic reasons. Lexicography, on these models, is a way of perceiving the world, like drawing: unexpectedly, at the beginning of the twenty-first century, lexicography is personal. Simultaneously, hypertextual dictionaries may expand to cover the universe of lexical knowledge, as the automated possibilities meet and then exceed our imaginations: we have imagined such utopian dictionaries for a while now (Revard 1973, Bailey 1973a, Bailey 1987a, and Adams 2007) and are likely to watch utopia transform into reality in our lifetimes.

The accelerating relationship of lexicography and automation illustrates the extent to which dictionaries are agents as well as artifacts of culture, texts that deserve study for all of the reasons we usually study texts. We have motives for writing dictionaries, but also reasons for writing about them. Recently, Julie Coleman and Sarah Ogilvie, both of them lexicographers and historians of lexicography, have described a methodology they call "forensic dictionary analysis, by which the dictionary researcher can examine, understand, and reconstruct lexicographic policies and practices—policies and practices that sometimes differ from the accounts given by the lexicographers themselves" (2009, 1).

The *OED* has undergone a considerable amount of forensic dictionary analysis, for instance, in books by K. M. Elisabeth Murray (1977), Lynda Mugglestone (2000, 2005), and Charlotte Brewer (2007). Such research reminds us of just how problematic dictionaries can be, not just in their conception and making, but for the cultures to which they are presented. *Webster's Third* excited so much controversy in the year after its publication in 1961 that James Sledd and Wilma R. Ebbit could publish *Dictionaries and* That *Dictionary* (1962). How could a dictionary cause so much trouble? How justified was the outraged response? Herbert C. Morton's *The Story of Webster's Third: Philip Gove's Controversial Dictionary and Its Critics* (1994) provides the entire story. There will always be as many opportunities to study the complex relations of dictionaries and cultures as there are dictionaries and cultures.

9

New Suckers from the Old Root

JOAN HOUSTON HALL
University of Wisconsin

In the introduction to the second series of *The Biglow Papers* (1867), James Russell Lowell took pains to justify both the use of vernacular speech in American literature in general and his own depictions of Yankee dialect in particular: "Very few American writers or speakers wield their native language with the directness, precision, and force that are common as the day in the mother country," he declared.

> And yet all the while our popular idiom is racy with life and vigor and originality . . . and proves itself no mere graft by sending up new suckers from the old root in spite of us. It is only from its roots in the living generations of men that a language can be reinforced with fresh vigor for its needs. (x)

After extending the metaphor by proclaiming our American language a "rich leaf-mould" from which the "vocal forest" might "clothe itself anew with living green" (xi), he asserted rather abruptly, "There is death in the dictionary; and, where language is too strictly limited by convention, the ground for expression to grow in is limited also; and we get a *potted* literature, Chinese dwarfs instead of healthy trees" (xi).

Twenty-one years later, Lowell might have been surprised to read James Murray's similar contention, in the preface to the first volume of the *New English Dictionary on Historical Principles*, that

> the creative period of the language, the epoch of 'roots,' has never come to an end. The 'origin of language' is not to be sought merely in a far-off Indo-European antiquity, or in a still earlier pre-Aryan yore-time; it is still in perennial process around us. A literary language, with . . . its constant appeals to an authoritative precedent . . . is hostile to word-creation. . . . But such is not the case with language in its natural state, where words are estimated simply as they serve their purpose of communicating the thought or feeling of the moment. . . . The unwritten dialects . . . approach in character to language in its natural state. . . . In the local dialects, then, in slang, and in colloquial use, new vocables and new expressions may at any time be abruptly brought forth to serve the needs of the moment, in accordance with feelings of inherent natural fitness, of imitative suggestiveness, or of subtle instinctive analogy with groups of words or parts of words already familiar. (qtd. in Raymond 1987, viii)

Clearly, Murray was committed to recording the ongoing vitality of English in this new dictionary, and the entries would include words "now in general use, or known to have been in use at any time during the last seven hundred years" (qtd. in Raymond 1987, viii).

The success of Murray's enterprise is legendary, and the *Oxford English Dictionary* or *OED* (as the *New English Dictionary on Historical Principles* came to be called) has served for nearly a century as the primary source of documentation of English from its earliest roots to its most recent branches. Language historians have relied heavily on it to understand such changes as the gradual loss of inflectional endings representing number, gender, and case, the tendency toward weakening of preterites and past participles of verbs, and the steady regularization of noun plurals. The *OED* also provides an almost-comprehensive record of the means by which new words come into the language, whether by the major processes of affixation, compounding, and the conversion of words from one part of speech to another (which together have yielded most additions to the lexicon) or such minor processes as back-formation, folk-etymology, metanalysis, metathesis, and blending.

Because of the *OED*'s broad overview of the evolution of word forms in English, a tendency among language historians has been to cite archaic forms to illustrate the processes of lexical change rather than to look at contemporary examples or those created from Lowell's "rich leaf-mould" or Murray's "local dialects."

In his excellent book *The Origins and Development of the English Language* (1964), for instance, Thomas Pyles has a chapter called "New Words from Old." In it he illustrates the common process of affixing with examples of such forms as *be-* (the unstressed form of *by* originally meaning 'about' and later 'at' or 'near') in *believe, beneath, beyond*, and the suffix *-ly* (from OE *līc* 'body') in *manly, godly*, and *homely* (267). His discussion of compounding points back to old words like *garlic* (OE *gār* 'a spear' + *lēac* 'leek'), *hussy* (OE *hus* 'house' + *wif* 'wife'), and *lord* (OE *hlāf* 'loaf' + *weard* 'ward') (280). Ancient words like *cherry* and *pea* are cited as examples of back-formation (284), with *acorn, cockroach, hangnail*, and *mandrake* (among others) serving as exemplars of folk-etymology (291). Pyles's consideration of blends begins with such sixteenth and seventeenth-century forms as *flush, luncheon, twirl, dumfound* and *flurry*, and moves forward to such recent examples as *cinemactor* and *infanticipate* (286–87). He acknowledges that many of these are well known examples that occur frequently in discussions of language change. While there is no question that they are useful and appropriate specimens, I suggest that they tend to contribute to the subliminal notion that processes of change are part of the historical development of English rather than continuing elements in the evolution of our language.

Convinced that many language historians had focused on the remote past while withholding sufficient respect for the remarkable changes that occurred in nineteenth-century English, Richard W. Bailey recently set out to explore that century in its social, economic, and linguistic contexts and to highlight the continuity of language change. His resulting book, *Nineteenth-Century English* (1996b), is a first-rate contribution to the canon. Examining the systems of writing, sounds, words, and grammar, along with the topics of slang and "voices" (those language differences occasioned by social and regional distinctions), Bailey details changes in English ranging from the patterned and predictable to others that were seemingly random.

In his chapter on words, Bailey shows that nineteenth-century writers reveled in the creation of new words by reviving the adverb-forming prefix *a-* as in *atingle, atremble, asway, asmear, asquirm, aswing,* and *awreck* (by Robert Browning, Elizabeth Barrett Browning, William Morris, Charles Dickens, William Dean Howells, Edward Dowden, and Joaquin Miller, respectively) (164). They seized on the prefix *non-*, extending it from the technical vocabulary of the law to any conceivable context, resulting in such forms as *non-beer-drinking, non-agricultural,* and *non-worker* (165–66). And they took the firmly established prefix *be-*, which by then had developed an extended sense 'covered with,' and made it a "living prefix" (165). Extending it even further so that it expressed the notion of 'overrun or afflicted by,' they created such inventive phrases as "*bedaughtered* dowagers," "*berailroaded* landscape," and "*behatted* doctor" (165). These kinds of creations, Bailey points out, may not necessarily express new ideas, but they "provide stylistic nuance and novelty, both aspects of innovation insufficiently appreciated in most treatments of English words" (165).

Looking at other word-forming processes in the nineteenth century, Bailey notes that back-formation produced such now commonplace verbs as *absorb, book-keep, burgle, legislate,* and *sculpt* (153); clipping gave us *cab, pants, pub, fan,* and *flu* (153); blending yielded *chortle, slanguage, insinuendo,* and *brunch* (154); the process of borrowing introduced *gneiss, feldspar, scherzo, beignet,* and *mauve* (151–61); medical and scientific word fervor (148) introduced such terms as *tonsillitis, appendicitis, appendectomy, brachycephalous,* and *prognathous* (140–41), while manufacturing generated *margarine, linoleum, vaseline,* and *aspirin* (150); and although compounding was already a well established linguistic mechanism, "the nineteenth century made it a principal method of forming new words" (230).

Just as Bailey's demonstration of vibrant linguistic change in the nineteenth century complements and updates earlier linguistic histories of English with their focus on roots and origins, data collected for the *Dictionary of American Regional English* (*DARE*) can extend Bailey's thesis of linguistic ferment through the twentieth century, at least for the millions of speakers of English in the United States. Based on a project of face-to-face fieldwork carried out in 1,002 communities across the country between 1965 and 1970, and supplemented by thousands of written sources ranging from government documents to novels, poems, plays, reports, histories, newspapers, and to ephemeral sources such as posters and overheard conversations, *DARE* illustrates the interactions of cultural and linguistic change.

Two features unique to *DARE* are the inclusion of population-adjusted maps of the United States that show where particular words and phrases were collected in the fieldwork, and the use of social labels based on statistical analysis of the categories of age, race, sex, education, and community type for each Informant. These allow *DARE*'s editors to describe regional distributions and to apply such labels as "*old-fashioned,*" "*chiefly among Black speakers,*" "*especially among women,*" "*chiefly among speakers with little formal education,*" and "*chiefly among rural speakers.*" But *DARE* also includes entries for "folk" speech—the language that we learn "in the home and in the community, from relatives and friends, not from schooling, books, or other outside forms of communication. It is traditional and largely oral; it includes anything that can be called 'dialect' in the United States" (*DARE* I.xvi).

DARE's focus on words that are *not* found throughout the country, that tend to have social restrictions in their use, or that are not considered "standard" means that it includes material ignored, marginalized, or "insufficiently appreciated" by other dictionaries and by histories of the lexicon. It can afford to give space to specimens that may not be widespread but that document the continuing linguistic creativity that, as Murray said, "may be abruptly brought forth to serve the needs of the moment"(quoted in Raymond 1987, viii).

It is those perhaps minor but very engaging examples of linguistic creativity that are the focus of this paper. Some might liken the lists that follow to Jean Aitchison's description of traditional lists that are reduced "to the level of stamp collecting, an assembly of colourful bits and pieces . . . [that] wrongfully give the impression that words exist in isolation from one another" (123). However, just as an understanding of the history of the postal system requires an examination of the colorful stamps it has produced, a full understanding of English language change should include the bits and pieces that illustrate the continuing vitality and diversity of our language, even if they ultimately prove to be ephemeral and exert no pressure on the structure of the system.

The resources, then, are now available with which we can survey linguistic change across a millennium, with illustrative examples from *Beowulf* to Google. For contemporary illustrations of language change to complement the old favorites in traditional histories, *DARE* can provide copious examples. And to make it easy to mine the data in the *Dictionary*, *DARE* staff members have produced *An Index by Region, Usage, and Etymology to the* Dictionary of American Regional English.[1] With it, scholars, teachers, and students can discover the larger patterns formed by the colorful bits and pieces of American English.

Back-Formation

An exploration of the process of back-formation as one way in which new words are created could surely start with Thomas Pyles's (1964, 284) clear explanation that

> the final consonant [-z] of *pease* is not, as it seems to the ear to be, the English plural suffix *-s*; it is in fact not a suffix at all. But by the seventeenth century *pease* was mistaken for a plural, and a new singular, *pea*, was derived from a word which was itself singular, precisely as if we were to derive a form **chee* from *cheese* under the impression that *cheese* was plural; then we should have *one chee, two chees*, just as we now have *one pea, two peas*.

In fact, precisely that interpretation of *cheese* as a plural had already been made long before Pyles suggested it in 1964. As *DARE* illustrates, the journal *Dialect Notes* reported in 1894 that in Connecticut "*Cheese* is sometimes used as plural = cheeses" (I.340), and the following year it noted that in Kentucky, western North Carolina, and Tennessee, "*Chee*, [is] singular; *cheese*, plural" (I.376). Later examples in *DARE*, from 1905 through 1954, of such phrases as "Those cheese haven't come yet"[2] and "Pass me them cheese," show that this back-formation had some staying power, at least for half a century.

Similar examples in *DARE*, gleaned from the *Indexes*, include the singular forms *Chinee, Maltee*, and *Portugee*, created on the assumption that the final consonants of *Chinese, Maltese*, and *Portuguese* must indicate plurality. Looking at the *DARE* entries for *Chinee* and *Portugee*, one can not only trace the history of these forms, but can also gain uncomfortable insights into the society that spawned them. A passage from the *Congressional Record* in 1890, quoting a Representative from eastern Pennsylvania, says: "It may be claimed that this bill . . . has something of a Heathen Chinee flavor about it and that it is framed with 'intent to deceive.'" Seventy-five years later, *DARE* informants were still using the term in response to the Questionnaire, offering such phrases as *Chinee food, Chinee pheasant, round eyes like a Chinee,* and *Heathen Chinee*. The fact that most of the *DARE* citations include regional labels allows readers to relate the presence of the linguistic form to the social history of the nation: *Chinee* is found primarily in the North and West, where Chinese immigrants were able to find work.

Likewise, those who view the *DARE* map showing the distribution of the forms *Portagee, Porte(r)gee, Portuguee,* and *Portyg(h)ee* (found at the entry for *Portuguese*), will see what looks at first like a highly unlikely regional pattern: the examples occur almost solely in southern New England, California, and Hawaii. However, the recognition that a huge percentage of the Portuguese people who immigrated to the United States made their living by fishing and that they moved to areas where they could maintain their traditional livelihoods makes the linguistic distribution easy to comprehend.

Other examples in the *DARE Indexes* of back-formations created from words mistakenly assumed to be plural comprise several categories: those coming from words ending in *x*, in which the sound resembles the plural marker [-ks], such as *appendic* (from *appendix*), *flock* noun (from *phlox*), *flommock* noun (from *flummox* as a noun), *galak* (as a verb 'to gather *galax*'—understood as *galacks*), *jink* noun (from *jinx* as a noun), and *link* noun (from *lynx*); those created from words with a plural-like final [-s] or [-z], such as *corp* (from *corpse*), *ho* (from *hose* 'stockings'), *mayonay* (from *mayonnaise*), *polonay* (from *polonaise* 'a type of overdress'), and *specie* (from *species*); and those from actual plural [-z] forms, creating parallel singular forms, such as *beef/beeve* (from plural *beeves*), *shaft/shav* (from *shavs*), and *sheaf/sheave* (from *sheaves*).

A different kind of back-formation with a long history and much contemporary vitality involves the process of creating a verb from an existing noun. Verbs ending in *-ate,* from nouns ending in *-ation,* are particularly productive: *alterate, applicate, botherate, combinate, consolate, interpretate, lamentate, mirate, norate,* and *perspirate* are good examples in *DARE.*[3] Verbs created from other noun forms are illustrated by *connip* (from *conniption*) and *deparch* (from *departure*). And verbs from adjectives include *antigogle* (from *antigoglin* 'askew, out of plumb'), *contage* (from *contagious*), *cose* (from *cozy*), *frivol* (from *frivolous*), and *hifalute* (from *hifalutin*). The virtue of studying these processes in *DARE* is that readers can determine who used the forms, when, and in what context. And while some of the users are well known authors, many others are "just folks."[4]

As editors working on the third edition of the *OED* have discovered, many of the words earlier thought to have been coined by Shakespeare had an independent existence prior to his using them in a play or a poem. He doubtless *was* the creator of hundreds of words, but his iconic stature in English literature has given him a huge advantage over other writers: his works have been scoured by lexicographers, while more obscure works have gone unscrutinized (Metcalf 2002, 61). With the availability of electronic access to large numbers of hitherto unstudied early texts, lexicographers and language historians will doubtless discover many more cases in which Shakespeare was not the coiner of new words but rather their popularizer. Those long unrecognized authors, bringing forth Murray's "new vocables" that served the needs of moments long ago, may ultimately get their day in the sun.

Some time ago in teaching a course on the structure of English, I used the preceding examples in a discussion of back-formations and then asked students to look out for similar forms as they read the newspapers or listened to the news. The thrill of the chase became evident as they returned with the following examples of linguistic creativity:

We had to surveil him closely.

All the troops that had attrited.

He was chosen to liaise.

The Vietnam War Memorial allowed veterans to catharse their feelings.

A check of the flotation cushions reveals they don't really flotate.

Pyles (1964, 285) discusses another kind of back-formation, "in which the secondary form could just as well have been the primary one, and in which no misunderstanding is involved." He cites *typewrite, housekeep, and baby-sit* as good examples of cases in which the *-er* ending in *typewriter, housekeeper*, and *baby-sitter* suggests nouns of agency derived from verbs, while in fact, the verbs were back-formed from the nouns. Similar forms in *DARE* are the verbs *appleknock* ('to act the yokel' or 'to curry favor,' from *appleknocker* 'a rustic' or 'an apple polisher'); *book-keep* ('to act as a bookkeeper,' which, as Bailey points out, was a nineteenth-century linguistic creation); *dressmake* ('to be a seamstress'); *middlebust* ('to use a middlebuster plow'); *mize* ('to act like a miser'); *pinhook* ('to act as a pinhooker [=a small-time speculator in farm products, especially tobacco]'); and *sharecrop* ('to act as a sharecropper' or 'to rent out [land] on shares').[5]

The process of back-formation takes a somewhat different course in the creation of the adjective *tush*; while the evidence is slight, the derivational path seems clear. In his 1934 glossary of prison slang, Kuethe defines *tush* as 'Dangerous; belligerent' (28); Wentworth and Flexner define it in *Dictionary of American Slang* in 1960 as 'Belonging to high society; wealthy, sophisticated and influential; ritzy.' This newly-derived adjective comes from the noun *tush hog*, which means, in its primary sense, 'a feral hog with prominent tusks.' In its extended senses, however, *tush hog* also denotes 'a tough, aggressive person; a bully, rowdy' and 'a city slicker, big shot.' A lack of familiarity with *tush* as a regional variant of *tusk* could easily lead to the understanding of *tush* as an adjective rather than an attributive noun.

Folk-Etymology

A similar kind of meaning-making occurs in the process of folk-etymology, by which an unfamiliar term is made understandable by assuming that it is made up of words that happen to sound similar but are actually unrelated. Standard examples in linguistic histories of English include *cockroach* (from Spanish *cucaracha*); *cold slaw* (from Dutch *kool* 'cabbage' + *sla* 'salad'); *hangnail* (from Old English *ang* 'tight, painful' + *naegl* 'an iron nail'); *muskrat* (from Algonquian *musquash*); and *sparrow grass* (for *asparagus*).

Pyles (1964, 289–93) includes a long list of such well known folk-etymologies, adding to them the wonderful recent example of *soda box*, used by ballet students after hearing the standard (but to them unfamiliar) French term *saut de basque* 'Basque leap' (290). In a similar way, adult participants in an aerobic dance class in Madison, Wisconsin, recently interpreted the instructor's use of the French term *sissonne* ['si,sɔ̃] (a dance jump named after its inventor) as *see-saw*, extrapolating from the up-and-down motion of the outstretched arm and leg. *DARE* contributes to the collection of folk-etymologies with quite a variety of forms. Some, like *soda box* and *seesaw*, are based on foreign terms that need some kind of plausible interpretation:

fat man and *fattyman*: from Norwegian *fattigmann*, in the phrase *fattigmanns bakkels* 'poor man's cookie'

hooligan: from *eulachon*, derived from Chinook Jargon *ulâkân* for a smelt-like food fish

never-sweat: from French *avocette*, for the bird known in English as the *avocet*

shoe-peg and *shoe-pick*: from French *choupique*, itself derived from Choctaw *shupik* 'mudfish,' in reference to the bowfin

skillpot: from Dutch *schildpad* 'shield-toad'(or from a similar Scandinavian form), referring to various turtles

sockeye salmon: from Salish *suk-kegh* 'red fish,' from the color of the flesh

tom fuller: from Choctaw *tahfula* 'hominy' for fresh, dried, or fermented hominy, or a dish made therefrom

Other misinterpretations of foreign words arise from the scientific names that refer to diseases or identify plants and animals:

acid anemia: for *acetonemia* 'an abnormal increase in ketone bodies in circulating blood' (a common affliction of cows)

Aunt Jericho: from the genus *Angelica*

dear Dora and *deer darrow*: from the species name for the deodar cedar *Cedrus deodara*

ladies'-streamer: from the genus *Lagerstroemia*, for a crape myrtle

our beauties: from the genus *Arbutus*, but used in reference to *Epigaea repens*, which is also known as *trailing arbutus*

tortoise collar: from *torticollis* 'an abnormal twisting of the neck so that the head does not face forward' (also known as *wry neck*)

Still other formations simply result from people's unfamiliarity with standard terms and an attempt to make the words have some sense:

bankrupture (bankruptcy)

brown kitties (bronchitis)

colored marbles or *collywobbles (cholera morbus)*

fist-to-cuff fight (fisticuff)

gypsum or *gypsy weed (jimson weed)*

high geranium (hydrangea)

leapfrog milk (Liebfrau milch)

old-timers' disease (Alzheimer's disease)

power doctor (powwow doctor)

prostrate cancer (prostate cancer)

roaches of the liver (cirrhosis of the liver)

Scotch chenille (cochineal)

scrapegoat (scapegoat)

separate (suppurate)

terrified fever (typhoid fever)

unkept (unkempt)

very close or *very coarse veins (varicose veins)*

Analogical processes can also contribute to the creation of new forms, with *highbelia* taking its place alongside *lowbelia* (itself a folk-etymology for *lobelia*), and *low-bred* (used of a non-hybridized corn) coming into contrast with *high-bred*, the 'logical' form of *hybrid*. Ironic reinterpretation can come into play as well. The adjective *soon*, in the sense 'smart, clever, shrewd,' yielded the noun *sooner*, meaning 'a clever, active person.' With that sense in mind, playful speakers extended the senses to include 'a lazy, good-for-nothing person' and 'an inferior or mongrel dog,' winking at the homonymy with *sooner*, meaning 'rather.' Typical explanations include these: "Sooners would just as soon lie in bed as get up" and "A sooner hound is a hunting dog that would sooner lie down than hunt."

Sometimes the folk-etymological process becomes even more extensively creative, with a setting and a plot devised to explain a word. Called *etymythologies* by linguist Laurence Horn (2004, 39), such stories are akin to etymological urban legends, and they are remarkably difficult to discourage once they become popularized. One example in *DARE* shows that a widely believed explanation for *anadama bread* (whose etymology is unknown) is that it comes from "Anna, damn her!" A more elaborate explanation goes from folk-etymology to etymythology, as the quotation in the 1956 *Betty Crocker Picture Cook Book* illustrates:

> An amusing story of the origin of Anadama Bread relates— The name *Anadama* comes from a New England fisherman whose lazy wife always served him corn meal mush and molasses for dinner. One day he came home and found the same corn meal and molasses. Tired of it, he mixed it with flour and yeast and baked it as bread, saying: "Anna damn her" (97).

Two of my favorite *DARE* folk-etymologies are not quite as scripted as the preceding, but are tangled with elements of a traditional folk custom with regional linguistic variants. One of the questions in the *DARE* questionnaire asked: "*When someone wants to pass on a compliment about you, in exchange for one about himself, he says, 'I have a _____ for you.'*" 203 informants, spread fairly widely across the country, but found less commonly in the Atlantic states, answered with the term *trade last*. That is, they would trade compliments, but the speaker would do it last, thereby ensuring the receipt of an ego-boosting comment. In the Mid and South Atlantic states, the corresponding term is the variant *last-go-trade*, reported by 37 informants. Two other informants, unfamiliar with the terminology, tried to make sense of the practice by interpreting it as a *lasso trade* (not unreasonable, given the notion of wresting a compliment from someone), and an *Alaskan trade* (so foreign that it must be from far away).

Metanalysis

Another process of linguistic creativity that is treated in many discussions of the history of English is that of metanalysis or 'false juncture.' Standard examples include the creation of *an adder, an apron* and *an umpire* from *a nadder, a napron* and *a numpire,* and the converse development of *a nickname* from *an ekename* (an 'also' name). Today's readers will all be aware of the existence of *nother,* as in "a whole nother ball game," but they may be intrigued to see that it is part of this recognized historical pattern of word development.

Additional contemporary examples of false juncture found in the *Index* to labels in *DARE* include *Adam's all fox* (from *Adam's off-ox,* as in "I wouldn't know him from Adam's off-ox") and the related *Madam's off-ox* (with *Madam* by metanalysis of *from Adam*); *a blige* ('an obligation,' from *oblige*); *an eye horse* (from *a nigh horse*); *a nagent, a naggie, a noration,* and *a numberell* (from *an agent, an aggie* [=an agate playing marble], *an oration,* and *an umbrella*); and the unusual but not unreasonable *teither* (as in "'I didn't either." "Yes, you did teither.")

Metathesis

New words created by the reversal of parts of existing words, whether by phonological, morphological, or phraseological shifting, have also been historically important contributors of new shoots from old roots. Histories of English often mention the reversal of phonemes that resulted in modern *bird* from *brid, curd* from *crud, thirty* from *thrity* (related to *three*), *tusk* from *tux,* and *wasp* from *waeps.* Similarly, the regionally distributed nouns *hoppergrass* and *peckerwood* and the adverb *right-down* (all common throughout the South and South Midland) have long been recognized as metathetic creations in which the two words of a compound have been switched. (Not surprisingly, these are also called *reversed compounds.*)

In *DARE,* examples of metathesis range from the switching of adjacent sounds in a syllable, to reversal across syllables, to reversed compounds, to the rearranging of the parts of a phrase. Within a syllable, metathesis seems to occur most frequently with the retroflex alveolars. The process of consonantal /r/ plus a vowel becoming optional vowel plus vocalic /ɝ/ occurs frequently, as illustrated by *carps* (for *craps*), *catasterfy* (for *catastrophe*), *curler* (for *cruller*), *egert* (for *egret*), *erligion* (for *religion*), and *purty* (for *pretty*). Just the opposite also occurs, as in *bittrun* (for *bittern*), *drindl* (for *dirndl*), *lantrun* (for *lantern*), *lectren* (for *lectern*), *modren* (for *modern*), *sogrum* (for *sorghum*), and *tuckrey* (for *turkey*). The /r/'s are not unique in participating in reversals, however, as illustrated by *collasp* (for *collapse*), *crips* (for *crisp*), *larnyx* (for *larynx*), and *unelse* (for *unless*).

When the reversal crosses syllable boundaries we get such examples as *aglore* (for *galore*), *brefkast* (for *breakfast*), *bronical* (for *bronchial*), *calvary* (for *cavalry*), and *dientical* (for *identical*). Sometimes the metathesis occurs at a slightly greater distance, as in *bass-ackwards* (for *ass-backwards*),[6] *gollylag* (for *lollygag*), *jassack* (for *jackass*), *Roly Holer* (for *Holy Roller*), and *slycoon* (for *cyclone*). (It should be pointed out, however, that both *bass-ackwards* and *jassack* may also be prompted by a perceived need for euphemism.)

Speakers of American English seem to be particularly fond of reversed compounds. Although the following examples (unlike *hoppergrass*, *peckerwood*, and *right-down*, mentioned previously) are neither longstanding nor widespread, nor, in most cases, regionally distributed, they do illustrate our yielding to the temptation to create words anew:

bucksaw (*sawbuck*)
bypasser (*passerby*)
carbox (*boxcar*)
cropout (*outcrop*)
cut-short (*shortcut*, noun and verb)
downcome (a *comedown*)
gunshot house (*shotgun house*)
gut-rot (*rotgut*)
hardblow (a *blowhard*)
jawlock (*lockjaw*)
layway (to *waylay*)
overlay (for *layover*)
pokeshite (*shitepoke*)
pour-down (*downpour*)
shot sling (*slingshot*)

One constellation of reversed compounds does exhibit strong regionality: *everhow, everwhat, everwhen, everwhere, everwhich*, and *everwho*. Used for the corresponding *however, whatever, whenever*, etc.,[7] these compounds had been found almost solely in the southern Appalachians and the Ozarks at the time *DARE* editors were working on Volume II (published in 1991). They seem to have emerged in this country early in the twentieth century, and they have retained their vigor up to the present, even expanding their range to other parts of the South. Because the research for the letter E in the *OED* was done between 1888 and 1893, and because Volume II of the *English Dialect Dictionary* was published in 1900, neither dictionary could have included these forms. Nor did the timing of publication of the second edition of the *OED* allow it to benefit from *DARE*'s research (though much of the evidence available to *DARE* was also in the public domain). Research tools currently available will make it possible for *DARE* editors perhaps to antedate and certainly to postdate the Volume II quotations in the forthcoming electronic edition of the *Dictionary*; those same tools, showing the spread of these forms from tightly restricted geographic regions to a much broader area of the southern United States, ought to justify their inclusion in *OED Online*, once the editors start revising the E's.

Finally, an unusual but understandable kind of phraseological metathesis (with a touch of folk-etymology) is recorded in *DARE* at *heaval*, where *in an upheaval* has morphed into *all up in a heaval*. Although *DARE* editors had only a single instance of the phrase when Volume II was published and could have rejected the entry of the basis of its status as a "oncer" (an item with a single quotation), inclusion of the phrase was the better decision. A recent quick check of digital resources shows the phrase to be relatively common today. Many of the examples were doubtless prompted by Piers Anthony's 2002 fantasy book *Up in a Heaval*, but other examples show the existence of the phrase before that date. The related phrase *heavalled up*, used to describe a state of confusion, occurs as a oncer in *DARE*; it does not seem to have survived with any frequency.

Blends

Still another linguistic process that is routinely treated in discussions of the creativity of speakers of English is that of blending, in which parts of two words (occasionally the entirety of one) are joined to fashion a new word that is relatively transparent and fills a lexical gap. The classic examples are Lewis Carroll's "portmanteau words" *chortle* (*chuckle* +

snort), *galumph* (*gallop* + *triumph*), and *snark* (*snake* + *shark*). Others that are frequently used to exemplify the process include *electrocute, motel, smog*, and *travelogue*. Bailey (1996b) notes that the nineteenth century yielded such blends as *brunch, Michigander*, and *slanguage* (154), which obviously filled a need and retained their vitality, as well as others like *visnomy* (*visage* + *physiognomy*) (284) and *gaselier* (*gas* + *chandelier*) (170), which did not.

In American English, the propensity to create blends is particularly vigorous, as the *Index* to *DARE* makes clear. Some of the resulting forms have become well established: *chifforobe*, a blend of *chiffonier* + *wardrobe*, goes back at least to the early twentieth century and still thrives, particularly in the South and South Midland; *chizzly* (*chilly* + *drizzly*) is perhaps appropriately more common in the North than elsewhere, as is *snirt* (*snow* + *dirt*); *haylage* and *oatlage* (modeled on *silage*) find their niche in farm country. It will doubtless surprise contemporary students to learn that *google* goes back at least to 1859: as a blend of *goggle* + *goozle* (all three words signifying the gullet or windpipe), this is found chiefly in the South and South Midland.

Many of the blends documented in *DARE* have had less prolific existences, with only a few examples, or even a single one. Our experience with *all up in a heaval*, however, suggests that a search of contemporary digital resources would yield additional citations for those singletons. Some inventive blends cluster in similar patterns: *aggravoke* (*aggravate* + *provoke*), used by William Faulkner, is a "oncer" from northern Mississippi in *DARE*; the usefulness of the type is corroborated, however, by entries for *aggerpervoke, aggervex*, and *aggrafret*, all of which occur somewhat more frequently than *aggravoke*. Judging by the *DARE* evidence, this kind of blend is a South Midland phenomenon.

Other blends highlight linguistic playfulness (or perhaps occasionally, confusion):

all get-outdoors (*all get-out* + *all outdoors*)

bapsouse (*baptize* + *souse*)

boocoodles (*boocoo*, variant of *beaucoup*, + *oodles*)

coffin stick (*coffin nail* + *cancer stick*)

coverhauls (*coveralls* + *overhauls*)

cuspitoon (*cuspidor* + *spittoon*)

downburst (*downpour* + *cloudburst*)

easy-go-lucky (*easy-going* + *happy-go-lucky*)

frizzle (*fry* + *sizzle*)

gawkward (*gawky* + *awkward*)

homekeeper (*homemaker* + *housekeeper*)

impity (*impudent* + *uppity*)

juvember (*June* + *November*)

nip and go (*nip and tuck* + *touch and go*)

Scowegian (*Scandinavian* + *Norwegian*)

scunnion (*scallion* + *onion*)

sheboodle (*shebang* + *caboodle*)

solemncholy (*solemn* + *melancholy*)

squadrol (*squad car* + *patrol*)

squeasy (*squeamish* + *queasy*)

umbersol (*umbrella* + *parasol*)

vog (*volcanic* + *fog* or *smog*)

Occasionally a lexical blend parallels a biological blend, as with *coydog* (a hybrid of a coyote and a wild dog) and *splake* (*speckled* + *lake*), a hybrid of the male brook trout and the female lake trout. The popular *jackalope* of Western lore and postcards, however, exists only in fertile imaginations.

Other Linguistic Processes

The *Index* to *DARE* also includes categories of less well known processes of language change, making it easy for language historians to bring American examples of aphetism, apocope, or syncope into the discussion; instances of assimilation and dissimilation, redundancy and reduplication are pin-pointed there; calques or loan translations in American English are identified, as are words borrowed directly from dozens of languages, from Algonquian to Danish, Japanese, Polish, and Yoruba; words that are now relics, or that are old-fashioned or archaic are also pointed out. In short, the *Index* to *DARE* serves as a handbook that, in concert with the published volumes, provides abundant evidence for James Murray's assertion that the creative period of language is indeed still in process around us. With such resources as the *Oxford English Dictionary*, groundbreaking books like Richard W. Bailey's *Nineteenth-Century English*, and the materials in the *Dictionary of American Regional English*, today's students of the history of our language can look at the old roots, trace the development of later shoots, and celebrate the vitality of a living language demonstrated by the new suckers that continue to sprout. Contrary to Lowell's assertion that "there is death in the dictionary," both the *OED* and *DARE* amply demonstrate that dictionaries can show concern for the new shoots, the hybridized varieties, and the healthy trees as well as all of the old roots and the potted palms.

NOTES

1. The *Index* to Volumes I and II and the *Index* to Volume III were published in 1993 and 1999 respectively; the integrated *Index* to the first four volumes was posted on the *DARE* web site in 2008, and that for the full five volumes will appear post-Volume V.
2. It is conceivable that *cheese* is here understood as a zero plural, analogous to *moose*.
3. *Conversate*, *notate*, and *orientate*, not included in *DARE*, are also good examples. A slightly different process, the creation of a noun from another noun ending in *-ation*, is exemplified by *vaccinate*, as in "I had a vaccinate for small pox" (cited in Wolfram and Christian 1976, 173).
4. Using the Informant List in the front matter to Volume I of *DARE*, readers can determine the age, sex, race, education level, community type, and specific community for every itemized *DARE* respondent.
5. Other well known examples include the verbs *beg* from *beggar*, *burgle* from *burglar*, and *edit* from *editor*, though these forms also involve reanalysis of a borrowed form.
6. This may also illustrate a kind of word play in that the switching of sounds is representative of the behavior described.
7. Illustrative examples include these: "I . . . jest offered t' teach a ten-night school for twenty-five dollars flat, an' let 'em raise it ever'how they could" (Randolph 1932, 236); "We'll do everwhat Jim wants to do" (Hall, n.p.); "Your old woman can get her water everwhen she wants it" (Chase 1943, 14); "Where do we go from here? . . . Everwhere the dog trees" (Hall, n.p.); "Ever which o' them 'ar saddles you-all want, jes' holler an' hit's yourn" (Randolph 1927, 474); ""They's a law in Arkansas pertectin' foxes, and if ary one should ever get caught it would be onfortunate for ever who owned the dawgs" (Wilson 1934, 107).

10

How Quotation Paragraphs in Historical Dictionaries Work: *The Oxford English Dictionary*

JESSE SHEIDLOWER
Oxford English Dictionary

Though chronologically arranged quotations are the most important part of a historical dictionary, the very thing that makes it what it is (see Aitken 1973a, 1973b), the quotation paragraph is one of the least understood components of such dictionaries. Many people, even synchronic lexicographers, do not fully appreciate what purposes quotation paragraphs serve. Books about lexicography typically discuss quotations in historical contexts, with no treatment of the issues that face a working historical lexicographer (see Willinsky 1994, though there are exceptions, such as Silva 2000). And while it is easy to find articles discussing the example sentences in learners' dictionaries (see Cowie 1978 and Stein 2002, 204–229), scholars tend not to focus on the details of the quotations in historical dictionaries, the work of Richard W. Bailey

(1980b and 1985), Charlotte Brewer (2004 and 2007), and Michael Adams (2002 and 2009) being notable exceptions. Certainly, there is little guidance for the would-be editor of a new historical dictionary or glossary. And readers take for granted the many editorial decisions underlying each and every quotation paragraph. Here, I discuss some basics of the quotation paragraph, its purpose and the process by which quotations are selected, focusing on the *Oxford English Dictionary*'s approach to the quotation paragraph, how it differs from that of other historical dictionaries, and how technology affects construction of quotation paragraphs.

The quotation tradition in English dictionaries started with Samuel Johnson in 1755. Some histories (for instance, Landau 2001, 46 and 64) state that John Florio first used quotations in *Worlde of Words* (1598), an Italian-English dictionary, but this is misleading. First, there were no quotations in the 1598 edition. In its revision, *Queen Anna's New World of Words* (1611), there are 105 quotations, but in almost all cases they are examples of dialect terms, foreign words, or archaisms that Florio couldn't define himself. In other words, these weren't illustrative examples: they were definitional replacements. And they were bibliographically quite spare; in fact, there was nothing to indicate that they were quotations at all. For instance,

> Giálda, al fedíre che fécero i Tedéschi di costa i
> Gialdoniéri lascióreno cadére le lóro giálde sópra i
> Nóstri cauallièri & mísersi in fúga.

This example is the complete text of the entry for *gialda*, an obsolete word denoting a type of spear used by the Germans, quoted from Giovanni Villani's fourteenth-century *Cronica*, but the reader has no way of knowing this (O'Connor 1972). Florio's practice was pedagogical: no historical claims were made in or about the quotations, nor metalinguistic claims about the style of the quotations, as in Samuel Johnson's *Dictionary of the English Language* (1755). *Queen Anna's New World of Words* was notable as being the first dictionary with an English component that included quotations, but none of Florio's dictionaries was a historical dictionary.

Johnson intended chiefly to illuminate English current in the mid-eighteenth century by quoting writers of quality who, he believed, deserved to be canonical, from Sir Philip Sidney to roughly his own period—no living writers were used. Of Johnson's 100,000 quotations, about a third were from works of Shakespeare, Milton, and Dryden, which helped cement the reputation of these writers. However, Johnson quoted them not because they were "good" in some abstract way, but because he felt they demonstrated important aspects of usage: proficiency, correctness, style, and linguistic merit. Thus, Johnson's practices do not really represent those of a historical dictionary, though his use of quotations inadvertently demonstrates the meanings of words.

Johnson's original plan was to have long, interesting, literary passages that could be read for pleasure in the dictionary itself (Johnson 1747, 31). But he later wrote in the "Preface" to his *Dictionary of the English Language* (1755, B2^{v}), "When the time called upon me to range this accumulation of elegance and wisdom into an alphabetical series, I soon discovered that the bulk of my volumes would fright away the student." It's worth noting the explicit acknowledgment that Johnson's dictionary not only can be, but also was *intended* to be read at least in part for the mere pleasure of doing so. The *OED* also can be read for pleasure, and choosing quotations to promote the reader's pleasure is an editorial goal.

Johnson's goal was to use only literary sources, but technical terms by nature are usually found in nonliterary places. Johnson aimed to provide quotations that truly exemplified the word being defined, but this wasn't always possible, as the *OED* later discovered. "Many quotations serve no other purpose, than that of proving the bare existence of words," Johnson continued in the "Preface" (Johnson 1755, B2^{v}). As for the *OED*, one is reminded of Murray's fulminating at William Craigie's inclusion of a quotation for *railway porter* reading "it was a railway porter": "Is there any purpose whatever," wrote Murray to Craigie, "served by . . . including this ridiculous quot[atio]n of 1894? . . . Only because . . .

you think you are obliged, by hook or by crook, to furnish an ostensible quot[atio]n for it! The mistake is in the principle which invokes such miserable failure in its application" (Murray 1977, 288).

Johnson was particularly interested in the difficulties inherent in selecting an appropriately wide range of evidence, as he explained in the "Preface" (Johnson 1755, C1^{r}):

> There is more danger of censure from the multiplicity than paucity of examples; authorities will sometimes seem to have been accumulated without necessity or use, and perhaps some will be found, which might, without loss, have been omitted. But a work of this kind is not hastily to be charged with superfluities: those quotations which to careless or unskilful perusers appear only to repeat the same sense, will often exhibit, to a more accurate examiner, diversities of signification, or, at least, afford different shades of the same meaning: one will shew the word applied to persons, another to things; one will express an ill, another a good, and a third a neutral sense; one will prove the expression genuine from an ancient authour; another will shew it elegant from a modern: a doubtful authority is corroborated by another of more credit; an ambiguous sentence is ascertained by a passage clear and determinate; the word, how often soever repeated, appears with new associates and in different combinations, and every quotation contributes something to the stability or enlargement of the language.

For useful and characteristic quotation paragraphs, a dictionary must rely on principled collection, selection, and arrangement of quotations. Arrangement is easy enough in most modern historical dictionaries (chronological order is typical); the collection, though difficult and time-consuming, is increasingly easy as full-text databases give us access to a vast range of material. The editor's work is in the selection, usually governed by extensive policies, and the results of these policies in the dictionary text are among the most significant factors distinguishing one historical dictionary from others.

Charles Richardson's *New Dictionary of the English Language* (1836–37) was a milestone in the use of historical quotations in dictionaries.

Richardson collected his evidence with the motive of justifying John Horne Tooke's theory that each word had its own immutable etymological meaning. Groups of supposedly related words would have a single body of quotations attached to it. Horne Tooke's beliefs are implausible, but they prompted Richardson to assemble an impressive variety of quotations, carefully chosen, and presented in historical order. For instance, his entry for *crack* v. (which included *crake* v., *crack* n., *cracker*, *crackle*, *crackling* n., and *cracknel*) has several brief definitions for each related word ("*Cracknel*, a kind of cake, which, when broken, *edit crepitum*, sends forth a *crack*"), presented without sense numbers, but continuing for over a full page, with quotations from Chaucer, Skelton, Donne, Jonson, Pope, Addison, Swift, and others, including some that Johnson had quoted, but adding earlier authors and thus putting the quotations more nearly to historical use.

When Richard Chenevix Trench presented his paper *On Some Deficiencies in our English Dictionaries* (1860) to the Philological Society, he praised Richardson's dictionary, which was an important model for the dictionary that was to become *OED* (Trench 1860, 44 and 65). Trench felt, however, that the literature still hadn't been adequately surveyed for quotations and realized that Richardson had focused too strongly on literary sources. In order to illustrate the entire language, it would be necessary to include a variety of text types and registers. Also, Richardson's practice of listing all of the quotations for a cluster of terms in one big block was also not appropriate for a dictionary committed to careful sense-analysis of one term at a time.

In planning the *OED*, various standards were suggested for the number and length of quotations. Frederick J. Furnivall, planning a "Concise Dictionary" (see Benzie 1983, 97–101), suggested having one quotation for each of three "periods" of the English language, with each quotation consisting of only three to four words—"short quotations (a few words long)" (Notices 1862–63, 328). An 1878 letter from Furnivall to Murray, by then the editor of the Philological Society's only planned dictionary, suggested one quotation for each of five "periods" of English (F. J. Furnivall to J. A. H. Murray, 28 March 1878, in the Murray Papers). And in 1879, Murray, summing up the aims of the project, set the goal of one quotation per century for established terms (Minute Book for Ordinary Meetings of the Philological Society, 7 February 1879, in the OED Archives). This was the guideline for the early work on *OED*, generally followed once editing began. A letter from Murray to Furnivall in 1892, when Murray was under great pressure to compress the dictionary, discusses this in practical terms: "Can we lay down the principle that we shall not seek to illustrate all or most of the spellings & shades of sense, but stick to 1 quotn for each century, with perhaps a bonus of 2, to be distributed when needed among the centuries, and to allow 2 or 3 for a 19th c word, so as not to leave these with only 1 quotn?" (Murray to Furnivall, 1 December 1892, in OED Archives [OED/B/3/1/6]).

For much of the work on the first edition of *OED*, the editors kept to a relatively pared-back policy regarding the number and extent of quotations, largely for practical reasons. A volunteer reader copying hundreds of quotations by hand would tend to give the least possible context on the citation slip, and it was not possible to re-check needed examples to expand them. With the costs of the printing and publication, space was at a premium; including longer quotations was regarded as a primarily aesthetic concern—anyone interested could always look up a desired example to get more context—that could not take precedence over the need for more entries, fuller etymologies, and everything else that could occupy space.

Robert Burchfield's *Supplement* to the *OED* (1972–86) had considerably more quotations per entry on average from the start. The quantity expanded further in the second volume, after the team had found their editorial footing, and yet again after the letter M, particularly in scientific areas, as a result of editorial practices developed and decisions made as work progressed. Burchfield's practice partly reflects one surprising fact about quotation paragraphs: counterintuitively, recent senses can have more quotations than older senses. Typically, the meanings of newer terms fluctuate considerably, so that a core meaning only stabilizes over time: at an early period, there might be several competing nuances or grammatical variations; over time, either the meaning coalesces, in which case the editor can simplify the definition to focus on the core sense and ignore the extra quotations, or it continues to diversify, in which case the editor can split the entry into additional subsenses and illustrate each one accordingly.

For example, consider part of the *OED*'s recently updated entry for *quill*:

> **quill** n. ...
> *U.S.* The whistle of a steam locomotive, esp. as sounded musically or distinctively; (also) the sound made by, or a blast on, such a whistle. Cf. QUILL v. 6.
> **1940** *Railroad Mag*. Apr. 50/2 *Quill*, Southern word for whistle. **1945** F. H. Hubbard *Railroad Avenue* ii. 9 With its interpretive tone the ballast scorcher could make that quill say its prayers or scream like a banshee... **1967** V. Williams *Greenbones* 138 'Like the sweetest quill I ever heard,' one said. He meant train whistles. **1999** J. Welsh *Amer. Railroad* 153/1 The most personal relationship an engineer had with his locomotive was with its steam whistle, or 'quill'. Many an engine and its hogger had a trademark sound, a musical wail. **2002** *Trains* Apr. 70, I..threw in a few quills to scare errant beasts from the track.

There are two subsenses to illustrate here: the meaning 'the whistle itself' (as in the 1945 and 1999 quotations), and the meaning 'sound made by a whistle' (2002 and possibly 1967; examples at the parallel verb sense are clearer). Here there are reasons for keeping most quotations: the 1940 is first, the 1945 is the first nonglossarial, the 1967 is a good example filling the gap nicely, the 2002 the only clear example in the sense 'sound of a whistle'. The 1999 could possibly be removed. Still, as currently envisioned, the sense will have five quotations over a period of less than seventy years, for an arguably marginal sense of *quill*. In time, OED editors will likely select even fewer examples to illustrate this subsense. The entry's subsequent sense of *quill*, referring straightforwardly to the pointed spines of a porcupine or hedgehog, is indisputably of broader interest than the railroad sense, but only ten quotations account for over 400 years of use.

OED3 is more generous with quotations than its predecessors. Its quotation paragraphs are larger: quotations themselves are longer, to give more context; bibliographical information is longer because new bibliographic policies encourage a more explicit treatment of citations.

Figure 10.1 shows how the sizes of *OED* quotations and quotation paragraphs have changed over time.

FIGURE 10.1. OED Citations

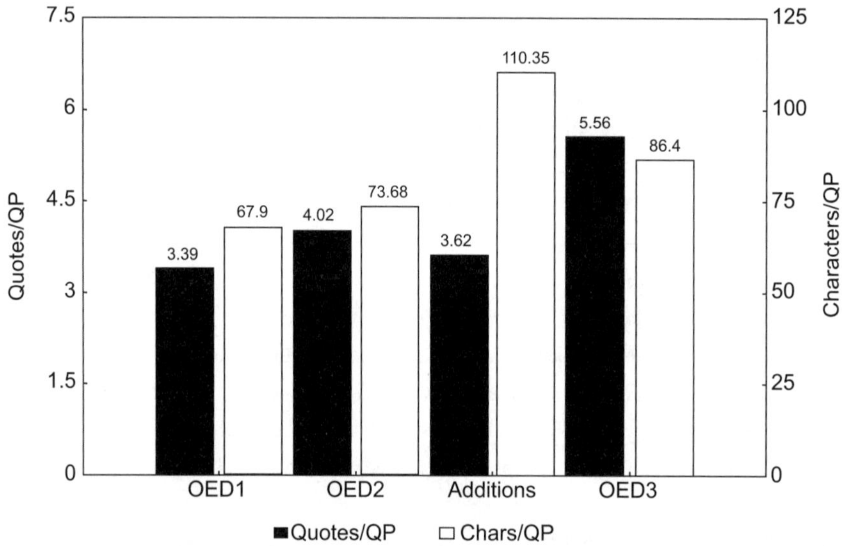

These figures measure the length of the quotation text, not the length of the entire quotation with its bibliographic reference. Note that some of these figures are estimates: it was not possible to get accurate measurements of the quotations in Burchfield's *Supplement*. Also, note the size of the quotations for the Additions Series volumes, three new-word supplements published in the 1990s. The data for *OED3*, while reflecting the revised entries, still show the effect of *OED1* research, because for existing entries we generally keep the quotations we have rather than rework every available quotation. Thus the Additions Series numbers more closely reflect the editorial practices of current work on entirely new terms.

Additions Series quotations are longer than those in the *OED* generally:

- There is an intentionally higher-than-average proportion of scientific terms in the Additions Series. Quotations from specialist sources are harder to shorten without risk of losing essential information. Also, simply put, technical terms are often longer than workaday words, and the graph measures length in number of characters, not words.

- Since the Additions Series volumes were published as separate books, it was decided to include more and longer quotations, both because the entries had to stand on their own (not alongside the rest of *OED*), and because they were being published as new-word additions, so we felt that they could bear more detailed quotations to support high-profile terms. In any case, the plan was always to shorten these entries when published within *OED*. A similar editorial practice is observed by other publications focused on new words; the *Barnhart Dictionary Companion* and the "Among the New Words" column in *American Speech*, for example, both typically include very extensive evidence for their entries, to illustrate them more fully and, to an extent, validate their inclusion.
- Finally, all of the character counts, apart from the Additions Series numbers, reflect the presence of *OED1* quotations, which were very short. Quotations for the first edition of *OED* were hand-gathered and written out painstakingly on slips: the tendency was to abbreviate drastically. Similar practices were in effect during the editorial process, as each character in *OED1* had a real impact on the cost of the printing. Since *OED2* and *OED3* continue to have a very large number of unexpanded *OED1* quotes, the average from these dictionaries will be rather lower than the average of any post-*OED1* source.

With this history of quotations and quotation paragraphs in dictionaries as background, I'd like to turn the discussion to the practical decisions and reasoning that lie behind the *OED*'s choice of quotations. The criteria behind these decisions are specific to the *OED*, and while the *OED*'s general model is widely followed, other historical dictionaries, such as the *Middle English Dictionary* (*MED*), the *Dictionary of American Regional English* (*DARE*), the *Dictionary of the Older Scottish Tongue* (*DOST*), and the *Historical Dictionary of American Slang* (*HDAS*), differ in the specifics. Each vocabulary poses its own problems of scope and faces unique semantic challenges. Historical dictionaries develop characteristic quotation paragraphs in response to those constraints. A very large number of factors bears on the selection of quotations for every entry in every historical dictionary, including, of course, the *OED*. Below is a list of some of the elements necessary to every *OED* quotation paragraph.

Earliest Quotation

First and foremost, a quotation paragraph records the earliest known use of an entry word, which establishes the age of a term, affects our understanding of its etymology (that is, its connection to related or semantically parallel terms), charts its formal and semantic development over time, and more. Much of the effort involved in the process of historical lexicography centers on antedating words or senses. Indeed, the date of a word's entry into the (usually written) record is one of the most distinctive features of historical dictionaries in the *OED*'s tradition.

In practice, it is almost always impossible to find the actual first quotation. We rarely know the true circumstances of coinage, derivation, or borrowing; we can only hope to get as close as possible. Typically, early evidence of a word is problematic or ambiguous. Consider the example of one sense of *joint*. Here is the entry from the *Historical Dictionary of American Slang*:

> **joint** *n*.... *Black E.* a film, song, or other production.
> **1988** S. Lee *School Daze* (film): A Spike Lee joint. **1991** Nelson & Gonzales *Bring Noise* 145: Pairing "joints that haven't been sampled yet" with recorded breaks and live music. **1991** *Source* (Oct.) 57: Singing that old hippie joint, "American Woman." **1993** *Source* (July) 36: His newest joint, *Looks Like a Job For...* was in my tape deck.

When Jonathan Lighter and I edited this in 1996, it was a solid entry: it included examples from different genres, starting off with Spike Lee's well-known use. We had the sense that Lee had used it earlier in his works but couldn't easily find it at the time. The problem with this entry is indeed the first quotation: Lee is pretty much the *only* person who uses this word in reference to movies. (It is possible, by plundering databases, to dredge up additional examples of the movie-related use, but these are rare and atypical.) Lee's influence, especially in the mid-1990s, made this nuance feel more important than it is, but generally the word is used of songs and albums.

When the *OED* came to edit this term ten years later, the facts were clearer—there were no additional examples of the movie nuance. Furthermore, Spike Lee's cultural influence had waned somewhat, so that the phrase "a Spike Lee joint" was no longer as prominent and recognizable as it had been. Thus, the *OED*'s draft entry begins:

> **joint** *n*[1]....*Music slang* (orig. *U.S.*). A song, a recording; an album.
> Perh. influenced by the earlier use of the word in the phrase *a Spike Lee joint*, used by the American film director Spike Lee (b. 1957) as a subtitle for his films: see quot. 1986.
> [**1986** *Los Angeles Times* 21 Aug. VI. 7/2 Lee calls his film a 'Spike Lee joint', but that's not a marijuana reference.... *Joint* is 'New York street talk for a cool place to be'.] **1991** H. Nelson & M. A. Gonzales *Bring Noise* 145 Pairing 'joints that haven't been sampled yet' with recorded breaks and live music.

Of course, there are many ways of handling this evidence; how to interpret and present it is an editorial decision. One could have a single definition encompassing all uses, as in *HDAS*, but with some kind of note indicating that the movie use is rare and associated with Lee. Or there could be a separate sense for the movie use, presenting Lee's examples in an unbracketed form, also with notes as appropriate. My feeling is that, based on the evidence, *OED*'s treatment is the best one: Lee's use, while real, does not reflect a core use of the word in English; anything that makes Lee's use explicit misrepresents its currency.

Semantic shifting is a problem particularly for treatment of newer words: they are moving targets, histories of which are captured largely in static texts. Even an editor personally familiar with the current use of such a term is not in a position to evaluate it, because he or she cannot predict how it will evolve. But the problem is not unique to new-word lexicography. If a corpus is entirely (or largely) known, as is the case for Old English or Latin, then one need not fear any (or many) revolutionary new discoveries; yet regardless of the nature of the corpus, thanks to large-scale databases it is quite common to find additional, especially early, evidence that forces us to rethink an entry.

Indeed, the more time one spends searching through databases for early examples, the more one realizes that early examples are very often quite unusual and unrepresentative. Often there's an early example for a sense that's otherwise extremely rare, or the early examples show unusual nuances. This is the case for Early Modern English (as we know from the Early English Books Online database) just as much as it is for modern musical terminology (thanks to, say, Nexis, music blogs, and the full text of *Rolling Stone* on DVD).

For example, the earliest sense of *rat race* n. in *OED2* was an effectively unique glossarial example referring to a dance. When revising this entry for *OED3*, we did find an earlier example in the broad sense 'a confused undertaking', but we also found something else:

rat race *n. Brit.* /ˈrat reɪs/, *U.S.* /ˈræt ˈreɪs/[< RAT *n.*[1] + RACE *n.*[1]]
1. A race contested by rats. *rare.*
1783 W. Jackson *Thirty Lett. var. Subj.* II. xxi. 40 The first time I was at a [horse-racing] course, it appeared but as a rat-race. **1851** W. Lennox *Percy Hamilton* I. v. 151 He was steward of a rat-race..where four of these 'varmin', decorated with different coloured ribands, were started for a sweepstakes, round the club-room, before a host of sportsmen. **1919** *Post Standard* (Syracuse, N.Y.) 22 Dec. 6/5 Sam, old son, you ought to been along. It was slicker'n a rat-race. **2002** C. H. Daly *Rats* 46/1 See how quickly your rat learns to navigate the course... Compare these times with those of other rats, in an Ultimate Rat Race.

This new sense 1 is literal, but only two of the four quotations provided are solid. The first is from an essay on perspective and uses *rat race* in a simile to denote the small appearance of horses in a race, from the observer's distant viewpoint. The second example is unambiguous, as is the fourth (though this presumably puns on the then-established usual sense); the third is similative and thus does not clearly represent the true use of the defined term.

Furthermore, these four quotations are effectively all the quotations for the literal sense that I was able to discover, even with extensive searching of electronic sources. Attempting to adhere to a moderate number of quotations creates a problem here, as the reader cannot tell the difference between an extremely rare sense such as this and a genuinely common word supported by only a moderate number of quotations. The sense cannot be omitted, because it is the earliest, but including it presents a misleading history of the term.

Latest Quotation

Within reason, editors of historical dictionaries want to include a very recent quotation for every current sense. It is not necessary to include something from 2008 when editing during that year; indeed, nothing makes a range of entries look more dated than having a string of quotation paragraphs, all with last quotations from the same very short timespan. But in general, if a sense is current, an editor should include a recent contextual quotation in the structure of the entry. If a term is historical, one can have a recent example in historical context together with a label of "Now hist." or an equivalent note is appropriate; but it would be inappropriate to use a glossarial example to provide a postdating for an obsolete term.

Quotations with Useful Context

The best quotes are contextual, unexplained examples. These show that the word is really in use, and they show how it is in use. The worst are glossarial quotes, which can, if the source is trustworthy, be helpful to the lexicographer in writing the definition, but which are not generally very useful to quote. Similar examples are also to be avoided, such as a use that is in running text, but which is followed by a definitional or explanatory phrase, or a use which is in scare quotes, indicating that the term is thought to be new, unnatural, non-serious, etc.

It is often necessary to include such quotations, when they are the first, or when they show seemingly reliable nuances that can't otherwise be captured, but one must be careful. For example, slang terms are often recorded chiefly or only in glossaries, and it is common for these glossaries to copy extensively from one another. A historical dictionary need not quote from a range of such glossaries, which would only demonstrate transmission among lexicographers, not any real-world usage. Such transmission (or piracy) is an object of scholarly interest; tracing the influence slang lexicographers had on one another is what makes Julie Coleman's *History of Cant and Slang Dictionaries* project so fascinating. But it is not helpful to the user who wants to understand the history of a slang word. If such a term were frequently discussed in secondary literature, or had been picked up from the dictionary record and used in historical fiction or similar contexts, the facts could be mentioned in notes, but to display more than two or three quotations from glossaries suggests a currency that glossaries alone cannot demonstrate.

Of course, the situation of slang is not identical to that of other vocabularies, and the *OED*'s use of glossarial evidence differs from that of other historical dictionaries. The *Middle English Dictionary* (*MED*), for instance, includes glossarial evidence in entries whenever it is available. When English words were glossed against Latin words, editors had an indication of semantic equivalence with defining value; and something about contemporary awareness of a word (arguably part of the word's history) might be reflected in the need for a gloss. As a result, a surprising percentage of the *MED*'s total quotations (between 3 and 4 percent) are glossarial, roughly half the number extracted from all of Chaucer's works (Adams 1992, 254).

The *MED* is a dictionary for scholars: scholars are likely to question HOW we know about words as well as WHAT we know about them. *OED* users may be less interested in such questions, and the *OED*, treating a larger vocabulary over a longer span of time, must choose among the evidence for the set of quotations that most efficiently abstracts a word's history. In part, the difference between the *OED*'s practice and the *MED*'s depends on different notions of what makes up a word's history: the *OED* confines itself to describing the semantic development of a word from quotation contexts; the *MED* considers facts about language use besides contextual semantics, such as sources and text types, as part of lexical history.

Good Chronological Spacing of Quotations

The number of quotations in a paragraph varies depending on many factors, but for an older, well established term with a straightforward meaning, two to three quotations per century should be more than adequate. Undefined compounds of obvious meaning can take even fewer, just two or three quotations for the term's entire history. For defined compounds appearing as part of an existing entry, one or two quotes per century, or more for newer ones, should do, depending on how complicated the compound is. (A compound with "(a)" and "(b)" definitions, or varying grammatical uses, would support a larger body of quotations.) If an editor has a compound where more quotations were genuinely necessary, or if there were a complicated group of meanings, it would be best to upgrade the item to main-entry status in order to afford the space for a fuller treatment.

Within these ranges, quotations should be distributed reasonably evenly. If a quotation from 1800 is followed by one from 1950, the gap should not be "filled" by another from 1803. (This is a point often missed by volunteer readers, who supply interdatings that cannot change the shape of an entry fundamentally.) Similarly, a term first cited in the 1920s should not be illustrated by a quotation paragraph with three quotations from the early 1970s, unless these are the only ones available to display variant semantic or grammatical patterns.

Quotations Demonstrating Range of Use

Examples should be chosen from as wide a range as possible, including register, region, ethnicity of writer, and other factors, particularly if they illustrate specific things about the types of sources in which they appear. Given a well-distributed term, it is best to take quotations from non-obscure sources; that is, avoid taking examples of a common, general-interest term from a scientific journal or an obscure regional newspaper. If they are available, an editor should prefer examples from fiction, literary criticism, sportswriting, a letter; examples from Britain and America and Australia; examples from writers of different sexes and ethnicities; and so forth.

On one hand, an editor certainly should not take all examples from the *New York Times* because it's "important" or because it is easily searchable on a particular database. On the other hand, choosing major, well-known sources is not a form of privileging canonical writers, but of ensuring that readers will see examples from potentially familiar sources, and not be mystified by an obscure quotation that cannot be easily checked. Expanding the range of texts, particularly for cases where the individual quotation itself could come from anywhere, should not be an end in itself. Diversity of authorship is a valuable goal only after the dictionary's primary purpose—of accurately representing the language—is satisfied. However, once this goal has been reached, then it paints a fuller picture of the language to show that a word has been used by as broad a range of writers, in as broad a range of circumstances, as possible.

Quotations Reflecting (and Being Reflected by) the Definition

Elements of the definition must be represented in the quotations; conversely, one cannot include quotations not covered by the definition. This is not to say that each semantic nuance must be exemplified by one quotation. But, if an editor says that something means "something general; esp. something specific," the quotation paragraph must illustrate both general and specific use. If quotations reflect transitive and intransitive uses of a verb, then the definition of that verb has to say so. If there are no modern quotations, there must be an "Obsolete" label.

Intrinsic Interest of Quotations

All quotations in a historical dictionary should be interesting. They should be fun to read, from authors a reader would want to track down. This isn't always possible, and because of all the other requirements, it is not the highest priority, but it is something that should always be sought. As mentioned, Johnson's dictionary is worth reading for its own sake, as is much of the *OED*; if one aim of the lexicographer is to make the dictionary something to enjoy, then seeking interesting examples should be a goal.

Quotations Capturing Typical Use (not Marginal or Esoteric Use)

The *OED*, perhaps especially, aims to describe the main features of the language, not to seek out unusual examples for their own sake. This is a problem at every level of the process: most people interested in dictionaries are familiar with James Murray's complaint at an early stage of editing that he had 50 examples of *abusion* to five of *abuse*. (J. A. H. Murray, Presidential Address, *Philological Society Transactions* (1877–79), pages 571–72, quoted in Murray 1977, 178). Editors should not choose quotations with unusual grammatical patterns or strange nuances just because they are unfamiliar.

A good example of this specific challenge, as well as of general problems with constructing quotation paragraphs, is the word *punchline*. There are three closely related subsenses best treated together: the main sense is 'the part of the very end of a joke that provides the humor'; but punchlines are not restricted to jokes, so there is a more general sense, 'a line at the end of a story carrying some rhetorical impact'; finally, there is an extended sense, 'any conclusion, especially a striking one'. (There is also the meaning 'a person or thing regarded as an object of ridicule; a laughingstock', e.g., "Paris Hilton became a punchline," but this would almost certainly be a separate sense.)

Here is what can happen when an editor, in fact, this editor, tries to craft a quotation paragraph to illustrate these senses:

> **1.** orig. *U. S.* The final phrase or sentence of a joke or story, providing the humour or some other crucial element. In extended use: a conclusion, esp. a striking one. **1916** *Marion* (Ohio) *Star* 10 May 5/3 A punch line falls flat; he looks dour, and the look gets a laugh. **1921** *Variety* 25 Nov. 8/1 All of their sure-fire punch~lines went over. **1937** *Dime Detective Mag*. Nov. 45/2 Go on..give me the punch line. **1957** *Oxf. Mail* 17 Oct. 1/2 It was Mr Dulles's punch-line and showed the Russians—and the American people—that President Eisenhower regards the Middle East crisis with great anxiety. **1971** *World Archaeology* 3 226 He [*sc.* V. G. Childe] was fond of dramatic punch-lines. **1977** *New Yorker* 27 June 67/1 Reaching the punch line, he erupted in laughter. **1993** *United Church Observer* June 2/2 Now here's the punchline: Any doubts I might have been harboring as to the appropriateness of calling myself a conservative were instantly dispelled last August when [etc.]. **2003** R. Dawkins *Devil's Chaplain* v. 198 The idea of science as 'the art of the soluble' provides the punchline for at least four of the essays. **2007** D. M. Hooley *Roman Satire* ii. 57 Shorter than any other satire, it begins with a standard joke-opening..and ends with a punchline pun on *Rex*.

When I initially assembled this quotation paragraph, I included an additional quotation:

> **2005** *Icon* Feb. 36/2 What you need for design is three things: the intention, the process and the punchline—the product.

This was an amateurish mistake on my part. The quotation is striking because its use is so unusual. The natural reaction is to call attention to it and to accommodate it in the definition. But the *OED* cannot include every semantic nuance; when one attempts to do so, one usually writes an unbalanced entry that doesn't accurately reflect usage. When quotation paragraphs lose focus and attempt to capture esoterica, they can grow beyond a size warranted by historical sense development. In the case of *punchline,* the quotations are weighted towards more recent examples, because those are the ones most likely to have non-core nuances. (The longer these senses exist, the more likely that one would separate them out into new subsenses.) Thus three quotations from the last fifteen years are more than one would prefer for a 90-year-old sense, but they are necessary to supply recent examples of all the nuances—and the core sense.

The belief that it is always better to have more evidence than less is widely held. After all, a reader can just ignore extra quotations. Especially in an online historical dictionary, where there are effectively no direct costs associated with delivering large number of quotations, there does not seem to be a good reason to keep good quotations out of entries. Lexicographers generally want to put in more, to show subtle semantic differentiae they have discerned, and in general to validate the time they have spent working on an entry.

Perhaps paradoxically, the availability of full text databases may have made it easier to find additional evidence, but it has also made it LESS necessary to include the many quotations that they allow us to find. The methodology has changed—it is no longer necessary to provide many examples just to show that one can, to demonstrate how comprehensive one's citation files are. Copiousness is no longer a virtue. What readers need is refinement, the distillation of the often copious available evidence into something useful. After all, for advanced users, that is the purpose of a dictionary in the first place—to show you what you probably COULD figure out on our own, if you were that determined, without making you bother. The *OED*'s authority is now in its discretion, not its bulk. This is something that is hard to convince volunteers about, in particular, and why managing "crowdsourced" work is so difficult. If one has a well-attested word with a gap in the quotation paragraph from 1715 to 1740, someone will find a 1717 example and send it in; the *OED* editor has to be appreciative, look at it, have someone key it—even though it is unlikely to find its way into the entry.

In fact, there are several important reasons to be careful about including extra quotations:

- The entry needs a structure that people can understand; too many quotations make an entry hard to follow, even if users can switch off the quotation view in an online version. A user (therefore an editor) does not need fifty quotations to demonstrate the relatively stable meaning of a term primarily from the fifteenth century; if all of those quotations are useful, the sense probably should be divided into subsenses.
- In the case of the *OED*, we want to leave room for other dictionaries. The public tends to believe that the *OED* is not only the largest dictionary, but also the only necessary one. But this simply is not true: if one calls up a range of entries in the letter N in *OED Online*, and compare them to an equivalent range in *DARE*, *DOST*, *HDAS*, *MED*, or the *English Dialect Dictionary*, one will see many things that *OED* has not taken: entire headwords, senses, grammatical patterns, quotations, historical descriptions. Our goal is broader than the goals of these other dictionaries. The reader who needs a general picture of older Scots vocabulary can get a good sense of it from *OED*, but the reader who needs a deep view should go to *DOST*. We have no intention to "outdo" these dictionaries; the *OED*'s mission takes it in one direction, their missions take them in others.

- Every additional quotation requires editorial time. Though electronic publication has lifted the space constraints that so afflict print dictionaries, there are a number of time-consuming editorial steps that apply to each quotation: every quotation requires some attention from the Bibliography Group, possibly requiring additional library research. Every quotation must be proofread, often multiple times. Several editors will judge every quotation during the editorial process.

And despite every effort, an additional quotation is an additional place where errors can occur.

The forces at work that pressure editors toward copiousness, however, are real. Here are some important ones:

- The opportunity to include additional quotations tempts editors to address marginal formal and semantic nuances. I have previously discussed cases where it is necessary to include unusual quotations, but the temptation is always strong to include any unusual quotation where possible, and a firm editorial policy against a multiplicity of examples can rein in editors who strain against economy and discretion.
- Editors may also be tempted to prove that a disputed or contentious term has genuine currency. The *OED* was once sued by a Jewish businessman, who objected to the inclusion of the verb *jew* in the sense 'to cheat or overreach, in the way attributed to Jewish traders or usurers'. In the revised entry for that word in the *Supplement*, Robert Burchfield included copious evidence for the use, mainly to show that it was not an occasional but a common, if dislikable, part of English. Similarly, *HDAS* included a large number of quotations in its entry for the prefix *Mc-*, in disparaging senses stemming from the name of the McDonald's restaurant chain, to forestall similar criticism.

- Editors hope to show the greatest variety of forms. The *OED* lists every form of a word it can find in a variant forms list near the start of every entry, but it does not require that these forms be fully reflected in the quotation paragraph itself. *DARE* and *MED*, on the other hand, do show every form in the quotations list as a matter of policy. Indeed, *DARE* will often include forms not specifically listed; in such cases, there will usually be a head note reading, "For additional forms, see the quotations."
- Editors struggle to suggest patterns of usage that would be hard to explain as clearly in definitions or annotations. For example, if a word is particularly common in one period, the editor can choose to add several quotations from that period to suggest its frequency at that time. Or, if a word is common in an unusual grammatical pattern, adding several quotations showing that pattern will clarify that it is not unusual for that word.
- Editors are inclined to achieve an extreme or exhaustive level of detail. While this is not necessarily useful for the *OED* or another relatively general dictionary, it can be the main point of a narrowly focused historical dictionary, such as the *Dictionary of Old English* or the *Dictionary of Smoky Mountain English* (Montgomery and Hall 2004) may as well show everything it reasonably can, as readers will expect it.
- Editors naturally hope to make positive use of the research they have done. One feels frustration to have spent hours on an entry, and hours finding and verifying quotations, having them checked by library researchers, and then cutting them because of a slightly newer discovery, a different editorial viewpoint, or the like. Having done the work, if the citation fits, why not show it?

Though protocols for quotation paragraphs undoubtedly impose a salutary discipline on editors of historical dictionaries, that is certainly not their only value. Principles of selection provide editors the means to discipline the exploding mass of online quotable data, and the application of any one dictionary's principles in the editorial practice of constructing quotation paragraphs reflects that dictionary's mission and establishes its unique style among dictionaries of the historical type. The *OED*'s quotation paragraphs are not a universal model: other historical dictionaries have their own missions and styles. But the *OED* is the first English dictionary on "historical principles" and the first to employ quotations in pursuit of often elusive lexical history. The quotation paragraph is often misunderstood, but it is at the centerpiece of the historical dictionary entry. Over nearly two centuries, the *OED* has ensured, too, that the quotation paragraph is the crowning achievement of the historical lexicographer's art.

11

The Core or the Periphery? The Lack of a *Dictionary of Irish English on Historical Principles*

MICHAEL B. MONTGOMERY
University of South Carolina

With the end of editing the *Oxford English Dictionary* in sight, Sir William Craigie stood before the English Association (apparently in 1916) to ask "what next?" in what he came thereafter to call "completing the record of English" (Craigie 1925–30, 1941).[1] No doubt he, like the three other principal editors of the *OED*, was daily and continually aware of sources unexcerpted and citations gathered that had to be discarded or archived. His now-classic address concerned avenues of treatment most conspicuously under-pursued in the grand work. These should lead to dictionaries typologically like the *OED*, which under the leadership of James Murray (1837–1915) had pioneered the basic principles of historical lexicography known so well today: documenting the record of each item's changes in form, meaning, and function; basing definitions on dated, referenced, illustrative quotations for each sense; organizing information chronologically within entries and senses; and presenting a pre-history of each item in a comprehensive etymological note.

Like Murray, Craigie (1867–1957) was a Scotsman and no doubt natively familiar with Lowland Scots.[2] Steeped in the ancient literature of their realm, they would have known of innumerable slighted texts from north of England's border.[3] The *OED* preface's well-known statement that "the circle of the English language has a well-defined centre but no discernible circumference" (Murray et al. 1989, xxiv) must have tinged with Anglo-centrism for Craigie. Murray could entertain no diversion from his main purpose; but because his training as a medievalist made him keen to further possibilities treating shoots from the Anglo-Saxon trunk and he expected to outlive the *OED*, Craigie could ponder what might lie beyond. He urged caution, lest self-satisfaction with publication lead the *OED* to fall victim to its own legacy:

> I trust that what I have said will not lead anyone to suppose that the task of English lexicography will end with the approaching completion of the Oxford dictionary . . . When we reflect how much the past century has done to swell the vocabulary of English, when we observe the new varieties of the language slowly but surely forming in the colonies and in the United States, it is obvious that there can be no talk of finality in the work. It is equally clear, I think, that the time must come when all the elements of such a language can no longer be conveniently or effectively treated in a single work, however many volumes it may consist. To my mind the future of English lexicography lies in concentration upon special periods and regions of the language, so that each of them may be dealt with more fully than is possible in a comprehensive work, even though this is on the scale of the Oxford Dictionary. (1941, 267)

By 1919 Craigie had answered "what next?" by identifying for the Philological Society a map of six dictionaries utilizing Murray's historical principles: four for British English, one for Scots, and one for American English (Craigie 1925–30). Organizations and institutions in Britain and the United States gave birth to four of these projects aimed to produce a second generation of dictionaries modeled on the *OED*.[4] Craigie had already commenced informal collection for his *Dictionary of the Older Scottish Tongue*, and fellow Scotsman William Grant, under the auspices of the Scottish Dialects Committee, had embarked on the *Scottish National Dictionary*, a work inspired by but independent of Craigie's "Completing the Record" proposal. The *SND* more resembled Wright's *English Dialect Dictionary* (1898–1905) in its greater concern with local variation than historical development.

The University of Michigan undertook sponsorship of the *Middle English Dictionary* (initiated in 1925, published as Kurath et al. 1952–2001) and the *Early Modern English Dictionary* (under Charles Fries), and by 1925 the University of Chicago was recruiting Craigie to edit the *Dictionary of American English. DAE*, as well as the period dictionaries, was to inherit citation slips amassed by the *OED* and undertake further excerption, producing more exhaustive, multi-volume works that would greatly clarify the picture of each period's characteristic English. With publication of *DAE* early on (Craigie and Hulbert 1938–44) and the final fascicle of the *MED* in 2001 and of *DOST* (Craigie et al. 1931–2002) the following year, the *EMED* (on which editing was actively pursued from 1927–42 but thereafter suspended pending completion of the *MED*) remains the only one of the four projects not finished (it never commenced publication; Bailey 1980b). Even with this gap in the record, the second generation of historical English lexicography was an undoubted success.

Regarding where Ireland might fit in his proposed map Craigie said nothing, but to him must go the principal credit for widening the circle of historical lexicography beyond England, a process still unfolding. The *DAE*, the first dictionary of overseas English on historical principles, inevitably aroused interest in citation-based dictionaries of other national streams. An ensuing generation of single-volume works recorded the English of South Africa (Branford 1978), Australia (Ransom 1988), Canada (Avis 1967), Jamaica (Cassidy and Le Page 1967/1980), the Bahamas (Holm and Shilling 1982), New Zealand (Orsman 1997), and the Caribbean (Allsopp 1996, among others). Continued collecting has led to expanded editions and to creation of institutions like the Australian National Dictionary Centre at the Australian National University.

Overlapping the previous group is an extension, a fourth generation of English historical lexicographical works utilizing the *OED*'s distinctive principles: comprehensive collection, chronological arrangement of dated citations for each sense, developmental sequencing (when possible) of senses and functions, etc., but having sub-national scope, treating regional and provincial varieties found in Newfoundland (Story et al. 1982/1990), Prince Edward Island (Pratt 1988), southern Appalachia (Montgomery and Hall 2004), and elsewhere. While formally similar to the third group, they show the narrowing focus of English historical lexicography.

All the aforementioned works are designed to complement the *OED*. What is conspicuously missing and seemingly left behind by the widening circle of *OED*-inspired works on "new," "extraterritorial," or "transplanted" forms of English that became native in lands beyond Britain is that of Ireland, sometimes dubbed "England's oldest colony," to which many in Ireland have derisively added, "yes, and the last." English has been used continuously on the island, varying in degrees, roles, and geographical domains, since arriving with Anglo-Normans in the twelfth century. Yet with a history of English speakers twice as long as anywhere else beyond Britain, Ireland remains (with the Indian subcontinent) the only long-time English-speaking territory with no dictionary based on *OED*-type historical principles.

From an Irish viewpoint the most obvious reason for this situation is political: Irish has long been considered the island's signature language, though Irish-speaking areas shifted overwhelmingly to English between 1600 and 1900 (Fitzgerald 1984, Hindley 1990), and few born in Ireland do not speak English natively today. Irish is named as the first official language in the 1921 and 1937 constitutions of the Irish Free State (which became the Republic of Ireland in 1947) and continues in use in its parliament, the Oireachtas, even if only conventionally employed by members in prefacing speeches delivered in English. English is the language of national as well as local discourse almost everywhere, but the symbolic status of Irish can hardly be underestimated. However far its use has now receded, Irish is intrinsic to Ireland's national identity.

For many with an English viewpoint, including academics, Ireland would seem too integral a part of the British Isles for a separate historical dictionary. English historians, even the eminent Macaulay and Trevelyan, have often seen Wales, Scotland, and Ireland as extensions of England, accessions produced by early imperial necessities. The English of Ireland would therefore be part of the core, too close to the center of the language. The *OED* has always featured citations from Ireland (albeit very few, as discussed below). Is the English language as used in Ireland (henceforth, for convenience, "Irish English" will be used as the island-encompassing, generic term) on the periphery looking in or in the core looking out? Might it be both?

Can the absence of a *Dictionary of Irish English on Historical Principles* (henceforth *DIEHP*) be simply a casualty to competing political status with Irish? At least some need for one has been perceived. A 1998 issue of the International Association for the Study of Irish Literature's newsletter headlined the story "H.E. [i.e., Hiberno-English] Dictionary—Again!" (Stewart 1998). The Association apparently considered fulfilling this need until the publication of Wall's *An Irish Literary Dictionary and Glossary* (2001). Hogan articulated the idea for a dictionary much earlier, stating in an endnote to a glossary of Dublin speech that "upon a set of similar collections a Dictionary of the English of Ireland could be based" (1944, 187). He set out twelve "Rules for Making a Glossary" and identified works in Scotland, England, and Ireland that could be models or contribute ideas or material to the enterprise. In 1969 Alan Bliss, on the faculty at University College Dublin and Secretary for the Committee on Anglo-Irish Studies at the Royal Irish Academy, began circulating an invitation to potential readers to submit citations for an *Anglo-Irish Dictionary* under the Academy's auspices.[5] Apparently in the early 1970s the project ran aground, however, for "lack of funds and a poor response for volunteer readers to supply quotations" (Wall 1990, 104).

What considerations, challenges, and obstacles face a historical dictionary of the English of Ireland? In considering why even the idea of a *DIEHP* has progressed little to date, this essay seeks to be a partial prolegomenon, profiling the state of English-language lexicography in Ireland and some needs and prerequisites for a *DIEHP*. It will offer as many questions as it does suggestions.[6]

Brief History of Irish English and Irish English Lexicography

More than the barest outline of the history of English in Ireland lies beyond the present essay's scope (for fullest treatments, see Kallen 1994, Hickey 2007), but the subject deserves fresher, more critical consideration of accepted views, especially using insights from modern sociolinguistics and language contact research. The English language came first to Ireland (to Dublin in 1169 and to Ulster[7] in 1177) with the Anglo-

Normans, with a modest migration from southwestern England thereafter consolidating English-speaking settlements in the southeast and around Dublin. In medieval times the use of English rarely penetrated beyond towns, and from no later than the early fourteenth century its territory began shrinking to only a few districts and fortified areas (e.g., Wexford and Waterford in the southeast, Carrickfergus in the northeast, "the Pale" around Dublin) as English speakers shifted almost entirely to Irish. A majority of linguistic scholars have held that spoken English sustained a radical discontinuity, essentially disappearing by the mid–sixteenth century, surviving in scattered places. It was then reintroduced from the late-sixteenth century, through plantations and especially the Cromwellian land settlement of the 1650s (Braidwood 1964, Hogan 1927, Bliss 1976, 1979, inter alia).

This received view (questioned more recently by historians and some linguists; cf. Kallen 1994), considers modern Irish English a product of both linguistic input from England and Scotland and a shift from Irish to English across many generations, both beginning in the seventeenth century (Kelly 2000). The dominant fact of linguistic life throughout Ireland for four centuries has been the decline of Irish in the face of English and (in Ulster) also of Scots. An overwhelmingly Irish-speaking island in 1600 has become one displaying universal command of English (i.e., there are many Irish/English bilinguals, but few if any Irish monolinguals). The process varied locally, with corresponding phases occurring inconsistently from area to area. Earlier stages, extrapolated to some degree from nineteenth-century census figures, show that any generalization must be scrutinized for its source and basis. For example, Ó Murchú asserts that "there is no reason to suppose that the retreat of Irish had seriously begun among the ordinary people before the beginning of the eighteenth century" (1986, 116), but Adams (1965, 25) emphasizes a different but important demographic fact: 38.8 percent of Ulster's population could speak English (or Scots) by c1659 and by the late eighteenth century, 90 percent of the population province-wide spoke English (1979, 69). (Any calculation necessarily treats speakers as monolingual, consequently limiting insights.)

Both scholarly literature and conventional thinking often show the situation exemplified above: statements that purport to pertain to Ireland island-wide but for which Ulster differs substantially because of the large influx of British, mainly Scottish, settlers. Generally speaking,

English and Scots were planted in much of rural Ulster in the seventeenth century, while elsewhere in Ireland English diffused from towns or from higher social ranks slowly at first, then often accelerating. Scholars from or who deal with Ulster tend to see the province as an exception in many regards, and this has profound implications for a prospective *DIEHP*. The long shift from Irish to English meant that in most areas bilingualism prevailed, the languages co-existed for generations, Irish Gaelic influence on the grammar and vocabulary of Irish English was extensive, and Irish English was still largely in flux in the nineteenth century.

Though Craigie never mentioned Ireland, in 1919 he would surely have declared that sources were insufficient for autonomous, much less multi-volume treatment like his other proposed works. Ireland lacked a diverse, unbroken textual record approaching the vast, continuous reservoir of sources and citations from Scotland or the United States. No matter how intensively excerpted, the record was too thin, too recent; nor was there a body of citations to consign to a *DIEHP* as to the other dictionaries he envisioned. Craigie would probably have claimed that Ireland was part of the center of English, not even on its margin (such a claim for Scotland was overridden by the latter's incomparable written record, comprising texts of all genres in the fifteenth and sixteenth centuries, when Scots was an institutional and near-standard, national language).

One wonders if the *OED* considered how its coverage of Ireland would gibe with its stated policy that "dialectal words and forms which occur since 1500 are not admitted, except when they continue the history of a word or sense once in general use, illustrate the history of a literary word or have themselves a certain literary currency, as is the case with many modern Scottish words" (Murray et al. 1989, xxv). *OED* policy was to eschew sources post-dating 1820, presumably thus excluding nearly all works from Ireland, so rudimentary was Anglo-Irish literature before that date. One must agree with Görlach that "the policy of the editors of the *OED* with regard to all kinds of regional lexis was ill-defined from the beginning" (1995a, 128). For instance, what is one to make of the label "Sc. and north." for *sheugh* 'furrow, trench, ditch, drain,' a term widely current in Ulster, especially in humorous reference to the north channel of the Irish Sea?

That the *OED* used few source texts from Ireland and generally under-used regional labeling is clear by searching the current on-line version, *OED3* in the making. As of this writing, it identifies 157 items as "Anglo Irish" and 34 as "Anglo Ir.," and it draws respectable numbers of citations from two nineteenth-century works: Carleton's *Traits and Stories of the Irish Peasantry* (1830ff.), with 114, and Patterson's *A Glossary of Words in Use in the Counties of Antrim and Down* (1880), with 81 (not all labeled as having Irish currency). However, that the vast majority of these has been incorporated recently is shown by their concentration in letters M-P, on which the third edition has worked so far. One can only conclude that *OED* editors (English and Scottish) have been myopic about Ireland as a source of citations.[8]

Lexical, if not necessarily lexicographical interest in the English and the Scots of Ireland is long-standing (for bibliographies, see Aldus 1976, Hickey 2002, and Erskine and Montgomery 2006). Most works have been published and known only in Ireland, indicating why the *OED* might have missed some, but surely not all, of them. Because with two or three exceptions this literature has not been produced by trained lexicographers or based on discernible, principled collection programs, its coverage may seem uneven and its analysis anecdotal. A tradition of collecting had commenced in Ulster late in the nineteenth century with Patterson's *Glossary*, from which the *EDD* and subsequent compilations drew heavily; later came substantial works by Marshall (1904-06), Russell (1910), and others in Ulster and by Joyce (1910) for Ireland as a whole. A separate tradition has prevailed in Ulster to the present day.[9] Major works of the twentieth century include Traynor's *The English Dialect of Donegal: A Glossary* (1953), Todd's *Words Apart: A Dictionary of Northern Ireland English* (1990), O'Kane's *You Don't Say: The Tyrone Crystal Book of Ulster Dialect* (1991), Fenton's *The Hamely Tongue* (1995/2000/2006), Macafee's *Concise Ulster Dictionary* (1996), Ó Muirithe's *A Dictionary of Anglo-Irish* (1996), Share's *Slanguage: A Dictionary of Irish Slang* (1997/2003), Dolan's *Dictionary of Hiberno-English* (1998/2004), and Wall's *An Irish Literary Dictionary and Glossary* (2001). These differ in almost every way: treatment, format, scope, emphasis, and so on. Some have limited historical features (e.g., Dolan, Ó Muirithe, Share, Todd, Traynor, and Wall have dated citations, though inconsistently and rarely from before the late nineteenth century), but one can find only rudimentary use of historical principles in any lexicography of the English of Ireland to date.

The most publicized recent volume is Dolan's. While many of its entries have dated citations (from literature occasionally as early as

Swift), Dolan declares his volume primarily one of speech and "intended to be a national dictionary, with material from all four provinces, which will confront the trivializing image of the dialect created by 'Stage Irish', by presenting its versatility and richness, at the same time explaining the sub-structure of such ostensibly humorous expressions as 'the dinner is on the table, and my wife is in it'" (2000, 323).[10] His popularity on the speaker circuit and as a radio commentator facilitated his gathering submissions from the public, and his dictionary is a continuing, indeed evolving, project (with a standing invitation to contribute at http://www.hiberno-english.com (Dolan 2002–). Such an offer would seem likely to attract a disproportion of exotic and obsolescing items of uncertain wider currency, and indeed Dolan's entries often do not appear elsewhere in Irish English lexicography, including many unassimilated from Irish or nearly so. He lists only four pages of published sources used. His etymologies provide minimal detail, citing Old or Middle English precursors but no semantic developments, and his catch-all label "E. dial." does not discriminate between England and Scotland or any region thereof.

Theoretical and Practical Issues

Vexed Historical, Linguistic, and Lexicographical Relations

After Henry VIII was proclaimed King of Ireland in 1542 and head of his newly established Protestant Episcopal Church there (which became the Church of Ireland, member of the Anglican communion), the British monarchy saw Ireland as integral to its realm, and with James I's ascension in 1603 it declared lordship over all three kingdoms in the British Isles, England, Scotland, and Ireland. That ecclesiastical, political, military, and other forces in Ireland have opposed this accession has been demonstrated by insurrections in 1641–49, 1688–90, 1798, 1916, 1969–97, and various other conflicts and campaigns of resistance. The Act of Union, which absorbed the Irish Parliament into the British one in 1801, essentially eliminated any remaining Irish autonomy. In 1921 the predominantly Protestant six-county state of Northern Ireland became a constituent of the United Kingdom, with the other 26 counties forming the Irish Free State. Official, formal distinctions aside, the ebb and flow of peoples, cultures, and languages from the late twelfth century, if not in some ways from pre-history, have produced interpenetration of cultures of the two main islands of the archipelago known today as the "British Isles." Especially facilitating movement between them is that the mainlands of Ireland and Scotland are only eleven miles apart at the closest point, such movement usually being *de facto* internal migrations and thus undocumented. So, are things "Irish" *ipso facto* "British"? In England "British" as a superordinate term including Ireland is not yet an anachronism, but is a usage that people in Ireland (universally in the Republic, but of course much less so in Northern Ireland) find presumptuous, hegemonic, and inaccurate. However, Americans are at least equally guilty (or sloppy) about appropriate distinctions. In the U.S. departments of English everywhere include Walter Scott, William Butler Yeats, inter alia, within the canon of "English literature," not seeing or unable to see the ambiguity of "English" in referring to both a language and a nation. In a trenchant historical critique Kearney (1989) shows how Scotland, Ireland, and Wales view the "British Isles" as far more differentiated than do the English and themselves as having multiple identities, with Scottish, Irish, and Welsh being the primary ones. Intrinsic to these identities have been differing linguistic heritages for nearly two millennia.

Is Irish English an extraterritorial variety, or is it integral to a larger entity, "British Isles English"? Can it thus be part of both the core and the periphery of English? The answer to the latter is almost certainly "yes." *OED3* will probably never use more than a relative handful of sources from Ireland, but many factors also favor seeing Irish English as an extraterritorial variety. Among the ways that Ireland is distinct from other territories in which English was taken in British colonial expansion are the following: (1) English was planted there more than once, centuries apart if not continuously over many centuries (which raises the question whether a *DIEHP* should include medieval Irish English); (2) arriving speakers of English and Scots found not several languages and thus a landscape on which English would be a unifying medium, but only one indigenous language (unlike all other colonies, with the exception of New Zealand, where only Maori was encountered); (3) the native language had a long-recognized literary, especially oral, tradition; (4) Ireland and England were both heir to some of the same heritage from the continent through the Catholic Church and its traditions; (5) since English was the language of the Reformation that Henry VIII sought to impose, this fact has tended to identify the Irish language with the Catholic population ever since and to consolidate it (Bliss 1979, 17); and (6) the English of Ulster was itself exported, as other former colonial varieties were not (Montgomery 2000, 2003, 2006).

So close are the two islands' historical experiences that Ireland could never have extricated itself from its larger neighbor's domination once the Normans consolidated power in England. That Ireland was monolingual (outside monastic and other religious life, where Latin often prevailed) when English first arrived sealed the eventual erosion of Irish, as happened to Welsh (i.e., "British") in England in the sixth and seventh centuries. The effects of the hegemony of England/Britain over Ireland has been reflected in the pursuit of lexicography as in other areas of life. Irish editors and compilers (e.g., Dolan) who claim that Irish English is distinct often do this by citing unassimilated loans from Irish, an act that asserts Irish national pride as much as linguistic facts. While usually stating that Irish English is also distinct in retaining English archaisms, they give these far less treatment as dictionary entries. The us (Ireland) vs. them (England) mentality has skewed presentation in existing works, which consequently lack historical depth and de-emphasize early citations. Insecurities produced by hegemonic relations likely prompt oft-heard claims that "the purest English in the world is spoken in Dublin" or that the English of Ireland has an Elizabethan character, supported by analogues from Shakespeare and the English Renaissance (Walsh 1911). The latter claim has been made for rural Ulster speech by Byers (1916) and O'Kane (1991, x), among others. Also reinforcing pride in the survival of archaisms in Ireland is their nostalgic value, in being redolent of older-fashioned life and its idyllic charms.

The political values associated with a language variety mean that a lexicographer inevitably endorses an ideology and must count on political capital and consensus when undertaking his or her work, especially in a post-colonial context. As Paulin puts it, "the disinterested scholar, laboriously and often thanklessly at work on a dictionary, cannot fail to have asked himself [*sic*] this fundamental question: for what nation am I compiling this lexicon?" (1985, 8). In most cases, including Ireland, it would be a group of motivated, multiply-skilled scholars and the institutions backing them for the long term that would ask and have to answer this question, and they would hardly be "disinterested." In the Irish mind today lingers resentment against "perfidious Albion," and for many the language of those considered the island's age-long oppressors is still viewed as an imposed colonial tongue. It may never be Irish enough to deserve investment, despite the constant urging of Daniel O'Connell (1775–1847), Ireland's "Emancipator" that his compatriots master English and ensure that their children did so for their self-advancement. However, in Irish folk memory O'Connell's arguments and the profound influence of English-medium National Schools, introduced in 1831, have dissolved as English gained repute as the language of that nation whose neglect contributed to the death of a million Irish people and the emigration of a million more, predominantly speakers of Irish, in the Great Potato Famine of the late 1840s. The 19th century made the Irish schizophrenic about themselves and the English language. The English language has both subjugated and freed the Irish, and in utterly different ways the Irish language has perhaps also done the same.

Over and above, then, any issue of the demography or prevalence of English in Ireland, and given the radically different valences English and Irish have there, does Irish English have adequate sociolinguistic status for the island's citizens to support a full-fledged historical dictionary project? Even electronic dictionaries are costly endeavors. What and how large would be the audience for a work requiring a decade or more and diversion of resources from existing priorities, probably including Irish-language ones? The Anglo-Irish literature of the late nineteenth century gave status to what outside the island had been considered merely a comic dialect of English. It provides core material for any dictionary and the reason why many would find interest in one. Beyond literary scholars and other academic specialists, would a *DIEHP* be valued throughout the island as a cultural asset, or would its appeal be mainly abroad? Such questions require energetic, thoughtful, and unambiguous resolution before work should commence.

Ambivalence about a project that in essence endorses the status of English in Ireland would be only part of the linguistic dynamic attendant to a *DIEHP* in Ireland; that Irish English lacks a standard spoken form further complicates the situation. Given the Republic of Ireland's preoccupation with Irish since that country's break from the United

Kingdom, especially in underwriting educational materials and reference works, a *DIEHP* would be a need less critical for students and teachers. This preoccupation is no mystery, since Irish was severely under-resourced in every way and lacking a de facto spoken form in 1921, but was set soon to become compulsory in the schools of the small, poor country. The belief that England/Britain had long suppressed Irish speakers and the language itself created an "Irish first" mentality and an over-simplified view of the historical linguistic landscape of Ireland as merely reflecting the political one, featuring competition between Irish and the "Standard" English of southeast England (Crowley 2005). That Ulster has been the most dynamic contact zone in the British Isles over the past four hundred years, involving two Celtic languages and two Germanic ones, would rarely if ever be suspected from dictionaries and other works produced beyond (or sometimes from within) Ulster. Lexicographers tend to specify, often speculatively, connections to Irish in their etymologies, e.g., Todd cites partial parallels to Irish terms differing in form or meaning, presumably suggesting reinforcement, when only a simple, direct borrowing from English would seem at play, as for *agin* 'against' she cites both Middle English *agein* 'against' and Irish *in-aghaidh* 'against, as a protection against' (1990, 21).

Terminology

This essay has employed "Irish English" as the over-arching term encompassing all the English (and Scots) used in Ireland. Given the complex, fraught history between Britain and Ireland and diverging views on the prominence and nature of Irish influence on English, not surprisingly there has been more disagreement about labeling the English(es) of Ireland than elsewhere. "Canadian English" and "New Zealand English" may be self-evident labels in their domains and beyond, but only recently has "Irish English" become a common generic term. Involving scholarly debate and contention, issues of labeling highlight substantially different views of the object and compass of study and point to potential dissension about what properly belongs in a *DIEHP* and what should be given priority.

"Anglo-Irish," for a long time the conventional term, was employed by the *OED1/OED2* in labeling entries and by earlier scholars such as McIntosh and Samuels (1968), Hogan (1927), and others for the English of Ireland. It remains a descriptor for literature by Irish writers (Swift, Synge, Joyce, etc.) in English, to avoid the ambiguity between the "Irish" language and those from Ireland who write in English. Henry (1958) uses "Anglo-Irish" for the English of areas shifting from Irish fairly recently and "Hiberno-English" for the predominantly urban English that germinated in the seventeenth century. Bliss, Todd, and Dolan define "Hiberno-English" quite differently, as the "English that has been profoundly influenced by features of the Irish language" (Dolan 2002–). While these scholars usually define their terms, their archetypal distinctions are impressionistic and opaque for those outside Ireland or who do not know Irish. Definitions also tend to conflate synchronic and diachronic criteria. Almost inescapable is the inference that scholars use their labels to press sub-gloss arguments about the prominence of input and influence from the Irish language. Barry, Corrigan, and Harris, also from Ireland, have used "Hiberno-English," especially in the 1980s/90s, as the generic term, but this has now been almost completely superseded by "Irish English," favored as parallel to "American English," "Australian English," etc. The fullest discussions and critiques of terminology are in Croghan (1988) and Kallen (1999).

The Case of Ulster Scots

Today in Northern Ireland, summer parades, bonfires, re-enactments, and other events keep alive popular memory and are reminders that crucial stories of rivalries between European powers were played out on the continent's northwest fringe in the seventeenth century. The organized peopling or planting of British settlers in Ireland aimed to ensure loyalty to a Protestant monarchy and to Protestant Christianity in a staunchly Catholic land that threatened to be Britain's Achilles heel until James II's defeat at the Battle of the Boyne in 1690. Mass plantations extended from one in Munster in the 1580s through the Cromwellian land settlements of the 1650s. The latter saw Catholic landowners dispossessed and moved west to Connacht, Ireland's poorest province, and thousands of commoners deported or enslaved to the Caribbean, Virginia, or elsewhere, replaced by the English supporters and soldiers of the Parliametarian Army given land in Leinster and Munster. Midway through this period King James I's Plantation of Ulster (1610–25) settled in that province tens of thousands of Scots from Lowland Scotland and

English (mainly from the northwest Midlands, and somewhat fewer from the south; London merchant companies contracted to populate the city of Derry and its hinterland) (cf. Robinson 1984). The differential linguistic inputs from east to west in the seventeenth century, each comprising a kaleidoscope of local dialects, account for what remains the most important English dialect boundary in Ireland, stretching from Carlingford Lough to Bundoran and closely paralleling the boundary of Ulster (Barry 1981). Many more Scots speakers made the crossing in the 1680s/90s, seeking relief from famine and haven from the persecution of Covenanters, bringing northeastern Ireland further into the Scottish linguistic and cultural orbit. The most comprehensive account of Ulster Scots as a language variety is Montgomery and Gregg (1997).

The two broad historical "streams" introduced into Ireland—Scots and northern English into Ulster and southern English elsewhere—have implications that are lexicographical, academic, political, and indeed ideological as well as linguistic. Within Ireland today common-place references to the "two main traditions" are cultural (i.e., Protestant and Catholic), not geographical, and any island-wide study of English must take account of them. Within Ulster one finds far more awareness of three traditions (sometimes referred to as "Catholic, Protestant, and Dissenter") and that Ireland has a plurality of heritages, not a polarity (Wood 1994, Erskine and Lucy 1997, and Kelly and Young 2004).

Should Ulster Scots be subsumed under "Irish English"? Here is not the place for detailed arguments of linguistic dendrology, i.e., whether structurally Ulster Scots is more properly seen as a branch of Lowland Scots or of Irish English and whether Lowland Scots is a branch of English or historically speaking of a superordinate variety (e.g., Old English). However, some perspective is useful. The name suggests, as do many linguistic features, close relationship to Lowland Scots. The first editor of the *SND* called Ulster Scots a "variant of w[est] m[id] Scots" (Grant 1931: xli), identifying its historical connections to be mainly to Ayrshire, Renfrewshire, and nearby districts of Scotland. The Linguistic Survey of Scotland included speakers in five Ulster counties (Mather and Speitel 1975, 1977, 1986). Gregg (1972) mapped Ulster Scots meticulously, differentiating it from Ulster English on the grounds of thirteen systematic phonological contrasts (e.g., /nixt/ vs. /naɪt/ 'night' and /tun/ vs. /taʊn/ 'town'), showing its prevalence across four Ulster counties, from Donegal to Down.

In contrast, overviews of English in Ireland by nearly every linguist in or from Ireland with whose work this writer is acquainted classify Ulster Scots as a variety of Irish English (Hickey 2002, 2007) or Northern Ireland English (Barry 1982, Harris 1984, Corrigan 1990, Kirk 1997, etc.) They presume, as Scots have not, geography as sufficient for considering the entire island a single linguistic territory. While a *DIEHP* not encompassing Ulster Scots is probably inconceivable, its lexicographers should recognize the historical nature of Ulster Scots, appreciate the justification for including it in Scottish dictionaries and surveys, and collaborate with and draw on the latter. A *DIEHP*'s etymologists should consult not only the *OED*, the *EDD*, the *Survey of English Dialects* (Orton and Dieth 1962–70) and other works on English, but also works on Scots, Irish, and Scottish Gaelic. As Macafee found with the *Concise Ulster Dictionary* (1996), not considering all of these can miss important information and result in gaps that can lead to speculative, if not spurious, etymologies.[11]

Nature of the Record

As the four stages of historical lexicography outlined earlier have proceeded, editors have faced dramatically different records on which to base their works. The *OED* and second-generation projects had abundant texts and ranges of citations from written, usually published sources. However, later-generation editors have had written sources less robust in number and size, more fragmented (particularly for earlier periods), less conventional (e.g., consisting of ephemeral literature), and having less-easily identified authors. They have therefore relied increasingly on oral sources and collateral programs such as surveys to confirm, compensate for, or elaborate on available written evidence.

A *DIEHP* would be a third-generation project. Its historical record would have the same longevity as Scotland's, though far thinner until the late nineteenth century. Some early sources were produced by transient outsiders (colonial officials, travelers, etc.), but a more serious–and contentious–issue for prospective editors is how to use the "mock" English of "stage Irish" characters (usually vagrants, servants, soldiers, and other types; see Duggan 1937) crafted by English writers since the early 17th century, for most of whom Irish English was already conventionalized and who probably had no direct experience with speakers of Irish English. Such evidence, which forms the bulk of the record before the late eighteenth century, does at least have the value of lacking pretense to being from speakers (however fictional) with education. Antiquarianism has prompted publication of numerous short word-lists in county and district historical journals, motivated in the Republic by interest in documenting Gaelicisms and thus declaring, rhetorically speaking, that Irish still lives in local English. The hundred local societies and clubs in Northern Ireland have published many compilations of local lore that include old-fashioned or curious words. For a *DIEHP* such sources should be mined exhaustively, as they reveal local currency, as do unsolicited citations such as those in Dolan's dictionary and website.

As suggested earlier, in the literature on Irish English two prominent characteristics are often cited. One is its wide-ranging manifestation of an Irish Gaelic substratum or influence in vocabulary and grammar, including phrases, idioms, calques (e.g., the "hot news" perfect with *after*, as in *I'm after drinking my tea* 'I have just drunk my tea'; see Harris 1986), and other products of English having had longer-term contact with an indigenous language in Ireland than in most, if not all, other extraterritorial contexts. The other is its preservation of archaisms from Early Modern English (e.g., incomplete late stages of the Great Vowel Shift, as in *tay* 'tea'). Gaelicisms in the literature on Irish English range widely beyond the lexical items usually found as dictionary entries. Joyce (1910) includes speech acts and other pragmatic phenomena, and these often involve English forms used in Irish ways or with far greater frequency in Ireland. One such covert Gaelicism is the tendency to answer yes-no sentences with truncated clauses, e.g., *We don't, They haven't*. Wall calls this phenomenon the "apparent proximity" of Irish English to "Standard" English (1991, 10). Joyce's *English as We Speak It in Ireland* remains refreshing and unrivaled after a century in discussing how the Irish use English in exclamations, terms of endearment and abuse, exaggerations and other speech acts, i.e., beyond lexical categories. Can or should these be captured in dictionary entries? Can an appropriate amount of historical data be found?

Lemmatizing Forms

Establishing head words in a *DIEHP* presents fundamental and persistent issues where a standard form does not exist for lemmatization. One is the familiar one Wright grappled with in his *English Dialect Diction-*

ary: which to choose among varying forms attested only in speech or in written representations of speech? A classic case from Irish English involves the second-plural personal pronoun most often spelled as *yous*. The *OED* enters both *yous* and *yez* (cross-referencing the second to the first, but not vice versa). *Yous* is normally taken to derive from *you* + *-s* (through false analogy of *you* with a noun), but this presumes the written form *you* as the base and that the vowel of the base form has historically been /u/. However, the earliest attested form is *yees* (1804). *Ye* as a second-plural form is well known in Ireland and represents a pronunciation typical of Ulster Scots. It comes then as no surprise that a lexicon of Ulster speech (Montgomery 2006) drawing on local fiction extensively found ten spellings (*yees, yeeze, yeis, yese, yez, yis, yiz, yous, youse,* and *yuhs*) of this speech-based word, most reflecting a high-front vowel and implying a derivational process of *ye* + *-s*. Thus, as Macafee (1996) found, a dictionary based substantially on speech forms requires painstaking cross-references even if including only forms that indicate the apparent range of pronunciations and omits those found in only one citation (thus eliminating nonce variants, some of which she determined to be "bad Irish"). *Yous/yez* is easier to treat than many, in having at least one plausible English source. How does an editor decide on a headword when there is no dominant form, but many competitors and no good citation for guidance? Macafee concluded that she could only enter the spelling(s) recorded (usually by a naive observer) and register "origin uncertain" or "origin unknown" (e.g., *bicker* 'a blow from a stone,' *gadlum* 'a strong, usually bad, smell') in etymologies.

A second major issue concerns loan words from Irish. Most are partially, if not entirely, assimilated into Irish English phonologically, though the only attestation may lie in a written Irish form. Because it has a long and prestigious history as a written language and is still studied by the great majority of primary and secondary school students on the island, the Irish language normally supplies a ready candidate for a headword. Macafee cites eleven forms *s.v. greesagh* 'embers, ashes of a fire,' from Irish *gríosach*, all differing orthographically from the Irish form, which appears only in the etymology. Other lexicographers adopt the Irish form as the headword. Among these Dolan is extreme, with 22 of 41 entries under N of this type, making his *Dictionary of Hiberno-English* substantially a compilation of loans assimilated marginally if at all, and Ó Muirithe's *Dictionary of Anglo-Irish* has only entries of this type, presented to indicate how Gaelic lexis has "continued to enrich daily speech in rural Ireland, thus continuing to fulfil a social function [even] in places where Irish had long since died" (1996, 13). With their works having so much Irish, Dolan, Ó Muirithe, et al. seem to see Irish English largely as the shadow of a fading Irish language, but this judgment is too facile and perhaps a little harsh. Dolan's conception of Irish English as a "macaronic dialect, a mixture of Irish and English" (1998, xix) differs little from some other lexicographers. More important, potential users of a *DIEHP* have as their usual points of reference only written Irish and written Standard English (to his credit, Dolan is the only editor other than Traynor to provide phonetic transcriptions for all entries). For two centuries Irish writers have mixed the two languages and peppered their English with Irish, doing so among other reasons in deference to their readers' bilingualism, however partial, asymmetrical, or symbolic it might be. William Carleton is foremost among them.

Confounding the Anglicization of Irish is the Gaelicization of Irish English. Concomitant with the Irish language revival of the past century or more has come the adoption or shift (sometimes conscious, as with surnames) from English forms to Irish ones. The most noted example of this is *craic* 'lively and engaging conversation, fun,' identified by Dolan (1998, 77) as a twentieth-century form historically from English *crack*, but the activity denoted is now so associated with Ireland that Irish English has appropriated and respelled the word as a pseudo-borrowing. Macafee (2002, 47) emphasizes that reborrowings are not always recent and that Irish has probably taken as much from English in Ireland as vice versa. While *craic* is invented, increased literacy in Irish has foregrounded historical forms of Irish as variants or replacements of ones partially or wholly Anglicized earlier. The 1991 census found that only three percent of the Republic's population reported that it spoke Irish natively and as much as one-third claimed some oral competence in the language. Considerably more, no doubt, had some recognition of written vocabulary items and the textbook spellings to go with them.

Illustrated above are only a few issues relating to the selection of entries and headword forms for a *DIEHP*. Would the dictionary's editors who are specialists in Irish accept Macafee's principles for inclusion and exclusion? Variant spellings can be ordered alphabetically after a headword, but how would a *DIEHP* enter variant pronunciations, many of which would need to be collected by a survey? How one might ask in English about words respondents perceive as Irish is another question. Editors can use principles to assign orthographic shape to spoken variants not otherwise attested, but on what basis can pronunciations be organized or ordered if words are migrating back and forth between the two languages? Even if generalist readers with some facility in Irish can look up loanwords, how to handle variation will consistently test the skills of editors.

The Irish English Lexicon

No well-researched outline of the lexicon of Irish English currently exists, much less a systematic diachronic or synchronic treatment. The research of Kallen, the only scholar to have begun examining the subject, suggests that the mental lexicon of many speakers may not separate Irish from Irish English, leading him to question the designation "English monolingual" (1996, 111). That lexicon "includes Irish-based items from [four] sources": loanwords, "apports," borrowings, and coinages (1996, 110). Further, phonological convergence between Irish English and Irish, produced by intimate contact, calls into question hard-and-fast criteria for entering an item in a *DIEHP*. Detailed lexical scholarship is a prerequisite to a historical dictionary, however, because editors need explicit, usable criteria for what lies within the bounds of the work and what does not. Introductions to regional historical dictionaries typically identify five to ten overlapping categories used to qualify entries, e.g., the *Dictionary of Jamaican English* includes "words or senses now (or once) general in English but of which the earliest or latest record is a book about Jamaica by one who had been there or otherwise had direct knowledge of the island" (Cassidy and LePage 1967, xiv). For Ireland the only serious thinking on this matter to date is Macafee's introduction to the *CUD*, for internal criteria (i.e., linguistic ones) pertaining to Ulster. External criteria such as a writer's Irish nativity should presumably play some role, since many of Ireland's most famous modern (Joyce, Beckett) and pre-modern (Goldsmith, Thomas Sheridan) writers lived most of their lives abroad. The old chestnut, asked of one whether he was "Irish" by having been born in Ireland, to which he responded, "Is a man a horse if he is born in a stable?" reminds us that Ireland claims an unusual proportion of expatriate writers as its own.

Borrowings and retentions, while obvious categories, need careful definitions, however much latitude editors retain in using them. How large and prominent are categories distinct from the English of England, such as derivations of entirely English material (e.g., *yous*), hybrid material (e.g., *girleen*), compounds, phrases, semantic extensions and other shifts (as *bold* 'naughty'; cf. Irish *dána* 'bold, naughty'), contrasts in register, and so on? Irish has often rubbed against English and Scots only gently, producing subtle semantic differences in Irish English. More elusive is the currency of variants, since many terms linger in the twilight of their existence or are attested only as recollected items. What labels, stylistic or otherwise, should a *DIEHP* employ beyond identifying technical terms?

Wall believes, no doubt wisely, that strict linguistic criteria for entries may be impractical and culturally insensitive: "To create and impose precise theoretical distinctions between the vocabulary of Hiberno-English and its parent languages would be to ignore the complexity of their relationships in life and literature and, from a practical point of view, greatly reduce the utility of a dictionary" (1990, 105). Virtually every dictionary or lexicon of Irish English contains proper nouns, i.e., culturally or historically significant items (anniversaries and other historical events, political movements and organizations, etc.; e.g., Dolan has *National University of Ireland*). For a *DIEHP* to become a quasi-encyclopedia would parallel works on South African, Australian, and other Englishes. But selecting proper nouns not on linguistic criteria but rather for their importance to history and culture, which would be inevitable, would require encompassing both the Republic of Ireland and Northern Ireland, jurisdictions having separate traditions and developments, and might double their number.

Conclusion

Many other complexities pertinent to a *DIEHP* project are as important and potentially thorny as ones considered in this essay. These include the practicalities of siting the project, establishing and organizing a team of editors and support staff (consultants, bibliographers, etc.), creating collection programs (excerptors, an island-wide survey of speakers and correspondents, etc.), agreeing on the scope and goals of the dictionary, and many other matters. Space constraints prevent even a glimpse at how these might be designed and implemented. Instead, the present essay has explored more underlying issues and challenges—historical, ideological, conceptual, among others—in order to understand why Irish English lacks a comprehensive dictionary on historical principles. Its absence is inescapably ironic when nothing so immediately and unambiguously reveals one's Irishness as how he or she speaks English, this fact stemming from one's intonation but also one's pronunciation, grammar, or vocabulary. Of how many varieties of English beyond Britain can it be said that nationality is revealed almost as one starts speaking? Also ironic is that most research on Irish English in recent decades has been undertaken either outside Ireland or by scholars who have emigrated to or studied there, not natives of the island.

Lexicographic endeavors of the past two decades fill half a shelf, but the deficit in information on the English language of life and literature in Ireland remains quite real. A full-scale, historically based reference work on Irish English probably remains a generation away, due primarily to the uncertainly of commitment, support, and cooperation. In Ireland scholars across institutions and the national divide still share few professional arenas in which to cultivate and pursue long-term cooperative ventures.

That the Republic of Ireland identifies itself with Irish rather than with English and invests considerable resources in its teaching and official (if mainly symbolic) use will constrain support for a *DIEHP*. An expensive project on Irish English, even if linguists, lexicographers, and other specialists resolve all logistical, institutional, and other issues between themselves, would be met with reservations by many, some less silent than others. Media outlets would parody any publicly funded project giving academic status to what they tend to consider a comic variety of English. Focus on the Irish language may increase in coming years because the Republic of Ireland has recently vowed to integrate it more fully into national life. In 2005 Irish became the twenty-first working, official language of the European Union. In Northern Ireland Irish-medium education is expanding, while activists press for more visibility and use of Irish in public life. Any long-term commitment in Ireland to a *DIEHP* would be a political manifesto, a declaration that Ireland, like so many other lands, had dissolved its previous association of the English language with England and henceforth claimed it as Ireland's own as much as anyone's, no longer the "grafted tongue" as portrayed by the poet John Montague:

> (Dumb, bloodied, the severed head now chokes to speak another tongue–
> As in a long-suppressed dream, some stuttering garbled ordeal of my own)
> An Irish child weeps at school repeating its English. After each mistake
> The master gouges another mark on the tally stick hung about its neck
> Like a bell on a cow, a hobble on a straying goat. To slur and stumble
> In shame the altered syllables of your own name; to stray sadly home
> and find the turf cured width of your parents' hearth growing slowly alien:
> In cabin and field, they still speak the old tongue. You may greet no one.
> To grow a second tongue, as harsh a humiliation as twice to be born.
> Decades later that child's grandchild's speech stumbles over lost syllables of
> an old order. (1988, 211–12)

The centenary of Sir William's vision approaches. The day when Ireland aspires to an equal place in English-language lexicography seems not yet on the horizon, but when it comes, the English language will have made full circle.

NOTES

1. I am most grateful to two colleagues in Ireland, Jeffrey Kallen and John Kirk, for many years of discussions informing my understanding of issues pertinent to this essay. Both have also graciously critiqued an earlier draft, but bear no responsibility for any views expressed herein.
2. Lowland Scots has a common ancestor with Modern English, i.e., Old English. Historically much more divergent from English, its status today as semi-autonomous or as a variety of English is a matter of debate, one that, not surprisingly, tends to differ between Scotland and England.
3. For example, from the early nineteenth century numerous serial publications, sponsored especially by local antiquarian societies and clubs, had brought into print hundreds of texts of medieval and Renaissance provenance. For the most detailed index of these, see Stevenson and Stevenson (1987).
4. Aitken's account of this evolution parallels the one in the present essay, but concentrates on the dictionaries proposed by Craigie. He says nothing about Ireland other than that a dictionary of "perhaps Ulster" could be a gleam in "scholars' eyes" (1987, 104), presumably meaning John Braidwood's *Ulster*

Dialect Dictionary, a project initiated by the Belfast Naturalists' Field Club in 1951 (Gregg 1951) and in 1964 put under Braidwood's editorship at Queen's University Belfast. The idea for a comprehensive dictionary of Ulster dialect dates back to at least Marshall (1904, 123). Braidwood collected material actively in the 1960s and sporadically thereafter and published extensive articles on bird names in *Ulster Folklife*, but otherwise his project never progressed beyond a large collection of notecards inaccessible since his death in 1988.

5. I am grateful to William Kirwin for details on Bliss's project from records of the *Dictionary of Newfoundland English* at Memorial University of Newfoundland.
6. Kallen (1996, 1997) has dealt most thoughtfully and extensively with the messy but crucial issues on what should be entered in such a dictionary and how. Görlach (1995b) also discusses some issues pertaining to a potential dictionary of Irish English.
7. Throughout this paper "Ulster" refers to the nine-county historical province, not the six-county state of Northern Ireland (popularly called "Ulster" today, especially in Protestant quarters and media) that was created in 1921. The counties of Donegal, Monaghan, and Cavan now lie within the Republic of Ireland.
8. The work invested in Montgomery (2006) shows what can be put on record for Irish English through one individual's assiduous scouring of local and archival materials. John Simpson, Editor-in-Chief of *OED3*, has acknowledged the deficit in citations from Irish materials, stating that one and sometimes two staff members had been assigned to ameliorate this situation (Simpson p.c., 2007).
9. For a review and comparative assessment of works published in both parts of Ireland through 1991, see Montgomery (1993).
10. Dolan gathered material over many years from university students, colleagues, respondents to solicitations in local newspapers, personal visits, and other sources. Why he included only a fraction of this in his dictionary is not clear. When the author asked Dolan whether he had utilized the resources of the Ulster Folk and Transport Museum's Dialect Archive or amassed much Ulster material, the latter replied with evident conclusiveness that he had some contributions from County Cavan (Dolan p.c., 1995).
11. She found it necessary to consult an American specialist in Old Irish to mitigate the excesses of a staff Celticist who insisted on positing Modern Irish forms as sources of Ulster English dialect in the dictionary's etymologies.

12

RESPONSE

Embracing the Digital Siren: Collaborative Lexicography in the Twenty-First Century

MARSHA L. DUTTON
Ohio University

In 1747, Samuel Johnson wrote in *Plan of an English Dictionary*, "The great labour is yet to come, the labour of interpreting these words and phrases with brevity, fulness, and perspicuity; a task of which the extent and intricacy is sufficiently shown by the miscarriage of those who have generally attempted it" (Johnson 1825, 5.13–14). As the great labor of dictionary making has evolved over the centuries, each generation of lexicographers has introduced new methods and new technologies in an effort to attain Johnson's aims of conciseness, thoroughness, and accuracy while remaining aware of the many ways in which they will surely fall short of all three. The struggle goes on today, as digital technology makes it less necessary to be brief and more possible to be thorough but poses new barriers to accuracy.

In *Dictionaries of English: Prospects for the History of our Language,* Richard W. Bailey (1987b, 1–2) anticipated the future impact of technological change on lexicography:

> Dictionary making [. . .] has heard at last the siren call of technology. [. . .] The slow introduction of information-processing machinery has, so far, mainly served only the purposes of the old handcrafts: alphabetizing slips, setting type, making up pages of dictionary copy. The future of our English dictionaries offers something more revolutionary.

Since these words appeared, Bailey's prophecy has been richly confirmed. Among the many changes effected by computerization, lexicography has become a populist endeavor, open to anyone with Internet access. What Michael Carr (1997, 209) called "bottom-up collaborative editing" has become the public face of lexicography.

Dictionaries and the New Technology

The last three decades have witnessed much scholarly speculation about how computers may change lexicography, with Bailey an early advocate for computer use (Bailey and Robinson 1973a; Robinson and Bailey 1973). Later Sidney I. Landau (1984, 272–293) focused on computer coding of entries, and Michael Carr (1997, 18–19) observed that digitalization would change not only the writing of dictionaries but also the process of publication: "Tomorrow's cyberdictionaries will be shaped by solutions to today's problems of copyright reinterpretation, search engineering, Net commerce, and collaborative editing." Frederic G. Cassidy (1987, 23), while noting advantages, foresaw some costs: "Future dictionaries, stored in computerized data banks, will be easier to update, if carefully and firmly directed, but I hope they will not totally displace the book which one can hold in one's hands, and in which one can leaf about as curiosity leads, or wild surmise and the gadding vine of thought."

The use of computers in creating print dictionaries has been a common scholarly theme. New technologies can resolve conflicts between dictionary publishers' need to limit costs for the benefit of purchasers, who want dictionaries that are comprehensive, clear, and current but still compact and cheap, and lexicographers' desire for enough time to be accurate and enough space to be thorough (Oppentocht and Schutz 2003, 215–227). Such hopes have been amply fulfilled. Major print dictionaries today rely heavily on computerization for compiling corpora and coding entries; most have online equivalents that allow searches not just for headwords but also for words within entries, often not requiring even correct spelling. Many dictionary websites also exist independently of print dictionaries.

One of the most ambitious of the freestanding dictionary sites, Onelook.com, claimed in early 2009 to index 1009 dictionaries with 13,549,061 words. *Onelook* allows wildcards to locate inflected forms or words whose spelling is unknown and has a reverse dictionary inviting readers to "describe a concept and get back a list of words and phrases related to that concept." With the chatty informality common to these sites, *Onelook*'s homepage explains its approach: "If you have a word for which you'd like a definition or translation, we'll quickly shuttle you to the web-based dictionaries that define or translate that word."

Dictionary.com situates itself between traditional print dictionaries and the comprehensiveness of *Onelook*, presenting results from a partial list of online dictionaries. A search for *siren* yields entries from eight dictionary sites (rather than *Onelook*'s forty-six). In addition to listing all eight full entries, with senses, pronunciation (three times with vocalization), syllabification, and etymology, Dictionary.com provides phrases containing the word, synonyms, and a list of "Nearby Entries." It also provides links to websites offering siren-related products, signaling the relationship between commercial interests and digitalized lexicography.

Many of the great historical dictionaries of English are electronically accessible. Both the *OED* and the *Compact OED* can be searched through their websites with an individual or institutional subscription. The *Middle English Dictionary* (*MED*) has been translated into electronic form, searchable by headword as well as by etymon, date, manuscript, stencil, language, and text. The *MED* is part of the online *Middle English Compendium*, which also includes the *Corpus of Middle English Prose and Verse* and the *HyperBibliography*, listing all the Middle English resources cited in the *MED*. As of January 2009, the *Dictionary of Old English* (*DOE*) website contained entries from A to G and hotlinks to a large number of bibliographic references, including the *Middle English Compendium*, the

OED, and four dictionaries. The *DOE* also provides electronic access to the *Dictionary of Old English Web Corpus*, "an online database consisting of at least one copy of every Old English text."

Users as Lexicographers

Although dictionaries in many formats continue to appear in print, the lexicographical wave of the present is digital. Increasing numbers of people who would not describe themselves as lexicographers and may not even know the word now contribute to online dictionaries. But the interest they show, as Landau (1984, 294) notes, is not new: "An astonishing number of people believe that new words are invented by individuals, and in an effort to be helpful they devise a list of neologisms of their own, which they kindly make available for inclusion in the next edition of one's dictionary." Today a growing number of online dictionaries, such as UrbanDictionary.com, PseudoDictionary.com, and Wordia.com, encourage people to submit current and even invented words and senses for immediate publication.

Aside from the invention of computers and the Internet, the change that has made the greatest difference in contemporary lexicography is the 1995 introduction of wiki technology, which allows anyone to add and emend entries. As Ward Cunningham, its developer, and Bo Leuf (2001, 16) explain, "A wiki [. . .] seeks to involve the visitor in an ongoing process of creation and collaboration that constantly changes the Web site landscape." Wiki technology has allowed a broad variety of people to become "amateur lexicographers" (Giles 2008). *Urban Dictionary*, for example, greets users with the header "Urban Dictionary is the slang dictionary you wrote. Define your world." In April 2009, it boasted "3,870,482 definitions written since 1999." A similar site is *Wordlustitude*, which its creator Mark Peters defines as "a growing dictionary of ephemeral words, also known as nonce or stunt words."

Another dictionary using wiki technology is *Wiktionary*, which currently lists dictionaries in 172 languages. *Wiktionary*'s homepage defines it as "a wiki-based Open Content dictionary" and "a multilingual free encyclopedia." Unlike most other wiki dictionary sites, which post submitted words and definitions with little editorial supervision by either site managers or users, *Wiktionary* allows users to edit the words and definitions, potentially leading to greater accuracy of entries than those on other sites.

On 8 April 2009, the English-language *Wiktionary* claimed to have "1,221,904 entries with English definitions from over 295 languages." The online wiki encyclopedia *Wikipedia* notes, however, that software robots (bots) furnished the bulk of those entries:

> Most of the entries and many of the definitions at the project's largest language editions were created by bots that found creative ways to generate entries or (rarely) automatically imported thousands of entries from previously-published dictionaries.

The article notes that while the English-language *Wiktionary* apparently depends less on bots than do many of the other Wiktionaries, without bots "the English Wiktionary would have about 137,000 entries [. . .] making it smaller than most monolingual print dictionaries." To a certain extent, then, *Wiktionary* resembles both the dictionary sites created by traditional print dictionaries and the other wiki dictionary sites.

Publishers of traditional dictionaries are also embracing wiki technology, to keep up with other dictionaries and to achieve greater lexical currency. Merriam-Webster's wiki-fueled *Open Dictionary* complements its non-wiki online dictionary and invites readers to join a collaborative lexicographical community by submitting and sharing entries, much like those who submitted slips for words to the *OED*. Collins Dictionaries also invites users to submit words and definitions to their online *Living Dictionary*. Jeremy Butterfield, Editor-in-Chief of Collins Dictionaries when *Living Dictionary* was created, explained the new dictionary as a response to the rapidity of language change: "Things change very quickly now [. . .] . Words can establish themselves within a month" (qtd. in Moss 2004).

Such sites contribute to the new two-way path between people and information. Michael Adams (2007, 9) suggests that frequent users of the Internet understand themselves as more than recipients of information: "Those who travel the Web for information and ideas [. . .] often expect to participate in the public construction of knowledge, contributing and editing Web content whenever they feel competent to do so."

Lexicographical Authority

Societal consensus has long granted to dictionaries authority not only over the existence and meaning of words but also over their spelling, pronunciation, etymology, morphology, and syntactic functions. Adams (2007, 11) notes that the etymologies in print dictionaries are generally regarded as "unassailable nuggets of expert conclusion." That normative authority rests to some extent on the lexicographer's obscurity. The traditional printed dictionary speaks in faceless absolutes, ruling on words acceptable in Scrabble™, the pronunciation of *err*, and the difference between *a while* and *awhile*. In living rooms, libraries, and bars, "the dictionary says" settles many disputes. But as lexicography becomes a public activity, requiring no learning and having few rules for form or authenticity of entry, most online dictionaries have abandoned even a tacit claim to authority and accuracy.

The *Double-Tongued Dictionary* builds on the goal of supporting professional lexicographers by attempting to mediate between the new wiki dictionaries, which encourage lexical innovation, and traditional dictionaries, whose scholarly pace keeps them always behind the times. It attempts to record words in use rather than those newly coined, to achieve currency without abandoning accuracy and authority. Its creator, Grant Barrett, defines it as concerned with "undocumented or under-documented words from the fringes of English, with a focus on slang, jargon, and new words." Recent entries include *dead arm* (n.), "shoulder inflammation" (used in baseball), *kettle* (v.), "to surround and contain protestors," and President Obama's *quo vadis haircut* (n.), "black parlance from the 1960s for close-cut locks."

Because Barrett's goal is currency rather than entertainment, his site asks that submissions be words in current use, "not coined, invented, or said for the first time ever by you, a friend, a family member, nor by someone else close to you," and that they "seem to have been used more than once, ever." He also attempts to exclude words already in dictionaries, requesting that contributors check intended submissions at *Onelook*, but he is finally dependent on the honesty and accuracy of his contributors.

The difficulty of knowing whether submitted words are in use is particularly great with *Urban Dictionary*, which indicates no concern with the origin or prior existence of contributions. Contributors register as editors; clicking on the heading "edit" brings up a page headed "Edit

Urban Dictionary," which promises, "Editors see the **newest defs** before they hit the streets, and decide what gets published." Directions for editors include "Don't reject an entry because you think it's inaccurate," "Reject nonsense," and "Publish if you think it looks plausible." Editors are also invited to reorder definitions within each entry by clicking "thumbs up" or "thumbs down," so providing some indication of the level of appreciation earned by each definition but minimal evidence of whether the words or senses are in use.

Thus the *Urban Dictionary* entry for *Bush doctrine*, prominent late in the 2008 presidential campaign, contains definitions ranging from factual precision to implausible solipsism. As of 28 January 2009, eight definitions had been posted, all after 13 September 2008, when journalist Charles Gibson asked Vice-Presidential candidate Sarah Palin in a television interview whether she agreed with "the Bush Doctrine." After Palin's flailing response, Gibson explained the phrase as meaning "that we have the right of anticipatory self-defense, that we have the right to a preemptive strike against any other country that we think is going to attack us." Six definitions refer to then-President George W. Bush's military policy, and three mention Palin. One entry simply defines the phrase as "Something Sarah Palin doesn't know." Nothing in the entry provides a way to distinguish between jokes and senses in use. While definitions referring to presidential policy are most intellectually persuasive, two others—"To pose a pedagogic question while hubristically ignorant as to the correct answer" and "A specialist in waxing, triming [sic] and removing female pubic hair"—are at best improbable.

Because the explicit goal of such dictionary sites is to amuse rather than to inform, their creators require no lexicographical or linguistic expertise and no evidence that anyone uses the words submitted. For an accurate record of the language, words or phrases known only from such sources rather than from published materials or oral interviews are thin gruel.

Truthiness and the New Lexicography

In privileging personal coinages over linguistic analysis, the lexicographical revolution facilitated by wiki technology is a postmodern phenomenon that rejects the authority long granted to the dictionary and its editors. Past lexicographers could presume that they and their users shared in valuing factual accuracy and evidence. Tacitly rejecting such values, collaborative digital lexicography instead rewards individuality and creativity. Jill Lepore (2006, 87) limns the implications of this change: "'Be your own lexicographer!' might be Wiktionary's motto. Who needs experts? Why pay good money for a dictionary written by lexicographers when we can cobble one together ourselves?"

However, only the print dictionary (though perhaps accessed digitally) still has enough authority to be cited in written or spoken argument, if not always by name. Even the side-by-side appearance in *Dictionary.com* of multiple entries, with differing etymologies, definitions, and pronunciations, does not hinder users from choosing among them and then giving as their authority "the dictionary." Students seldom cite *Urban Dictionary* and *Wiktionary*, no matter what pleasure they may find in reading or contributing to them.

The competing claims of traditional authority grounded in fact and expertise and of an individualistic preference for opinion and originality achieved lexical embodiment in Stephen Colbert's introduction of *truthiness* on 17 October 2005. During the first episode of his satirical television news show *The Colbert Report*, Colbert explained the term as referring to "things that a person claims to know intuitively or 'from the gut' without regard to evidence, logic, intellectual examination, or facts." In his monologue he rejected the authority of traditional lexicography because of its reliance on facts:

> I will speak to you in plain, simple English. And that brings us to tonight's word: "truthiness." Now I'm sure some of the "word police," the "wordinistas" over at Webster's are gonna say, "hey, that's not a word." Well, anybody who knows me knows that I'm no fan of dictionaries or reference books. They're elitist. [. . .] I don't trust books. They're all fact, no heart. And that's exactly what's pulling our country apart today. 'Cause face it, folks; we are a divided nation. [. . .] we are divided between those who think with their head, and those who *know* with their *heart*.

Later Colbert expanded the point in an interview with Nathan Rabin (2006) of *The Onion's A.V. Club:* "It used to be, everyone was entitled to their own opinion, but not their own facts. But that's not the case anymore. Facts matter not at all. Perception is everything."

As lexicographers quickly pointed out, the *OED* had already recorded *truthiness* from 1824 with the meaning 'truthfulness, faithfulness'. But its reintroduction by Colbert gained widespread attention. The *New York Times* included *truthiness* among "some of the more interesting words and expressions to crop up in 2005" (Kennedy 2005; Steinberg 2005), the American Dialect Society named *truthiness* its 2005 Word of the Year, and on 13 February 2006, the *Macmillan English Dictionary* declared *truthiness* its Word of the Week, noting its association with "political spin and fabrication in general" (Maxwell 2006).

Though *truthiness* defines a social reality extending well beyond dictionaries and their makers, it has a particular relevance to wiki lexicography. But lexicography has always breathed the spirit of its age. As Robert Cawdrey and other creators of hard-word dictionaries reacted to the rapidly growing vocabulary of Early Modern England, as Samuel Johnson's *Dictionary* emerged from eighteenth-century England's desire to systematize and regularize the language, and as Noah Webster's *An American Dictionary of the English Language* enunciated the new geographical and political realities of nineteenth-century America, so today's lexicographers share twenty-first-century values of individuality, perpetual accessibility, and digitalization. The question is how to incorporate this new reality without yielding to—well, to truthiness.

English Lexicography Today

The three chapters in this section focus on traditional forms of lexicographical scholarship, usefully maintaining the balance that would be lost if one perceived online dictionaries as the sole or even best representatives of today's lexicography. While all three indicate the value of digital technology to lexicographers and lexicologists, they also suggest the many questions that remain intransigent to digital solutions. For while language change is systematic, it can also be illogical, so attempts to investigate or catalogue inconsistencies in English require intellectual freedom, creativity, and painstaking labor beyond that available in binary code. Thus even though both traditional and non-traditional lexicographers welcome computer technology's transformations, scholars must go on grappling with the linguistic problems and innovations created by human speculation, imagination, and necessity, so to develop appropriate non-digital resources and human skills and insights.

Joan Houston Hall's chapter on the formation of new English words found in *DARE* represents an intersection of traditional scholarship and online resources such as the electronic *OED*, the *Dictionary of the Scots Language*, and *DARE*'s own Index. Although *DARE* itself contains an extensive collection of linguistic data, much of what makes it so valuable as a source for the history and development of American English is its pioneering use of technology to map, label, and analyze the collection. As Hall has used digital tools and resources to locate words new in twentieth-century American English, other scholars will be able to use sources like the *Old English Web Corpus* and the *Middle English Compendium* to survey the process of linguistic change in earlier historical periods.

The intellectual underpinnings of Hall's work, however, are not technological but human, her literary and scholarly predecessors and contemporaries, including James Russell Lowell, James A. H. Murray, Thomas Pyles, and Bailey, each of whom has written about the continuing lexical vitality of English and the value of recording the products of that vitality. Hall thus provides evidence of the way in which speakers of American English daily continue to produce new forms and senses—new growth emerging from Lowell's "rich leaf-mould" of English.

Jesse Sheidlower writes about the problematic relationship between access to a limitless reservoir of text and the principled and practical requirements of historical lexicography. Undoubtedly, recourse on the Web to the widest variety of texts, from digitized medieval works to Web text itself, serves the lexicographer's interest. And, on the practical side of things, it is useful indeed to trawl for evidence of a thinly attested word: a generation ago, one had to search for evidence of a word book by book; now with a few keystrokes one can search for the word through all digitized books. Also, by networking the dictionary staff, computers facilitate the editing of material, as well as the passage of workaday copy into "print," whether "print" means paper or finished online text. So, one imagines, if J. A. H. Murray, instead of sorting paper slips into pigeonholes, had surfed the universe of English texts on the Internet, or if the Scriptorium had been networked with subeditors across the world, an even more compendious *OED* would have been published in what is for historical lexicography no time at all.

Sheidlower does not allow imagination to ignore the realities of twenty-first century lexicography, however. A dictionary entry is an abstract of a word's meaning, not a concordance of a word's use. Given all the evidence available, Sheidlower admits, historical lexicographers are tempted to incorporate more and more evidence into entries—but to what effect? The lexicographer's job is partly to write a comprehensible entry, but as the abstract expands to accommodate the available evidence, the entry loses its explanatory value. So more evidence, in fact, requires more editorial time and judgment, not less. Technology enables a new lexicography, as Bailey suggested, but "the old handcrafts" are as essential to twenty-first-century dictionaries as they ever were.

Michael Montgomery begins with Sir William Craigie's concern for "completing the record of English" and the creation of such great historical dictionaries as the *OED*, the *MED*, and the *Dictionary of American English.* To explain the non-existence of a *Dictionary of Irish English on Historical Principles* (*DIEHP*), he cites the variety of historical and lexicographical difficulties that continue to hinder its creation. Among the most difficult is the complex status of English in a nation where Irish is a symbol of national identity but English is universally used and is the medium of education, religion, commerce, and politics.

For the lexicographer, however, the most vexed questions have to do with what constitutes Irish English: Should the English of Ireland be considered simply an extension of British English (and so already included in the *OED*) or an independent national variety like Newfoundland English or Jamaican English? Would a historical dictionary of Irish English include the English spoken and written in Ireland during the medieval centuries given the apparently widespread disuse of English between the early periods and the late sixteenth century? How correct are scholars' claims for such a discontinuity, anyway? How valid are Early Modern English dramatists' representation of spoken Irish? How much influence has Irish Gaelic exercised on Irish English? And where would the English of Ulster fit in? As Montgomery explains the significance of such questions, it becomes clear both why there is as yet no *DIEHP* and why it should be the next big project of English lexicography.

Creators of a *DIEHP* would have to begin their work by resolving all such historical, political, and linguistic problems through scholarly investigation, dialogue, and what Bailey and Robinson (1973a, 39) refer to as "that most human of attributes, judgment." At the same time, computer technology would surely be at the center of the gathering and organizing of the corpus of Irish English, however it might be defined. The project would certainly rely on digitalization from beginning to end. The corpus would be placed online as a *Compendium of Irish English*, perhaps accompanied by wiki technology so that users could contribute new words and texts to achieve currency. The *DIEHP* itself would be published online, with resources facilitating its full exploitation by users. Such a project in all its complexity would certainly involve editorial drudgery, but drudgery informed by intellectual challenge, endeavor, and achievement.

Although technology cannot solve some fundamental problems of lexicography, all three of these chapters reveal the rapidly disappearing barrier between print and digital dictionaries and indicate some of the ways dictionary editors and users may work together today to their mutual benefit. As scholars use a combination of printed resources and digital tools, their work in turn will become part of the digital record, to be used by lexicographers and non-lexicographers alike.

Lexical Collaboration Today

All lexicography is collaborative. Dictionary editors consult over email or at one another's desks about the etymology of *shark* or the shape of a *lof de sugre* or the difference between *still* adj. and *still* adv. In the past, most users of dictionaries remained isolated from the collaborative endeavor. Now that traditional lexicographers are being joined and assisted in achieving lexical currency by amateurs wanting to share in the fun, however, lexicography is more collaborative than ever, as lexicographers, having answered the digital siren, have survived the encounter and come to rejoice in her embrace.

PART IV

English Language Studies and Education

Introduction

The professional study of English has long been associated with the teaching of English, arguably since the first English school grammar, William Bullokar's *A Short Introduction of Guiding to Print, Write, and Reade Inglish Speech* (1580), and the first English dictionary, the schoolteacher Robert Cawdrey's *A Table Alphabeticall* (1604). That relationship has had many benefits, but it has not been without tensions. Fred Newton Scott (1913, 1), a professor at the University of Michigan, identified a central "problem" of English Language Studies:

> It is the fortune of teachers of English—whether good or ill . . . —that they have to do with a subject of universal interest. Not everybody cares about algebra and geometry. A limited number are interested in Cicero and Virgil. Even history and civics and manual training are allowed to be the special property of a fraction of the community. But English is everybody's subject. Everybody uses it; everybody thinks he knows how it should be taught; everybody has some opinion about the success or failure of current methods of teaching it.

The problem isn't that everyone has a stake in the English language, obviously, but that many of the opinions about it are insufficiently informed linguistically, historically, or both. Further, schoolteachers, even those who have taken university courses in the structure and history of English, are often not much more linguistically aware than the educated population at large.

The problem of a century ago has only intensified. Today's English teachers are responsible for increasingly linguistically diverse classrooms, classrooms filled with students who speak a multitude of languages and dialects of English at home—and, outside formal contexts, at school. Teacher education programs and school curricula lag behind the needs of teachers, who ideally should equip these linguistically diverse populations to meet successfully the varied linguistic demands of their lives. These demands go far beyond speaking and writing in a standard variety of English, the traditional goal of much language arts schooling. Students do need to control a standard variety in order to have access to specific educational, social, and professional opportunities; but they also have many reasons to be multilingual/multidialectal in order to navigate their social and sometimes their professional worlds. For too long, the study and celebration of linguistic diversity in courses on language and linguistics at the university has been seen as somehow at odds with the educational aims of the school system, though both share (or at least English language scholars would argue should share) the same social goal: to equip students with the most versatile linguistic repertoire possible.

Achieving this goal may require more information, more deliberation, and less regulation. Imagine a classroom where students are debating when the word *ain't* is and is not acceptable in formal writing—as well as who gets to decide what is "acceptable" in formal writing. Or a classroom where students analyze nonstandard dialects that don't employ third-person singular present tense *-s* (e.g., *she walk*) next to standard varieties that do (e.g., *he walks*) as part of the study of subject-verb agreement. Or a classroom where students critically examine their own language shifting practices—when do they speak one language/dialect versus another, and why?—as part of a conversation about the expectations and linguistic demands of "school language." Such practice would newly envision language arts education at the beginning of the twenty-first century, inspired by research in linguistics and education. It is a vision that aims to affirm students' home languages while expanding their linguistic repertoires, both spoken and written. It is a vision playing out in classrooms throughout Great Britain and Australia—but right now in only a handful of classrooms in the United States. The conversation between educators and linguists in the U.S. has been halting at best, and yet it is of the greatest importance.

The struggle to influence curricula and expand the base of teacher knowledge spanned the twentieth century and endures today. Albert H. Marckwardt (1965, 159) summarized a National Council of Teachers of English report on the relationship between English Language Studies at the university and teaching of English in the schools:

> Published in the December, 1928, issue of the *English Journal*, the report began by calling attention to the considerable gap between a competent knowledge of the English language and the totally unrealistic and inaccurate attitudes and prescriptions of textbooks and classroom teachers. The obvious remedy was the development of a proper course in the English language as part of an adequate teacher training program.

Courses were duly established and required of future teachers of English, but the results were not quite those intended, because school teachers and school curricula are inevitably more responsive to community attitudes and expectations than to ivory tower requirements. So, over the past several decades, some of the most prominent scholars in the field, including William Labov, Geneva Smitherman, Richard W. Bailey, John R. Rickford, Walt Wolfram, Orlando Taylor, and John Baugh, have reached outside the academy and striven to shape educational policy and practice. As the essays in this section suggest, however, the efforts have not always had lasting impacts. Why have linguists, and specifically in this case those with expertise in English Language Studies, had such trouble being heard outside the academy?

It is not for a lack of exciting new scholarship at the intersection of Linguistics and Education. Rickford, Sweetland, and Rickford (2004) provides a comprehensive bibliography of recent research in the area, which is now an invaluable resource for this subfield of English Language Studies. Leading researchers continue to do hands-on work with educators, from Labov's work with the Urban Minorities Reading Project at the University of Pennsylvania to Smitherman's directorship of the African American Language and Literacy Project at Michigan State University. Rebecca Wheeler's work demonstrates the inroads linguists can make working directly with partner teachers in schools (Wheeler and Swords 2006). David W. Brown (2009) has created a curriculum focused on code-switching and academic writing that teachers with no background in linguistics can implement. Walt Wolfram and his students have been more successful than perhaps anyone else at producing resources for the public that explain language variation in American English in accessible, entertaining yet informative ways—including videos, pamphlets, and short books. Recent doctoral dissertations provide persuasive evidence about the effectiveness of different kinds of intervention with teachers and students (e.g., Alim 2004, Reaser 2006, Sweetland 2006). Rickford and Rickford (2000) offers a model for how linguists can write about existing knowledge in the field of English Language Studies in a way that is accessible to a broader audience. And the United States can look to the United Kingdom and Australia for inspiration and exemplars, as these countries have implemented linguistically informed curricula at the national level (cf. Denham and Lobeck forthcoming). Those working in English Language Studies must also look inwards to determine how we can share what we know more effectively.

In 2004, the University of Michigan hosted two panels to commemorate the twenty-fifth anniversary of the Ann Arbor "Black English case" (*Martin Luther King Junior Elementary School Children et al. v. Ann Arbor School District Board*), in order to reflect on gains and remaining challenges in the relationship between Linguistics and Education. Controversy over the status of African American Vernacular English in the schools was not a matter of the distant past: only seven and a half years had passed since the Oakland School Board Resolution on Ebonics, and the public argument that followed proved that, despite the efforts of linguists of several generations, we had made little progress in promoting knowledge about linguistic diversity in order to overcome prejudice against nonstandard varieties of English.

The Ann Arbor Black English case had a promising outcome: the judge determined that Boards of Education are responsible for providing teachers with the best "existing knowledge" about language variation and language attitudes. Yet, thirty years later, and a discouraging eighty years after the NCTE report mentioned previously, most teachers, practicing and in training, still encounter relatively little about American dialects, language variation and change, and common attitudes about variation in English as part of their teacher education or in-service training. The frustration among linguists is almost palpable, and clearly many educators don't yet accept the knowledge linguists have to offer.

John Rickford addressed this frustration directly in his talk in Ann Arbor in 2004, suggesting that linguists may have been heard but not often enough:

> . . . We do need to be more persistent and more skilled in communicating the assumptions and findings of our field to the public. I say persistent because I'm always struck by the fact that linguists always say ... back in 1969 we told the public this. You know, and the analogy I always make is look at advertisers: Colgate doesn't say in 1969 we told you that if you brush with Colgate, your teeth are going to be whiter. They tell you 5200 times a day. And they're going to tell you 5200 times again tomorrow. So I don't know why we should be so surprised that we have to keep saying the message again and again.

Rickford also argued that linguists need to communicate effectively (e.g., in sound bytes for the media and with less jargon for non-linguists), to know more about the scholarship in Linguistics and Education, as well as specifically about reading and writing (different skills from speaking Standard English), and to spend more time working directly with schools and teachers.

The contributions to this section reflect on the valuable work that has been done and contemplate how far there is to go. They also reflect the determination that scholars in English Language Studies bring to the table, to promote the conversation between linguists, those studying and teaching rhetoric and composition, K–12 teachers, teacher educators, students, and the public at large. In a volume published two years after the Ann Arbor Black English case, Richard W. Bailey (1981a, 125) eloquently summarized what is at stake in this work: "In a broader context, the Black English case and others like it address profound issues of national unity and of our willingness to accept the cultural and linguistic diversity that characterizes our society." Schools represent one of the most critical sites for intervention, to bring existing linguistic knowledge to teachers and thereby to students. The high value placed on multiculturalism and diversity in today's educational system can only be enhanced by richer—and righter—understandings of linguistic diversity.

13

African American Language and Education: How Far Have We Come?

GENEVA SMITHERMAN AND
MINNIE QUARTEY-ANNAN
Michigan State University

Only before God and the linguist are all languages equal.

—*W.F. Mackey, 1978*

From the vantage point of the more linguistically enlightened twenty-first century, the "Black Dialect Debates," as they were called back in the day, might strike many readers of this volume as relics of some prehistoric era. That any reasonably sane American, let alone one who was highly educated, would declare "Black Dialect" to be evidence of cognitive deficiency is an assertion beyond racism, bordering on lunacy. Yet that is precisely what twentieth-century linguists were up against as they attacked this line of thought about Black Language behavior, which emanated not only from some sectors of the general public, but also from the Academy (e.g., Deutsch 1963; Bereiter 1965; Bereiter and Engelmann 1966). As linguists stepped up to this challenge, their counter arguments took the form of, for example, the studied deliberation of J. L. Dillard's "Negro Children's Dialect in the Inner City" (1967), the sedate eloquence of William Labov's *The Logic of Nonstandard English* (1970; first published in 1969), and the bold indictment of James Sledd's "Bidialectalism: The Linguistics of White Supremacy" (1969). One of the authors of this chapter, Geneva Smitherman, then a young graduate student, cast her argument in the rhetorical framework of the Black Liberation Movement of that period, asserting that "Black Language is Black Power" (1968).

As we seek to sum up half a century of the Black Linguistic Experience in the educational system, linguist W.F. Mackey's statement haunts us. What has been the impact of English Language Studies on the African American Language Question in the Nation's schools and colleges? In short, how far have we come? In our investigation of this question, we situate language education scholarship on African American Language (hereafter AAL) within the context of the changing, evolving socio-political, legal, ideological, and intellectual currents that spawned this work. While we may mention some descriptive studies of AAL, our emphasis in this chapter is on pedagogical intervention from 1959 to the present day, that is, programs and studies in which knowledge from scholarly research on AAL was applied to language and literacy instruction for AAL-speaking students. Readers interested in a descriptive bibliographic survey are invited to consult Rickford, Sweetland, and Rickford's comprehensive essay-bibliography "African American English and Other Vernaculars in Education" (2004), which assembles and categorizes almost 700 references.

The Black Freedom Struggle and the "New Linguistics"

Beginning around the mid-1950s, two seemingly unrelated movements formed the underpinning of language education programs for AAL speakers from pre-school to college: (1) the societal struggle of Blacks, i.e., "The Black Movement"; and (2) the paradigm shift in conceptions of English grammar, often referred to as the "New Linguistics."

In popular historical chronicles of the Black Freedom Struggle of the mid–twentieth century, particularly in mass media, the origin of the Civil Rights Movement is commonly marked by Rosa Parks's refusal to surrender her seat to a White passenger and the subsequent bus boycott which catapulted Dr. Martin Luther King, Jr., to national leadership. However, many Black historians contend that the Movement began the year before Parks's historic action, on May 17, 1954, with the U.S. Supreme Court ruling in *Brown* that mandated an end to separate and (un)equal education. As Black resistance took center stage, the System sought to address Black grievances about centuries of educational neglect by pouring massive funding into language (as well as other) educational programs. The rationale was that since language is the foundation stone of education, and since AAL was not the language of the school, it needed to be dealt with in order for Blacks to advance in the (soon-to-be) desegregated school systems of the Nation. Further, according to the rationale of that era, since AAL was not the language of the socio-economic mainstream, in order for Blacks to be absorbed into the (soon-to-be) equal work force, they would need to master the speech of the dominant group.

In this same historical moment American linguistics was reinventing itself, breaking away from anthropology, philosophy, literary studies, and rhetoric, and emerging as a distinct discipline that would challenge not only behaviorist conceptions of language but also Latinate-based, prescriptivist paradigms of English that had reigned for generations in classrooms. A major consequence of this paradigm shift was the development of descriptive grammars of English based on objective observation, rather than preconceived norms. English language pedagogy was fundamentally influenced by the theory, in both Structural and Generative Linguistics, of a descriptive linguistics, grounded in the organic grammar of English. As Beryl Loftman Bailey (1968, 15), the first Black woman linguist, put it, "If we have in recent years come to regard pattern practice as an essential feature of our language program, it is because the linguist has substituted his more scientific view of the structure of the language for the rules of an earlier era." Accompanying this paradigm shift was a sense of optimism and excitement about the potential of these new conceptualizations of language for English teachers. Lloyd even went so far as to contend that the "New Linguistics" was "a promised land for the English teacher" (1953, 43). Linguistics seemed to hold the potential to contribute to the resolution of a host of social and pedagogical issues, including an accurate and sophisticated understanding of AAL and its speakers. Bailey stated that "more and more teachers are learning that linguistics can help both inside and outside the classroom" (1968, 15). Central to these efforts were William Labov's 1960's pioneering methods and frameworks, with which he analyzed the language system and reading failures of Black children in Harlem.

Typically, the application of what came to be called the "linguistic method" in pedagogy for AAL speakers took the form of oral pattern practice drills and contrastive analysis exercises. Instruction focused on explicit comparisons of features in AAL and "Standard English" (hereafter, Language of Wider Communication/LWC) in order to call the student's attention to the differences between them and provide practice in using LWC patterns. For example,

> John <u>work</u> every day.
>
> John <u>works</u> every day.

In some versions of the "linguistic method," the above patterns would be labeled "Home Talk" and "School Talk" respectively.

A repetition drill technique was often used. For example, in teaching copula use, a taped voice would use a sentence with a form of *be*, and the student would repeat that sentence, thus:

> We're in the English class.
>
> I'm in my seat.
>
> The teacher is near the desk.

Feigenbaum (1970) provides an exhaustive discussion, with illustrative examples in AAL and LWC, of the techniques used in this kind of pedagogical intervention.

In the 1960s and '70s, dozens, if not hundreds, of programs of this nature were established in K–12 curricula and schools, community and technical colleges, four-year colleges and research universities, job corps training programs, and in other institutional venues in Black communities across the Nation. However, the written historical record is sparse because so many educators and other professionals administering and teaching in such programs did not publish nor widely disseminate information about their programs or the results of these endeavors. As linguist Orlando Taylor states, ". . . a search of the literature reveals few reports of on-going programs . . . or comparative analyses of the ones which do exist. . . . The result is that researchers and practitioners typically have little knowledge of the extent to which educational philosophy and linguistic theory . . . have been translated into pedagogical practice, or the results of those efforts which have been attempted" (1983, 36).

Ruth Golden's 1959 study at Detroit's Central High School is the first documented language education study of AAL speakers using the "linguistic method" (Golden 1960, 1962). Golden's research consisted of a control group that followed the standard, traditional, Latinate-based grammar outline for the course while the experimental group followed contrastive analysis and pattern practice methodology. They participated in 13 half-hour speech and listening drills on tape, based on patterns of AAL that "deviated" from "Standard English." The same oral test was administered to both groups before and after the experiment. Golden reports that the experimental group's post-test score was almost twice as high as that of the control group. Notwithstanding her claims of success, there was no measurement of the students' oral language in natural, extemporaneous discourse, nor was there any follow-up to assess whether or not their acquisition of those "Standard English" patterns was lasting.

In 1965, Charles G. Hurst, a high school dropout who later became a college president, was head of the Speech Department at Howard University. He took a group of 1,209 first-year college students and performed a battery of tests to divide the population into three proficiency groups: high, moderate, and low. He then randomly selected 140 students from the low-proficiency group for experimental and control groups that focused on treatments for what he termed *dialectolalia,* a speech condition that "interferes with communication, and often causes its possessors to be maladjusted" (1965, 1). He equated dialectolalia with Negro Dialect. The study evenly divided the students into seven groups, ranging from no treatment to varying degrees of involvement in the university's Speech Clinic, remedial language/speech classes, and counseling sessions. All students were administered pre- and post-tests of phonological discrimination, a reading passage, and a one-minute impromptu speech. Each subject's performance was recorded, and a panel of judges rated the speakers' proficiency levels.

Hurst's results were less dramatic than he had predicted. The most surprising and crippling result was the performance of the group whose treatment incorporated all elements of a complete remedial speech/language program: these students increased a mere 0.03 points, far from the average increases of groups who did not receive "the more extensive and inclusive treatment [and] remedial procedures" (50). Hurst's study, however, did confirm that ignorance is not bliss: the students in the control group—who received no treatment and no information about their performance on the battery of tests they had taken at the outset of the experiment—showed a 0.34 point *drop*. Nonetheless, he concluded that a "comprehensive and efficacious remedial program" could cure all students of dialectolalia, i.e., Negro speech (59). For the historical record, it is important to note that Hurst (1968) later repudiated this work.

Language programs of this period, like Golden's and Hurst's, reflect design problems, inconsistent and incomplete results, and a questionable pedagogical philosophy. The implicit (and sometimes explicit) goal of such programs was linguistic eradication, eliminating the student's Black speech patterns and replacing them with LWC. Yet, these students' speech community—home, community, church, peers, social life, etc.—was immersed in AAL; its use was appropriate. Thus, there was little or no real world reinforcement of the LWC patterned drills they heard and practiced in the language lab or the speech classroom. And significantly, on the larger social level, such linguistic eradication programs were completely out of step with the "I'm Black and I'm proud" language ideology of 1960s and '70s African America.

More realistic applications of the "New Linguistics" to the complex language issues confronting AAL speakers were the programs under San-Su C. Lin at Claflin University, South Carolina, and the summer research program of Beryl L. Bailey at Tougaloo College, Mississippi. Lin's research design encompassed both speech and writing from 1961–1964. Rather than pattern practice and contrastive analysis drills of stilted, artificial sentences, Lin recorded language patterns from a wide range of real-world sources—literary selections, humorous stories and anecdotes, and informative selections on a variety of topics of general interest. Students developed essay topics from the recordings and read their essays aloud for discussion and feedback from their peers. Practice with extended, extemporaneous discourse came with small group role-playing activities to practice the patterns they had worked on in the language laboratory. Although Lin reports some success in giving students greater control in the use of LWC patterns, she cautiously notes that this control was in "delicate balance" and that a different mood or speech situation could trigger the use of the students' community speech (1965, 142).

Bailey's research compared the speech and writing of 100 pre-freshmen students at Tougaloo College during the summer of 1965. The written language of students entering Tougaloo each year "fell well below national norms" (1968, 20); Bailey hypothesized that this was due to the influence of the students' speech. For example:

In the speech:	*It was* about fifteen girls participating in this. *It's not* enough room for one thing.
In the written language:	*It's one* thing about the building that makes it really unique. *It isn't* but two ways to spend a vacation. (1968, 21)

A clear exception to the replication of the students' speech patterns in their writing was in the case of what Rickford calls the "showcase variable" (1999, 62), that is, invariant *be* (as in *He be slow*). This pattern was found only infrequently in the Tougaloo students' writing although it occurred with great frequency in their speech. For this feature, Bailey's results are consistent with all later studies of the writing of AAL-speaking students, including Smitherman's large-scale writing research on 17-year-old students in the National Assessment of Educational Progress (see Smitherman and Wright 1983; Smitherman 1992, 1994). While not a pedagogical intervention as such, Bailey's Tougaloo research is significant because it was one of the first language education studies to investigate the question of the relationship between AAL students' speech and writing. While Bailey's discussion and descriptive lists lack the rigor of quantitative analysis and tests of statistical significance, her pioneering work laid the foundation for future studies of AAL-speaking students. Smitherman's (1969) doctoral dissertation, comparing the speech and writing of Grade 7–9 students, was one of these "future studies." Her research was conducted under the wise, guiding hand of Dr. Richard W. Bailey, to whom this volume is dedicated. Bailey was at that time a new, young Assistant Professor at the University of Michigan (Ann Arbor), who, as Smitherman told one of her Movement comrades, is the "only one, this low-on-the-totem-pole-professor, among all these big-time ranking full prof. White cats on my committee, who understand what uhm doin." Smitherman's dissertation project and her subsequent writing studies expanded Beryl Bailey's research vision to encompass a language variation research design, discourse framework, and statistical analyses.

Last, we note that research in ethnolinguistic communities enjoyed the support of the Center for Applied Linguistics (CAL) in Washington, DC. Among other things, CAL established an "Urban Language Series" to make the results of sociolinguistic research on African American and other socio-ethnic urban groups available to disciplines and audiences beyond linguistics. Under the editorship of linguist Roger W. Shuy, CAL published six important volumes in these early years (Labov 1966; Shuy, Wolfram, and Riley 1968; Baratz and Shuy 1969; Wolfram 1969; Fasold and Shuy 1970; and Loman 1968).

The Emergence of Black Linguists and Other Black Scholars

One major result of the fierce struggles of Black people for equity, social justice, and power in the Black Freedom Struggle of the 1960s and 1970s was the emergence of a critical mass of Black intellectuals, academic scholars, and researchers. According to Blackwell (1981), more than 80 percent of all Black PhDs in the four hundred–year existence of U.S. slave descendants were produced between 1960 and 1980. The fruits of the Civil Rights and Black Power Movements were clearly evident in this unparalleled emergence of sizable numbers of Black scholars in most of the disciplines of the Academy, particularly the Humanities and Social Sciences. These scholars had borne witness to the turbulent social transformation of the 1960s and '70s. Some had been Movement activists, and even though the Reagan-Bush Presidency was beginning to launch the "Second Reconstruction" (Walters 1993), they still, to borrow from a popular Hip Hop saying, had Black Liberation on they minds and they minds on Black Liberation.

In his analysis of *King v. Ann Arbor* (the "Black English" Federal court case of 1977–1979), Labov addresses the impact of the emergence of Black linguists in the field:

> [B]lack scholars now . . . define the role that their white allies can play in advancing the study of Black English. The significance of these events has to be seen in a larger context of the history of the black people in America. Members of an oppressed people have entered an academic field, taken up the tools of linguistic research, and used them for the advancement of their nation. The forerunners of this movement were isolated and ignored during their lifetimes. In Lorenzo Turner's last years, he could not find anyone to take his notes and records into safe keeping; he died believing that his work was wasted and forgotten. When Beryl Bailey died, she was bitterly aware that her research was for the most part set aside, her book out of print, her contributions ignored. This is the experience of the black scholar in the white man's world. The Ann Arbor trial marks a turning point in this dismal history. The trial was the initiative of black people: the mothers of the Green Road children, the lawyer Kenneth Lewis, the linguist Geneva Smitherman, and many other members of the black community. The whites who have been privileged to play an auxiliary role in this affair know that they are marginal to the success that was achieved. The only permanent advance in the condition of life in any field occurs when people take their own affairs into their own hands. I believe that this is true of the study of Black English as it is true everywhere. (1982, 195–196)

Among the critical mass of Black scholars that emerged during the 1960–1980 era was the powerful interdisciplinary team of Gary Simpkins (clinical psychologist), Grace Holt (linguist), and Charlesetta Simpkins (reading specialist). Simpkins, Holt, and Simpkins were architects of the *Bridge* reading series (1974, 1977), designed to raise the literacy skills of AAL-speaking youth. We shall return to their particular pedagogical intervention after a brief overview of the issues surrounding "dialect readers" for AAL-speaking students.

In the 1960–1980 era, there were furious debates over the necessity for and usefulness of "dialect readers." One line of thought was that the problem of Black children's reading failures should be addressed by changing teacher attitudes toward AAL and training teachers to understand the patterns of AAL (e.g., Goodman and Buck 1973). Thus teachers would be able to differentiate between a child's actual mistakes in decoding words in a reading text and mere variations in the pronunciation of words in the text. An opposing line of thought was that the mismatch between the child's AAL and the language of school reading materials was a significant factor in "reading retardation" (Cullinan 1974) in Black youth. To reduce this mismatch, some educators and language scholars proposed the development of dual reading materials, one in AAL and a companion version in LWC. For example, the Education Study Center in Washington, DC, under the direction of educator Joan Baratz and linguist William Stewart, produced readers like *Ollie*:

Here go Ollie.	This is Ollie.
Ollie have a big family.	Ollie has a big family.
He have three sisters.	He has three sisters.
A sister name Brenda . . .	A sister named Brenda . . .

(Education Study Center, 1970, quoted in Cullinan, 1974, 146)

Such readers—and there were others around the country—were problematic for a number of reasons. Not only did they lack cultural depth, but the language used was often stilted and unnatural. Additionally, there were slippages in the printed representations of AAL, and they displayed content and characterization reflective of, or at least bordering on, stereotype. Further, some of these interventions had no systematic evaluation component; others lacked controls or had very small sample sizes.

Although *Bridge* falls into the category of "dialect readers," its vision, creative material, rootedness in Black Cultural Reality, East and West Coast pilot studies, and national field test locate it in a class all its own. The vision for *Bridge* originated with the late Gary Simpkins, who had experienced and witnessed miseducation and reading failure in school, especially among young Black males. On a break from Black

Power activism, he created *Bridge* while a Harvard graduate student in psychology, reflecting on his own educational experiences and those of his peers during their journey through the K–12 system and committing himself to producing work that would break the cycle of educational failure and powerlessness of Black people.

Grounded in the Associative Bridging technique—from the known to the unknown, in this instance, from reading in AAL to reading in LWC—*Bridge* pushed the envelope for "dialect readers." The stories, some from Black Folk Tradition (e.g., "Shine," "Stagolee," "the Signifyin Monkey") and others written by Simpkins himself, were sophisticated enough to hold the attention of an AAL-speaking adolescent used to running the streets, who was several grades behind in reading level. The Program consisted of five reading booklets, beginning with stories in AAL and ending with stories in LWC, with booklets in between containing stories written in a transitional language variety, a combination of AAL and LWC. Stories told in more than one linguistic version were not simple, literal, word-for-word translations but language constructed as it would be used in a natural language environment. To ensure that students didn't rely solely on their memory of earlier versions of a story as they worked through the series, names of characters and certain other details were changed although the basic plot remained the same. There were study books with questions and exercises (e.g., on figures of speech, vocabulary or "word bridging"), Peer Control stories, and cassette recordings of Black voices reading some of the stories. Finally, there was an annotated Teacher's Edition for each study book and a comprehensive Teacher's Guide to the entire program.

The national field test of *Bridge*, conducted in 1975, was designed to assess the effectiveness of the Program in the real world conditions of classrooms in five distinct locations to capture the ubiquity of the problem and the universality of a common solution. The subjects were 540 students in 27 classes, Grades 7–12. Fourteen teachers participated in the experiment, teaching both experimental (*Bridge*) and control (traditional remedial reading program) classes. Students spent four months (one hour a day, five days a week) in the Program. Pre- and post-test reading scores were obtained using the Iowa Test of Basic Skills in Reading Comprehension, Level 12. The results indicated that the *Bridge* students had a mean gain of 6.2 months in reading level in the four months of instruction whereas the control group only had a mean gain of 1.6

months in the four months of instruction (Simpkins and Simpkins 1981, Simpkins 2002). These statistically significant results demonstrate the crucial importance of pedagogical intervention if Black students are ever to catch up. Further, the fact that the control group did not even make at least a four-month gain in four months of reading instruction lends credence to the tragic axiom that the longer Black kids stay in school, the further behind they get (see, e.g., Rickford and Rickford 2000; Simpkins 2002).

In addition to the need for the national field test, the Simpkins team (which included Grace Holt along with Gary and Charlesetta Simpkins) also thought it imperative to address teacher knowledge about and attitudes toward language in general and AAL in particular. The Simpkins team approached Smitherman about developing a handbook for teachers to accompany the *Bridge* Series; their thinking was that Smitherman's manuscript-in-progress might serve as that handbook. The manuscript was Smitherman's *Talkin and Testifyin: The Language of Black America* (1977). Amidst voluminous works on AAL by Whites during the 1960s and '70s, *Talkin and Testifyin* stood alone as a major contribution to the subject by a Black scholar, widely and favorably reviewed in both scholarly and mainstream (e.g., *New York Times*) circles. It did not, however, become a companion piece to *Bridge*, which was doomed. Despite its proven effectiveness in the pilot studies and especially in the national field test, and despite a reasoned and rather favorable article on *Bridge* by Sheils and Manning in *Newsweek* (December 20, 1976), Houghton Mifflin capitulated to social pressure, delayed the release of the series, and eventually canceled its publication altogether.

Opposition to *Bridge* centered on its use of AAL as pedagogical intervention, coupled with the Program's "failure" to condemn AAL and put forth a linguistic eradicationist message (see, e.g., Simpkins 2002). Even though the end goal is school/academic/LWC literacy, implicit in the conceptualization and implementation of *Bridge*—which celebrates Black folk and community heroes talkin that talk—is the ideological value of bilingualism/biculturalism. This was fundamental to motivating students to buy into the Program and to addressing their linguistic insecurity. While objection to *Bridge* came from a variety of societal sectors, including White professionals, it was the vociferous opposition from the Black middle class that sounded the death knell for the Program. At the same time, the *Bridge* team's experience with Black community leaders, working class parents, activists, and inner-city teachers was highly positive. Once they understood the pedagogical philosophy, goals, and vision of *Bridge*, that the Program was designed to raise the reading levels of students by bridging the known (AAL) with the unknown (LWC), they were strongly supportive.

Another group of scholars who emerged during the 1960-1980 period whose story parallels that of the *Bridge* team was the Language Curriculum Research Group (LCRG), comprised of Carol Reed, Milton Baxter, and Sylvia Lowenthal, college writing instructors. Their pedagogical intervention, launched from 1969–1974, grew out of their teaching of composition in SEEK (Search for Education, Elevation, and Knowledge), an academic support program for open admissions students at City University of New York (CUNY). The LCRG developed a student text and a teachers' manual "for teaching standard English writing to speakers showing Black English influences in their writing" (1973). The LCRG also conducted teacher training workshops for composition instructors at Brooklyn College and other colleges in the CUNY system. The student text included folk and popular song lyrics, short stories—some presented in several English varieties, e.g., "Black English Vernacular (BEV)," "Guyanese Creole," "White nonstandard English"—taped excerpts reflecting various dialect voices, mass media excerpts, Black Arts poetry, disc jockeys' and entertainers' raps, and sample essays for discussion and revision. The explicit philosophy of the intervention was bilingualism, with instruction designed to teach written literacy in the LWC, as well as to convey to students the systematic, complex, and varied nature of their language. Contrastive analysis of grammatical patterns was taught in the context of essays and reading selections, rather than as isolated, decontextualized sentences. In this connection, the teachers' manual distinguished patterns of spoken AAL in these college students' compositions (e.g., *She at they house now*) from errors common to all student writers (e.g., *who/whom* distinction). Importantly, these SEEK students conducted ethnographic research on AAL in their communities, including their own language use, and the LCRG team incorporated these data into the textbook. Although course evaluations by students and teachers using the LCRG materials were highly positive, Reed, Baxter, and Lowenthal were not only unsuccessful in getting their manual published—they were rejected by every publisher they contacted—but they also eventually lost their Ford Foundation backing.[1]

The failure of Black progressive pedagogical interventions can be read as a master narrative of class conflict in the Black community. Class contradictions in the previously unified, segregated Black Nation were just beginning to form in the desegregating social order of the 1970's with the beginnings of a historically unparalleled middle class formation of U.S. slave descendants made possible by the social, economic, and political fruits of the Black Movement. In the case of the LCRG, as with *Bridge*, rejection by the Black middle class was crucial; some even objected to the LCRG's inclusion of too much Black Arts ("Black Pride") literature. Typical of Black middle class reaction was the pronouncement of Roy Wilkins, then HNIC (head Negro in charge) of the National Association for the Advancement of Colored People (NAACP), who dismissed the project as "black nonsense" in *Ebony* Magazine. Additionally, in "Black Nonsense," an editorial in *Crisis,* the NAACP journal, the argument was put forth that these Black CUNY students' language was "basically the same slovenly English spoken by the South's under-educated poor white population" and that "it is time to repudiate this black nonsense and to take appropriate action against institutions which foster it in craven capitulation to the fantasies of the extreme black cultists and their pale and spineless sycophants" (1971, 78).

There was even deep-seated middle class Black rejection of the Federal court case, *Martin Luther King Junior Elementary School Children Et Al. v. Ann Arbor School District Board.* Although it came to be sensationalized as the "Black English Case," the broader, and in a sense, the more profound issue was about the School District's violation of the children's right to equal educational opportunity, as provided for in the 1974 Equal Educational Opportunity Act. As Richard W. Bailey, who joined the expert witness team a few months before the trial in 1979, stated, the *King* case "can easily be summed up . . . by saying that it concerned the task of teaching little children to read" (1981a, 94). Smitherman served as the chief expert witness for the children from 1977, when Attorneys Kenneth Lewis and Gabe Kaimowitz filed the lawsuit, through the four-week trial in July, 1979. In his ruling, Judge Joiner quoted extensively from linguistic research on AAL and relied on expert witness testimony in his decision. He mandated that the Ann Arbor School Board had to "take into account" the children's "Black English" in the teaching of literacy skills.

As local and national media focused on *King,* word spread about the "Black English Case." From the very beginning, Lewis, Kaimowitz, and Smitherman, along with the mothers of the children, endured the slings and arrows of Black middle class consciousness, such as that from June Brown, then a popular local journalist, who attacked the morality of the children's single mothers as cause for the poor performance of the children. Writing in *The Detroit News* a month before the trial in June, 1979, she argued that "mothers whose children can't read should get the boyfriends out and get the books in."[2]

Post-*King* Pedagogical Interventions

By the time of the *King* trial in July of 1979, pedagogical intervention studies for AAL speakers had come to a halt. The U.S. was increasingly conservative on the social, political, and educational fronts. For Blacks, the mood of America shifted from change and promise to stagnation and dreams deferred. In the previous generation, there had been a plethora of studies and language education programs for AAL speakers, with generous support and resources from government agencies, private foundations, and school systems. However, beginning with what late political scientist Ronald Walters calls the "Second Reconstruction" in 1980, this support was significantly reduced. And the "numerous" interventions that educators and linguists had predicted would be conducted after the *King* decision failed to materialize.

While there has been important AAL research since 1979, most has been descriptive or theoretical, rather than pedagogically grounded, though there are exceptions (e.g., Brooks 1985). To be sure, in the 1980's and 1990's, some teachers within the confines of their individual classrooms had to have been takin care of bidness for at least some of the country's AAL youth. Otherwise, a young language scholar like Minnie Quartey-Annan, from Valdosta, Georgia, would not have emerged to co-author this chapter. Nonetheless, the earlier momentum of pedagogical intervention for AAL speakers has never been regained.

One effort at resurrecting this momentum is the *Academic English Mastery Program* (AEMP) of the Los Angeles Unified School District, established in 1990-91 under the direction of Noma LeMoine. AEMP focuses on the success of several groups of students of Color—African Americans, Native Americans, Mexican Americans, and Hawaiian Americans—referred to as Standard English Learners (SELs). Integrating contrastive analysis, African American literature, rhetoric and culture, and instructional strategies for enhancing writing and speaking, with the goal of increasing and enhancing students' general and academic use of "Mainstream English Language (MEL)," while leaving intact their competency and use of their home language, AEMP strikes us as the pedagogical offspring of LCRG and *Bridge*.

Maddahian and Sandamela (2000) evaluated AEMP and found the results positive and promising. They studied students at 16 elementary schools (treatment/experimental group) drawn from the 31 AEMP schools and 4 comparable schools without AEMP (control group). All of the schools had over 50 percent African American enrollment. Researchers analyzed data from three instruments: (1) pre- and post-tests of writing and speaking; (2) teacher survey; (3) observation check list. Results indicated that while there was a trend (though not statistically significant) in favor of the AEMP group on the speaking assessment, the most "statistically significant and educationally meaningful difference" between the two groups was on the writing assessment, with the AEMP students well outperforming the control group.

In addition to AEMP's innovative curriculum, a major component of the Program is the professional development of teachers. This involves a weeklong summer institute, an educational seminar series, intersession courses, demonstration lessons, and a weekend professional development conference. The goal is to increase teachers' knowledge about linguistic research and provide proven instructional strategies to help SELs achieve positive outcomes (LeMoine and Hollie 2007, 44; see also LeMoine 1999). Further, focus is on teacher language attitudes, an area that several researchers have shown can have negative adverse effects on student performance (e.g., Guskin 1970; Baugh 1999; Smitherman 2000b). However, a major concern for the Program involves the degree of teacher adherence to the Program's instructional strategies. In Hollie's study (2000) and Ai's program evaluation (2002), the issue of implementation was raised. For example, contrastive analysis, a key AEMP instructional strategy, was not practiced in 82.9 percent of the 41 second and third grade AEMP classrooms observed in Ai's 2001 evaluation. (One limitation to this finding might be that each teacher was observed only once, albeit for an entire day.) Both Hollie and Ai investigated the relationship between degree of implementation and student performance, but with conflicting results. Hollie found that the student writing scores of the teacher implementing the program at the highest level showed the greatest gains (155). In contrast, Ai concluded that degree of implementation "did not matter with respect to. . .the writing test" (35). That said, Ai did find that several AEMP instructional strategies were "positively related to student achievement in reading, language, and attitudes toward reading: modeling correct language use, having a positive attitude toward African American language, and incorporating technology into instruction" (2002, 37).

Carol Lee's concern about AAL speaking students' low reading levels led her to develop an instructional approach focusing on the Black Verbal Tradition of Signification, a.k.a. Signifyin(g). This communication style invokes figurative language, double-voicedness, humor, and social critique and employs commonly used ritual insults, or novel, extended discourse (see e.g., Labov 1972; Smitherman 1977, 2000b). Although Signification has existed in the Black Oral Tradition at least since 1619, the work of Dr. Claudia Mitchell-Kernan (1968) brought this long-standing AAL discourse pattern to the attention of linguists. More recently, Henry Louis Gates established the case for an expanded form of Signifyin(g) as a fundamental trope in African American Literature, particularly that written by women (1988).

Lee (1993) hypothesized that instruction that tapped into Black students' prior social knowledge and their skill in signifyin would advance students' achievement in "the broad category of inferential levels of [reading] comprehension" and in "complex implied relationships" (46). She selected six classes in two public, urban, virtually all-Black high schools in Chicago (N=160). Four of the classes were taught using the experimental instructional unit; there were two control classes which received no treatment and were taught according to the regular high school English curriculum. The instructional unit was comprised of signifyin dialogue, instruction in the characteristics of signifyin, articles by African American writers and scholars, students composing their own signifyin dialogues, and reading and interpreting two novels, Hurston's *Their Eyes Were Watching God* (1935) and Walker's *The Color Purple* (1982), focusing on signifyin in the texts.

Lee's "signifyin" intervention resulted in the experimental group gaining significantly more skill than the control group in reading skills and in interpreting fiction. The gain was "a broad ratio of three to one"

(91). Further, signifyin knowledge and prior social knowledge correlated with gains in reading scores from pre- to post-test. Lee's qualitative discourse analysis of classroom talk concluded that "the experimental classes were characterized by an on-going focus on difficult, inferential questions, by an on-going expectation that students would consistently refer to the text as an initial source of explication, and by a concern with the figurative or metaphoric aspects of the texts" (126). In the control classes, the level of discussion tended to focus simply on the plot of the texts and discussions about characters' motives and intentions. Lee concludes that "the effectiveness of this instructional model is important precisely because it enabled students who are academically marginal to interpret figuratively dense works of fiction and answer difficult inferential questions of those texts. The students who started out the weakest were the students who achieved the greatest gain" (135).

While Lee focused on AAL speakers and reading, Hanni U. Taylor and Elaine Richardson concentrated on AAL speakers and writing. As a teacher of college writing for AAL speakers, Taylor (1989) tapped into her experiences as a native German speaker of a variety (Hessian) far from "Hoch Deutsch" and as an immigrant to the U.S. who spoke English with an accent. She began her research in the late 1970's at Aurora University, located in one of Chicago's western suburbs. Taylor notes that her interest in the educational achievement of AAL-speaking students was sparked when "Lester," a fifth-year senior at Aurora, from the South Side of Chi-town, was sent to her office by the Dean of Students because "he didn't talk right and didn't write right" (1). Yet, Lester was "bright, an athlete and assistant coach, as well as a leader" among his peers. Her initial work with the Lesters among Aurora's Black student body focused strictly on "linguistic performance, specifically writing performance," but she came to realize that this approach was "overly constrictive" (24). She learned that she had to be attuned to the "entire *gestalt* of their cultural experience" (24; emphasis hers). In 1983, she formalized her approach, and launched her experiment, "Project Bidialectalism." Twenty student volunteers participated for one semester, meeting for weekly sessions in Aurora's Learning Assistance Center. Half of the students were assigned to the control group, who were taught according to the regular first-year writing curriculum, which focused only on LWC. The other half were taught by Taylor's "Project Bidialectalism" method, which used not only contrastive analysis, but also incorporated "cultural frameworks in which linguistic choices are embedded" (101), the counseling-learning method, and heightened "ethnosensitivity" (103).

Students produced pre- and post-test essays which Taylor and an English Department colleague used to assess writing progress. Taylor coded "10 categories of interference from black English to standard English" (149), which had been produced in essays by Black students over a period of five years—e.g., third person singular *-s* ("home is where everybody know you and feel special there"); deletion of the copula ("There __ a path that leads from the farmhouse to the wooden barn") (149). At the end of the semester, the experimental group reduced the total occurrence of the 10 AAL patterns in their writing by 59.3 percent. The control group, however, *increased* the total occurrence of these features by 8.5 percent. On the one hand, Taylor's study is significant for its creative use of cultural materials as well as its philosophical, sociocultural perspective—what she refers to as "ethnosensitivity"—in combination with Contrastive Analysis and audio-lingual skills instruction. On the other hand, the focus on ten grammatical patterns as the sole criterion for assessing the students' writing is insufficient to measure their acquisition of written academic discourse.

Elaine Richardson (1996; see also Richardson 2003) implemented her pedagogical intervention in the college writing classroom at two different Midwestern universities. She designed and taught semester-long courses with five orientations: (1) Afrocentricity, (2) politicizing literacy and difference, (3) position, (4) Signifyin(g), and (5) bi-dialectal/contrastive approach to teaching academic writing (1996, 59). Students produced three essays: an impromptu pre- and post-writing sample and a "polished" essay that they worked on for several weeks during the semester. The prompt for the pre- and post-essay was excerpted from Gates (1988): "What does it mean to be a member of the AAVE culture (Black) and literate (write)?" This inquiry was designed "to explore an aspect of AAVE political-literate tradition, writing/speaking the self into subjectivity" (72). For the polished essay, Richardson used a passage from Bormann (1971) that explored the rhetorics of unity and divisiveness.

Richardson and a panel of Composition Studies experts rated students' pre- and post-essays using a 4.0 scale. These ratings were the basis for dividing students into three groups (high, medium, and low). Although the results did not reach statistical significance, change was apparent in the students' writing: the number of students in the low category decreased by 20 percent while those in the high category more than doubled.

Of course we can only hope, but there must be several programs going on every day, many of them unreported or undocumented, although many may be falling by the wayside. An unfortunate loss in the struggle. But all ain't lost yet. Notable, established, and up-and-coming programs are still on the grind, tightening the slack. Walt Wolfram has been making dents in the education of linguistically diverse students for a long time (see e.g., Wolfram 1999; Wolfram et al. 1999). He and Ralph Fasold created *The Study of Social Dialects in American English* (1974), believed to be the first textbook on social dialectology. Through the use of dialect awareness programs, which Wolfram defines as "activities that are directed toward promoting an understanding of and appreciation for language variation" (2004, 16), students are introduced to the different varieties of a language, which are taken as different but equal systems. The approach demands that students conduct hands-on data collection, analysis, and presentation of findings; they are encouraged to become researchers and "observant participants" in their own communities.

The DeKalb Bidialectal Communication Program in DeKalb County, Georgia, under the direction of Kelli Harris-Wright, has been in operation since the late 1980s (Harris-Wright 1999). The program focuses on students in grades five through eight, emphasizing the "explicit teaching" model, which employs Contrastive Analysis and a "mind map." As students become more familiar and comfortable with the process, teachers transition them into literary texts and employ the same strategy. Harris-Wright reports greater gains for students on the Iowa Test of Basic Skills, and teachers report that as a result of this pedagogical intervention, students begin to make the transition from home to school language more easily.

Arthur Palacas, linguistics and composition professor at the University of Akron, has created a curriculum focusing on the "liberation of Ebonics from English." He argues that "an unbridgeable chasm separates the grammatical systems of these two languages" (2001, 340) and that students perform better when they view their home language and the language of the academy as two separate entities, not simply the former being a broken form of the latter. Currently amassing evaluative data, Palacas reports a number of testimonial examples of student success. For example, one of his students had failed Business Writing three times with the same professor. When she took Palacas's composition class and the Business Writing class simultaneously, she passed the Business Writing class with a B+. That professor asked her what had changed, and she explained that she now had an understanding that Standard English and Black English were different languages, allowing her to "split the two languages in her thinking and to monitor the difference more effectively" (346).

Writing continues to be a major concern in twenty-first century pedagogical interventions for AAL speakers, whether on the college or elementary school level. Sweetland (2006) created a ten-week program that infuses the writing process with a sociolinguistic flavor by focusing on language variation in the elementary classroom. Contending that "learning about sociolinguistic variation makes a positive difference for teachers and for learners" (4), Sweetland implemented a program in Cincinnati that incorporated four elements: the writing process, dialect awareness, teacher awareness, and contrastive analysis. Previous intervention programs generally included a cross-section of two or three of these elements at most.

Data was gathered from thirteen classes, Grades 4–6, with 188 students and 13 teachers. There were three groups of students in the study: (1) a no treatment (NT) group whose teachers received no training or support from the researcher and taught the school district's mandated curriculum; (2) a partial treatment, writing process group (WP) whose teachers received a three-day training course and an entire quarter's worth of materials and lesson plans for teaching writing; (3) a full treatment, sociolinguistic approach (SA) group whose teachers were given all of the treatment of the WP group, plus seven literature-based lessons on language variation, and direct instruction on four points of grammar that differentiate AAL from Standard English.

Measures to evaluate the treatments included pre- and post-writing samples, a Writer Self-Perception Survey, teacher attitude surveys, lesson evaluations, and interviews. Sweetland concluded that the SA group produced the most positive results, in terms of teacher language attitudes and impact on student literacy and language achievement. Students in the SA group demonstrated "greater facility with Standard English grammar than students . . . taught using either traditional, textbook-based methods or the writing process approach" (212). Further, according to the Six Traits model of writing (ideas/content, organization, voice, word choice, fluency, conventions), the SA group made greater gains in each area of writing than the other two groups. Importantly, when the writing was gauged in terms of overall writing scores, the SA group's performance was also outstanding. Considering the SA group's greater gain over that of the WP group, Sweetland concluded that "absent culturally responsive adaptations, such as attention to sociolinguistic differences, the writing process approach does not fulfill its promise for African American learners" (217).

Minnie Quartey-Annan (2006) has created a set of materials to better equip teachers to deal with students from diverse linguistic backgrounds. CUSP (Cultural Understanding and Specialized Praxis) looks at the language and literacy learning process as involving three levels of interaction: the community, the classroom, and the individual. Designed to expose educators (for all age groups) to critical classroom issues involved in teaching linguistically diverse students, CUSP is a set of supplementary materials educators can customize to fit the needs of particular classes or students. CUSP employs a blend of contrastive analysis with dialect awareness and culturally nuanced materials. Consonant with the goals of programs like LCRG, *Bridge,* and AEMP, Quartey-Annan's introduces culturally sensitive material and understanding into the classroom to mirror the cultural diversity of the students. Focus is on teacher language awareness and understanding. CUSP educates teachers on the differences between AAL and LWC and offers them resources and models they can implement in their classrooms to enhance AAL-speaking students' understanding and use of LWC. CUSP charges educators to use diversity in the classroom as a stepping stone, not a stumbling block, extending "the three R's to include literature that incorporates language variation, writing that looks not at commas but at content, and adding all students into the equation of success, not just LWC speakers"(19).

What Have We Learned? Lessons of the Blood

Turn of the century and early twenty-first century educational intervention research reflects sophisticated research designs and the best that quantitative sociolinguistics, critical discourse analysis, and statistical paradigms have to offer. We are greatly encouraged by the (long overdue!) collaboration of research/academic linguists and educational practitioners— for example in the Linguistic Society of America's establishment of the Language in the School Curriculum Committee, which "explores and pursues ways in which the linguistics community can have an effect on school instruction in language-related topics, including linguistics." Following that mandate, the Committee has opened up professional dialogue and communication with the Language Commission of the National Council of Teachers of English. Another example is the publication of *Code-Switching: Teaching Standard English in Urban Classrooms* (2006), a co-authored textbook by an academic linguist, Rebecca Wheeler, and a classroom teacher, Rachel Swords. It is designed for primary and secondary school classrooms, and is constructed in two segments: (1) theory and research and (2) classroom practice.

What we are seeing today, in 2011, is clearly high quality work. Yet for thousands of African American Language speakers, the literacy achievement gap persists. We need to mount massive, large-scale pedagogical interventions, based on our decades of experience, to address the serious language and literacy achievement gaps among the hundreds of thousands of AAL-speaking students around the country. What we have learned from the past half-century of pedagogical intervention research is that both cognition and affect must be tapped into in order to teach language and literacy skills to AAL-speaking youth. That language must be approached holistically, as a total communication system, not piecemeal. That surface features must be dealt with in the context of larger rhetorical and discourse patterns. That language ideology still ensnares and entraps teachers, students, and the public. As this summary of research and programs demonstrates, lay attitudes are often a huge obstacle to educational initiatives. Educational change can be blocked by public responses (not always well-informed, unfortunately) from parents, teachers, well-known public figures, and journalists.

Finally, we have learned that linguists must be part and parcel of the country's sociopolitical process—we cannot live by research alone—and that the U.S. needs a national multilingual language policy, whereby every citizen will know and respect not only their own native language but will learn and come to know at least one or two other languages (e.g., CCCC 1988; Smitherman 2006). Otherwise, Mackey's admonition, that only before God and the linguist are all languages equal, will continue to hold true.

NOTES

1. Wible (2006) provides a more complete account of the work of Reed, Baxter, and Lowenthal as members of the Language Curriculum Research Group, situating this history within the "Students' Right to Their Own Language" policy of the Conference on College Composition and Communication.
2. A generation later, in 1996, it was members of the Black middle class, such as Maya Angelou, who led the attack against the Oakland, California School Board for its Ebonics Resolution. That Resolution simply put forth the view that the primary/home language of its Ebonics/AAL-speaking children would be used to teach them "Standard English." It should be noted that this is the same Maya Angelou who had achieved literary fame through poetry and fiction imbued with the cadence, rhythms, and sometimes the syntax of AAL.

14

Language and Education: The More Things Change

DENNIS BARON
University of Illinois at Urbana-Champaign

> "You know what you taught us about using descriptive grammar instead of prescriptive, and not covering student papers with lots of red marks? Well, you were wrong."
>
> —*a former student, on seeing me again after three years of teaching English in his own high school classroom*

In this essay I explore the ways that some of the major developments in language use and language scholarship of the past 50 years affected, or failed to affect, the American classroom. The past half-century has seen an explosion in our knowledge about what language is and how it works, and while almost everyone's experience supports the resulting model of language as a dynamic, highly-nuanced, and ever-changing set of practices occurring in complex and fluid social settings, American high schools have often ignored the new linguistic knowledge, retaining the traditional picture of language as a fixed set of universal standards that students must master in order to ensure both successful communication and a good grade.

Research seldom translates directly into class work, and schools have always been slow to incorporate new knowledge, linguistic or otherwise, into the curriculum, but in most fields, once ideas gain currency among specialists, they begin to appear in lesson plans as well. Newtonian principles dominated high school physics long after Einstein's first forays into relativity in the early 1900s, and evolution remains a flash point in the schools well over a century after Darwin's speculations on the origin of species. Nonetheless, today's physics teachers take $e=mc^2$ and the Big Bang as givens, and biologists do the same with DNA and the fossil record. Science teachers tell their students that the world is round, or pear-shaped, or perhaps, for AP students, an oblate spheroid. But twenty-first-century English teachers have typically sidestepped advances in linguistics, content instead with a flat-earth view of grammar and usage that has changed little since it emerged in the eighteenth century.

Over the past two centuries linguistics has deepened our understanding of language history and change, relationships among language families, language acquisition and loss, and the social and political dynamics of language use. In the decades since the 1950s, transformational grammar deepened understanding of the nature of language and provided new tools for analyzing the grammatical structure of English. Sociolinguistic research during the same period has focused closely on the contexts of language use and forced us to consider anew the nature of linguistic variation and change. And at the same time, scholars have broadly expanded our definitions of literacy and how it works, complicating the notions of how to measure reading and writing competence.

Thinking about English has changed in the past half-century, and so have the speakers of English. The U.S. Supreme Court decision in *Brown v. Board of Education* (1954) and the Civil Rights movement of the 1960s forced American schools to confront, as one of the results of school integration, a racial component to language that they had previously ignored. In addition, the Immigration Reform Act of 1965 reopened American borders that had been effectively closed to immigration since

1924, and for the first time since World War I the United States found itself assimilating large numbers of nonanglophones into schools and the workplace, as well as into the social and political fabric of the nation. Government policy makers struggled with the issues sparked by the new American demographic, while linguistic researchers studied the impact of changing integration and immigration patterns on language variety, code switching, language loyalty, bilingualism, and both language and dialect loss.

Sociolinguists during this time came to view standard language, or more neutrally, the language of wider communication, as one of several varieties operating in speech communities, demonstrating as well that speakers often master several varieties of their language, standard and not, in the course of their linguistic development, switching between them as context requires. Nonetheless, American schools cling fast to their traditional goal of teaching the more reductive notion of standard English as correct English, perpetuating the correctness model of language well beyond the schoolroom.

New linguistic knowledge asks us to think of language as—to borrow an analogy from physics—both wave and particle: at the same time certain and ambiguous, logical and erratic, predictable and unexpected, formulaic and innovative. But English teachers have opted to retain a view of language as a stable and finite set of teachable rules, some dealing with language structure but most of them a series of "thou shalt nots" that are essentially linguistic etiquette. They see themselves as the gatekeepers of English, with red pencils and standardized tests poised to measure their students' success, or lack thereof, in mastering the formulas they teach.

It's not that American teachers haven't been exposed to the new linguistic knowledge. Many teacher training programs have given prospective teachers forward-looking ways to work with students speaking stigmatized varieties of English or other languages entirely. As a result, many of today's teachers have learned to reframe traditional subjects like vocabulary and grammar, teaching them not as stand-alone units but integrating them into their literature-based curriculum. These teachers' students look up the meaning of words used in an assigned short story or parse sentences drawn from literature instead of grammar books or grade-level lists created by state departments of education. Teachers chart students' writing progress by means of portfolios rather than fill-in-the-bubble tests. Traditional sentence diagrams give way to the tree diagrams made popular by newer syntactic theories. Teachers are taught to apply their new awareness of the language diversity to help students come to terms with the academic English necessary for school success. A whole-language methodology encourages the teaching of reading and writing as complex, creative, contextualized activities.

All this sounds progressive, and in some cases it actually is. Not all schools, and not all individual teachers, are saying No to new linguistic developments. But all too often, educators do little more than dress up their rigid language attitudes with new catch phrases to make them *seem* up to date.

I have been working with prospective English teachers for more than 30 years, and I've met many teachers whose approach to language is far from regressive. But I learned as well that far too many teachers are not incorporating the lessons they learn into the lessons they teach. Former students regularly report that veteran colleagues and supervisors in the schools tell them to forget what they learned about language in college. In many cases, this reprogramming isn't even necessary. When I question my current students about their language attitudes at various points during the year, I find that despite what we have been reading in class, many of these prospective teachers form their attitudes toward language and their models of appropriate language arts teaching not from what they acquire in college, but from models they absorbed during their own school days. Whatever happened in college doesn't seem to have changed their minds about what school's supposed to be, at least in terms of language and literacy.

We're all immersed in language from cradle to grave, but because the language arts are a major focus of the American classroom, we think of school, not the home, the neighborhood, or the workplace, as the primary site where literacy is taught, refined, and measured. And we consider school the primary site where students speaking languages other than English make their transition to English. It is in the schools, both through periodic testing and through day-to-day interaction, that students may first discover that some people's language use is different from the norm, and perhaps more significantly, that some people's language—maybe even theirs—just isn't up to snuff. At the same time that schools perpetuate misconceptions about standard English, they stimulate the linguistic insecurity that causes many students to doubt their own abilities as competent users of a language they learned long before arriving at school.

We've come to recognize over the past half-century that the classroom is one place where children's language attitudes are challenged, altered, or reinforced, where linguistic confidence is built, eroded, or even shattered. But as the epigraph to this essay suggests, many teachers, once they have students of their own, address issues of language in the classroom much as teachers always have. Teachers today still tend to think of language as a discrete set of skills that can be taught incrementally, then carefully measured and rigorously corrected. When it comes to grammar, usage, spelling, and pronunciation, many teachers still see themselves as arbitrators who must correct every bit of written prose and shape every bit of speech so that it comes out better.

Teachers are pressured to take this corrective approach to English by older colleagues, and by school authorities who see new teachers not as professionals creating and transmitting knowledge, but as employees obliged to follow a preset, teacher-proof curriculum. Whether their aims are idealistic or practical, whether they want to prepare students to think critically, to take their place as well-informed citizens of a strong democracy, to embrace liberal education and pursue life-long active learning, or to simply be employable, many teachers feel their mission is also to teach students not that our language choices are always contextually nuanced, but that there's one and only one appropriate way to speak and write. Looking at how schools have responded to new linguistic developments, we see that somehow they always manage to come back to standard English.

From Black English to Ebonics: The Schools and Language Variety

Two events that call up issues of how the schools respond to language variety frame the period covered by this survey of language and education: the Ann Arbor Black English case in 1979, which underscored the need for educators to understand the language their students bring to the classroom; and the Ebonics resolution in 1996 that put the Oakland, California, School Board on the nation's front pages. While the Ann

Arbor decision promised a progressive approach to educating speakers of nonstandard varieties of English, the controversy over Ebonics showed that thinking about language variety both in the schools and in American society more generally had not progressed at all.

Linguists turned their attention to the English of African Americans in the 1960s. Responding to the claim by the psychologists Carl Bereiter and Siegfried Engelman (1966) that African American four-year-olds were coming to preschool unable to make "statements of any kind" and appeared to have "no language at all," the sociolinguist William Labov clearly demonstrated in his pioneering essay "The Logic of Nonstandard English" (1969) and his book *Language in the Inner City* (1972) that African Americans spoke an expressive, sophisticated, and grammatical dialect of English that followed logical rules that differed in systematic ways from those of standard English. Some educators sought to apply this new knowledge to the education of African American children, either by developing African American English reading texts or creating programs for teaching children to translate from their dialect to standard English. But most schools continued to treat the language of black children as "bad English" in need of correction, or they accepted Bereiter and Engelman's disproven "deficit theory," which suggested that such children needed to be taught English from the ground up once they got to school.

What Happened in Ann Arbor

In 1978, a group of parents sued the Ann Arbor, Michigan School Board in federal court for failing to overcome significant linguistic barriers that prevented their children from becoming academically successful. Supported by expert testimony from linguists like Richard W. Bailey and Geneva Smitherman, attorneys for the plaintiffs argued that the Black English the children spoke was "so different from the English commonly spoken in the public schools as to constitute a language barrier which impedes their equal participation in King School's instructional programs" (King 1978; for a more detailed account of the events surrounding the King decision, see Smitherman 1981, esp. Bailey 1981a, 1981b).

In deciding the case, Judge Charles Joiner acknowledged that "a major goal of a school system is to teach reading, writing, speaking and understanding standard English" (King 1978). He noted that African American parents did not want their students to be taught Black English, a language variety that they already used extensively in their informal communication. The judge acknowledged that the teachers at King School had no trouble understanding their students' variety of English, and the students had no trouble understanding their teachers. Even so, Joiner found that, though not used by all African Americans, yet used by many who are not black, Black English is a dialect related to race. More to the point, he agreed with the plaintiffs' claim that a language barrier prevented children at the school who used Black English in their informal communication from learning to read standard English texts.

Because federal law required the school system to overcome that language barrier, in finding for the plaintiffs the court directed the school district to remedy the situation. In response, the Ann Arbor School Board offered a two-part plan. It would create a program to teach the district's teachers about "the contrasting features of black English and standard English, the identification of black English speakers, [and] the accommodation of code-switching needs in black English speakers." And teachers would learn to apply their new linguistic knowledge "to help individual students read standard English."

What Happened in Oakland

Court-ordered linguistics in Ann Arbor prompted the educational establishment to study the language that students bring to school, but it didn't affect the language arts curriculum in most schools or national reading scores. Almost twenty years after the King decision, the School Board of California's Oakland Unified School District, desperate to improve the test scores of its African American students, passed a resolution declaring that Ebonics, the speech of the majority of students in the Oakland schools, was not a dialect of English but a separate language derived from West African roots (Oakland 1996; see also Baron 2000; Baugh 2000; and Delpit and Perry 1998). The Board ordered teachers to "devise and implement the best possible academic program for imparting instruction to African-American students *in their primary language* for the combined purposes of maintaining the legitimacy and richness of such language . . . and to facilitate their acquisition and mastery of English-language skills" (emphasis added).

Oakland felt driven to this position because their African American students consistently underperformed on achievement tests compared to other groups. In addition, black children were disproportionately represented in remedial programs, were suspended from school more frequently, and had unacceptably high drop-out rates. But by recognizing these students' speech as constituting a separate language from English, Oakland went well beyond the claims of a language barrier made by the plaintiffs in the Ann Arbor case. And by explicitly requiring schools to *use* and *maintain* Ebonics, while also helping students *acquire* English, the Board provoked a national controversy.

Oakland's use of the term *Ebonics* rather than the more common Black English, or the term most linguists now use, African American Vernacular English (AAVE), reinforces the claim that their students weren't speaking English. That assertion of separateness in turn allowed Oakland to target federal bilingual education funds. By declaring linguistic independence, the School Board was also expressing the community's frustration that plans like the one mandated in the King decision had changed nothing.

The Ann Arbor decision succeeded in the courts but not in the classroom, where according to the evidence of standardized tests, black students continued to perform below the level of other groups at school. Many also failed to transition to standard English. The Oakland resolution initially failed in the arena of public opinion. Americans in general, even those college-educated Americans who had taken linguistics courses, were convinced that Ebonics was little more than "lazy English" or "bad grammar." While the Linguistic Society of America quickly passed a resolution attempting to explain the linguistic basis of Ebonics to the American public (Rickford 1997), and the American press fairly presented the linguistic point of view to explain Oakland's actions (Nunberg 1997), sociolinguistic tolerance was not the order of the day, and African American leaders like Jesse Jackson and NAACP head Kweisi Mfume seconded the general public's response that the Oakland resolution sought to elevate the status of slang and corrupt English. The Ebonics resolution generated so much opposition that within days the school district hired a public relations firm to repair the damage, and within a couple of weeks it issued a clarification backing away from its insistence on separating Ebonics and English (Oakland 1997).

In an amended resolution passed on 15 January 1997, the Board sought to clarify matters by asserting that Ebonics was genetically *descended from*—that is, based on or related to—African languages and not merely a dialect of English. The Oakland Board repeated the parallel between African American students and other students classified as having limited proficiency in English, though it played down its request for bilingual education dollars. And the Board insisted that it never intended for Ebonics to be *taught* in the classroom, nor did it envision a program of language maintenance. Instead, without referring to the King decision, Oakland indicated that it wished to proceed much as Ann Arbor had done, educating teachers in the language their students used so that these teachers would be better able to lead their students from Ebonics toward standard English.

The U.S. Department of Education quickly ruled that Ebonics was not a foreign language and Oakland was not eligible for federal bilingual education funds for its African American students (Bennett 1996). But after Oakland softened its stand on Ebonics, Jesse Jackson, on a fact-finding trip to the city, revised his opinion of the School Board's efforts. They were just trying to teach students good English, he concluded, and that was fine with him. But the School Board's revision came too late—the political damage was already done, and just as the fallout from the Ann Arbor decision quickly subsided, Oakland eventually abandoned its efforts to put Ebonics on the national agenda.

The program that Oakland sought to implement, called Standard English Proficiency (SEP), was already in place (and federally funded) in a number of California schools. SEP uses foreign language methodologies to teach standard English to children who speak a nonstandard dialect, or whose proficiency in English is otherwise suspect. SEP avoids the term *dialect* altogether, substituting the label "home language" instead. SEP students whose home language is AAVE are regularly asked to translate from their home language into standard English, much as Spanish speakers are asked to translate from Spanish to English, or English speakers learning a foreign language are asked to translate from English into the target language. SEP assumes that a student's home language is not an incorrect variety of English, but a different language altogether, or perhaps a different variety of English; learning standard

English should not cause students to feel that their own variety of English is being devalued.

In practice, however, SEP is no different from traditional methods based on a good English/bad English model, methods whose goal is to correct students' language and get them to use a prescribed norm. In accomplishing this, students' "home language," whether or not it is English, is routinely devalued, sometimes implicitly, sometimes directly. Fifth grade teacher Carrie Secret, a member of the Oakland School Board Task Force that came up with the original Ebonics resolution, used SEP in her classes, teaching her students that their home language is their L1, the conventional linguistic term for 'first language.' According to Secret, "Telling [students] that black English is different, not wrong, makes them feel better about themselves" (Walker 1996). Secret adds, "If a child says, 'You was sitting in my chair,' I say to them, 'L2 please—you were sitting in my chair.'" However, telling English-speaking students that they are speaking a foreign language, a patent fiction to students and teachers alike, does not disguise the fact that the students' English is being corrected. Moreover, the pretense that SEP methodology deals with bilingualism, or even bidialectalism, rather than a conventional notion of right and wrong, quickly falls away in actual practice. Secret's teaching clearly emphasizes 'correctness' rather than 'translation' from L1 to L2:

> Yesterday, Secret had her students read essays aloud and told them to *enunciate.*
> "Jist for seven days ..." one boy began.
> Secret interrupted him. "You said, 'jist.' Use it *right.*"
> The boy *corrected* himself using 'just,' the standard English *translation.*
> (Walker 1996; emphasis added)

As this vignette shows, even teachers like Secret, despite their exposure to language theory, often cannot resist the prescriptive approach to language—shared by most Americans—that focuses on correction. Secret wants her students to say "just" because it's "right." But she's actually legislating a standard of correct "enunciation" that is not shared by language experts. All the major English dictionaries record the common pronunciation "jist" without marking it as nonstandard. Students are well aware that the school language standard often differs from conversational and written norms outside the classroom. That's a "teaching moment" that the language arts curriculum would do well to explore. But this sort of opportunity to discuss language variation in context, to show that there may be several acceptable or standard forms, not just one, is typically rejected in favor of a more rigid, testable, and traditional approach to usage.

If what happened in Ann Arbor and in Oakland signals anything, it signals the ability of the schools to embrace language theory even as they ignore its implications. In the name of sociolinguistics they reject language diversity. Celebrating Ebonics in one breath, in the next they campaign to stamp out bad English, which their students readily understand as the home language that they bring to school with them.

When Languages Collide: From *Lau v. Nichols* to Proposition 227

The diversity inherent in English is one aspect of language study that the schools routinely gloss over as if it were an embarrassment. Our educational system seems equally helpless in the face of students who don't speak English at all or who have limited command of the language. Another pair of legal actions that bracket the time period of this study delineates how American schools educate—or fail to educate—their non–English speaking students. The U.S. Supreme Court decision in the case of *Lau v. Nichols* (1974) ushered in an era of court-mandated bilingual education designed to erase the language barrier that prevented nonanglophones from succeeding in school. And the passage by 61 percent of the voters of California's Proposition 227 in June, 1998, which ordered an end to bilingual education, signaled a national backlash against attempts by the schools to accommodate the educational needs of students whose English was limited.

Before 1974, schools dealt with non–English speakers in two ways Most commonly, they ignored these children—a method called by its proponents "immersion," but often referred to by its critics as "sink or swim," since most students immersed in English-only classes effectively sank. The few attempts to meet the problem head-on had little impact. In the early twentieth century, at the height of the pre–World War I immigration boom, New York City offered special "steamer" classes for immigrant children to ease their transition to English, but there were never enough seats to meet student demand. Instead, the formal teaching of English as a second language (ESL) was generally reserved for foreign-born adults attending night school, while mainstream classrooms, full of nonanglophone children, dealt with the problem randomly and sporadically, focusing for example on eradicating foreign accent through repetitive phonics exercises and speech therapy rather than systematic language instruction (on school responses to nonanglophones, see Baron 1990; Padilla et al. 1990; González 2001).

There were some bilingual programs before the 1974 Lau decision. In the late nineteenth century, a few midwestern school systems—among them Cincinnati, Milwaukee, and St. Louis—offered bilingual English-German schools in order to woo students from the German-language parochial schools into public classrooms (at the time, German was the second most-commonly-spoken language in the U.S., after English). These programs promised both English and L1 language maintenance—preserving the students' German, not replacing it. But World War I put an end to public support for German-language instruction in the United States; for a time several states made the teaching of all foreign languages, not just German, illegal. That ban was overturned by the U.S. Supreme Court in the case of *Meyer v. Nebraska* in 1923, but the damage had already been done, and in the isolationist period that followed World War I the U.S. turned inward both politically and linguistically. Before the war, 25 percent of American high school students studied German, but after 1917 few Americans studied any foreign language in school at all.

The 1924 immigration law put an end to a long period of massive immigration. As a result, American schools no longer worried about integrating great waves of immigrant children or teaching them English. The bilingual problem of the early twentieth century managed to resolve itself largely without the schools' intervention. Immigrant children always quickly took to English, becoming fluent enough, for example, to translate for their limited–English speaking parents. Unfortunately, the English they mastered wasn't always the academic register of English necessary for school success. Following this largely bilingual second generation was a third generation who were mostly monolingual English speakers. But with the Immigration Reform Act of 1965 the schools once again saw an influx of children whose English was tentative or nonexistent.

Responding to this new wave of immigration, some schools developed both ESL and bilingual education programs. But once again they failed to meet demand, and once again many children were left behind. The plaintiffs in *Lau v. Nichols* claimed that the San Francisco schools were ignoring the majority of their nonanglophone Chinese children and that the inability of these children to speak English presented an insurmountable language barrier in violation of the Fourteenth Amendment and the 1964 Civil Rights Act.

The U.S. Supreme Court agreed unanimously with the Lau plaintiffs. As in the Ann Arbor decision, it ordered the schools to remedy the situation without specifying how. But because the Lau decision came from the Supreme Court, unlike the Ann Arbor case, it had national implications. Following *Lau v. Nichols,* schools across the nation began implementing programs of transitional bilingual education calculated to move non-English speakers to English while keeping them up to speed in terms of their academic work.

The theory behind bilingual education was elegant and appealing. During the time it takes for nonanglophones to learn English—usually several years—children often make little progress in basic school subjects such as reading, history, math, and science. The bilingual methodology provides students with an opportunity to learn English, while at the same time receiving instruction in basic subjects in their first language. That way they don't fall behind their English-speaking peers in content mastery.

As with other theories of the language arts, the ideal didn't always play out in practice: many schools did not implement bilingual education programs that were adequate or effective. Schools struggled to find staff trained to deliver instruction in the many languages that immigrant children bring to school and who were also trained to teach ESL. Observers complained that children were not being taught English; that their academics were being ignored; that students speaking a variety of languages were lumped together in a single bilingual education class that was taught, for example, only in Spanish; and that anglophone children still benefited from the best teachers and the strongest curricula.

Of course there were exceptions, programs with effective academic components, as well as a few programs that emphasized the need for all students to learn an additional language, not just the nonanglophones. However, the success stories didn't allay fears that schools were failing to teach English to immigrant children. This, together with a growing resentment of immigration itself, both illegal and legal, led to the kind of backlash represented by Proposition 227, which moved California's schools from bilingual education to structured immersion—a year of "sheltered" intensive English instruction for students whose knowledge of the language is weak or nonexistent, followed by a return to the mainstream, English-only classroom. Proposition 227 also permitted parents to sue schools that violated the law's provisions.

It was politics, not linguistics or educational theory, that decided the matter for Californians. For one thing, the public rejected bilingual education because it takes too long. Language learners need several years to gain fluency in a new tongue. Nonanglophones may pick up conversational English from their peers fairly quickly, but mastering the technical vocabulary and the reading and writing skills necessary for school success takes much longer. A key aim of bilingual education is to keep students from falling behind in essential subjects as they learn English. Ideally, once their new language is up to speed, such students can move to English instruction in these subjects and be at grade level. In many cases these students switch to English as their dominant language, but some remain fluent in their first language. That outcome, when it occurs, doesn't play well with voters interested in keeping the U.S. English-only.

Bilingual education was only tolerated so long as it seemed a way to replace students' first language with English. But the same voters and politicians who complain that America can't compete in the global market or assure its defenses unless more Americans master foreign languages argue that maintaining a first language alongside English is unpatriotic and should be illegal. And so they either treat their bilingual programs as a place to warehouse students with unpromising futures, or they cut them altogether. Unfortunately, as it was in the early twentieth century, the result for many nonanglophone children is that, while English comes easily enough to them, school English remains for many a closed book.

Grammar in the Classroom

Each semester I ask my students what they've been told about language by their previous English teachers, and each semester they spout the same list of rules:

- Don't use the first person.
- Don't use the second person.
- Don't use the verb *to be.*
- Avoid the passive voice.
- Never end a sentence with a preposition.

Recently a new rule has appeared:

- Don't use *he.*

When advances in linguistics do penetrate the English classroom, concepts tend to be simplified, to be sure, to fit the educational level of the students, but they tend to become rigidified as well. In the 1970s linguists began looking at language and gender, motivated in part by a renewed focus on women's rights that came out of second wave feminism. Studies both confirmed and questioned the linguistic differences between women and men, complicated discussions about the relationship between language and power, and tracked numerous proposals for gender-neutral vocabulary (for further reading, see Baron 1986, 2007, and Coates 1998). How American schools integrated this new knowledge about language and gender represents a case where schools took new linguistic information and turned it into yet another a rule: Don't use *he.*

Even if the teachers explained to students exactly why inclusive pronouns might be more appropriate in certain kinds of discourse than generic masculines, most students automatically place this rule alongside the other school rules they categorize as arbitrary and irrational. They reply, when I ask why use coordinate *he or she* instead of *he,* "Because the teacher told us to."

Students are accustomed to having their language corrected by teachers, and they're well aware that even if a rule comes with a rationale, the schools are just not buying any linguistic approach that isn't going to focus on correctness: that's the academic bottom line. The model of standard English that schools perpetuate goes uncontested since standard English is prized for academic discourse and it's considered—by parents, teachers, employers, and the students themselves—the key to a good job. But the connection between mastering a particular dialect and getting hired may be more myth than reality, and many who have adopted a model of precise, standardized speech and writing to escape racial, ethnic, or gender discrimination find that employers determined not to hire them will find another reason not to do so.

But the main problem with a school model based on standard English isn't that standard language may not pay off the way it's supposed to. The difficulty is that like all varieties, the standard dialect is itself not monolithic and invariant. The school's model of standard English, focusing narrowly on uniform spelling, punctuation, and a handful of grammatical features such as subject-verb agreement, allows for little in the way of flexibility or variation. In actual use, standard English permits its users a great deal of latitude. It even accommodates significant numbers of highly stigmatized forms like *ain't* and double negatives, forms that would be marked wrong on a standardized test of standard English.

Confronted with a linguistic model of standard discourse that does not offer a neat package with easy-to-follow instructions, schools either reject it as inaccurate or argue that students have to learn the rules before they can deal with the exceptions (and the schools are hoping that students won't discover the exceptions until long after they graduate). However, this common walk-before-you-run methodology, while it seems logical, doesn't fit well with actual language learning.

In foreign language classes, students who master the textbook rules invariably encounter difficulties when they begin negotiating the rough and tumble of language use outside the classroom, and students enrolled in ESL classes run the risk of coming away with the same kind of inflexible textbook English rather than a fluent, idiomatic style. When we teach English in schools to speakers of English, we often forget that these students have already mastered that idiomatic language at a very young age. In telling such students that they have to abide by rules and choose words that their own experience already marks as stiff or unnatural, teachers are not giving them the structure they need, but adding instead to their sense that the language rules they learn in school bear little relevance to what goes on beyond the schoolhouse door.

Nonetheless, the schools reject the descriptive model of standard English or any other language variety. After 50 years of folding linguistic theory into the training of classroom teachers, students still leave high school thinking that a noun is the name of a person, place, or thing. They still think it best not to end a sentence with a preposition, although many aren't even sure what a preposition is—though some of them will hazard that it's probably not the name of a person, place, or thing. And they learn, in school, that no matter how high their grades, their language is still prone to error. But most of all they learn that, while grammar may be a game they're either good at or clueless about, grammar lessons are designed to make their eyes glaze over. Most instructors are not trained effectively to teach the traditional, prescriptive school grammar, and even those who have benefited from the new advances in linguistics aren't well-enough prepared in that subject to teach a linguistically informed language curriculum. English teachers typically choose the profession because they love literature, and when they think of the beauty inherent in language they are almost always thinking of elevated poetic diction and limpid prose, not the witty, resourceful, and thoroughly creative language of their students, and certainly not the syntactic analysis of such speech. Few of these teachers take more than one or two language courses, not much compared to the eight to ten literature classes and the huge number of units in curriculum and instruction necessary for professional licensing.

Certainly one or two language classes can change a prospective teacher's focus on matters linguistic, but working against that is a school culture bent on nonstop correcting and testing. Teaching to the test was driving the curriculum long before the federal No Child Left Behind law forced schools to fit a one-size-fits-nobody pattern, but we are now faced with the possibility that standardized testing will move up from K–12 and permeate the college environment as well. Inevitably, large-scale testing is multiple-choice rather than a more direct measure of language production and analysis. And it reinforces the kind of grammatical instruction that has already failed to give either teachers or their students any insight into how language actually works.

Since a major concern of the schools has been the teaching of standard English—a concern reinforced by court decisions like King and Lau—the focus of grammatical instruction and testing is on the structure of that code. This is supposed to help students who are still learning the school's language, and it's supposed to deepen the linguistic understanding of the students who come to school already using the linguistic code that matches the one being taught. Some curricula fold grammar instruction into the larger study of literature, but whether sample sentences are drawn from a worksheet or a novel doesn't really change the school's focus on correct usage, and it doesn't help students to understand why some forms are considered proper while others aren't.

Linking writing instruction to linguistic correctness further reinforces the school's list of don'ts. Despite several decades of research into how writers create texts and how readers evaluate them, and a curriculum in many schools that claims to focus on the "writing process" model, high school writing instruction in many instances reduces the process to a series of required steps, and it focuses not on rhetorical sophistication or the ways in which different writers work through a writing assignment, but on the creation of a final product containing well-formed sentences that are punctuated correctly, and fancy, correctly spelled vocabulary.

The schools may defend their focus on correctness as test-driven. But testing alone doesn't drive the prescriptive approach to language that remains endemic in our schools. American society simply expects its English teachers to be language experts, even if their interests are not in language but in literature. College English majors are routinely asked by friends in other disciplines to correct their papers or settle disputes about the proper form or meaning of a word. And those who go on to become English teachers find that whether they accept the role of language guardian willingly or with reluctance, they must do so or risk their jobs.

Making Things Different

I and many of my colleagues in English and linguistics departments around the country regularly teach prospective English teachers everything they will need to know about language and linguistics, but were afraid to ask. We focus on the history, structure, and great variety of English in the U.S. and around the world; on the dynamics of multidialectal and multilingual societies; on the nature of standard language varieties and the role of language education in the schools. I myself begin and end my classes with intense discussions of the differences between language description and prescription: the analysis of language as it is compared to the vision of language as some might like it to be.

And while I try to redirect my students' preference away from what seems to be an ingrained acceptance of prescription to the more scientific aspects of linguistic description and analysis, too often I learn from their final exams that my efforts are in vain. Every once in a while a student will blurt out what many of them are thinking, as this student did in response to an exam question calling for her to weigh the benefits of prescriptivism and descriptivism in terms of how best to teach language topics in high school:

> I think I support prescriptivism. I believe that some words are absolutely unacceptable in any situation. I think there should be an accepted way of speaking and deviation would not be tolerated. I believe in a set of absolute values. I believe there is one right and wrong for everyone. Perhaps what I think is right is not what you think is right but in the final analysis that isn't going to matter. What God thinks is right is what really matters and He doesn't have one right for you and one right for me.

Granted, the phrasing is extreme. Not all my students equate fundamentalism with linguistic correctness, and most speakers of English recognize that standards of correctness, like highway speed limits, allow for some wiggle room when the authorities aren't watching. But even students who leave my class raving descriptivists determined to celebrate their students' language while revolutionizing Americans' language attitudes find the odds stacked against them once they get their own classroom. Veteran high school teachers regularly complain to me that they have to train new teachers to root out student spelling and grammar errors. As my returning student so bluntly put it in summarizing my own futile attempt to get him to think of his students' language not as a wrong-headed approximation of an idealized standard model of discourse, but as an exciting, developing, highly competent variety of language in its own right, I was wrong.

For the past half-century linguists have been trying, with little success, to change this situation. We're not proposing to do away with notions of correctness—ideas about appropriate usage form a solid part of the way that English speakers function, and like everyone else, linguists have some definite opinions about what's right and wrong when it comes to language use. Instead, we hope to complicate the traditional right-or-wrong approach to language in the schools by demonstrating that in most situations there isn't a single way to be correct, by suggesting that there are usually multiple standards in play at any given time, and by transmuting the correctness dichotomy of right and wrong language into a contextually dependent sliding scale of language that works in particular situations, and language that may not work so well.

The title of this essay is pessimistic: in the case of the language arts in the United States, the more things change, the more they seem to stay the same. Still, language researchers don't give up trying to make them different. However, to succeed at this means reconfiguring some very basic conceptions that Americans have about language use. That's something that education is supposed to do.

But the situation isn't really as bleak as that. Outside the classroom things linguistic are not so monochromatic. It's true that when put on the spot, most people will assert that there's a right and a wrong way to speak or write, parroting the idea they learned at school and from parents as well. But in actual practice most people take a more relaxed and pragmatic approach to language. They recognize correct usage as a set of rules, but they also see that it consists of what works in a given situation, not what's categorically good or bad. Perhaps the most important English lesson that schools can give their students is not a set of testable rules to memorize, but rather an ability to weigh linguistic options and a predilection to trust their language instincts. Instead of convincing students that they need to speak and write language that may not conform to some unattainable ideal (an ideal that's really a moving target, since it differs from teacher to teacher), schools should strive for language that—whatever the language purist who rants in the local newspaper or the Educational Testing Service thinks about it—is simply good enough to do the job.

15

Written Language in Use: An Essay on Returning Language to Writing Studies

AMY J. DEVITT
University of Kansas

Standing in the hallway at a national conference on composition, a colleague and I were discussing our shared research interest in genre theory. "You do language-based genre study," he asserted with no doubt in his voice. "Oh no," I first replied. "My work is rhetorical." Feeling as if I had denied my mother, I added that I supposed I was indeed most interested in how genre instantiates in texts, and more typical convention conversation followed. I was so taken aback at first by my colleague's assertion that I did language-based genre study because I could not imagine any other kind of genre study. Genres are elements of writing. Why doesn't the study of writing necessarily entail language?

I am making much of an idle hallway comment, one my colleague might explain differently. My initial denial, though, recognized that many who study writing and the teaching of writing contrast language-based study with rhetorical study, and some consider language-based study of writing to be old-fashioned, apolitical, and ideologically suspect. Some of that reaction comes from unfortunate past experiences with linguistics, badly applied to teaching writing. Some surely also comes from a limited understanding of English language study and what it contributes to our knowledge and practice of writing. Claiming both English language and composition and rhetoric as my areas of expertise, I find it difficult to envision the study of writing without the study of all its components: its rhetorical contexts, its composing acts, and its language features. Writing is, after all, a rhetorical act composed through language. Ignoring any element of that complex act minimizes what writers must achieve. Today, English language study stands in a unique position to help return language to the study and teaching of writing.

When I completed my doctorate at the University of Michigan, I considered myself a scholar of writing, not of either language or composition alone. I wanted to understand better how, why, and what people write, as well as when and where—the social and cultural contexts of writing. My first years as a graduate student introduced me to the fields of English language and composition studies as overlapping and shared endeavors. The primary books in composition I studied then would today likely be considered language-based: Mina Shaughnessy's *Errors and Expectations* (1977), E. D. Hirsch's *The Philosophy of Composition* (1977), James Kinneavy's *A Theory of Discourse* (1971), Frances Christensen's *Notes Toward a New Rhetoric* (1967), and Frank D'Angelo's *A Conceptual Theory of Rhetoric* (1975). Shaughnessy showed how the textual forms students write reveal experiences with and knowledge and assumptions about language. Hirsch emphasized the written variety of language, the grapholect, and the differences between spoken and written discourse. Kinneavy classified texts according to rhetorical aim, with one of four components being the language signal. Christensen analyzed the grammatical components of sentences and paragraphs and translated that grammar into a method for teaching sentence and paragraph elaboration. These language-based approaches to composition seemed cutting edge at the time, vast scholarly improvements over previous emphases on a single version of "correctness," obliviousness to the influences of speech on writing, instructions to elaborate sentences and paragraphs with no instructions on how to do so, and such arhetorical classifications as the modes and such static textual models as five-paragraph themes.

Although works of composition study in the late 1970s were based in language, some also suggest the beginning of a shift from study of and instruction in text to study of and instruction in the act of writing itself, what became shorthanded as the shift from product to process. Shaughnessy strategized *why* students wrote as they did; Christensen helped writers *generate* writing; D'Angelo theorized the *thinking* behind the structures. At the same time, we read Perl's (1979) and Sommers' (1980) studies of composing strategies of college writers, studies of what people *do*, though nonetheless grounded also in what people wrote, in textual forms. Emig (1971) and Britton et al. (1975) examined how students thought about and acted on their writing assignments, at times independent of what they wrote. Flower and Hayes' (1980, 1981) research into and theories of composing processes took us new directions into cognitive processes. Like Emig, they used composing-aloud protocols to expose the invisible cognitive processes of writers writing—what they thought, not what they wrote.

While psycholinguistics offers language-based approaches to cognition, this new approach treated spoken language as an almost transparent route into the mind (a method later criticized and little used today). Cognitive studies of how people write developed insights into invention and prewriting, into revising strategies, and into the recursiveness of writing activities as writers loop back and forth between discovering what they want to say, attempting to say it, reading and changing what they have written, and thinking and drafting some more. Applications of these studies provided a correction especially to writing instruction, which had too long shown students what to produce without adequate guidance on how to produce it.

By 1982, when Maxine Hairston published her summation of the "new" process approach as a replacement for a product approach, the study as well as teaching of writing had shifted largely toward the principles she espoused: it focused on "the" writing process, including teaching invention; it was "rhetorically based," making audience, purpose, and occasion central in varied assignments and their evaluation; it viewed writing as recursive, intuitive as well as rational, creative as well as disciplined, and as a way of learning as well as of communicating. Hairston's list of twelve principal features mentioned language explicitly only twice, both times naming linguistics as a discipline whose research informs composition but without any clear application for that research in the other ten features.

With this turn from product to process came a perhaps necessary but unfortunate turn away from language-based study and teaching of writing. Language came to be associated with product, and *product* was a bad word. Connors (2000, 100) described the turn away from product through the lens of the sentence, noting an "anti-formalism" of the time, "the idea that any pedagogy based in form rather than in content was automatically suspect." Work with linguistic forms like sentences was viewed especially as arhetorical, as taking the form out of its context. Sentences were considered only as parts of the whole discourse, which was treated only as a unit of meaning. For process proponents in particular, form became antithetical to effective writing instruction because instruction in form was inauthentic. Authentic writing instruction involved the learner writing and rewriting with response from a sympathetic reader (Connors 2000, 123). Although renewed emphasis on individual expression and the meaning of form was probably due, the pendulum swung too far, knocking form not only off its pedestal but out of the picture. Effective teaching practices like generative rhetoric, imitation, and sentence-combining—which did in fact help students learn how as well as what to write and, as some empirical research demonstrated, helped students write more complex sentences and holistically higher-rated texts—became associated with formalism. "The loss of all defense of formalism," Connors (2000, 122) writes, "has left some curious vacuums in the middle of our teaching."

In recent years, composition studies has left behind, for the most part, study or teaching of sentences, diction, style, organizational patterns, and cohesion, in favor of theorizing and investigating the contexts of writing. Valuable work has examined how rhetorical purpose and audience affect writing; the varied social settings of writing, in school, work, and public spheres; how identities of race, gender, class, sexuality, and disability influence and interact with and through writing; the ideologies of literacy and literacy programs, including new attention to visual literacy and writing technologies. Scholars examine such topics theoretically, historically, pedagogically, politically—but, for the most part, not formally. All of this has expanded our understanding of writing considerably: the field of study is now a rich web of approaches to the complex act that is writing. Meaning and content are understood as only partly created by the writer, inevitably linked with readers and cultures and standing in many ways outside the text. Processes of writing are seen as individual, multiple, and variable, though embedded in multi-layered rhetorical situations and cultural contexts and, in some ways, less amenable to instructor or student intervention. Although without agreement yet on precisely what the term means, some describe the field of composition as now post-process. Less belief, perhaps, exists in the individual expression of meaning. Less faith, perhaps, exists in the sufficiency of learners writing and rewriting with a sympathetic reader. More belief, perhaps, exists in the power of context, individually influential and ideologically powerful.

This richer, more complex understanding of writing and writers is ripe for the reintroduction of form. Language has already reappeared in feminist composition studies and other studies of identity, though largely in its ideological power as a negative or constraint. Literacy studies have addressed the demands of academic writing conventions for students from less academic backgrounds. The spreading influence of digital media has focused attention on writing as medium and on the increasing interaction of images with words. And, of course, language and form have never been completely absent from the study and teaching of writing, even if they have received less attention. It is time, I argue, to rebuild knowledge about text as well as context. It is time to integrate form with this fuller, more complex understanding of meaning. The field of English language study stands in a particularly important position to contribute to that rebuilding because it has always focused on language in use. Rather than decontextualized formalism, English language study offers the understanding that form is always fused with meaning. Combining English language study with contemporary composition and rhetoric studies, we can fill that curious vacuum that Connors notes in our study and teaching of writing with a view of language not as rigidly formalist but as actively used.

English language study attends to the form that instantiates rhetorical purposes and complicates the composing act. Yet English language study does not attend to that form in isolation. Rather, the heart of English language study is the study of language in use, in all its process and product, rhetorical and formal, individual and social complexity. Even the name for it that we are using in this collection—*English language study*—indicates that combination: scholars in the field study not language in the abstract, but a particular language used by particular peoples in particular contexts. Applied to writing, English language study enables the study of language forms as rhetorically, socially, ideologically, and historically contextualized; it enables the study of written forms as resulting from and revealing of writing activities; it enables the integration of product and process, text and context, individual and social.

If form is to regain inclusion in writing study and teaching, scholars and students alike will need ways of describing formal elements. Discourse analysis and pragmatics provide some descriptive methods and vocabulary for larger units (Barton and Stygall 2002). At the sentence and word level, the tools for describing forms must exhibit special sensitivity to context in order to counteract composition's earlier rejection of isolated forms at those levels. English language study supplies us with grammars and dictionaries. While reputable dictionaries place word meanings into their contexts, the contexts of grammars are not always so visible. Detailed grammars of English, such as Quirk, Greenbaum, et al. (1985) and Biber, Johansson, et al. (1999) try to account for the complexity of sentences as they actually occur in a range of contexts, in contrast to the static Latin-based grammars familiar to many teachers of writing.

Yet the distinction between grammars may not be evident immediately to non-linguists, and the more detailed ones might be better promoted to teachers. New grammars might even more thoroughly describe syntactic variation. Since English language scholars have already developed multiple grammars to describe English for different purposes and from different theoretical perspectives, well-informed scholars, teachers, and students of writing can choose a grammar to help achieve their own purposes, whether describing syntactic patterns, analyzing stylistic choices from among alternative possibilities, or instructing students in expanding their syntactic range for fluency in multiple writing contexts. In light of composition's history, the fact that no single grammar represents the one "true" or "best" description of English sentences needs emphasis. Replacing one grammar with another to support theory abstracted from language use may serve linguistics well, but English language and writing scholars less well. Having multiple grammars to serve different research and teaching purposes is helpful.

Dictionaries are less static than they appear and more visibly describe language form in context. Entries in dictionaries for words with multiple senses often specify the settings for those senses, whether a scientific discipline or a regional dialect. Less evident, though, are the historical and cultural contexts. Scholars of lexicography know that editors construct reputable dictionaries by interpreting instances of a word gathered from particular places at particular times. Such dictionaries provide good examples of how forms can be described in their contexts. Yet only such extensive dictionaries as the *Oxford English Dictionary* clearly situate each word historically, offering some of the evidence the editors interpreted. One small change that might remind users of dictionaries' historical and social embeddedness would be to include the year and place of publication in the dictionary's title—*The Dictionary of American English in 2011*.

Popular books about dictionaries and their makers by Winchester (2003) and Green (1996), among others, and historical studies of lexicography, such as Sledd and Ebbitt's (1962) study of reactions to *Webster's Third* or Landau's (2001) account of how dictionaries are made, help to ensure that dictionaries are understood as texts created in particular contexts, editorialized interpretations of what counts as a word and whose meanings matter. Through them, readers understand that *blog* "is a word," even if it has not yet entered dictionaries; that *inflammable* does mean not flammable to most people, even if its origins meant the opposite; and that *hopefully* commonly means 'one hopes that,' no matter what the usage label might state.

Those in English language study might seek ways to share their knowledge of language use more widely within composition and rhetoric and to apply that knowledge to the teaching of writing. Users of English grammars would benefit from knowing of historical studies of grammar, such as Traugott (1972) or Visser (1963–1973), to ensure that no one grammar stands as the true description of English syntax and that sentence structure in use is flexible and changeable. Applying that knowledge of grammars and syntactic history to the difficulties of many second-language learners of English, for example, could illuminate why they often have trouble with modals and verbals, structures in English that developed late and that grammarians still have difficulty describing fully and accurately. If they knew historical studies of usage and attitudes toward "correct" English—those by Milroy and Milroy (1999),

Finegan (1980), Baron (1982), Smitherman (2006), and Bailey (1991a), for example—writers would understand that usage guides represent dynamic and power-laden pictures of English status at a moment in time.

Writing scholars and teachers versed in the history of usage can better contextualize the preference for Standardized Edited English (SEE) in edited written texts and can better prioritize the teaching of specific usage items. Battling the split infinitive, a late "error" created by language mavens in the eighteenth century and largely unnoticed today, seems insignificant compared to teaching students to edit non-standard subject-verb agreements like *He don't* that are socially stigmatized. Since all the tools for describing English language are ideologically embedded, fuller knowledge of English language studies helps scholars, teachers, and students of writing to use customary writing tools more consciously as well as effectively. Fully understood as observations of current forms in specific contexts, the reference works created by English language scholars can serve scholars, teachers, and students of writing as they analyze existing texts, study the choices writers make, or advise students in achieving their rhetorical aims.

English language scholars might also share more widely and apply more explicitly the extensive scholarship on variation in English. Though variation studies tend to be explicit about the contexts within which forms occur, they also tend to emphasize speech, so they might demonstrate how scholarship on spoken variation applies to writing and writers (as does Biber 1988). Numerous studies of English in different regions and groups show how dialects vary in the United States and England, even worldwide, including the dialect features of spoken English visible in writing. Knowing that young Americans may have been laxing or lowering their tense vowels before /l/, as James Hartman reported in 1984, for example, helps teachers understand new spellings of *really* as *rilly.* That knowledge might give teachers better ways to correct the spelling to standard usage than by referring to the word's pronunciation—not saying to the student, as I heard a fellow teacher say, "But it's '/ri:li/' not '/rɪl:i/.'"

The extensive research into social variation (Labov 1973b, Smitherman 2006, and Eckert 2000, for three notable examples) contributes to understanding how writers' identities influence writers' choices. The knowledge of how English in the United States varies by social class, for example, would enhance composition scholars' increasing attention to the effects of social class on writers (see, for example, Hurlbert and Blitz (1991), Soliday (1999), Beech (2004), or Ashley (2001). Such concepts as linguistic insecurity, hypercorrection, code switching, and social stratification of linguistic variables can help explain how and why writers might resist some instruction and require specific other types of instruction. Gender, ethnicity, and age differences also have a body of scholarship in English language study, scholarship relevant to those same issues in the study of written language. All this knowledge of how English varies among individuals and groups is critical knowledge for anyone trying to understand or teach writing with individuals from varied backgrounds and in varied settings.

Individual use of language, in fact, is a critical context for scholars and teachers of writing, one that English language study might gain from working with composition and rhetoric. Even with its current emphasis on group identities and social contexts, composition and rhetoric remains strongly aware of writing as an individual act. Each writer's identity differs in some ways from others, and each piece of writing differs from others. Since so many scholars of writing also teach writing, they are keenly aware of the application of scholarship to individual cases. Both composition and rhetoric and English language study benefit from the perspective that language is both unique and shared. Although much of English language study would seem to emphasize the social over the individual, with its emphasis on groups over individuals, its scholarship repeatedly demonstrates the significance of the individual as well, and some explicitly focuses on the individual (see Johnstone 1996, for example).

Whether descriptive, historical, or social, English language research recognizes the individual variation that occurs with using English. Each individual speaks and writes from a unique background at a unique moment, with an idiolect that bespeaks the individual's community membership. Since regional and social dialect patterns represent clusters of use rather than uniformity, individual use always varies. Since English is always in the process of change, with changes spreading gradually through different groups, individuals will always differ in how much change they have adopted. Since word meanings vary according to users' experiences and backgrounds, the same word will have unique resonances for each user. Some people style-shift more than others, though trends by social class and network position are visible (see, for example, Tannen 2005 or Milroy 1987). The language of two lames (Labov 1973a) or two jocks (Eckert 2000) will not be identical, though their use of the group's markers might have more in common than the use of two members of other groups.

Scholarship in variation reveals that much of English is variable yet patterned. Scholarship in the history of English reveals that much of English is changing, though the spread of that change takes time and varies as it goes. Grammars, dictionaries, and style guides grapple with variation and change, even as they attempt to record English at that moment for some of its users. Scholars in both English language studies and composition and rhetoric could better balance their attention to both the individual and the social: each writer and each piece of writing is unique, yet they share identifiable patterns with other writers and pieces of writing. To capture those commonalities is not to deny individuality. Communication requires both.

With form deeply embedded in the individual as well as the social and in the context as well as the text, the knowledge, perspectives, and practices that English language study has to offer can inform the study and teaching of writing in concrete ways. They provide methods and vocabulary for describing textual structure in different contexts, whether organizational patterns, discourse units, sentences, or diction. They help characterize voice and style and call attention to the range of voices and styles writers use in different settings. They contextualize SEE, clarifying its historical and social situatedness, and providing information about specific features and their social significance. Knowledge of the English language has also contributed to responsible and ethical treatment of students' language and offers extensive examples for studying the ideological power of language expectations and writers' language choices. As writing teachers turn increasingly to developing students' awareness of the ideologies of writing, they might point out what has been learned about the English used on Martha's Vineyard (Labov 1973b), in "Belten High" (Eckert 2000), or in postcolonial settings (Bailey 1991a, 151–177).

Combining English language study with composition and rhetoric can add to language-in-use a vision of writing as text-in-context. My own scholarship has blended English language study and composition and rhetoric in ways that might illustrate their compatibility in more detail. Two areas of my work derive most directly from my background in English language study and apply to the study and teaching of writing: the study of standardization and SEE; and the study of genres. They illustrate how English language study, applied to the study of writing, can integrate the individual and the social, text and context, and language with its use.

I began studying SEE as part of my doctoral work. I developed a dissertation project to study Scots writers from 1520–1659, as they shifted in their writing from using a Scots-English standard variety to an Anglo-English standard. I found writers shifting usage gradually over time, with some features changing more rapidly than others and those changes occurring differently in different written contexts. I discovered that the changes appeared in the form of an S-curve, suggesting a classic pattern of diffusion of a language change in progress (Devitt 1989). In the first decade of this study, none of the texts used predominantly the Anglo-English preterite inflection *-ed*, opting instead for the Scots English *–it*; but by the final decade all but one text did. Yet writers did not simply shift from following Scots-English standards to following Anglo-English standards. Change happened gradually and spread unevenly, with different texts showing more or less use of the new forms at the same time. In the midst of this change, writers mixed forms: one text would use both the old Scots-English and the new Anglo-English form. For example, in the period 1600–1619, two texts used only the Scots-English form of the preterite inflection *-it*, as in "intendit," while four texts used only the Anglo-English form *-ed*, as in "intended." Fourteen texts used both forms, however, with eight texts using over 50 percent *-it* and six texts using more than 50 percent *-ed*. As the conventions for standardized English changed in this century and a half, these Scots writers found themselves mixing forms.

At any given time, then, the written language standard was variable and individual even as the patterns and direction of change were evident. The implications for understanding SEE today are not difficult to suggest. Since the conventions of SEE continue to change (though certainly not at the rate they were changing in Scotland in the sixteenth and seventeenth centuries), observing that writers are using two versions of a convention may suggest a convention susceptible to change (asserting that such a convention is undergoing change would make language much more predictable than it is). Knowing that conventions have changed gradually in the past, we would expect that changes in

SEE today would spread gradually. We should also expect that many changes are occurring without our noticing. Those of us interested in the role that SEE plays in writing today can register that, if the results of this study proved true today as well, changes in conventions likely spread slowly at first, then take off in an S-curve before leveling off to nearly completed change. This study and others that track changing standards in English, combined with historical studies of how attitudes toward English standards change, provide a complex account of how conventions of "correct" English operate in writing.

The implications for teaching SEE are also clear. Conventions with widespread "misuse" might well be undergoing change. Different approaches toward student writers might develop if they were seen not as error-makers but as participants in language change. Writers who use multiple forms of the same convention—who use both *affect* and *effect* as verbs meaning 'to influence,' for example, or who use both *proved* and *proven* without noticing the inconsistency—are showing the same pattern as did writers in 1610 who used both *-it* and *-ed* for the preterite inflection. Like those Scots writers, current writers who mix conventions might also be unaware of the inconsistency and therefore not easily open to changing that pattern. If multiple writers demonstrate the same inconsistency, some teachers might decide not to push those conventions that show signs of potential historical change, focusing instead on those conventions that individuals "violate" in unique ways. Scholarship on error in composition, such as Shaughnessy (1977) or Bartholomae (1980), already argues for treating errors as revealing individual students' thinking. This research opens the possibility of treating nonstandard usage as revealing not just the individual but also the social, revealing the shared language community.

This view of errors as social as well as individual can also enlighten students. Even though the writer might still need to learn to edit the nonstandard usages that are most stigmatized socially, the student's confidence and education surely benefit from knowing that others share the usage, that inconsistency may signal change in progress, and that designations of error change over time. The extensive scholarship on SEE from English language study enables teachers to help students understand SEE as a socially powerful but changing set of expectations.

Students also should know that SEE is appropriate for some contexts but not all. My research into Scots-English standards also demonstrated the complex ways that language standards vary in different settings. These results led to my research into genre, for I found that genre was a significant variable in how and when these conventions changed. In fact, genre was as significant a variable as was date. Writers followed different standards at the same time when writing different genres. Explaining these genre differences required me to reinterpret genre as both language-based and rhetorical. My education in both English language and composition and rhetoric studies enabled these results to lead me to genre theory.

In the 1980s and after, genre study shifted from largely formal and classificatory to rhetorical and action-based, but that shift did not leave language or form behind. Rhetoric no more studies purposes without their instantiations than English language study considers form without its contexts. Carolyn Miller, whose 1984 article "Genre as Social Action" is often cited as helping to create this shift in genre study, describes genre as one of many meaningful actions in discourse that emerge from combining form and substance. Genre does not exist without both. The context is neither easily visible nor important without the language that gives it shape; the linguistic structures are neither important nor interpretable without the context that gives them meaning. Since both text and context are essential for writing, neither can be neglected.

Genres are recognized through similarity of rhetorical situations as well as through textual features (though the degree of actual similarity of either is questionable—see Miller 1984). Consider how one knows one has received a letter from a friend. In the old snail-mail days, the genre was evident upon first picking up a hand-addressed envelope from the home mailbox. A return address might make it even more visible, but the context—including its differences from other types of mail—is what first and most marks the genre of letter from a friend. Context alone is not enough, however. Opening the envelope might reveal a party invitation instead, that genre evident in textual features. Knowing the context, though, again helps interpret the textual markers of a party invitation: Was the sender a personal friend or boss? Is this the genre of invitation or command appearance? In another genre, the notification e-mail requiring the recipient to confirm bank account information, the necessity of context is even more obvious. All textual information marks the genre as notification e-mail from a bank; only context, specifically knowledge about e-mail scams, easily identifies the genre as attempted theft or fraud. These extreme examples make the routine ones more visible. Genres exist as both text and context, a synthesis of form and meaning. Rather than attending to one in order to understand the other, attending to both is necessary for understanding either (Flowerdew 2005).

My background in English language study as well as composition and rhetoric also has enabled me to see genres as simultaneously individual and social. I have argued elsewhere (Devitt 2004, 137–62) that genres necessarily entail both constraint and choice for writers. The most telling comparison returns to language standards. The conventions of SEE concern mostly those linguistic features where speakers and writers vary in their use. The distinction between *affect* and *effect* matters because each is used by some people to mean 'have influence on'; the distinction between *gamble* and *gambol* is not one commonly noted in descriptions of SEE because they are not confused. Without variation, then, standardization is unnecessary; uniformity of language goes unremarked. Similarly, the constraint of genres makes visible the choices possible within genres. The popular view of genres as formulas that require writers to conform recognizes the side of genre that regularizes language-use.

If genres were only regularities, though, all texts of one genre would be identical. Rather, genres entail both the social expectations for kinds of rhetorical actions and the individual possibilities for unique variations. Letters to friends entail usual forms of address and closings, a certain tone, and intimate subjects. With those patterns ensuring the relationship, friends are free to choose specific topics, to greet one another by nicknames, to express their unique relationship. Even more rigidly specified genres require variation. A job application permits only blanks for the writer to fill in, but the writer must choose which employment experiences to list, what titles to give references, how to describe relevant skills. The individual writes always within a social context, so writing involves always what is unique and what is shared. Like dialects and rhetorical situations, genres are both unique and shared. As language in use, they necessarily entail both the uniformity and the variation that enable communication.

When I studied the writing of tax accountants, then, I needed to study the situational context: the professional community's set of genres and the expectations it has for how those genres will be used (Devitt 1991). I also needed to study the linguistic structures: the textual features of those genres and the variations within the community's expectations. Because I wanted to understand both the context and the texts, I was able, among other findings, to discover and interpret the common practice of "plagiarism" of tax codes and regulations in some of the genres tax accountants wrote. Accountants at all levels of experience copied passages from the tax codes and regulations into opinion letters to clients, for example, directly and without quotation marks; yet, in tax protests to IRS agents, passages from the tax codes and regulations were explicitly quoted. Exploring that link between a textual strategy and a generic context led me to a broader understanding of both. Both their textual practices and their rhetorical strategizing supported their field's enmeshment with and necessary belief in the inviolability of the Tax Codes and Regulations, a larger epistemology that in turn helped to explain other textual practices. Without studying the context and the texts, I would not have understood either.

The role of the individual was less clear in this study initially since my attention had focused on shared practices over individual variation. Although there are notable exceptions, currently both composition and rhetoric and English language study tend to focus on the social over the individual. Advances in both fields of study might come from attempting to balance attention on both what is shared and what is unique in writing.

Within genre studies, some interesting questions emerge from a "language-based" approach to genre that attends to language in use. If form and context are so inextricably linked, how does the form of a genre change over time while the genre remains? Popken's (1999) study of the résumé, for example, found dramatic changes in the genre over time, yet it remains a résumé with the purpose of listing an applicant's qualifications and experience. Perhaps even more telling might be changes in literary genres. People still read novels, even though some of the novels they now read contain magical realism, can be read starting from either cover, or exist in digital links whose ordering the reader decides. How much can an individual writer vary within a genre and still fulfill readers' expectations? Did James Joyce vary too much at the time? How much personal voice can I use in a scholarly article and still be published? Such questions intimately link linguistic forms and rhetorical situations, and they make evident the significant role of individual writers in creating shared genres. Some of my current work is investigating how individuals use past rhetorical and textual knowledge of genres when they write unfamiliar genres. How does fluency in one genre influence development of new genres in a writer's repertoire? Do linguistic forms transfer from one writing situation to another without rhetorical context, or, as I suspect, do linguistic forms stay enmeshed with context when they transfer? If genres morph into new genres and individuals write unfamiliar genres through familiar ones, how do new genres distinguish themselves? Can a writer create a new genre?

The tools, knowledge, and perspectives of English language study make answering some of these questions possible. Analytical descriptions of forms make it possible to associate those forms with their contexts. Methods of studying historical change make it possible to trace textual changes along with social and cultural changes, and they provide models of language change, like the S-curve, to help interpret results. I suspect that patterns of linguistic variation might appear in generic variation as well, revealing how widespread a generic pattern is, whether its use is stratified, which variations are marked and which are most closely tied to group membership. The study of language acquisition within the study of English as a second language is proving helpful to me as I grapple with how first-language writers acquire new genres. All of this established scholarship within English language study extends our understanding of and reach into knowledge about writing.

And all of this scholarship can help with teaching writing as well (Devitt 2004, 191–213). Genre awareness involves consciousness of how language features and rhetorical contexts interact and the ability to make writing choices based on that knowledge. Teaching writing can involve teaching students that their textual choices have contextual significance and that their contexts become embodied in texts. Genres make that reciprocal relationship visible, so teaching genre awareness gives students access to that insight and a way to carry it out. Students can study genres historically, seeing how texts and contexts have changed over time with different effects. They can study genres of other cultures, noting how different cultures instantiate rhetorical situations differently. And they can study their own uses of genres, practicing using language differently in different contexts and varying its use to create their own situations. Such meta-linguistic and meta-contextual awareness surely precedes effective and educated writing.

Which parts of my teaching of genre awareness and of Standardized Edited English come from my education in English language study and which parts come from my education in composition and rhetoric, I could not say. To associate English language study only with form and composition and rhetoric only with context is to minimize both fields. I can say that both fields have much to offer the other. With so much to offer in tools, knowledge, and perspectives, English language study could expand its range and influence by spreading more fully into composition and rhetoric studies. Applying current English language study to the teaching of writing might even enable us to reclaim the benefits of textual practices like sentence combining, generative rhetoric, and even imitation, and—rather than abandon style, usage, organization, and other textual features—reinvigorate, reinterpret them into writing theories and practices. With a respect for both fields, we might develop new, "language-based" understandings of why, when, where, how, and what people write, a vision of writing that integrates the individual and the social, text and context, and written language with its written uses.

16

RESPONSE

Watch the Language: Scholarship, Teaching, and Change

SUSANMARIE HARRINGTON
University of Vermont

We expect a lot from English and its speakers: we want the language to flow trippingly off the tongue in public settings, we want it to mark boundaries between in groups and out groups, we want it to cultivate our dreams, and we want it to do our business. We also expect a lot from other people's English, and here the harsher side of humanity shows its face: too many speakers of English expect everyone else's English to sound like theirs and draw mean-spirited conclusions about people whose English is different. Such attitudes about English fly in the face of what philologists and linguists have demonstrated time and again: language variation and language change are a normal part of human experience, and every dialect of English is a full and complete language. The essays in this section tackle questions arising from the tensions between public (mis)understandings of language and scholarly approaches to language. They consider how scholarly attitudes about language have shaped paradigms in composition studies and affected litigation around language, as well as how popular attitudes about language have shaped school curricula. Questions running through this section include: *What can we usefully teach about language? What difference does language knowledge make? What do people need to know about the language they speak? What do people need to know about how language shapes their world?*

One might conclude, after reading this section, that modern language educators have a sorry lot. Dennis Baron's review of the last 50 years of language education suggests that American education has been largely unable to dent the perception that Good English is, well, Good, and that nonstandard Englishes are Not Good. Baron ends his essay by arguing back with the pessimism of his own essay's title, citing "a more relaxed and pragmatic approach to language" that prevails in everyday use. Good Enough English, Baron seems to say, would be a fine educational standard: English that's simply good enough to accomplish whatever needs doing. Though Good Enough English is, in fact, what most people speak and write, Baron's essay provides evidence that the barriers to embracing Good Enough English are formidable.

Those barriers arise from several public and scholarly issues. Amy Devitt's history of twentieth-century rhetoric and composition identifies the process movement as having inadvertently turned attention away from language itself. As scholars devoted increasing attention to studies of the rhetorical situation, an emphasis on writers' motives and understanding of rhetorical context seemed to draw attention away from language choices. Talking specifically about language came to be associated with retrograde pedagogies, and so language lost its place in composition studies. Geneva Smitherman and Minnie Quartey-Annan cite language tensions within the Black middle class and the public more broadly as factors that interfered with the translation of Black linguistic scholarship into pedagogical materials for public schools. Dennis Baron similarly cites English speakers' willingness to hold onto prescriptive notions of English grammar—and their own low self-esteem as language users—as factors in language curricula that reify Good English as an easily identifiable, easily taught, easily learned variety. Two accounts of the Ann Arbor case highlight the difficult public relations schools have encountered as they try to adapt curriculum in the face of narrow public attitudes about language and the realities of language variety on the schoolyard and in the classroom.

Taken together, these chapters suggest that dominant attitudes about English are influenced by social politics as well as individual attitudes. It hardly takes new scholarship to make that point; to say that institutions and individuals interact in a politically charged context to create language attitudes restates the assumption underlying sociolinguistics. But it bears repeating, for the chapters here prove that scholars who seek to shift public attitudes about Good English must strive, at every opportunity, to upend what appears to be common sense. It is, after all, common sense that drives people like Baron's student to think that prescriptive grammar is what must be taught in school. It is common sense that leads people to conclude that standard English is both necessary for business success and that the ability to speak/write it somehow creates success for individuals. It is common sense, that is, until language scholars find ways to change the stories about language that circulate in the public sphere.

Unexamined assumptions about standard English have enormous consequences, particularly for speakers of non-mainstream varieties. We need only a sample of two English speakers to find language variation: none of us uses exactly the same range of pronunciations, diction, grammar, and style as anyone else, no matter how closely our backgrounds and education match. But not all variations carry significant social weight. Rosina Lippi-Green's work demonstrates the ways that variation in the language of middle-class speakers draws little, if any, attention. As Lippi-Green (1997, 240) puts it, "People do not lose jobs because they wait *on line* rather than *in line*." But language discrimination indeed causes job loss: "people do lose jobs and schoolchildren are belittled because their native language makes it difficult for them to differentiate between *l* and *r* sounds; because their sentence intonations are Latino; because they say *y'all* rather than *all of you, aks* rather than *ask*" (Lippi-Green 1997, 241). Language attitudes are bound up in attitudes about diversity and culture. The intimate relationship of language and identity insists that public discussions of language acknowledge the complexity of language in use. Only then will speakers and writers rejoice in the competencies they bring to school and take pleasure in expanding their competencies through further study and application.

The chapters here share some pessimism about the ability of language scholarship to change society, but they share a hopeful vision. Innovative pedagogies and the rise of genre studies suggest that scholarship can get students and teachers to simply *pay attention* to language. In paying attention to language, students and teachers can see the richness of human experience reflected in and created by language. The message of this section is clear: when we take language seriously, carefully considering what choices speakers and writers make, we celebrate the power of language to create connections, to craft relationships, to influence others, to articulate identities. The power to use language—in all its varieties—is the power to use one's voice. The work of language scholars encourages the study of English, and most importantly, the ability to listen to English, all English, with generous ear and open mind.

Current Politics and Language Attitudes

When language scholars turn to educational settings in order to apply their work, they move into a context facing particular challenges. As I write, a particular challenge for English language scholar-teachers lies in calls for assessment and accountability. For the past decade, questions of assessment and standards have increased pressures on American educational institutions. These pressures have had mixed effects. John Bean (1996), Barbara Walvoord and Virginia Anderson (1998), and Grant Wiggin (2001) link assessment and learning. Yet the mainstream discourse about assessment and education pushes away from local and context-sensitive approaches to discussions of language and performance. Public debates about education and language default to broad strokes discussions that allegedly promote quality but in reality undermine an appreciation for the rich variation in American language.

Several recent initiatives, all purporting to raise levels of student performance via increased accountability, illustrate the tensions between reform efforts and language awareness. The No Child Left Behind Act (NCLB), signed in 2002, has heightened calls for school success to be measured in ways that suppress interest in language variation. The effects of NCLB are debatable, but it is clear that there has been an increase in tests taken by school children, with a concomitant focus on teaching to the test, an effect that has been roundly criticized by educational reformers and teachers alike (see Kohn 2007 and Nichols and Berliner 2008). The Spellings Commission's 2006 report on American higher education added to the discourse emphasizing narrow approaches to standards and accountability (U.S. Department of Education). The American Diploma Project, working to coordinate high school curricula, emphasizes the virtues of a curricular "common currency" based on expectations that would be "portable to other states" (2004, 4).

The challenge for language scholars is clear: in an atmosphere dominated by debates over high-stakes testing, how can we influence conversations to promote broader views of language competence and standards? The complicated stories language scholars tell about language—stories that affirm the value of African American Vernacular English not just at home but in public, stories that see bilingualism as a business asset, not a problem, stories that value regional vocabulary as a crucial part of a nation's heritage and present culture—don't fit well into school curricula dominated by a focus on tests and narrow views of assessment. English teachers are learning to tell stories more effectively in public. In 2005, the National Council of Teachers of English successfully reframed the public debate about including writing in the new SAT and ACT tests, adeptly deploying its task force report to highlight concerns about the test (NCTE 2005). National commentary on the test featured English professors—like Robert P. Yagelski, chair of the NCTE task force and Les Perelman of MIT—whose comments conveyed both the discipline's theoretical knowledge about writing and the pragmatic consequences of limiting classroom assessments (see Winerip 2005 and Baron 2005).

New stories are important: narrow conceptions of language performance in high-stakes testing will only further limit public perception about language (as well as further limiting what students learn about language in school). Successful language use encompasses a wide array of rhetorical, linguistic, and social components, and good assessments should honor the complexity of language. Bad assessments ignore what we know about English and undermine efforts to incorporate it into English curricula at all levels, so obstruct the progress of what we know into public understanding and public discourse. The public discourse about language and testing is thus an important context for the scholarly study of English. Students enter our classrooms with attitudes about education affected by their prior assessment experiences. State legislators, boards of trustees, and the interested public similarly hold views about language that take shape within the public discourse on education. Continued public calls for transparency, accountability, and portability of standards in education encourage the belief that language learning and language itself can be transported, unchanged by local or regional context. The wonders of language variation—of different lexical items, pronunciations, grammars, and politeness strategies—appear to be problems in a discourse— that of mainstream debates about education—that emphasizes sameness. No wonder Dennis Baron's former student resists incorporating descriptive grammatical precepts into his curriculum: prescriptive grammatical approaches fit into mainstream educational discourse much more smoothly, and that discourse exerts a powerful influence on day-to-day life in American high schools.

Public Perceptions of Language

Dennis Baron's *The Web of Language* comments on language stories in the news. Taking entries posted between December 2007 and June 2008 as one way to characterize popular attitudes about language, we see that fears about language change or conflicts regarding language account for about half the postings. Technology is frequently assumed to be stifling literacy or intelligibility (Baron 2008a and 2008c). It's not uncommon, especially on slow news days, to see reports about the dangers of netspeak: "IM shorthand slips off the screens and into the classroom" explains a headline in a typical story about students who can't keep clear boundaries between their online and academic worlds (Aratani 2006).

Such critiques favor a world in which formal language expectations hold sway and language change never occurs. The reality of language in action is more complicated. Despite media fondness for quoting statements like the Librarian of Congress's claim that texting was causing the death of the sentence, careful research shows a more nuanced effect. University of Toronto researchers found that IM text blends formal and informal features, and the researchers conclude: "these results challenge the adverse perceptions of IM promulgated in the media and suggest that they have been overblown…if our results are indicative, adolescents appear to abandon the 'funky' IM features at a very young age" (Tagliamonte and Denis 2008, 24; see also Baron 2008b). Nonetheless the media eagerly emphasizes what it sees as the negative.

Baron's posts repeatedly highlight supposed threats to language. The geographic proximity of languages leads to problems—lawsuits about English only, school districts banning Spanish on school buses, concerns about the encroachment of English in France, language tensions in Quebec—and in North America and Europe there seems to be no shortage of people worrying about the future of English. In their worrying, they seek to regulate technology, focus on standards, or eliminate bilingualism in efforts to protect and strengthen English.

The Role of Education

Worry about English is hardly a new story. Literacy crises have come and gone in America for the past two centuries. The current crisis as framed in the NCLB/Spellings Commission debates is only the latest crisis over the alleged failures of American schools. The charge that students aren't ready for higher education was one that Fred Newton Scott responded to in the late nineteenth century, challenging elite eastern universities' entrance examinations. When Richard W. Bailey was named the Fred Newton Scott Professor at the University of Michigan, he emphasized Scott's contributions to a democratic notion of American English built on a regard for both American English teachers and speakers. In Scott's day, eastern colleges preferred a system of college entrance examinations that would vet applicants' knowledge. Scott characterized such an approach as "feudal," and he favored instead the system in use in American's western universities, where accreditation processes ensured that high school graduates would be welcomed in western universities. The system trusted the teachers, and as Scott put it, what should be sought "in preparatory English is sympathetic, broad-minded, well-trained teachers. If such teachers can be found, we are willing to trust them implicitly" (qtd. in Bailey 2002a). Scott trusted not only teachers of English, but its speakers. This is a language tradition as old—if not as newsworthy—as the traditions of suspicion and critique that play so well in modern media. Bailey's address, in part, traces the trusting vibrancy of American English through the moves of American nationalists and literary figures, notably Walt Whitman. As students of Richard W. Bailey, many contributors to this volume are fifth generation students of Fred Newton Scott and figure in the legacy Bailey (2002a) described:

> Like Whitman, Scott saw the speech of ordinary people—those of "good moral character" that is—as a source of wisdom and potential excellence. Both Whitman and Scott, of course, were rooted in the Romanticism of Wordsworth who had famously celebrated the "real" language of leech- gatherers and others representative of the folk. It was from such language that poetry (or a future standard English) should be made, not from the affectation of the drawing rooms or the halls of academe.

Perhaps in the study of ordinary language we can hope to influence the language debates of the future. Professional organizations have done their share. For example, the NCTE's Conference on College Composition and Communication's *Students' Right to Their Own Language* resolution, passed in 1974, called on college teachers to value the language diversity of their students: "A nation proud of its diverse heritage and its cultural and racial variety will preserve its heritage of dialects. We affirm strongly that teachers must have the experiences and training that will enable them to respect diversity and uphold the right of students to their own language" (Conference on College Composition and Communication). Geneva Smitherman (1999, 349) argues that the CCCC "has served as the site of dialogues about language controversies" since its inception and has a "past record as advocate for those on the linguistic margins [that] is, on balance" worthy of praise. She highlights the politics of the "Students' Rights" resolution as well as its more recent Language Policy Committee, which works against English Only efforts. In addition to these organizational moves, we can look to decades of scholarship (like that quoted in Smitherman and Quartey-Annan) that have made concerns about identity, race, and language important in composition and language studies.

Amy Devitt's chapter, however, reminds us that transformations in language attitudes come not simply from professional and social contexts but also from quite personal ones. Her essay charts the transformation of her own willingness to embrace the study of language as part of her professional identity. Her introduction looks at the ways scholars in some parts of English studies reject the study of language itself as something that is "old-fashioned, apolitical, and ideologically suspect." It is easy to dismiss those conclusions with logic: no part of English Studies can really be said to be divorced from language study, and any part of English is self-conscious about its language. Richard W. Bailey's *Images of English* (1991a) illustrates the socio-political consequences of the ways English has been imagined by its speakers over time. Devitt likely knows these works. Her opening reflects, rather, the affective position of language in English Studies. In this response I join her in the project of looking to "help return language to the study and teaching of writing." She reminds us that even established language scholars need to engage with the emotional side of language study. Language and identity are intertwined, and part of that identity is emotional. Language educators and scholars need to address emotional needs as well as cognitive ones.

Those emotional needs are complicated. Dennis Preston's studies of speakers' perceptions of language variation demonstrate the interaction of self-esteem, regional politics, and national stereotypes (see pages 17–33 in this volume). Lippi-Green and Preston have both noted that to some extent, the South serves as a foil to the rest of the United States, providing a (real or imagined) basis of comparison against which speakers can rate themselves more highly. Yet, as Baron notes in this collection, most students don't rate their own language very highly. Preston's most recent scholarship reveals two factors at play in language judgments: cognitive judgments about correctness and affective judgments about pleasantness. This mixing of judgments complicates everyday language politics, creating a "middle ground" where stigmatized varieties move into mainstream discourse. This middle way offers hope for a way out of the pessimism of this section. Language prejudice abounds—but the energy of American democracy pushes against strict language standards even as it enforces them.

Nonstandard Englishes have a long history in political satire and social commentary. While Bailey's *Images of English* (1991a) and *Nineteenth-Century English* (1996b) illustrate the long history of disdain for nonstandard forms that emerges with the process of standardization over time, they also illustrate the function of nonstandard varieties beyond serving as regional or local in-group language. The proliferation of vernacular writing served to parody nonstandard speakers, highlight regional differences, and participate in political debates (see "Voices" in *Nineteenth-Century English*). Students and teachers alike are caught up in this tension between the emergence of standards and a celebration of the rough vernacular. We all work out the identities we claim, balancing our regional or social identifications as well as broader academic or social ambitions. Language choices aren't ever simple, and in the complexity of those choices, there is room for language scholarship to make a difference.

Everyday Scholars

Every American student is (at some point) a speaker of English whose experiences and attitudes matter—and every student is thus a scholar of English who can learn to see language as basic to our common humanity. Most students won't join us in making language scholarship their life's work, but we can ask them to join us in the life project of understanding language. That's what an everyday language scholar embodies.

A framed, hand-lettered admonition, *Watch the Language*, sits on a shelf in my office. A holiday gift from Richard Bailey to the Philology Reading Group at the University of Michigan in 1990, it reminded us to pay attention to language around us. We met monthly, studying a yearly theme. We paid attention to the language of the past, and in so doing, learned to pay attention to the language of the future. Robert Connors, historian of composition, noted:

> Since, more than other college-level course, the teaching of writing is tied in with larger cultural goals, dreams, and fears, our history, to be useful, must show us how this connection has developed and worked in the past....Composition history cannot exist in a narrow valley of the 'history of ideas' because all of our disciplinary ideas have been based in people's struggle for a better life. Purely philosophical history is mandarin history. Meaningful historical writing must teach us what people in the past have wanted from literacy so that we may come to understand what we want. (qtd. in Gaillet and Miller 2001, 147)

As the work in this collection demonstrates, the same frame applies to the relationship between language scholarship, language teaching, and education. The teaching of language itself is inextricably linked with "cultural goals, dreams, and fears." In learning to watch the language, we learn to watch a culture unfold. If the best hopes of those assembled here come to pass, we will watch the language carefully, and in so doing, influence the future culture it creates.

References

Adams, G. B. 1965. Materials for a Dialect Map of 17th Century Ireland. *Ulster Dialect Archive Bulletin* 4: 15–30.

Adams, G. B. 1979. The 1851 Language Census in the North of Ireland. *Ulster Folklife* 20: 65–70.

Adams, Michael. 1992. Review of Jürgen Schäfer, *Early Modern English Lexicography* (Oxford, U.K.: Clarendon Press, 1990). *Modern Philology* 90(2): 251–254.

Adams, Michael. 2002. *DARE*, History, and the Texture of the Entry. *American Speech* 77(4): 370–382.

Adams, Michael. 2007. The Critical Dictionary and the Wiki World. *English Today* 23(2): 9–15.

Adams, Michael. 2009. The Period Dictionaries. In *The Oxford History of English Lexicography*, 2 volumes, ed. A. P. Cowie, 1.326–352. Oxford, U.K.: Oxford University Press.

Adams, Michael. 2010. Legacies of the *Early Modern English Dictionary*. In *Adventuring in Dictionaries: New Studies in the History of Lexicography*, ed. John Considine, 290–308. Newcastle-upon-Tyne, U.K.: Cambridge Scholars Publishing.

Adams, Michael, and Richard W. Bailey. 2009. "Shut Up and Listen": An Interview with Richard W. Bailey. *Journal of English Linguistics* 37: 356–374.

Adamson, Bob. 2004. *China's English. A History of English in Chinese Education.* Hong Kong: Hong Kong University Press.

Adelung-Johann C. Adelung, *Grammatisch-kritisches Wörterbuch der Hochdeutschen Mundart.* Leipzig, Germany: J. G. I. Breitkopf, 1793–1801.

Ai, Xiaoxi. 2002. *Academic English Mastery Program: 2000–2001 Evaluation Report.* Los Angeles: Los Angeles Unified School District, Planning, Assessment and Research Division.

Aitken, A. J. 1973a. Definitions and Citations in a Period Dictionary. In *Lexicography in English, Annals of the New York Academy of Sciences 211*, ed. Raven I. McDavid and Audrey Duckert, 259–265. New York: New York Academy of Sciences.

Aitken, A. J. 1973b. Sub-sense Analysis for a Historical Dictionary. In *Lexicography and Dialect Geography: Festgabe for Hans Kurath*, ed. Harald Scholler and John Reidy, 5–16. Zeitschrift für Dialektologie und Linguistik 9. Wiesbaden, Germany: Franz Steiner Verlag.

Aitken, A. J. 1987. The Period Dictionaries. In *Studies in Lexicography*, ed. Robert Burchfield, 94–116. Oxford, U.K.: Clarendon.

Aitken, A. J., Richard W. Bailey, and N. Hamilton-Smith, eds. 1973. *The Computer and Literary Studies*. Edinburgh: Edinburgh University Press.

Aldus, Judith. 1976. Anglo-Irish Dialects: A Bibliography. *Regional Language Studies Newfoundland* 7: 7–28.

Alim, H. Samy. 2004. *You Know My Steez: An Ethnographic and Sociolinguistic Study of Style-shifting in a Black American Speech Community*. Publication of the American Dialect Society (PADS) 89. Durham, NC: Duke University Press.

Alim, H. Samy. 2006. *Roc the Mic Right: The Language of Hip Hop Culture*. New York: Routledge.

Allen, Don Cameron 1968. *The Ph.D. in English and American Literature*. New York: Holt, Rinehart and Winston.

Allsopp, Richard A., ed. 1996. *Dictionary of Caribbean English Usage*. Oxford, U.K.: Oxford University Press.

American Diploma Project. 2004. *Ready or Not: Creating a High School Diploma That Counts*. Washington DC: Achieve, Inc. www.achieve.org/files/ADPreport_7.pdf

Anthony, Piers. 2002. *Up in a Heaval*. New York: TOR.

Aratani, Lori. 2006. IM Shorthand Slips off Computer Screens and into Schoolwork. *The Washington Post* (December 25): A1.

Ashley, Hannah. 2001. Playing the Game: Proficient Working-Class Student Writers' Second Voices. *Research in the Teaching of English* 35: 493–524.

Avis, Walter S., ed. 1967. *Dictionary of Canadianisms on Historical Principles*. Toronto: Gage.

Bacon, Alan, ed. 1998. *The Nineteenth-Century History of English Studies*. Aldershot, U.K.: Ashgate

Bailey, Beryl Loftman. 1968. Some Aspects of the Impact of Linguistics on Language Teaching in Disadvantaged Communities. In *On the Dialects of Children*, Urbana, IL: National Council of Teachers of English, ed. A. L. Davis, 15–24. (Reprinted from *Elementary English* 45 (5): 570–578, 626.)

Bailey, Guy. 2001. The Relationship between African American Vernacular English and White Vernaculars in the American South: A Sociocultural History and Some Phonological Evidence. In *Sociocultural and Historical contexts of African American English*, ed. Sonja Lanehart, 53–92. Amsterdam: John Benjamins.

Bailey, Guy, Natalie Maynor, and Patricia Cukor-Avila. 1991. *The Emergence of Black English*. Amsterdam: John Benjamins.

Bailey, Guy, and Jan Tillery. 1999. The Rutledge Effect: The Impact of Interviewers on Survey Results in Linguistics. *American Speech* 74(4): 389–402.

Bailey, Richard W. 1965. *The Public and Private Styles of the Earl of Chesterfield*. Ph.D. dissertation, University of Connecticut.

Bailey, Richard W. 1973a. Reflections on Technology in Lexicography. In *Lexicography in English*, ed. Raven I. McDavid and Audrey R. Duckert, 293–297. New York: New York Academy of Sciences.

Bailey, Richard W. 1973b. Write Off vs. Write On: Dialects and the Teaching of Composition. In *Varieties of Present-Day English*, ed. Richard W. Bailey and Jay L. Robinson, 384–412. New York: Macmillan.

Bailey, Richard W. 1978. *Early Modern English: Additions and Antedatings to the Record of English Vocabulary, 1475–1700*. Hildesheim, Germany: Georg Olms.

Bailey, Richard W. 1979. The Future of Computational Stylistics. *Association for Literary and Linguistics Computing Bulletin* 7: 4–11.

Bailey, Richard W. 1980a. Determining Authorship in Ancient Greek. In *Proceedings of the International Conference on Literary and Linguistics Computing*, ed. Zvi Malachi, 279–290. Tel Aviv: The Katz Research Institute.

Bailey, Richard W. 1980b. Progress toward a Dictionary of Early Modern English 1475–1700. In *Proceedings of the Second International Roundtable on Historical Lexicography*, ed. W. Pijnenburg and F. de Tollenaere, 199–226. Dordrecht, The Netherlands: Foris.

Bailey, Richard W. 1980c. Our Readers Write: Black English and the Ann Arbor Public Schools. *English Journal* 69(6): 74.

Bailey, Richard W. 1981a. Education and the Law: The *King* Case in Ann Arbor. In *English and the Education of Black Children and Youth*, ed. Geneva Smitherman, 94–129. Detroit: Wayne State University Press.

Bailey, Richard W. 1981b. Press Coverage of the *King* Case. In *English and the Education of Black Children and Youth*, ed. Geneva Smitherman, 359–389. Detroit: Wayne State University Press.

Bailey, Richard W., ed. 1982. *Computing in the Humanities*. Amsterdam: North-Holland.

Bailey, Richard W. 1983. Litigation and Literacy: The Black English Case. In *Fforum: Essays on Theory and Practice in the Teaching of Writing*, ed. Patricia L. Stock, 128–132. Upper Montclair, NJ: Boynton-Cook.

Bailey, Richard W. 1985. Charles C. Fries and the *Early Modern English Dictionary*. In *Toward an Understanding of Language: Charles C. Fries in Perspective*, ed. Peter H. Fries and Nancy M. Fries, 171–204. Amsterdam: John Benjamins.

Bailey, Richard W. 1986. Dictionaries of the Next Century. In *Lexicography as an Emerging International Profession*, ed. Robert Ilson, 123–137. Manchester, U.K.: University of Manchester Press.

Bailey, Richard W. 1987a. On Some Discontiguities in Our English Dictionaries. In *Dictionaries of English*, ed. Richard W. Bailey, 136–161. Ann Arbor: University of Michigan Press.

Bailey, Richard W., ed. 1987b. *Dictionaries of English: Prospects for the Record of Our Language*. Ann Arbor: University of Michigan Press.

Bailey, Richard W. 1990a. The Period Dictionary: English. In *Wörterbücher/Dictionaries/ Dictionaries*, ed. Franz Josef Hausmann, Oskar Reichmann, Herbert Ernst Wiegand, and Ladislav Zgusta, 1436–1457. Berlin: Walter de Gruyter.

Bailey, Richard W. 1990b. *The Politics of the English Language: Issues to Consider in the Chinese Context. In ELT in China: Papers Presented at the International Symposium on Teaching English in the Chinese Context (ISTEC)*. Guangzhou, China 1985. Beijing Foreign Language and Research Press, 11–28.

Bailey, Richard W. 1991a. *Images of English: A Cultural History of the Language*. Ann Arbor: University of Michigan Press.

Bailey, Richard W. 1991b. Scots and Scotticisms: Language and Ideology. *Studies in Scottish Literature* 26: 65–77.

Bailey, Richard W. 1992. The First North American Dialect Survey. In *Old English and New: Studies in Language and Linguistics in Honor of Frederic G. Cassidy*, ed. Joan H. Hall, Nick Doane, and Dick Ringler, 305–326. New York: Garland.

Bailey, Richard W. 1996a. Centennial Celebration of *The Century Dictionary*: Origins. *Dictionaries: Journal of the Dictionary Society of North America* 17: 1–16.

Bailey, Richard W. 1996b. *Nineteenth-Century English*. Ann Arbor: University of Michigan Press.

Bailey, Richard W. 1996c. Attitudes toward English: The Future of English in South Asia. In *South Asia English: Structure, Use, and Users*, ed. Robert J. Baumgardner, 40–52. Urbana: University of Illinois Press.

Bailey, Richard W. 1997. The English Language in Japan. In *Englishes Around the World*. Vol. 2: *Caribbean, Africa, Asia, Australasia. Studies in Honour of Manfred Görlach*, ed. Edgar W. Schneider, 177–187. Amsterdam: John Benjamins.

Bailey, Richard W. 1998. Majority Language, Minority Misery: The Case of Sri Lanka. In *Language, Legislation, and Linguistic Rights*, ed. Douglas A. Kibbee, 206–224. Amsterdam: John Benjamins.

Bailey, Richard W. 2000a. The *OED* and the Public. In *Lexicography and the OED*, ed. Lynda Mugglestone, 253–284. Oxford, U.K.: Oxford University Press.

Bailey, Richard W. 2000b. This Unique and Peerless Specimen: The Reputation of the *OED*. In *Lexicography and the OED: Pioneers in the Untrodden Forest*, ed. Lynda Mugglestone, 207–227. Oxford, U.K.: Oxford University Press.

Bailey, Richard W. 2000c. Language at the Edges. *American Speech* 75: 385–386.

Bailey, Richard W. 2002a. Democracy in American English. Inaugural lecture delivered at the University of Michigan, 27 September 2002. www-personal.umich.edu/

Bailey, Richard W. 2002b. A Thousand Years of the History of English. *Studies in the History of the English Language: A Millennial Perspective*, ed. Donka Minkova and Robert Stockwell, 449–471. Berlin: Mouton de Gruyter.

Bailey, Richard W. 2003a. Ideologies, Attitudes, and Perceptions. In *Needed Research in American Dialects*, ed. Dennis R. Preston, 123–150. Publication of the American Dialect Society 88. Durham, NC: Duke University Press.

Bailey, Richard W. 2003b. *Rogue Scholar: The Sinister Life and Celebrated Death of Edward H. Rulloff*. Ann Arbor: University of Michigan Press.

Bailey, Richard W. 2004. D-Day Minus One. *Dictionaries: Journal of the Dictionary Society of North America* 25: 160–163.

Bailey, Richard W. 2007a. Centers and Peripheries. Paper presented at the 123rd Convention of the Modern Language Association, Chicago, 30 December.

Bailey, Richard W. 2007b. The Greatest Atlas Ever. Review of *The Atlas of North American English: Phonetics, Phonology, and Sound Change*, by William Labov, Sharon Ash, and Charles Boberg. *American Speech* 82: 292–300.

Bailey, Richard W. 2009. National and Regional Dictionaries of English. In *The Oxford History of English Lexicography: Volume 1: General-Purpose Dictionaries*, edited by A. P. Cowie, 279–301. Oxford, U.K.: Oxford University Press.

Bailey, Richard W. Forthcoming. *Speaking American*. Oxford, U.K.: Oxford University Press.

Bailey, Richard W., and Dolores M. Burton. 1968. *English Stylistics: A Bibliography*. Cambridge: The MIT Press.

Bailey, Richard W., and Anne Curzan. 1997. The Diary of Henry Machyn: An Electronic Text. In *Tracing the Trail of Time: Proceedings from the Second Diachronic Corpora Workshop*, ed. Raymond Hickey, Merja Kytö, Ian Lancashire, and Matti Rissanen, 25–31. Amsterdam: Rodopi.

Bailey, Richard W., and Lubomír Doležel. 1968. *An Annotated Bibliography of Statistical Stylistics*. Ann Arbor: Michigan Slavic Contributions.

Bailey, Richard W., James W. Downer, Jay L. Robinson, and Patricia V. Lehman. 1975. *Michigan Early Modern English Materials*. Ann Arbor: Xerox University Microfilms and the University of Michigan Press.

Bailey, Richard W., and Robin Melanie Fosheim, eds. 1983. *Literacy for Life: The Demand for Reading and Writing*. New York: Modern Language Association.

Bailey, Richard W., and Manfred Görlach, eds. 1982. *English as a World Language*. Ann Arbor: University of Michigan Press.

Bailey, Richard W., Marilyn S. Miller, and Colette V. Moore, eds. 2006. *A London Provisioner's Chronicle, 1550–1563, by Henry Machyn: Manuscript, Transcription and Modernization*. Ann Arbor: University of Michigan Press and the Scholarly Publication Office, the University of Michigan Library.

Bailey, Richard W., and Jay L. Robinson. 1973a. The Computer in Lexicography. In *Lexicography and Dialect Geography: Festgabe for Hans Kurath*, ed. Harald Scholler and John Reidy, 37–45. Zeitschrift für Dialektologie und Linguistic 9. Wiesbaden, Germany: Franz Steiner Verlag.

Bailey, Richard W., and Jay L. Robinson. 1973b. *Varieties of Present-Day English*. New York: Macmillan.

Baratz, Joan C., and Roger W. Shuy, eds. 1969. *Teaching Black Children to Read*. Washington, DC: Center for Applied Linguistics.

Baron, Dennis. 1982. *Grammar and Good Taste: Reforming the American Language*. New Haven, CT: Yale University Press.

Baron, Dennis. 1986. *Grammar and Gender*. New Haven, CT: Yale University Press.

Baron, Dennis. 1990. *The English-Only Question: An Official Language for Americans?* New Haven, CT: Yale University Press.

Baron, Dennis. 2000. Ebonics and the Politics of English. *World Englishes* 19: 5–20.

Baron, Dennis. 2005. The College Board's New Essay Reverses Decades of Progress toward Literacy. *The Chronicle of Higher Education* 51(35): B14.

Baron, Dennis. 2007. Illinois Bans Male Pronoun. http://go.illinois.edu/webof language

Baron, Dennis. 2008a. Is the Internet Killing Literacy, or Pumping New Life into It? *Web of Language* (26 January). http://illinois.edu/blog/view?topicId=1362

Baron, Dennis. 2008b. Researchers: IM definitely infectious, but associated linguistic damage short-lived, haha. *Web of Language* (25 April). http://illinois.edu/blog/view?topicId=1828

Baron, Dennis. 2008c. Txting blamed for the decline of French. *Web of Language* (30 May). http://illinois.edu/blog/view?topicId=1922

Baron, Dennis. *The Web of Language*. http://webtools.uiuc.edu/blog/view?blogId=25

Baron, Dennis E., Richard W. Bailey, and Jeffrey P. Kaplan. 2009. Brief in Support of Petitioners. *District of Columbia v. Heller*. 2008 Westlaw 157194 (U.S.). Eagan, MN: Thomson Reuters/West.

Baron, Naomi. 2008. *Always On: Language in an Online and Mobile World*. New York: Oxford University Press.

Barry, Michael V. 1981. The Southern Boundaries of Northern Hiberno-English Speech. In *Aspects of English Dialects in Ireland, Volume 1*, ed. Michael V. Barry, 52–95. Belfast: Institute of Irish Studies.

Barry, Michael. 1982. The English Language in Ireland. In *English as a World Language*, ed. Richard W. Bailey and Manfred Görlach, 84–133. Ann Arbor: University of Michigan Press.

Bartholomae, David. 1980. The Study of Error. *College Composition and Communication* 31: 253–269.

Barton, Ellen, and Gail Stygall, eds. 2002. *Discourse Studies in Composition*. Cresskill, NJ: Hampton Press.

Baugh, John. 1983. *Black Street Speech: Its History, Structure, and Survival.* Austin: University of Texas Press.

Baugh, John. 1999. *Out of the Mouths of Slaves: African American Language and Educational Malpractice.* Austin: University of Texas Press.

Baugh, John. 2000. *Beyond Ebonics: Linguistic Pride and Racial Prejudice.* New York: Oxford University Press.

Baugh, John. 2001. Applying Linguistic Knowledge of African American English to Help Students Learn and Teachers Teach. In *Sociocultural and Historical Contexts of African American English,* ed. Sonja Lanehart, 319–330. Amsterdam: John Benjamins.

Baugh, John. 2003. Linguistic Profiling. In *Black Linguistics: Language, Society, and Politics in Africa and the Americas,* ed. Cinfree Makoni, Geneva Smitherman, Arnetha F. Ball, and Arthur K. Spears, 155–168. New York: Routledge.

Bautista, Maria Lourdes S., ed. 1997. *English Is an Asian Language: The Philippine Context. Proceedings of the Conference Held in Manila on August 2–3, 1996.* Sydney: Macquarie Library.

BBC Radio 4 "Today." 2007. John Humphrys' interview of Frank Luntz, February 14, 2007. Accessed March 3, 2007 at www.bbc.co.uk/radio4/today/listenagain/zwednesday_20070214.shtml

Bean, John. 1996. *Engaging Ideas: The Professor's Guide to Integrating Writing, Critical Thinking and Active Learning in the Classroom*. San Francisco: Jossey-Bass.

Beech, Jennifer. 2004. Redneck and Hillbilly Discourse in the Writing Classroom: Classifying Critical Pedagogies of Whiteness. *College English* 67(2): 172–186.

Benfey, Theodor, 1839–1842. *Griechisches Wurzellexikon.* Berlin: M. Reimer.

Bennet, James. 1996. White House Rejects Federal Aid for Black English Courses. *New York Times* (December 25). http://www.nytimes.com

Benzie, William. 1983. *Dr. F. J. Furnivall: A Victorian Scholar Adventurer*. Norman, OK: Pilgrim Books.

Bereiter, Carl. 1965. Language Programs for Culturally Deprived Children. In *Language Programs for the Disadvantaged* (Report of the National Council of Teachers of English Task Force on Teaching English to the Disadvantaged), 195–203. Urbana, IL: National Council of Teachers of English.

Bereiter, Carl, and Siegfried Engelmann. 1966. *Teaching Disadvantaged Children in the Preschool.* Englewood Cliffs, NJ: Prentice-Hall.

Bereiter, Carl, Siegfried Engelman, Jean Osborn, and Philip A. Reidford. 1966. An Academically Oriented Pre-school for Culturally Disadvantaged Children. In *Pre-school Education Today*, ed. Fred M. Hechinger, 105–135. New York: Doubleday.

Bezzenberger, Adalbert 1907. *Weib* und *Weibel. Zeitschrift für vergleichende Sprachforschung* 41: 282.

Biber, Douglas. 1988. *Variation across Speech and Writing*. New York: Cambridge University Press.

Biber, Douglas, Stig Johansson, Geoffrey Leech, Susan Conrad, and Edward Finegan. 1999. *Longman Grammar of Spoken and Written English*. New York: Pearson ESL.

Bilderdijk, Willem. 1822. *Geslachtlijst der Nederduitsche Naamwoorden, op stellige taalgronden gevestigt.* Amsterdam: J. C. Sepp en Zoon.

Black Nonsense. 1971. *The Crisis* 78(3) (April/May): 78.

Blackwell, J.E. 1981. *Mainstreaming Outsiders: The Production of Black Professionals*. Bayside, NJ: General Hall.

Bliss, Alan. 1976. The English Language in Early Modern Ireland. In *A New History of Ireland: Volume III Early Modern Ireland 1534–1691*, ed. T. W. Moody, F. X. Martin, and F. J. Byrne, 546–560. Oxford, U.K.: Clarendon.

Bliss, Alan. 1979. *Spoken English in Ireland 1600-1740*. Dublin: Dolmen.

Bolton, Kingsley. 2003. *Chinese Englishes. A Sociolinguistic History*. Cambridge, U.K.: Cambridge University Press.

Bolton, Kingsley, and Braj B. Kachru, eds. 2006. *World Englishes*. 6 vols. Abingdon, U.K.: Routledge.

Bonfiglio, Thomas P. 2002. *Race and the Rise of Standard American*. New York: Mouton de Gruyter.

Bormann, E. G. 1971. *Forerunners of Black Power: The Rhetoric of Abolition*. Englewood Cliffs, NJ: Prentice-Hall.

Boswell, James. 1934. *The Life of Samuel Johnson LL.D*, Volume II, *1766–1776*, ed. L. F. Powell. Oxford, U.K.: Clarendon Press.

Bourdieu, Pierre. 1991. *Language and Symbolic Power*. Cambridge, MA: Harvard University Press.

Braidwood, John. 1964. Ulster and Elizabethan English. In *Ulster Dialects: An Introductory Symposium*, ed. G. B. Adams, 5–109. Hollywood, Ireland: Ulster Folk Museum.

Branford, Jean, ed. 1978. *A Dictionary of South African English*. Oxford, U.K.: Oxford University Press.

Brewer, Charlotte. 2004. The "Electronification" of the *OED*. *Dictionaries* 25: 1–43.

Brewer, Charlotte. 2007. *Treasure-House of the Language: The Living OED*. New Haven, CT: Yale University Press.

Britton, James, et. al. 1975. *The Development of Writing Abilities (11–18)*. London: Macmillan.

Brooks, Charlotte K., ed. 1985. *Tapping Potential: English and Language Arts for the Black Learner*. Urbana, IL: National Council of Teachers of English.

Brown, David West. 2009. *In Other Words: Lessons on Grammar, Code-Switching, and Academic Writing*. Portsmouth, NH: Heinemann.

Bucholtz, Mary. 2003. Sociolinguistic Nostalgia and the Authentication of Identity. *Journal of Sociolinguistics* 7: 398–416.

Burling, Robbins. 1973. *English in Black and White*. New York: Holt, Rinehart, and Winston.

Byers, John W. 1916. Shakespeare and the Northern Dialect. *Northern Whig* 22 (April).

Campbell, Charles D. 1905. *The Names of Relationship in English: A Contribution to English Semasiology*. Strasbourg, France: J. H. Ed. Heitz (Heitz & Mündel).

Cantor, Geoffrey. 1991. *Michael Faraday: Sandemanian and Scientist*. Houndmills, U.K.: Macmillan.

Carleton, William. 1830. *Traits and Stories of the Irish Peasantry*. Dublin: W. F. Wakeman.

Carpenter, Jeannine. 2004. *The Lost Community of the Outer Banks: African American Speech on Roanoke Island*. M.A. thesis, North Carolina State University.

Carpenter, Jeannine. 2005. The Invisible Community of the Lost Colony: African American English on Roanoke Island. *American Speech* 80: 227–256.

Carr, Michael. 1997. Internet Dictionaries and Lexicography. *International Journal of Lexicography* 10: 209–221.

Cassidy, Frederic G. 1987. The *Oxford English Dictionary* and the *Dictionary of American Regional English*: Some Differences of Practice. In *Dictionaries of English: Prospects for the History of Our Language*, ed. Richard W. Bailey, 22–29. Ann Arbor: University of Michigan Press.

Cassidy, Frederic G., and R. B. LePage, eds. 1967. *Dictionary of Jamaican English*. 2nd ed., 1980. Cambridge, U.K.: Cambridge University Press.

Center for Applied Linguistics. 1979. *Ann Arbor Decision, The Memorandum, Opinion, and Order & The Educational Plan*. Washington, DC: Center for Applied Linguistics.

Chase, Richard. 1943. *The Jack Tales*. Boston: Houghton Mifflin.

Childs, Becky, and Christine Mallinson. 2006. The Significance of Lexical Items in the Construction of Ethnolinguistic Identity: A Case Study of Adolescent Spoken and Online Language. *American Speech* 81: 3–30.

Childs, Becky, and Christine Mallinson. 2004. African American English in Appalachia: Dialect Accommodation and Substrate Influence. *English World-Wide* 25: 27–50.

Christensen, Francis. 1967. *Notes toward a New Rhetoric: Six Essays for Teachers*. New York: Harper & Row.

Claridge, Claudia. 2009. Historical Corpora. In *Corpus Linguistics: An International Handbook*, ed. Anke Lüdeling and Merja Kytö, 242–259. Berlin: Mouton de Gruyter.

Coates, Jennifer, ed. 1998. *Language and Gender: A Reader.* Oxford, U.K.: Blackwell.

Coleman, Julie. 2004. *A History of Cant and Slang Dictionaries. Volume 1: 1567–1783. Volume II: 1753–1858*. Oxford, U.K.: Oxford University Press.

Coleman, Julie, and Sarah Ogilvie. 2009. Forensic Dictionary Analysis: Principles and Practice. *International Journal of Lexicography* 22(2): 1–22.

Conference on College Composition and Communication (CCCC). 1974. Students' Right to Their Own Language. *College Composition and Communication* 25(3): 1–32. http://www.ncte.org/ about/over/positions/category/lang

Conference on College Composition and Communication (CCCC). 1988. *National Language Policy.* Urbana, IL: National Council of Teachers of English.

Congressional Record. 1873–. Washington, DC: U.S. Congress.

Connors, Robert J. 2000. The Erasure of the Sentence. *College Composition and Communication* 52(1): 96–128.

Corrigan, Karen. 1990. Northern Hiberno-English: The State of the Art. *Irish University Review* 20(1): 92–119.

Court, Franklin E. 1992. *Institutionalizing English Literature: The Culture and Politics of Literary Study.* Palo Alto, CA: Stanford University Press.

Cowie, A. P. 1978. The Place of Illustrative Material and Collocations in the Design of a Learner's Dictionary. In *In Honour of A. S. Hornby*, ed. P. Strevens, 127–139. Oxford, U.K.: Oxford University Press.

Craig, Holly, and Julie Washington. 2006. *Malik Goes to School: Examining the Language Skills of African American Students from Preschool–5th Grade*. Mahwah, NJ: Lawrence Erlbaum.

Craigie, William A. 1925–1930. New Dictionary Schemes Presented to the Philological Society, 4 April 1919. *Transactions of the Philological Society*: 6–11.

Craigie. William A. 1941. Completing the Record of English. *Society for Pure English Tract 58*, 267–304. Oxford, U.K.: Clarendon.

Craigie, William A., et al., eds. 1931–2002. *Dictionary of the Older Scottish Tongue.* 12 vols. Chicago: University of Chicago Press/Oxford, U.K.: Oxford University Press.

Craigie, William A., and James R. Hulbert, eds. 1938–1944. *Dictionary of American English on Historical Principles.* 4 vols. Chicago: University of Chicago Press.

Crocker, Betty. 1956. *Picture Cook Book.* 2d ed. New York: McGraw-Hill.

Croghan, Martin. 1988. A Bibliography of English in Ireland: Problems with Names and Boundaries. In *Anglo-Irish and Irish Literature: Aspects of Language and Culture*, ed. Birgit Bramsback and Martin Croghan, 103–115. Uppsala, Sweden: Almqvist and Wiksell.

Croghan, Martin. 1990. Demythologizing Hiberno-English. *Irish Studies Working Papers* 90-1.

Crowley, Tony. 2005. *The War of Words: The Politics of Language in Ireland 1537–2004.* Oxford, U.K.: Oxford University Press.

Crystal, David. 1997. *English as a Global Language.* Cambridge, U.K.: Cambridge University Press.

Crystal, David. 2004. *The Language Revolution.* Cambridge, MA: Polity Press.

Cukor-Avila, Patricia. 1995. *The Evolution of AAVE in a Rural Texas Community: An Ethnolinguistic Study.* Ph.D. dissertation. Ann Arbor: University of Michigan.

Cukor-Avila, Patricia. 2001. Co-existing Grammars: The Relationship between the Evolution of African American and Southern White Vernacular English in the South. In *Sociocultural and Historical Contexts of African American English*, ed. Sonja L. Lanehart, 93–128. Amsterdam: John Benjamins.

Cukor-Avila, Patricia, and Guy Bailey. 2001. The Effects of the Race of the Interviewer on Sociolinguistic Fieldwork. *Journal of Sociolinguistics* 5(2): 252–270.

Cullinan, Bernice E., ed. 1974. *Black Dialects and Reading.* Urbana, IL: National Council of Teachers of English.

Cunningham, Ward, and Bo Leuf. 2001. *The Wiki Way: Quick Collaboration on the Web.* Boston: Addison Wesley.

Curzan, Anne. 2008. Corpus-based Approaches to the History of English. In *A Companion to the History of the English Language*, ed. Michael Matto and Haruko Momma, 596–607. Malden, MA: Wiley Blackwell.

Dale, Thomas 1829. An Introductory Lecture Delivered in the University of London, on Friday, October 24, 1828. *Ten Introductory Lectures Delivered at the Opening of the University of London.* 4th ed. London: Printed for John Taylor.

D'Andrea, Kristy D. 2005a. The Shifting Significance of 3rd singular *–s* absence as Compared to *r*-lessness in Princeville, NC. Unpublished manuscript. North Carolina State University.

D'Andrea, Kristy D. 2005b. African American English in Princeville, NC: Looking at Dialect Change through the Feature of *r*-lessness. Paper presented at annual meeting of the American Dialect Society Annual Meeting, in Oakland, California.

D'Angelo, Frank J. 1975. *A Conceptual Theory of Rhetoric.* Cambridge, MA: Winthrop.

D'Angelo, James F. 2005. Educated Japanese English: Expanding Oral/Aural Core Vocabulary. *World Englishes* 24: 329–349.

Davis, Marcus. 1865. *Everybody's Business. A Guide to Correct Speech*. London: Longman.

Delpit, Lisa, and Theresa Perry. 1998. *The Real Ebonics Debate: Power, Language, and the Education of African-American Children*. Boston: Beacon Press.

Denham, Kristin, and Anne Lobeck. Forthcoming. *Linguistics at School: Language Awareness in Primary and Secondary Education*. Oxford, U.K.: Oxford University Press.

Deterding, David. 2006. The Pronunciation of English by Speakers from China. *English World-Wide* 27: 175–198.

De Tollenaere, F. 1987. [Rev. of] Meijerling, H. D. [1985]. *Leuvense Bijdragen* 76: 205–208.

Deutsch, Martin. 1963. The Disadvantaged Child and the Learning Process. In *Education in Depressed Areas*, ed. A. Harry Passow, 163–179. New York: Columbia University Press.

Devitt, Amy J. 1989. *Standardizing Written English: Diffusion in the Case of Scotland 1520–1659*. New York: Cambridge University Press.

Devitt, Amy J. 1991. Intertextuality in Tax Accounting: Generic, Referential, and Functional. In *Textual Dynamics of the Professions: Historical and Contemporary Studies of Writing in Professional Communities*, ed. Charles Bazerman and James Paradis, 336–357. Madison: University of Wisconsin Press.

Devitt, Amy J. 2004. *Writing Genres*. Carbondale: Southern Illinois University Press.

Dialect Notes. 1890–1939. New Haven, CT: American Dialect Society.

Dickens, Charles. 1853. *Bleak House*. London: Bradbury & Evans.

Dickens, Charles. 1861. *Great Expectations*, 3 vols. London: Bradbury and Evans.

Dictionary of American Regional English. 1985–. Volume I (Introduction and A–C), 1985; ed. Frederic G. Cassidy; Volume II (D–H), 1991; ed. Frederic G. Cassidy and Joan Houston Hall; Volume III (I–O), 1996; ed. Frederic G. Cassidy and Joan Houston Hall; Volume IV (P–Sk-), 2002; ed. Joan Houston Hall. Cambridge, MA: Belknap Press of Harvard University Press.

Dictionary of Old English. 1986– . Ed. Angus Cameron, Ashley Crandall Amos, Antonette diPaolo Healey, and others. A–G published to date. Toronto: Pontifical Institute of Mediaeval Studies.

Dictionary of the Older Scottish Tongue. 1931–2001. Ed. W. A. Craigie, A. J. Aitken, J. A. C. Stevenson, and others. Chicago: University of Chicago Press.

Diefenbach, Lorenz. 1851. *Vergleichendes Wörterbuch der gothischen Sprache*. Frankfurt am Main: Joseph Baer.

Dillard, J. L. 1967. Negro Children's Dialect in the Inner City. *The Florida FL Reporter* (Fall): 2–4.

Dolan, Terence P., ed. 1998. *Dictionary of Hiberno-English*. Dublin: Gill & Macmillan. 2nd ed. 2004.

Dolan, Terence P. 2000. The Compilation of a Dictionary of Hiberno English. In *Celtic Englishes II*, ed. Hildegard L. C. Tristram, 323–328. Heidelberg, Germany: Winter.

Dolan, Terence P. 2002– . *Dictionary of Hiberno-English*. <http://www.hiberno-english.com/index.html>. Dublin: University College.

Doležel, Lubomír, and Richard W. Bailey, eds. 1969. *Statistics and Style*. New York: American Elsevier.

Douglas, Sylvester. 1991 [1779]. *A Treatise on the Provincial Dialect of Scotland*. Ed. Charles Jones. Edinburgh: Edinburgh University Press.

Duanmu, San. 2000. *The Phonology of Standard Chinese*. Oxford, U.K.: Oxford University Press.

Duggan, G. C. 1937. *The Stage Irishman: A History of the Irish Play and Stage Characters from the Earliest Times*. London: Blom.

Eagleton, Terry 1996. *Literary Theory: An Introduction*. Second edition. Minneapolis: University of Minnesota Press.

Eckert, Penelope. 2000. *Linguistic Variation as Social Practice: The Linguistic Construction of Identity in Belten High*. Malden, MA: Blackwell Publishers.

Ellert, Ernest E. 1946. *The Etymology and Semantic Development of Words of Family Relationship in the Germanic Languages*. Unpublished Ph.D. dissertation, University of North Carolina.

Ellis, A. J. 1869–1889. *Early English Pronunciation*. 5 volumes. London: Asher & Company for the Philological Society and Trübner & Company for the Early English Text Society and the Chaucer Society.

Ellis, J. 1956. [Untitled.] In *Proceedings of the Seventh International Congress of Linguists, London, 1–6 September 1952*, ed. F. Norman and P. F. Ganz, 169–170. London: [n.p.].

Emig, Janet. 1971. *The Composing Processes of Twelfth Graders*. NCTE Research Report 13. Urbana, IL: National Council of Teachers of English.

English Dialect Dictionary. 1898–1905. Ed. Joseph Wright. London: H. Frowde/New York: G.P. Putnam's Sons.

Erskine, John and Gordon Lucy, eds. 1997. *Varieties of Scottishness: Exploring the Ulster-Scottish Connection*. Belfast: Institute of Irish Studies.

Erskine, John G. W., and Michael Montgomery. 2006. Annotated Bibliography of Ulster-Scots Language and Literature. In *The Academic Study of Ulster-Scots: Essays for and by Robert J. Gregg*, ed. Anne Smyth et al., 99–118. Holywood, Ireland: Ulster Folk and Transport Museum.

Faraday, Michael. 1816–1846. Lectures on Oratory by M[r] B. H. Smart. *Common Place Book*. IEE UK0108 SC MSS 002/1/4. London: The Institution of Electrical Engineers.

Faraday, Michael. 1859. Observations on Mental Education. *Experimental Researches in Chemistry and Physics*. London: Taylor & Francis. 463–491.

Fasold, Ralph W. 1972. *Tense Marking in Black English: A Linguistic and Social Analysis*. Arlington, VA: Center for Applied Linguistics.

Fasold, Ralph W., and Roger W. Shuy. 1970. *Teaching Standard English in the Inner City*, Washington, DC: Center for Applied Linguistics.

Fasold, Ralph W., and Walt Wolfram. 1970. Some Linguistic Features of Negro Dialect. In *Teaching Standard English in the Inner City*, ed. Ralph W. Fasold and Roger Shuy, 41–86. Washington, DC: Center for Applied Linguistics.

Fasold, Ralph W., William Labov, Fay Boyd Vaughn-Cooke, Guy Bailey, Walt Wolfram, Arthur K. Spears, and John R. Rickford. 1987. Are Black and White Vernacular Varieties Diverging? Papers from the NWAVE-16 Panel Discussion. *American Speech* 56: 3–80.

Feigenbaum, Irwin. 1970. The Use of Nonstandard English in Teaching Standard: Contrast and Comparison. In *Teaching Standard English in the Inner City*, ed. Ralph Fasold and Roger Shuy, 87–104. Washington, DC: Center for Applied Linguistics.

Fenton, James. 1995. *The Hamely Tongue: a Personal Record of Ulster-Scots in County Antrim*. Newtownards: Ulster-Scots Academic Press. 2nd ed. Belfast: Ullans Press, 2000; 3rd ed. Belfast: Ullans Press, 2006.

Finegan, Edward. 1980. *Attitudes toward English Usage: The History of a War of Words*. New York: Teachers College Press.

Fitzgerald, Garret. 1984. Estimates for Baronies of Minimal Levels of Irish-Speaking amongst Successive Decennial Cohorts, 1771–1781 to 1861–1871. *Proceedings of the Royal Irish Academy* 84, Section C, 117–155.

Florio, John. 1598. *World of Wordes*. London: Printed by Arnold Hatfield for Edw. Blount.

Florio, John. 1611. *Queen Anna's New World of Words*. London: Printed by Melch. Bradwood [and William Stansby] for Edw. Blount and William Barrett.

Flower, Linda, and John R. Hayes. 1980. The Cognition of Discovery: Defining a Rhetorical Problem. *College Composition and Communication* 31: 21–32.

Flower, Linda, and John R. Hayes. 1981. A Cognitive Process Theory of Writing. *College Composition and Communication* 32(4): 365–387.

Flowerdew, Linda. 2005. An Integration of Corpus-Based and Genre-Based Approaches to Text Analysis in EAP/ESP: Countering Criticisms against Corpus-Based Methodologies. *English for Specific Purposes* 24: 321–332.

Free, John 1968 [1749]. *An Essay Towards an History of the English Tongue.* Facsimile edition. Menston, U.K.: Scolar Press.

Gaillet, Lynee, and Thomas Miller. 2001. Making Use of the Nineteenth Century: The Writings of Robert Connors and Recent Histories of Rhetoric and Composition. *Rhetoric Review* 20(1/2): 147–157.

Gates, Henry Louis. 1988. *The Signifying Monkey.* New York: Oxford University Press.

Giles, Jim. 2008. Words Nerd Sites are Helping the Dictionary Pros. *New Scientist* 2 (February): 22–23.

Gladstone, J. H. 1872. *Michael Faraday.* London: Macmillan and Co.

Gneuss, Helmut 1996. *English Language Scholarship: A Survey and Bibliography from the Beginnings to the End of the Nineteenth Century.* Binghamton, NY: Center for Medieval and Early Renaissance Studies.

Golden, Ruth I. 1960. *Improving Patterns of Language Usage.* Detroit: Wayne State University Press.

Golden, Ruth I. 1962. *The Effectiveness of Instructional Tapes for Changing Regional Speech Patterns.* Detroit: Detroit Public Schools.

González, Roseann D., with Ildikó Melis. 2001. *Language Ideologies: Critical Perspectives on the Official English Movement.* Vols. 1 and 2. Urbana, IL: National Council of Teachers of English.

Goodman, Kenneth and Catherine Buck. 1973. Dialect Barriers to Reading Comprehension Revisited. *Reading Teacher* 27: 6–12.

Gordon, Matthew. 2006. Interview with William Labov. *Journal of English Linguistics* 34: 332–351.

Görlach, Manfred. 1991. *Englishes.* Amsterdam: John Benjamins.

Görlach, Manfred. 1995a. Dictionaries of Transplanted Englishes. In *More Englishes: New Studies in Varieties of English 1988–1994,* 124–163. Amsterdam: John Benjamins.

Görlach, Manfred. 1995b. "Irish English and Irish Culture in Dictionaries of English." In *More Englishes: New Studies in Varieties of English, 1988–94,* 164–191. Amsterdam: John Benjamins.

Görlach, Manfred. 1995c. *More Englishes.* Amsterdam: John Benjamins.

Gould, Peter, and Rodney White. 1974. *Mental Maps.* Baltimore, MD: Penguin.

Graff, David, William Labov, and Wendell A. Harris. 1986. Testing Listeners' Reactions to Phonological Markers of Ethnic Identity: A New Method for Sociolinguistic Research. In *Diversity and Diachrony,* ed. David Sankoff, 45–58. Amsterdam: John Benjamins.

Graff, Gerald. 1987. *Professing Literature: An Institutional History*. Chicago: University of Chicago Press.

Graff, Gerald, and Michael Warner, eds. 1989. *The Origins of Literary Study in America: A Documentary Anthology*. New York: Routledge.

Grant, William. 1931. Introduction. *Scottish National Dictionary*. Vol. 1 viii–xlvi. Edinburgh: Scottish National Dictionary Association.

Green, Jonathon. 1996. *Chasing the Sun: Dictionary-Makers and the Dictionaries They Made*. New York: Henry Holt & Co.

Green, Lisa J. 2002. *African American English: A Linguistic Introduction*. New York: Cambridge University Press.

Green, Lisa. 2004. African American Vernacular English. In *Language in the USA: Themes for the Twenty-first Century*, ed. Edward Finegan and John R. Rickford, 76–91. Cambridge, U.K.: Cambridge University Press.

Gregg, Robert J. 1951. The Ulster Dialect Dictionary. *Ulster Education* (September: 24–25).

Gregg, Robert J. 1972. The Scotch-Irish Dialect Boundaries in Ulster. In *Patterns in the Folk Speech of the British Isles*, ed. Martyn Wakelin, 109–139. London: Athlone.

Grimm, Jacob 1831. *Deutsche Grammatik*. Vol. 3. Göttingen, Germany: Dietrichsche Buchhandlung.

Grimm, Jacob. 1835. *Deutsche Mythologie*. Göttingen, Germany: Dietrichsche Buchhandlung.

Guskin, J. 1970. Social Perceptions of Language Variation: Black Dialect and Exceptions of Ability. Paper presented at the American Research Association Conference, Minneapolis, MN, March.

Hairston, Maxine. 1982. The Winds of Change: Thomas Kuhn and the Revolution in the Teaching of Writing. *College Composition and Communication* 33(1): 76–88.

Halimah, Mohd Said, and Ng Keat Siew, eds. 2000. *English Is an Asian Language: The Malaysian Context*. Kuala Lumpur: Persatuan Bahasa Moden Malaysia/ Sydney: Macquarie Library.

Hall, Joseph S. Unpublished collection of dialect materials from the Great Smoky Mountain National Park, Tennessee and North Carolina, 1937–1987.

Hamilton, James. 2002. *Faraday: The Life*. London: HarperCollins.

Hannah, Dawn. 1997. Copula Absence in Samaná English: Implications for Research on the Linguistic History of African-American Vernacular English. *American Speech* 72(4): 339–372.

Harris, John. 1984. English in the North of Ireland. In *Language in the British Isles*, ed. Peter Trudgill, 115–134. Cambridge, U.K.: Cambridge University Press.

Harris, John. 1986. Expanding the Superstrate: Habitual Markers in Atlantic Englishes. *English World-Wide* 7: 171–199.

Harris-Wright, Kelli. 1999. Enhancing Bidialectalism in Urban African American Students. In *Making the Connection: Language and Academic Achievement Among African American Students*, ed. Carolyn T. Adger, Donna Christian, and Orlando Taylor, 53–60. Washington, DC: Center for Applied Linguistics.

Hartley, Laura C. 1999. A View from the West: Perceptions of US Dialects by Oregon Residents. In *Handbook of Perceptual Dialectology: Volume 1*, ed. Dennis R. Preston, 315–332. Amsterdam: John Benjamins.

Hartman, James W. 1984. Some Possible Trends in the Pronunciation of Young Americans (Maybe). *American Speech* 59(3): 218–225.

Hempl, George. 1896a. American Speech-maps. *Dialect Notes* 1: 315–318.

Hempl, George. 1896b. *Grease* and *Greasy*. *Dialect Notes* 1: 438–444.

Hempl, George. 1902. Stovepipes and Funnels. *Dialect Notes* 2: 250–256.

Hempl, George. 1904. The Teacher of English and His Attitude toward His Subject. *PMLA* 12: xxxi–liii.

Henry, Patrick L. 1958. *A Linguistic Survey of Ireland: Preliminary Report.* Lochlann 1: 49–208.

Hickey, Raymond. 2002. *A Source Book for Irish English.* Amsterdam: John Benjamins.

Hickey, Raymond. 2007. *Irish English: History and Present-Day Forms.* Cambridge, U.K.: Cambridge University Press.

Hindley, Reg. 1990. *The Death of the Irish Language: A Qualified Obituary*. London: Routledge.

Hirsch, E. D., Jr. 1977. *The Philosophy of Composition*. Chicago: University of Chicago Press.

Hirt, Herman 1909. *Etymologie der neuhochdeutschen Sprache.* Handbuch des deutschen Unterrichts IV/2. München: C. H. Beck. 2nd ed., 1921.

Historical Dictionary of American Slang. 1994– . 2 volumes to date. Ed. J. E. Lighter. New York: Random House.

Hogan, James Jeremiah. 1927. *The English Language in Ireland.* Dublin: Educational Company of Ireland.

Hogan, James Jeremiah. 1944. Notes on the Study of Anglo-Irish Dialect. *Béaloideas* 14:187–191.

Hollie, Sharroky. 2000. *African American Students as Standard English Language Learners: An Alternative Approach.* Ph.D. dissertation, University of Southern California.

Holm, John A., and Allison Watt Schilling. 1982. *Dictionary of Bahamian English.* Cold Spring, AR: Lexik House.

Holthausen, Ferdinand 1920. Worterklärungen. *Germanisch-romanische Monatsschrift* 8: 182–184, 249–250, 366–369.

Horn, Laurence. 2004. *Spitten Image*: Etymythology and Fluid Dynamics. *American Speech* 79: 33–58.

Hume, David. 1757. *Four Dissertations.* Vol. 4, *Of the Standard of Taste.* London: Millar.

Hurlbert, C. Mark, and Michael Blitz. 1991. *Composition and Resistance.* Portsmouth, NH: Boynton/Cook.

Hurst, Charles, G. 1965. *Psychological Correlates in Dialectolalia.* Washington, DC: Communication Sciences Research Center, Cooperative Research Project No. 2610.

Hurst, Charles G. 1968. Participant, Seminar on Social Dialects, National Council of Teachers of English Annual Convention. Milwaukee, Wisconsin, November 30.

An Index by Region, Usage, and Etymology to the "Dictionary of American Regional English," Volumes I and II. 1993. Ed. Luanne von Schneidemesser and Allan Metcalf. Publication of the American Dialect Society 77. Tuscaloosa: University of Alabama Press.

An Index by Region, Usage, and Etymology to the "Dictionary of American Regional English," Volume III. 1999. Ed. Luanne von Schneidemesser. Publication of the American Dialect Society 82. Durham, NC: Duke University Press.

International Phonetic Association. 1999. *Handbook of the International Phonetic Association.* Cambridge: Cambridge University Press.

James, F. A. J. L. (ed.) 1991–1999. *The Correspondence of Michael Faraday.* Volume 1, *1811–1831* (1991); Volume 2, *1832–1840* (1993); Volume 3, *1841–1848* (1996); Volume 4, *1849–1855* (1999). London: The Institution of Electrical Engineers.

James, F. A. L. J. 2004. Faraday, Michael (1791–1867). *Oxford Dictionary of National Biography* Oxford: Oxford University Press. http://www.oxforddnb.com/view/article/9153, accessed 18 Jan 2007

Johansson, Karl F. 1893. Sanskritische Etymologien. *Indogermanische Forschungen* 2: 1–64.

Johnson, Sally. 2001. Who's Misunderstanding Whom? Sociolinguistics Debate and the Media. *Journal of Sociolinguistics* 5: 591–610.

Johnson, Samuel. 1747. *Plan of a Dictionary of the English Language.* London: J. & P. Knapton, T. Longman and T. Shewell, C. Hitch, A. Millar, and R. Dodsley.

Johnson, Samuel. 1755. *A Dictionary of the English Language.* London: W. Strahan.

Johnson, Samuel. 1825. *The Works of Samuel Johnson, L.L.D.* 11 volumes. Oxford, U.K.: Talboys.

Johnstone, Barbara. 1996. *The Linguistic Individual: Self-Expression in Language and Linguistics*. New York: Oxford University Press.

Jones, H. Bence. 1870. *The Life and Letters of Faraday*. London: Longmans, Green, and Co.

Joseph, John E. 2002. *From Whitney to Chomsky: Essays in the History of American Linguistics*. Amsterdam: John Benjamins.

Joyce, Patrick W. 1910. *English as We Speak It in Ireland*. London: Longmans, Green. Reprinted in 1981 by Wolfhound, Dublin, with a new introduction by Terence Dolan.

Kachru, Braj B., ed. 1982/1992. *The Other Tongue: English across Cultures*. 2nd ed. Urbana: University of Illinois Press.

Kachru, Braj B. 1986. *The Alchemy of English: The Spread, Functions, and Models of Non-native Englishes*. Oxford, U.K.: Oxford University Press.

Kachru, Braj B., ed. 1992. *The Other Tongue: English across Cultures*. Urbana: University of Illinois Press.

Kachru, Braj B. 1997. English as an Asian language. In *English Is an Asian Language: The Philippine Context. Proceedings of the Conference Held in Manila on August 2–3, 1996*, ed. Maria Lourdes S. Bautista, 1–23. Sydney: Macquarie Library.

Kachru, Braj B. 2005. *Asian Englishes. Beyond the Canon*. Hong Kong: Hong Kong University Press.

Kachru, Braj, Yamuna Kachru, and Cecil Nelson, eds. 2006. *The Handbook of World Englishes*. Malden, MA: Blackwell.

Kachru, Yamuna, and Cecil L. Nelson. 2006. *World Englishes in Asian Contexts*. Hong Kong: Hong Kong University Press.

Kallen, Jeffrey L. 1994. English in Ireland. In *The Cambridge History of the English Language: Volume V English in Britain and Overseas Origins and Development*, ed. Robert Burchfield, 148–196. Cambridge, U.K.: Cambridge University Press.

Kallen, Jeffrey L. 1996. Entering Lexical Fields in Irish English. In *Speech Past and Present: Studies in English Dialectology in Memory of Ossi Ihalainen*, ed. Juhani Klemola, Merja Kytö, and Matti Rissanen, 101–129. Frankfurt: Peter Lang.

Kallen, Jeffrey L. 1997. Irish English and World English: Lexical Perspectives. In *Englishes Around the World I: General Studies, British Isles, North America: Studies in Honour of Manfred Görlach*, ed. Edgar W. Schneider, 139–158. Amsterdam: John Benjamins.

Kallen, Jeffrey L. 1999. Irish English and the Ulster-Scots Controversy. *Ulster Folklife* 45: 70–85.

Kauffmann, Friedrich. 1913. *Deutsche Altertumskunde.* München, Germany: Oskar Beck.

Kearney, Hugh. 1989. *The British Isles: A History of Four Nations.* Cambridge, U.K.: Cambridge University Press.

Keller, Margrit. 1938. *Die Frau und Mädchen in den englischen Dialekten.* Diss. Zürich [n.p.: n.p.].

Kelly, Patricia. 2000. A Seventeenth-Century Variety of Irish English: "Spoken English in Ireland 1600–1740" Revisited. In *Celtic Englishes II,* ed. Hildegard L. C. Tristram, 265–279. Heidelberg, Germany: Winter.

Kelly, William, and John R. Young, eds. 2004. *Ulster and Scotland 1600–2000: History, Language and Identity.* Dublin: Four Courts.

Kendall, Tyler, and Walt Wolfram. 2009. Local and External Language Standards in African American English. *Journal of English Linguistics* 37(4): 305–330.

Kennedy, Randy. 2005. Saying It, and How, This Year. *The New York Times* (25 December). nytimes.com/2005/12/25/weekinreview/25kennedy.ready.html

Kinneavy, James L. 1971. *A Theory of Discourse: The Aims of Discourse.* New York: Prentice Hall.

Kirk, John M. 1997. Ulster English: The State of the Art. In *Celtic Englishes,* ed. Hildegard L. C. Tristram, 135–179. Heidelberg, Germany: Winter.

Kluge, Friedrich 1916. Etymologien. *Beiträge zur Geschichte der deutschen Sprache und Literatur* 41: 180–82.

Kluge, Friedrich 1918. Althochdeutsches. *Beiträge zur Geschichte der deutschen Sprache und Literatur* 43: 145–149.

Kohn, Alfie. 2007. Too destructive to salvage. *USA Today* (May 31): 11.

Kortmann, Bernd, Kate Burridge, Rajend Mesthrie, Edgar W. Schneider, and Clive Upton, eds. 2004. *A Handbook of Varieties of English.* Vol. 2: *Morphology and Syntax.* With *Multimedia CD.* New York: Mouton de Gruyter.

Kretzschmar, William A., Jr. 1992. Isoglosses and Predictive Modeling. *American Speech* 67: 227–249.

Kretzschmar, William A., Jr. 1995. Dialectology and Sociolinguistics: Same Coin, Different Currency. *Language Sciences* 17: 271–282.

Kretzschmar, William A., Jr. 1996. Quantitative Areal Analysis of Dialect Features. *Language Variation and Change* 8: 13–39.

Kretzschmar, William A., Jr. 2003. Mapping Southern English. *American Speech* 78: 130–149.

Kretzschmar, William A., Jr. 2006. Art and Science in Computational Dialectology. *Literary and Linguistic Computing* 21: 399–410.

Kretzschmar, William A., Jr. 2008. Neural Networks and the Linguistics of Speech. *Interdisciplinary Science Reviews* 33: 336–356.

Kretzschmar, William A., Jr. 2009. *The Linguistics of Speech*. Cambridge, U.K.: Cambridge University Press.

Kretzschmar, William A., Jr., Virginia G. McDavid, Theodore K. Lerud, and Ellen Johnson, eds. 1993. *Handbook of the Linguistic Atlas of the Middle and South Atlantic States*. Chicago: University of Chicago Press.

Krogmann, Willy. 1958–1959. Nhd. *Weib. Indogermanische Forschungen* 64: 136–145.

Krogmann, Willy. 1960. Urfriesisches. *Us Wurk* IX(4): 73–76.

Kuethe, J. Louis. 1934. Prison Parlance. *American Speech* 9: 25–28.

Kurath, Hans. 1949. *A Word Geography of the Eastern United States*. Ann Arbor: University of Michigan Press.

Kurath, Hans, et al., eds. 1952–2001. *Middle English Dictionary*. Ann Arbor: University of Michigan.

Kurath, Hans, Marcus L. Hansen, Bernard Bloch, and Julia Bloch. 1939. *Handbook of the Linguistic Geography of New England*. Providence, RI: Brown University.

Kurath, Hans, Miles L. Hanley, Bernard Bloch, Guy S. Lowman, Jr., and Marcus L. Hansen. 1939–1943. *Linguistic Atlas of New England*. 3 vols. in 6 pts. Providence, RI: Brown University for ACLS.

Kurath, Hans, and Raven I. McDavid, Jr. 1961. *The Pronunciation of English in the Atlantic States*. Ann Arbor: University of Michigan Press.

Labov, William. 1966. *The Social Stratification of English in New York City*. Washington, DC: Center for Applied Linguistics.

Labov, William. 1969. The Logic of Non-standard English. In *Georgetown Monograph on Languages and Linguistics 22*, ed. James Alatis, 1–31. Washington, DC: Georgetown University Press.

Labov, William. 1972. *Language in the Inner City: Studies in the Black English Vernacular*. Philadelphia: University of Pennsylvania Press.

Labov, William. 1973a. The Linguistic Consequences of Being a Lame. *Language in Society* 2(1): 81–115.

Labov, William. 1973b. *Sociolinguistic Patterns*. Philadelphia: University of Pennsylvania Press.

Labov, William. 1982. Objectivity and Commitment in Linguistic Science: The Case for the Black English Trial in Ann Arbor. *Language in Society* 11: 165–201.

Labov, William. 1998. Co-existent Systems in African American English. In *The Structure of African American English: Structure, History, and Use*, ed. Salikoko Mufwene, John R. Rickford, Guy Bailey, and John Baugh, 110–153. London: Routledge.

Labov, William, Sharon Ash, and Charles Boberg. 2005. *Atlas of North American English: Phonetics, Phonology and Sound Change.* Berlin: Mouton de Gruyter.

Labov, William, Paul Cohen, Clarence Robins, and John Lewis. 1968. *A Study of the Non-Standard English of Negro and Puerto Rican Speakers in New York City.* Washington, DC: United States Office of Education Final Report, Research Project 3288.

Landau, Sidney I. 2001. *Dictionaries: The Art and Craft of Lexicography.* 2nd ed. New York: Cambridge University Press.

Lanehart, Sonja L., ed. 2001. *Sociocultural and Historical Contexts of African American English.* Amsterdam: John Benjamins.

Lanehart, Sonja L. 2002. *Sista, Speak! Black Women Kinfolk Talk about Language and Literacy.* Austin: University of Texas Press.

Language Curriculum Research Group (Milton Baxter, Carol Reed, et. al.). 1973. Teachers' Manual *For Teaching Standard English Writing to Speakers Showing Black English Influences in Their Writing* (Draft). Brooklyn, NY: Department of Educational Services, Brooklyn College, January.

Lau v. Nichols. 1974. 414 U.S. 563.

Lee, Carol D. 1993. *Signifying as a Scaffold for Literary Interpretation: The Pedagogical Implications of an African American Discourse Genre.* Urbana, IL: National Council of Teachers of English.

Lee, Jay, and William A. Kretzschmar, Jr. 1993. Spatial analysis of Linguistic Data with GIS Functions. *International Journal of Geographical Information Systems* 7: 541–560.

Legum, Stanley E, Carole Pfaff, Gene Tinnie, and Michael Nichols. 1971. *The Speech of Young Black Children in Los Angeles.* Inglewood, CA: Southwest Regional Laboratory.

LeMoine, Noma, and Hollie Sharroky. 2007. Developing Academic English for Standard English Learners. In *Talkin Black Talk: Language, Education, and Social Change*, ed. H. Samy Alim and John Baugh, 43–55. New York: Teachers College Press.

LeMoine, Noma, and Los Angeles Unified School District. 1999. *English for Your Success: A Language Development Program for African American Students. Handbook of Successful Strategies for Educators.* New Jersey: The Peoples Publishing Group.

Lepore, Jill. 2006. Noah's Ark. *The New Yorker* (6 November): 87

Liberman, Anatoly 2007. An Additional Note on Tautological Compounds. *NOWELE* 52: 67–73.

Liberman, Anatoly. 2008. With the assistance of J. Lawrence Mitchell. *An Analytic Dictionary of English Etymology: An Introduction.* Minneapolis: University of Minnesota Press.

Lin, San-Su C. 1965. *Pattern Practices in the Teaching of Standard English to Students with a Non-Standard Dialect*. Washington, DC: U.S. Office of Education Project 1339.

Lindquist, Axel. 1943. Bidrag till svensk ordhistoria 3. *Meijerbergs Arkiv för svensk ordforskning* 5: 76–88.

Lippi-Green, Rosina. 1997. *English with an Accent: Language, Ideology, and Discrimination in the United States*. London: Routledge.

Lloyd, Donald J. 1953. An English Composition Course Built Around Linguistics. *College Composition and Communication* 4(2): 40–43.

Lockwood, William B. 1991. Old Norse *fljóð, sprund, víf. Maal og Minne:* 25–28.

Loman, Bengt. 1968. *Conversations in a Negro American Dialect*. Washington, DC: Center for Applied Linguistics.

Lowell, James Russell. 1867. *The Biglow Papers*. 2nd series. Boston: Ticknor and Fields.

Macafee, Caroline, ed. 1996. *A Concise Ulster Dictionary*. Oxford, U.K.: Oxford University Press.

Macafee, Caroline. 2002. The Under-representation of Irish Etymologies in English Dictionaries. *Studia Indogermanica Lodziensia* 4:43–49.

Mackey, William F. 1978. The Importation of Bilingual Education Models. In *Georgetown University Round Table on Language and Linguistics*, ed. James E. Alatis, 1–18. Washington, DC: Georgetown University Press.

Maddahian, E., and A. Sandamela. 2000. *Academic English Mastery Program 1998–1999 Evaluation Report*. Los Angeles: Los Angeles Unified School District Research and Evaluation Unit.

Makovskii, M. M. 1989. [Rev. of] Taylor Starck and J. C. Wells, *Althochdeutsches Glossenwörterbuch . . . .* Heidelberg: Carl Winter, 1971–87. *Voprosy iazykoznaniia* 1: 134–141.

Makovskii, M. M 1999. *Istoriko-etimologicheskii slovar' sovremennogo angliiskogo iazyka*. Moscow, Russia: Dialog.

Mallinson, Christine. 2004. The Construction of Ethnolinguistic Groups: A Sociolinguistic Case Study. In *Linguistic Diversity in the South: Changing Codes, Practices and Ideology*, ed. Margaret Bender, 66–79. Athens: University of Georgia Press.

Mallinson, Christine. 2006. *The Dynamic Construction of Race, Class, and Gender through Linguistic Practice among Women in a Black Appalachian Community*. Ph.D. dissertation, North Carolina State University.

Mallinson, Christine, and Walt Wolfram. 2002. Dialect Accommodation in a Bi-ethnic Mountain Enclave Community: More Evidence on the Development of African American Vernacular English. *Language in Society* 31: 743–775.

Mallory, J. P., and D. Q. Adams, eds. 1997. *Encyclopedia of Indo-European Culture.* London: Fitzroy Dearborn Publishers.

Marchand, James W. 1973. Observations on the Use of Dialect in Historical Linguistics. In *Lexicography and Dialect Geography: Festgabe for Hans Kurath*, ed. by Harald Scholler and John Reidy, 122–133. Zeitschrift für Dialektologie und Linguistick 9. Wiesbaden, Germany: Franz Steiner Verlag.

Marckwardt, Albert H. 1965. Courses in Language and Linguistics. In *The College Teaching of English*, ed. John C. Gerber, John H. Fisher, and Curt A. Zimansky, 153–177. New York: Appleton-Century-Crofts.

Marshall, John J. 1904–06. The Dialect of Ulster: A Glossary of Words in the Ulster Dialect, Chiefly Used in the Midland and North-Western Counties. *Ulster Journal of Archaeology* n.s. 10:121–130; 11:64–70, 122–125, 175–179; 12:18–21.

Martin Luther King Junior Elementary School Children v. Ann Arbor School District Board. 1978. 451 F. Supp. 1324.

Martin Luther King Junior Elementary School Children et al., plaintiffs, v. Ann Arbor School District Board. 1979. 473 F. Supp. 1371.

Martin, Peter. 2000. *A Life of James Boswell.* New Haven, CT: Yale University Press.

Martynov, V. V. 1972. Slavianskie etimologicheskie versii. In *Russkoe i slavianskoe iazykoznanie k 70-letiiu chlena-korrespondenta AN SSSR R. I. Avanesova*, 185–192. Moscow, Russia: Nauka.

Mather, J. Y., and H. H. Speitel. 1975, 1977, 1986. *The Linguistic Survey of Scotland. Scots Section.* 3 vols. London: Croom Helm.

Maurice, F.D. 1840. Introductory Lecture by the Professor of English Literature and Modern History, King's College, London. *The Educational Magazine* n.s. 2.

Maxwell, Kerry. 2006. Word of the Week. macmillandictionaries.com/wordoftheweek/archive/060213-truthiness.htm

McArthur, Tom. 1998. *The English Languages.* Cambridge, U.K.: Cambridge University Press.

McArthur, Tom. 2002. *Oxford Guide to World English.* Oxford, U.K.: Oxford University Press.

McArthur, Tom, and others, eds. 1992. *The Oxford Companion to the English Language.* Oxford, U.K.: Oxford University Press.

McIntosh, Angus and M. L. Samuels. 1968. Prolegomena to a Study of Mediæval Anglo-Irish. *Medium Ævum* 37:1–11.

Meijerling, H. D. 1985. *Chindh uuirdit uns chiboran. Over het woord 'kind' in het oudere Duits.* Amsterdam: VU Boekhandel/Uitgeverij.

Meineke, Birgit 1987. *CHIND* und *BARN im Hildebrandslied vor dem Hintergrund ihrer althochdeutschen Überlieferung.* Studien zum Althochdeutschen 9. Göttingen, Germany: Vandenhoeck & Ruprecht.

Mesthrie, Rajend, and Rakesh Bhatt. 2008. *World Englishes.* Cambridge, U.K.: Cambridge University Press.

Metcalf, Allan. 2002. *Predicting New Words.* Boston: Houghton Mifflin Company.

Mezger, Fritz. 1948. IE *se-* and Derivatives. *Word* 4: 98–105.

Michael, Ian 1987. *The Teaching of English: from the Sixteenth Century to 1870.* Cambridge, U.K.: Cambridge University Press.

Middle English Dictionary. 1952–2001. Ed. Hans Kurath, Sherman M. Kuhn, Robert E. Lewis, and others. Ann Arbor: University of Michigan Press.

Miller, Carolyn R. 1984. Genre as Social Action. *Quarterly Journal of Speech* 70: 151–167.

Milroy, James. 1992. *Linguistic Variation and Change: On the Historical Sociolinguistics of English.* Oxford, U.K.: Blackwell.

Milroy, James, and Lesley Milroy. 1999. *Authority in Language: Investigating Standard English.* 3rd ed. London: Routledge.

Milroy, Lesley. 1987. *Language and Social Networks.* 2nd ed. Oxford, U.K.: Blackwell.

Mitchell-Kernan, Claudia. 1968. *Some Aspects of Social Interaction in a Black Urban Community.* Berkeley: University of California Language-Behavior Research Laboratory.

Mitchell-Kernan, Claudia. 1971. *Language Behavior in a Black Urban Community.* Berkeley: University of California Language Behavior Research Laboratory.

Mollin, Sandra. 2007. New Variety of Learner English? Criteria for Variety Status and the Case of Euro-English. *English World-Wide* 28: 167–185.

Montague, John. 1988. A Grafted Tongue. In *Contemporary Irish Poetry*, ed. Anthony Bradley, 211–212. Berkeley: University of California Press.

Montgomery, Michael. 1993. The Lexicography of Hiberno English. In *Irish Studies Working Papers* 93-3, 19–35.

Montgomery, Michael. 2000. The Celtic Element in American English. *Celtic Englishes II*, ed. H. L. C. Tristram, 231–264. Heidelberg, Germany: Winter.

Montgomery, Michael. 2003. The Scots Language Abroad. *Edinburgh Companion to Scots*, ed. John Corbett et al., 233–250. Edinburgh: Edinburgh University Press.

Montgomery, Michael. 2006. *From Ulster to America: The Scotch-Irish Heritage of American English.* Belfast: Ulster Historical Foundation.

Montgomery, Michael, and Robert J. Gregg. 1997. The Scots Language in Ulster. In *The Edinburgh History of the Scots Language*, ed. Charles Jones, 569–622. Edinburgh: Edinburgh University Press.

Montgomery, Michael B., and Joseph S. Hall, eds. 2004. *Dictionary of Smoky Mountain English*. Knoxville: University of Tennessee Press.

Morgan, Marcyliena. 2001. Nuttin but a G thang?: Grammar and Language Ideology in Hip Hop Identity. In *Sociocultural and Historical contexts of African American English*, ed. Sonja Lanehart, 187–209. Amsterdam: John Benjamins.

Morgan, Marcyliena. 2002. *Language, Discourse, and Power in African American Culture*. Cambridge, U.K.: Cambridge University Press.

Morris, William 1886. Letter on English Literature at the Universities. *Pall Mall Gazette*, 1 November 1886. Reprinted in the *Pall Mall Gazette Extra* 32, 27.

Morton, Herbert C. 1994. *The Story of Webster's Third: Philip Gove's Controversial Dictionary and Its Critics*. New York: Cambridge University Press.

Moss, Stephen. 2004. Collins Launches Online Dictionary to Debate New Words. *The Guardian* (16 December). guardian.co.uk/technology/2004/dec/16/books.pressandpublishing

Mugglestone, Lynda, ed. 2000. *Lexicography and the OED: Pioneers in the Untrodden Forest*. Oxford, U.K.: Oxford University Press.

Mugglestone, Lynda. 2005. *Lost for Words: The Hidden History of the Oxford English Dictionary*. New Haven, CT: Yale University Press.

Mugglestone, Lynda C. 2007. *"Talking Proper": The Rise of Accent as Social Symbol*. Rev. 2nd ed. Oxford, U.K.: Oxford University Press.

Murray, James A. H. et al., eds. 1989. *Oxford English Dictionaries*. 2nd ed., 20 vols. Oxford, U.K.: Clarendon.

Murray, K. M. Elisabeth. 1977. *Caught in the Web of Words: James Murray and the* Oxford English Dictionary. New Haven, CT: Yale University Press.

National Council of Teachers of English (NCTE). 2005. *The Impact of the SAT and ACT Timed Writing Tests*. Urbana, IL: NCTE.

New English Dictionary on Historical Principles. 1888–1928. Ed. James A.H. Murray, et al. Oxford, U.K.: Clarendon Press.

Newbrook, Mark, ed. 1999. *English Is an Asian Language. The Thai Context*. Sidney: Macquarie Library.

Nichols, Patricia C. 1983. Linguistic Options and Choices for Black Women in the Rural South. In *Language, Gender, and Society*, ed. Barrie Thorne, Cheris Kramarae, and Nancy Henley, 54–68. Rowley, MA: Newbury House.

Nichols, Sharon, and David C Berliner. 2008. Testing the Joy Out of Learning. *Educational Leadership* 65(6): 14–18.

Niedzielski, Nancy, and Dennis R. Preston. 2000. *Folk Linguistics*. Berlin: Mouton de Gruyter.

Noble, W. Vernon. 1984. Words from Wool. *Lore and Language* III(10): 70–74.

Notices of the Meetings of the Philological Society in 1862, and to June 19, 1863. 1862–63. *Transactions of the Philological Society* 8: 327–335.

Nunberg, Geoffrey. 1997. Double Standards. *Natural Language and Linguistic Theory* 14: 667–675.

Oakland Unified School District. 1996 (December 18). Synopsis of the Adopted Policy on Standard American English Language Development.

Oakland Unified School District. 1997. (January 15). An amended resolution. Jan. 15.

O'Connor, D. 1972. J. John Florio's Contribution to Italian-English Lexicography. *Italica* 49: 49–67.

Ode, A. W. M. 1927. Reflexe von "Tabu" und "Noa" in den indogermanischen Sprachen. *Mededeelingen der Koninklijke Akademie van Wetenschappen*. Afd. Letterkunde 69, A/3: 73–100.

O'Kane, William. 1991. *You Don't Say?: The Tyrone Crystal Book of Ulster Dialect*. Dungannon, Ireland: Irish World.

Ó Muirithe, Diarmaid. 1996. *A Dictionary of Anglo-Irish: Words and Phrases from Gaelic in the English of Ireland*. Dublin: Four Courts.

Ó Murchú, M. 1986. "The Retreat from Irish: The Statistical Analysis and Other Aspects." In *Ireland in the Contemporary World: Essays in Honour of Garret FitzGerald*, ed. James Dooge, 112–121. Dublin: Gill & Macmillan.

Oppentocht, Lineke, and Rik Schutz. 2003. Design of Dictionaries. In *A Practical Guide to Lexicography*, ed. Piet van Sterkenberg, 215–227. Amsterdam: John Benjamins.

Orsman, H. W., ed. 1997. *The Dictionary of New Zealand English: A Dictionary of New Zealandisms on Historical Principles*. Oxford, U.K.: Oxford University Press.

Orton, Harold and Eugene Dieth, eds. 1962–1970. *Survey of English Dialects*. 4 vols., 12 parts. Leeds, U.K.: Arnold.

Oxford English Dictionary (*OED1*). 1933. 13 volumes. Ed. J. A. H. Murray, H. Bradley, W. A. Craigie, C. T. Onions, and others. Oxford, U.K.: Clarendon Press.

Oxford English Dictionary, Second Edition (*OED2*). 1989. 12 volumes. Ed. J. A. Simpson and E. S. C. Weiner. Oxford, U.K.: Clarendon Press.

Oxford English Dictionary, Third Edition (*OED3*). Ongoing and available online. Ed. J. A. Simpson and others. Oxford, U.K.: Oxford University Press.

Oxford English Dictionary Additions Series. 1993/1997. Ed. J. A. Simpson and E. S. C. Weiner (Volumes 1 and 2, 1993) and Michael Proffitt (Volume 3, 1997). Oxford, U.K.: Clarendon Press.

Padilla, Anthony M., Halford H. Fairchild, and Concepción M. Valadez. 1990. *Bilingual Education: Issues and Strategies.* Newbury Park, CA: Sage Publications.

Palacas, Arthur L. 2001. Liberating American Ebonics from Euro-English. *College English* 63 (3): 326–352.

Partridge, Eric. 1958. *Origins: A Short Etymological Dictionary of Modern English.* London: Routledge & Kegan Paul.

Patterson, William Hugh. 1880. *A Glossary of Words in Use in the Counties of Antrim and Down.* London: Trübner for the English Dialect Society.

Paulin, Tom. 1985. A New Look at the Language Question. In *Ireland's Field Day Pamphlet 1,* 4–17. London: Hutchinson.

Pedersen, Holger. 1942. Angl. *wife* et *woman. Studia Neophilologica* 14: 252–254.

Perl, Sondra. 1979. The Composing Processes of Unskilled College Writers. *Research in the Teaching of English* 13: 317–336.

Pictet, Adolphe. 1863. *Les origines indo-européennes.* Vol. 2. Paris: Joël Cherbuliez.

Picton, James A. 1862–63. The Ancient Gothic Language, in Its Relation to the Other Indo-European Tongues. *Proceedings of the Philosophical Society of Liverpool* 17: 37–62.

Picton, James A. 1863–64. On Sanscrit Roots and English Derivations. *Proceedings of the Philosophical Society of Liverpool* 18: 36–64.

Pisani, Vittore. 1934. *Tamfana. Beiträge zur Geschichte der deutschen Sprache und Literatur* 58: 456–457.

Pollock, Jane. 1870. 'Michael Faraday', *St.Paul's Magazine* 6, 293.

Polomé, Edgar C. 1961. [Rev. of] IEW, fasc. 11–12, 1957–1958. *Belgisch Tijdschrift voor Philologie en Geschiedenis/Revue Belge de Philologie et d'Histoire* 39: 554–555.

Popken, Randall. 1999. The Pedagogical Dissemination of a Genre: The Resume in American Business Discourse Textbooks, 1914–1939. *JAC: A Journal of Composition Theory* 19: 91–116.

Poplack, Shana, ed. 2000. *The English History of African American English.* Malden, MA: Blackwell.

Poplack, Shana, and Sali Tagliamonte. 1989. There's No Tense like the Present: Verbal -s Inflection in Early Black English. *Language Variation and Change* 3: 47–84.

Pratt, T. K., ed. 1988. *Dictionary of Prince Edward Island English.* Toronto: University of Toronto Press.

Preston, Dennis. 1989. *Perceptual Dialectology.* Dordrecht, Germany: Foris.

Preston, Dennis R. 1996. Where the Worst English is Spoken. In *Focus on the USA,* ed. Edgar Schneider, 297–360. Amsterdam: John Benjamins.

Preston, Dennis. 1997. The South: the Touchstone. In *Language Variety in the South Revisited*, ed. Cynthia Bernstein, Thomas E. Nunnally, and Robin Sabino, 311–351. Tuscaloosa: University of Alabama Press.

Preston, Dennis, ed. 1999a. *Handbook of Perceptual Dialectology*. Amsterdam: John Benjamins.

Preston, Dennis R. 1999b. A Language Attitude Approach to the Perception of Regional Variety. In *Handbook of Perceptual Dialectology: Volume 1*, ed. Dennis R. Preston, 359–373. Amsterdam: John Benjamins.

Preston, Dennis R. 2004. Three Kinds of Sociolinguistics: A Psycholinguistic Perspective. In *Sociolinguistic Variation: Critical Refelctions*, ed. Carmen Fought, 140–160. New York: Oxford University Press.

Printz, Wilhelm. 1932. Nhd. *Weib*, Skr. *kálatram*, Urdū *'aurat* u. a. *Indogermanische Forschungen* 50: 132–135.

Pyles, Thomas. 1964. *The Origins and Development of the English Language*. New York: Harcourt, Brace, & World, Inc.

Quartey-Annan, Minnie. 2006. Teachers' Manual *On the C.U.S.P. of a Breakthrough: Cultural Understanding and Specialized Praxis. A Guide to Help Teachers Teach Students from Diverse Linguistic Backgrounds.* Unpublished manuscript, Michigan State University.

Quirk, Randolph, Sidney Greenbaum, Geoffrey Leech, and Jan Svartvik. 1985. *A Comprehensive Grammar of the English Language*. New York: Longman.

Randolph, Vance. 1927. More Words from the Ozarks. *Dialect Notes* 5: 472–479.

Randolph, Vance. 1932. *Ozark Mountain Folk*. New York: Vanguard Press.

Ransom, W. S., ed. 1988. *The Australian National Dictionary: A Dictionary of Australianisms on Historical Principles.* Oxford, U.K.: Oxford University Press.

Raymond, Darrell R., ed. 1987. *Dispatches from the Front: The "Prefaces" to the Oxford English Dictionary*. Waterloo, ON: University of Waterloo Centre for the New Oxford English Dictionary.

Reaser, Jeffrey Leo. 2006. *The Effect of Dialect Awareness on Adolescent Knowledge and Attitudes*. Ph.D. dissertation, Duke University.

Renn, Jennifer. 2007. *Measuring Style Shift: A Quantitative Analysis of African American English*. M.A. thesis, University of North Carolina at Chapel Hill.

Revard, Carter. 1973. How to Make a N.U.D.E (*New Utopian Dictionary of English*). In *Lexicography in English*, ed. Raven I. McDavid and Audrey R. Duckert, 91–98. New York: New York Academy of Sciences.

Richardson, Charles. 1836–37. *A New Dictionary of the English Language*. 2 volumes. London: William Pickering.

Richardson, Elaine. 1996. *An African Centered Approach to Composition: Freedom through Culturally Relevant Literacy Instruction*. Ph.D. dissertation, Michigan State University.

Richardson, Elaine. 2003. *African American Literacies*. New York: Routledge.

Rickford, John R. 1992. Grammatical Variation and Divergence in Vernacular Black English. In *Internal and External Factors in Syntactic Change*, ed. Marinel Gerritsen and Dieter Stein, 175–200. Berlin: Mouton de Gruyter.

Rickford, John. 1997. LSA Resolution on the Oakland "Ebonics" Issue. http://www.lsadc.org/info/lsa-res-ebonics.cfm

Rickford, John. 1999. *African American Vernacular English: Features, Evolution, Educational Implications*. Malden, MA: Blackwell.

Rickford, John R., and Faye McNair-Knox. 1994. Addressee- and Topic-Influenced Style Shift: A Quantitative Sociolinguistic Study. In *Sociolinguistic Perspectives on Register*, ed. Douglas Biber and Edward Finegan, 235–276. Oxford, U.K.: Oxford University Press.

Rickford, John R., and Russell J. Rickford. 2000. *Spoken Soul: The Story of Black English*. New York: John Wiley and Sons.

Rickford, John R., Julie Sweetland, and Angela E. Rickford. 2004. African American English and Other Vernaculars in Education: A Topic-Coded Bibliography. *Journal of English Linguistics* 32(3): 230–320.

Roberts, Joanne, Walt Wolfram, Sandra Jackson, Jennifer Renn, and Danai Kasambira. 2006. Language of African American Children: School Achievement and Vernacular Variants. Paper presented at American Speech-Language-Hearing Association Convention, in Miami, Florida.

Robinson, Jay L., and Richard W. Bailey. 1973. Computer-produced Microfilm in Lexicography: Toward a Dictionary of Early Modern English. In *The Computer and Literary Studies*, ed. A. J. Aitken, R. W. Bailey, and N. Hamilton-Smith, 3–14. Edinburgh: Edinburgh University Press.

Robinson, Philip. 1984. *The Plantation of Ulster: British Settlement in an Irish Landscape 1600–1670*. Dublin: Gill & Macmillan.

Ross, Claudia, and Jing-heng Sheng Ma. 2006. *Modern Mandarin Chinese Grammar. A Practical Guide*. London: Routledge.

Rowe, Ryan D. 2005. *The Development of African American English in the Oldest Black Town in America: Plural -s Absence in Princeville, North Carolina*. M.A. thesis, North Carolina State University.

Royen, Gerlach 1929. *Die nominalen Klassifikations-Systeme in den Sprachen der Erde* . . . . Anthropos: Collection internationale de monographies linguistiques . . . . 4. Wien: Mechitharisten-Buchdruckerei, 1929.

Russell, Charles C. 1910. *The Language and People of Ulster*. Belfast: Linenhall.

Ryan, Ellen Bouchard, Howard Giles, and Richard J. Sebastian. 1982. An Integrated Perspective for the Study of Attitudes toward Language Variation. In *Attitudes Towards Language Variation*, ed. Ellen Bouchard Ryan and Howard Giles, 1–19. London: Arnold.

Sakai, Sanzo, guest ed. 2005. Symposium on World Englishes in the Japanese context. *World Englishes* 24: 321–382.

Scalia, Antonin. 2009. Opinion for the Majority. *District of Columbia v. Heller* 128 S. Ct. 2783 (2008). Eagan, MN: Thomson Reuters/West.

Schilling-Estes, Natalie. 2002a. American English Social Dialect Variation and Gender. *Journal of English Linguistics* (Special Issue: *Language and Gender*) 30: 122–137.

Schilling-Estes, Natalie. 2002b. Investigating Stylistic Variation. In *Handbook of Variation and Change*, ed. J. K. Chambers, Peter Trudgill, and Natalie Schilling-Estes, 375–401. Malden, MA: Blackwell.

Schmidt, Klaus T., and Klaus Strunk. 1989. Toch. B. *kwīpe* 'Scham, Schande', A. *kip* 'Scham' und germ. **wība-* 'Weib'. In *Indogermanica Europaea. Festschrift für Wolfgang Meid zum 60. Geburtstag am 12.11.1989*, ed. Karin Heller, Oswald Panagl, and Johann Tischler, 251–284. Grazer Linguistische Monographien 4. Graz: Institut für Sprachwissenschaft der Universität Graz.

Schneider, Edgar W. 2004. Global synopsis: phonetic and phonological variation in English world-wide. In *A Handbook of Varieties of English*. Vol. 1: *Phonology*, ed. Edgar W. Schneider, Kate Burridge, Bernd Kortmann, Rajend Mesthrie, and Clive Upton, 1111–1137. Berlin: Mouton de Gruyter.

Schneider, Edgar W. 2007. *Postcolonial English: Varieties around the World*. Cambridge, U.K.: Cambridge University Press.

Schneider, Edgar W. 2011. *English Around the World*. Cambridge, U.K.: Cambridge University Press.

Schneider, Edgar W., Kate Burridge, Bernd Kortmann, Rajend Mesthrie, and Clive Upton, eds. 2004. *A Handbook of Varieties of English*. Vol. 1: *Phonology*. With *Multimedia CD*. Berlin: Mouton de Gruyter.

Schreier, Daniel. 2005. *Consonant Change in English Worldwide. Synchrony Meets Diachrony*. Houndmills, U.K.: Palgrave Macmillan.

Schutz, Paul A., Courtney B. Chambless, and Jessica T. DeCuir. 2004. Multimethods Research. In *Research Methods in the Social Sciences: Frameworks for Knowing and Doing*, ed. Kathleen B. deMarrais and Stephen D. Lapan, 267–281. Hillsdale, NJ: Lawrence Erlbaum.

Schwenck, Konrad 1834. *Wörterbuch der deutschen Sprache in Beziehung auf Abstammung und Begriffsbildung*. Frankfurt am Main: Johann D. Sauerländer. 2nd ed., 1837; 3rd ed., 1838; 4th ed., 1855.

Schwenter, Ernst. 1927. Nhd. *weben* und *schweben*. *Beiträge zur Geschichte der deutschen Sprache und Literatur* 51: 18–23.

Schwink, Frederick W. 2004. *The Third Gender: Studies in the Origin and History of Germanic Grammatical Gender.* Heidelberg, Germany: Winter.

Semerano, Giovanni. 1994. *Le origini della cultura europea.* Vol. 2. *Dizionari etimologici. Basi semitiche delle lingue indeuropee. Dizionario della lingua latina e di voci moderne.* Firenze, Italy: Leo S. Olschki.

Share, Bernard. 1997. *Slanguage: A Dictionary of Irish Slang.* Dublin: Gill & Macmillan. 2nd ed., 2003.

Shaughnessy, Mina P. 1977. *Errors and Expectations: A Guide for the Teacher of Basic Writing.* New York: Oxford University Press.

Shea, Ammon. 2008. *Reading the OED: One Man, One Year, 21,730 Pages.* New York: Perigee.

Sheridan, Thomas. 1762. *A Course of Lectures on Elocution.* London: J. Dodsley.

Sheridan, Thomas. 1780. *A General Dictionary of the English Language.* London: Charles Dilly.

Shuy, Roger W., and Ralph W. Fasold. 1973. *Language Attitudes: Current Trends and Prospects.* Washington, DC: Georgetown University Press.

Shuy, Roger W., Walt Wolfram, and William K. Riley. 1967. *Linguistic Correlates of Social Stratification in Detroit Speech.* USOE Final Report No. 6-1347.

Shuy, Roger W., Walt Wolfram, and William K. Riley. 1968. *Field Techniques in an Urban Language Study.* Washington, DC: Center for Applied Linguistics.

Silva, Penny. 2000. Sense and Definition in the OED. In *Lexicography and the OED: Pioneers in the Untrodden Forest*, ed. Lynda Mugglestone, 77–95. Oxford, U.K.: Oxford University Press.

Simpkins, Gary. 2002. *The Throwaway Kids.* Brookline, MA: Brookline Books.

Simpkins, Gary, Grace Holt, and Charlesetta Simpkins. 1974, 1977. *Bridge: A Cross-Culture Reading Program.* Experimental edition. Boston: Houghton Mifflin.

Simpkins, Gary, and Charlesetta Simpkins. 1981. Cross-Cultural Approach to Curriculum Development. In *Black English and the Education of Black Children and Youth: Proceedings of the National Invitational Symposium on the King Decision*, ed. Geneva Smitherman, 221–240. Detroit: Wayne State University Center for Black Studies.

Sledd, James. 1969. Bi-Dialectalism: The Linguistics of White Supremacy. *The English Journal* 58 (9): 1307–1329.

Sledd, James, and Wilma R. Ebbit. 1962. *Dictionaries and That Dictionary: A Casebook on the Aims of Lexicographers and the Targets of Reviewers.* Chicago: Scott, Foresman, and Company.

Smart, Benjamin H. 1810. *A Practical Grammar of English Pronunciation.* London: John Richardson.

Smart, Benjamin H. 1812. *A Grammar of English Sounds or the First Step in Elocution.* London: John Richardson.

Smart, Benjamin H. 1814. 'Advertisement for course of lectures in elocution,' *The Times* 12 Aug 1814, 1.

Smart, Benjamin H. 1815. 'Advertisement for course of lectures in elocution,' *The Times* 15 April 1815, 1.

Smart, Benjamin H. 1836. *Walker Remodelled. A New Critical Pronouncing Dictionary of the English Language.* London: T. Cadell.

Smith, Geoff P., and Stephen Matthews, eds. 2005. *Chinese Pidgin English: Texts and Contexts.* Special Issue of *Hong Kong Journal of Applied Linguistics.*

Smitherman, Geneva. 1968. Black Power is Black Language. Talk presented at Black Power Conference. Chicago. Revised version, 1972, *Black Culture: Reading and Writing Black*, ed. Gloria Simmons, 78–89. New York: Holt, Rinehart and Winston.

Smitherman, Geneva. 1969. *A Comparison of the Oral and Written Styles of a Group of Inner-City Black Students.* Ph.D. dissertation, University of Michigan.

Smitherman, Geneva. 1977. *Talkin and Testifyin: The Language of Black America.* Boston: Houghton Mifflin.

Smitherman, Geneva., ed. 1981. *Black English and the Education of Black Children and Youth: Proceedings of the National Invitational Symposium on the 'King' Decision.* Detroit: Wayne State University Center for Black Studies.

Smitherman, Geneva. 1992. Black English, Diverging or Converging?: The View from the National Assessment of Educational Progress. *Language and Education* 6 (1): 47–61.

Smitherman, Geneva. 1994. "The Blacker the Berry, the Sweeter the Juice": African American Student Writers and the National Assessment of Educational Progress. In *The Need for Story: Cultural Diversity in Classroom and Community*, ed. Anne Haas Dyson and Celia Genishi, 80–101. Urbana, IL: National Council of Teachers of English.

Smitherman, Geneva. 1999. CCCC's Role in the Struggle for Language Rights. *College Composition and Communication* 50(3): 349–376.

Smitherman, Geneva. 2000a. *Black Talk: Words and Phrases from the Hood to the Amen Corner.* Boston: Houghton Mifflin.

Smitherman, Geneva. 2000b. *Talkin That Talk: Language, Culture and Education in African America.* London: Routledge.

Smitherman, Geneva. 2006. *Word from the Mother: Language and African Americans.* London: Routledge.

Smitherman, Geneva, and Sandra Wright. 1983. Black Student Writers in the NAEP. Unpublished research report to National Council of Teachers of English. Chicago.

Soliday, Mary. 1999. Class Dismissed. *College English* 61(6): 731–741.

Sommers, Nancy. 1980. Revision Strategies of Student Writers and Experienced Adult Writers. *College Composition and Communication* 31(4): 378–388.

Sommer, Ferdinand. 1921. *Vergleichende Syntax der Schulsprachen* . . . . Leipzig and Berlin: B. G. Teubner.

Spears, Arthur. 1982. The Semi-auxiliary "Come" in Black English Vernacular. *Language* 58: 850–872.

Spears, Arthur K. 1999. Race and Ideology: An Introduction. In *Race and Ideology: Language, Symbolism, and Popular Culture*, ed. Arthur K. Spears, 11–58. Detroit: Wayne State University Press.

Stack, Carol B. 1996. *Call to Home: African Americans Reclaim the Rural South*. New York: Basic Books.

Stanlaw, James. 2004. *Japanese English. Language and Culture Contact*. Hong Kong: Hong Kong University Press.

Stein, Gabriele. 2002. *Better Words: Evaluating EFL Dictionaries*. Exeter, U.K.: University of Exeter Press.

Steinberg, Jacques. 2005. Truthiness. *The New York Times* (25 December). nytimes.com/2005/12/25/weekinreview/25track.ready.html?sq=truthiness%20 2005&st=cse&scp-1&pagewanted=print

Stevenson, David, and Wendy B. Stevenson. 1987. *Scottish Texts and Calendars: An Analytical Guide to Serial Publications*. Edinburgh: Scottish History Society.

Stewart, Bruce. 1998. H. E. Dictionary–Again! *IASIL Newsletter*, new series 4: 1–2 (March), 1–3.

Stewart, William A. 1967. Sociolinguistic Factors in the History of American Negro Dialects. *The Florida FL Reporter* 5 (2): 11, 22, 24, 26.

Story, G. M., W. J. Kirwin, and J. D. A. Widdowson, eds. 1982/1990. *Dictionary of Newfoundland English.* 2nd ed.Toronto: University of Toronto Press.

Supplement to the Oxford English Dictionary. 1972–1986. 4 volumes. Ed. Robert W. Burchfield and others. Oxford, U.K.: Clarendon Press.

Sutcliffe, David. 2001. The Voice of the Ancestors: New Evidence on 19th-century Precursors to 20th-century African American English. In *Sociocultural and Historical Contexts of African American English*, ed. Sonja L. Lanehart, 129–168. Amsterdam: John Benjamins.

Sweetland, Julie. 2006. *Teaching Writing in the African American Classroom: A Sociolinguistic Approach.* Ph.D. dissertation, Stanford University.

Szemerényi, Oswald. 1977. Indo-European Kinship. *Acta Iranica.* Textes et mémoires 7. Varia: 1–240.

Tagliamonte, Sali, and Shana Poplack. 1988. How Black English "Past" Got to the Present: Evidence from Samaná. *Language in Society* 17(4): 513–533.

Tagliamonte, Sali A., and Derek Denis. 2008. Linguistic Ruin? LOL! Instant Messaging and Teen Language. *American Speech* 83(1): 3–34.

Tamasi, Susan. 2003. Cognitive Patterns of Linguistic Perceptions. Ph.D. dissertation, University of Georgia.

Tannen, Deborah. 2005. *Conversational Style: Analyzing Talk among Friends.* New York: Oxford University Press.

Tavernier-Vereecken, C. 1954. De etymologie von 'wijf'. *Belgisch Tijdschrift vor Philologie en Geschiedenis/Revue Belge de Philologie et d'Histoire* 32: 97–101.

Taylor, Hanni U. 1989. *Standard English, Black English, and Bidialectalism.* New York: Peter Lang.

Taylor, Orlando. 1983. A Survey of Bidialectal Language Arts programs in the United States. *Journal of Negro Education* 52 (1): 35–45.

Terry, Michael. 2004. *On the Articulation of Aspectual Meaning in African American English.* Ph.D. dissertation, University of Massachusetts at Amherst.

The Late Professor Faraday. *The Times.* 1867 (August 7) 28.

Thill, Jean-Claude, William A. Kretzschmar, Jr., Irene Casas, and Xiaobai Yao. 2008. Detecting Geographic and Socio-economic Associations in English Dialect Features with Self-Organising Maps. In *Self-Organising Maps: Applications in GI Science*, ed. Pragya Agarwal and André Skupin. London: Wiley.

Thomas, Erik R. 2002. Sociophonetic Applications of Speech Perception Experiments. *American Speech* 77: 115–147.

Thomas, Erik R., and Jeffrey Reaser. 2004. Delimiting Perceptual Cues for the Ethnic Labeling of African American and European American Voices. *Journal of Sociolinguistics* 8: 54–87.

Todd, Loreto. 1990. *Words Apart: A Dictionary of Northern Ireland English.* Gerrards Cross, U.K.: Smythe.

Tolkien, J.R.R. 1983. Valedictory Address to the University of Oxford. *The Monsters and the Critics and Other Essays*, ed. Christopher Tolkien, 224–240. London: George Allen & Unwin.

Toon, Thomas. 1983. *The Politics of Early English Sound Change.* New York: Academic Press.

Torbert, Benjamin. 2004. *Southern Vowels and the Social Construction of Salience.* Ph.D. dissertation, Duke University.

Traugott, Elizabeth Closs. 1972. *A History of English Syntax: A Transformational Approach to the History of English Sentences.* New York: Holt, Rinehart and Winston.

Traynor, Michael, ed. 1953. *The English Dialect of Donegal: a Glossary Incorporating the Collections of H. C. Hart, etc.* Dublin: Royal Irish Academy.

Trench, Richard Chenevix. 1860. *On Some Deficiencies in Our English Dictionaries.* London: John W. Parker and Son.

Tyndall, John. 1870. *Faraday, as a Discoverer*. London: Longman, Green, & Co.

U.S. Department of Education, 2006. *A Test of Leadership: The Future of U.S. Higher Education.* A report of the commission appointed by Secretary of Education Margaret Spellings. www.ed.gov/about/bdscomm/list/hiedfuture/reports/final-report.pdf

Van Hofwegen, Janneke, and Walt Wolfram. 2010. Coming of Age in African American English. *Journal of Sociolinguistics* 14.

Visser, F. Th. 1963–1973. *An Historical Syntax of the English Language*. Leiden, The Netherlands: E. J. Brill.

Walker, John. 1791. *A Critical Pronouncing Dictionary and Expositor of the English Language*. London: G. G. and J. Robinson.

Walker, Thaai. 1996. How Ebonics Works: Teachers Help Kids Translate to English. *San Francisco Chronicle* (December 21): A1.

Wall, Richard. 1990. Towards a Dialect Dictionary and Glossary for Irish Studies. *Canadian Journal of Irish Studies* 16:104–117.

Wall, Richard. 1991. Dialect in Irish Literature: The Hermetic Core. *Irish University Review* 20(1): 8–18.

Wall, Richard, ed. 2001. *An Irish Literary Dictionary and Glossary*. Gerrards Cross, U.K.: Smythe.

Walsh, James J. 1911. A Survival of Elizabethan Speech. *Harper's Monthly* 123: 191–197.

Walters, Ronald W. 1993. *Pan Africanism in the African Diaspora: The African American Linkage*. Detroit: Wayne State University Press.

Walvoord, Barbara, and Virginia Anderson. 1998. *Effective Grading: A Tool for Learning and Assessment*. San Francisco: Jossey-Bass.

Watts, Isaac. 1721. *The Art of Reading and Writing English*. London: T. Longman.

Watts, Isaac. 1743. *The Improvement of the Mind; containing a variety of Remarks and rules for the Attainment and Communication of Useful Knowledge in Religion, in the Sciences, and in Common Life,* 2nd edition. London: printed for J. Brackstone and T. Longman.

Wee, Lionel. 2004. Singapore English: Phonology. In *A Handbook of Varieties of English.* Vol. 1: *Phonology*, ed. Edgar W. Schneider, Kate Burridge, Bernd Kortmann, Rajend Mesthrie, and Clive Upton, 1017–1033. Berlin/New York: Mouton de Gruyter.

Weldon, Tracey. 2004. African American English in the Middle Classes: Exploring the Other End of the Continuum. Paper presented at NWAV 33, in Ann Arbor, Michigan.

Wentworth, Harold, and Stuart Berg Flexner. 1960. *Dictionary of American Slang*. New York: Thomas Y. Crowell.

Wheeler, Rebecca S., and Rachel Swords. 2006. *Code-Switching: Teaching Standard English in Urban Classrooms*. Urbana, IL: National Council of Teachers of English.

Wible, Scott. 2006. Pedagogies of the "Students' Right" Era: The Language Curriculum Research Group's Project for Linguistic Diversity. *College Composition and Communication* 57 (3): 442–478.

Wiedemann, Oskar. 1902. Etymologien. *Beiträge zur Kunde der indogermanischen Sprachen* 27: 193–261.

Wiggin, Grant. 2001. *Educative Assessment*. San Francisco: Jossey-Bass.

Williams, L. Pearce. 1965. *Michael Faraday: A Biography*. London: Chapman and Hall.

Willinsky, John. 1994. *Empire of Words: The Reign of the* OED. Princeton, NJ: Princeton UP.

Wilson, Charles Morrow. 1934 (1970). *Backwoods America*. Chapel Hill: University of North Carolina Press.

Wilson, Woodrow 1896. Mere Literature. *Atlantic Monthly*, 1893. Reprinted in *Mere Literature, and Other Essays*. Boston: Houghton Mifflin Company, 1–27.

Winchester, Simon. 2003. *The Meaning of Everything: The Story of the* Oxford English Dictionary. New York: Oxford University Press.

Winerip, Michael. 2005. SAT Essay Test Rewards Length and Ignores Errors of Fact. *The New York Times* (4 May): B9.

Winter, Werner. 1998. Lexical Archaisms in the Tocharian Languages. In *The Bronze Age and Early Iron Age Peoples of Eastern Central Asia/Zhang Ya dong bu qing tong he zao qi tie qi shi dai de ju min*, ed. Victor H. Mair, 347–357. (Journal of Indo-European Studies Monograph 26.) Washington, DC: The Institute for the Study of Man in Collaboration with The University of Pennsylvania Museum Publications.

Wittmann, Judith J. 1982. *A Semantic Study of Five Words for 'Girl' and 'Woman' from Wulfila through Luther*. Ph.D. dissertation, University of Colorado.

Wolfram, Walt. 1969. *A Sociolinguistic Description of Detroit Negro Speech*. Washington, DC: Center for Applied Linguistics.

Wolfram, Walt. 1974. The Relationship of White Southern Speech to Vernacular Black English. *Language* 50: 498–527.

Wolfram Walt. 1991. *Dialects and American English*. Englewood Cliffs, NJ: Prentice-Hall.

Wolfram, Walt. 1993. Ethical Considerations in Language Awareness Programs. *Issues in Applied Linguistics* 4: 225–255.

Wolfram, Walt. 1995. On the Sociolinguistic Significance of Obscure Dialect Structure: NP_i *call* NP_i V-*ing* in African American Vernacular English. *American Speech* 69: 339–360.

Wolfram, Walt. 1999. Repercussions From the Oakland Ebonics Controversy—The Critical Role of Dialect Awareness Programs. In *Making the Connection: Language and Academic Achievement Among African American Students,* ed. Carolyn T. Adger, Donna Christian, and Orlando Taylor, 61–80. Washington, DC: Center for Applied Linguistics.

Wolfram, Walt. 2003. Reexamining the Development of African American English. *Language* 79: 282–316.

Wolfram, Walt. 2004. Dialect Awareness in Community Perspective. In *Linguistic Diversity in the South: Changing Codes, Practices and Ideologies,* ed. M. C. Bender, 15–36. Athens: University of Georgia Press.

Wolfram, Walt. 2007. Sociolinguistic Myths in the Study of African American English. *Linguistic and Language Compass* 1: 288–313.

Wolfram, Walt, and Jeannine Carpenter. 2006. Trajectories of Change in African American English. Paper presented at the annual meeting of the Linguistic Society of America, in Albuquerque, New Mexico.

Wolfram, Walt, and Donna Christian. 1976. *Appalachian Speech.* Arlington, VA: Center for Applied Linguistics.

Wolfram, Walt, Donna Christian, and Carolyn Temple Adger. 1999. *Dialects in Schools and Communities.* Mahwah, NJ: Lawrence Erlbaum Associates.

Wolfram, Walt, and Ralph W. Fasold. 1974. *The Study of Social Dialects in American English.* Englewood Cliffs, NJ: Prentice-Hall.

Wolfram, Walt, and Natalie Schilling-Estes. 2006. *American English: Dialects and Variation,* 2nd edition. Malden, MA: Blackwell.

Wolfram, Walt, and Erik R. Thomas. 2002. *The Development of African American English.* Malden, MA: Blackwell.

Wolfram, Walt, and Ben Ward. 2006. *American Voices: How Dialects Differ from Coast to Coast.* Malden, MA: Blackwell.

Wood, Ian S. 1994. *Scotland and Ulster.* Edinburgh: Mercat.

Wright, Joseph, ed. 1898–1905. *English Dialect Dictionary.* 6 vols. London: Henry Frowde.

Yip, Virginia, and Stephen Matthews. 2000. *Basic Cantonese: A Grammar and Workbook.* London: Routledge.

Zimmer, Stefan. 1999. Comments on a Great Book: *The Encyclopedia of Indo-European Culture,* ed., J. P. Mallory and D. Q. Adams. *The Journal of Indo-European Studies* 27: 105–163.

CONTRIBUTORS

Michael Adams teaches at Indiana University–Bloomington. He is author of *Slayer Slang* (2003) and *Slang: The People's Poetry* (2009), and co-author, with Anne Curzan, of *How English Works: A Linguistic Introduction* (3rd ed., 2012), and editor of *"Cunning passages, contrived corridors": Unexpected Essays in the History of Lexicography* (2010). Once editor of *Dictionaries*, he is currently editor of the quarterly journal *American Speech*.

Dennis Baron is professor of English and linguistics at the University of Illinois. His most recent book is *A Better Pencil: Readers, Writers, and the Digital Revolution* (2009). He has also written *Grammar and Good Taste* (1982), *Grammar and Gender* (1986), and *The English-Only Question* (1990). He blogs regularly on language and technology issues on the Web of Language: http://bit.ly/weblan. You can follow him on Twitter @DrGrammar.

Anne Curzan is Associate Professor of English at the University of Michigan, where she also holds appointments in the Department of Linguistics and the School of Education. She is author of *Gender Shifts in the History of English* (2003) and co-author of *How English Works: A Linguistic Introduction* (with Michael Adams, 3rd ed., 2012) and *First Day to Final Grade* (with Lisa Damour, 3rd ed., 2011). She currently serves as co-editor of the *Journal of English Linguistics*.

Amy Devitt is Chancellors Club Teaching Professor and Professor of English at the University of Kansas. Her publications include three books—*Writing Genres* (2004), *Scenes of Writing* (with Anis Bawarshi and Mary Jo Reiff, 2004), and *Standardizing Written English* (1989). She received her Ph.D. from the University of Michigan in 1982 under the direction of Richard W. Bailey.

Marsha L. Dutton is Professor of Medieval Literature and Chair of the Department of English at Ohio University, Athens, Ohio. After receiving her Ph.D. in English at the University of Michigan, she was for five years Associate Editor of *Dictionaries* while Richard W. Bailey was its editor and was for three years an assistant editor on the *Middle English Dictionary*. She is a scholar of twelfth-century English Cistercian writing, having published widely on the works of Aelred of Rievaulx.

Joan Houston Hall is Chief Editor of the *Dictionary of American Regional English*. She began as an Assistant Editor of *DARE* in 1975, became Associate Editor in 1979, and succeeded Frederic G. Cassidy as Chief Editor following his death in 2000. She has served as President of the American Dialect Society and the Dictionary Society of North America, and she was named a Fellow of DSNA in 2009.

Susanmarie Harrington is Professor of English and Director of the Writing in the Disciplines Program at the University of Vermont. She is the author, co-author, or editor of three books and numerous articles exploring the ways values about writing are enacted in curricula, program design, and assessment. Her most recent publications address the ways claims about responsibility and accountability are used to construct understandings of literacy.

William A. Kretzschmar, Jr., teaches English as Willson Professor in Humanities at the University of Georgia. His most recent major publications are *The Linguistics of Speech* (2009) and the *Oxford Dictionary of Pronunciation for Current English* (2001). He is the Editor of the American Linguistic Atlas Project and maintains a community-language field site in Roswell, GA. He is Past President of the American Dialect Society.

Sonja L. Lanehart is Professor and Brackenridge Endowed Chair in Literature and the Humanities at the University of Texas at San Antonio. She is author of *Sista, Speak! Black Women Kinfolk Talk about Language and*

Literacy (2002), editor of *Sociocultural and Historical Contexts of African American English* (2001), editor of *African American Women's Language: Discourse, Education, and Identity* (2009), and co-editor of the *Oxford Handbook of African American Language* (projected 2013).

Anatoly Liberman is a professor of Germanic Philology at the University of Minnesota (Minneapolis). His main areas of expertise include general and Germanic linguistics, medieval literature and folklore, poetic translation, the golden age of Russian poetry, and literary criticism. His work on a new etymological dictionary of English resulted in the publication of the book *Word Origins . . . and How We Know Them, An Analytic Dictionary of English Etmology: An Introduction* (2005) and *A Bibliography of English Etymology* (2010).

Michael Montgomery is Distinguished Professor Emeritus of English at the University of South Carolina. His books include *Language Variety in the South: Perspectives in Black and White* (with Guy Bailey, 1986), *Dictionary of Smoky Mountain English* (with Joseph Sargent Hall, 2004), and *From Ulster to America: The Scotch-Irish Heritage of American English* (2006). He has served as President of the American Dialect Society and has been Senior Associate Editor of the journal *American Speech* since 1996.

Colette Moore is an assistant professor of English at the University of Washington. Her research on the history of the English language draws upon historical pragmatics, historical sociolinguistics, and stylistics. Her forthcoming book, *Quoting Speech in Early English* (2011), investigates reported speech in premodern English.

Lynda Mugglestone is Professor of History of English at the University of Oxford, and a Fellow of Pembroke College, Oxford. Recent work includes *Lexicography and the OED* (2002), *"Talking Proper": The Rise of Accent as Social Symbol,* revised and extended ed. (2007), *Lost for Words: The Hidden History of the Oxford English Dictionary* (2005), and *The Oxford*

History of English (2006). *Dictionaries: A Very Short Introduction* will be published by Oxford University Press in 2011.

Dennis R. Preston is Regents Professor and Co-Director of the Center for Oklahoma Studies, Oklahoma State University, and University Distinguished Professor Emeritus, Michigan State University. He was Director of the 2003 LSA Institute at Michigan State and has served as president of the American Dialect Society. His most recent books are, with James Stanford, *Variation in Indigenous Languages* (2009), and, with Nancy Niedzielski, *A Reader in Sociophonetics* (2010). He is a fellow of the Japan Society for the Promotion of Science and holds the Officer's Cross of the Order of Merit of the Polish Republic.

Minnie Quartey-Annan received her B.A. and M.A. degrees from Georgetown University and is a doctoral student at Michigan State University studying sociolinguistic variation in nonstandard forms of English, namely African American Language.

Edgar W. Schneider is Chair Professor of English Linguistics at the University of Regensburg, Germany, after previous appointments in Bamberg, Georgia, and Berlin. He has written and edited about 20 books—most recently, *Handbook of Varieties of English* (2004/2008), *Postcolonial English* (2007), and *English Around the World* (2011)—and edits the scholarly journal *English World-Wide*.

Jesse Sheidlower is Editor at Large of the *Oxford English Dictionary*. His interests include the practice of historical lexicography, the history of the American lexis, and American slang.

Geneva Smitherman is University Distinguished Professor of English at Michigan State University, co-founder and Executive Committee Member of African American and African Studies, and founder and Co-Director of My Brother's Keeper mentoring program for middle school males in Detroit. She is the author of six books, including *Talkin and Tes-*

tifyin: The Language of Black America (1986). She has published more than 100 articles and book chapters and is editor/co-editor of eight books. Her awards include the 2005 NCTE James R. Squire Award.

Walt Wolfram is William C. Friday Distinguished University Professor at North Carolina State University, where he also directs the North Carolina Language and Life Project. He has pioneered research on social and ethnic dialects of American English since the 1960s. His current research focuses on the development of AAE during its early lifespan, based on a unique longitudinal database that spans 17 years.

INDEX

Page numbers followed by f indicate figure

African-American English: and Black social movements, 255–256, 261–262; characteristics, 35–51, 257–260, 270–273; debate about, 38–39, 254–255, 265–268, 283; origins of, 45–46; teaching with, 257–261, 263–277. *See also* Black English case, Ann Arbor (MI); Ebonics

Ann Arbor School Board, King v. See Black English case, Ann Arbor (MI)

Asian speakers of English, 136–154

back-formation, 178–181

Bailey, Beryl L., 256–257, 260

Bailey, Richard W.: about, 2–8, 17–18; on culture and language, 68–69; on diversity, 253; on Kurath and Labov's work, 59; on language change, 175–176; on *OED,* 169–170; on technology, 171, 238; on 19th Century English, 87–88

bilingual education, 288–291

Black English case, Ann Arbor (MI), 252–253, 262, 267–268, 283–284

blends, 187–189

Bridge reading series, 263–266

China, English use in: background, 142–143; characteristics of, 152–154; grammar and pronunciation, 145–152; research methodology, 144–146

code-switching, 49–51, 251–252

DARE (Dictionary of American Regional English), 170, 175–180, 182–189, 246

dialectolalia, 258–259

dialect readers, 263–266

dialects: early studies on, 12–14; identification of, 56–57; influences on study of, 75–78; social consequences of, 11–12; and subjectivity, 72–76. *See also* mapping, linguistic

dictionaries: about, 168–172; authority, 242–245; forensics analysis of, 172; quotation paragraphs, 191–212; technology impacts on, 171–172, 237–241, 245–248. *See also* lexicography; *Oxford English Dictionary (OED)*

Dictionary of American Regional English (DARE), 170, 175–180, 182–189, 246

Dictionary of Irish English on Historical Principles (DIEHP), 217, 224–225, 228–234, 248

Dolan, Terence P., 220–221, 230–231

Ebonics, 273–274, 284–287

elocution, 89–94

English Dialect Dictionary, 215, 229–230

English language: Asian speakers of, 136–155; globalization impacts, 135–137; need for research, 317–318; research methods, 78–81; and standardized testing, 318–320. *See also* dialects; language attitudes

English language, history. *See* History of English Language (HEL)
English language, teaching of. *See* teachers and teaching
English Language Studies: background, 5–8; diversity and, 249–253; research methods, 78–81; and writing, 302–303
etymology: difficulties with, 108–109; *wife* study, 109–130

Faraday, Michael: about, 88, 89, 94; influence of Watts, 94–96; motivations, 105; relationship with Smart, 89–90, 100–104; speaking skills, 98–100; writing style, 96–98
folk-etymology, 181–184
forensic dictionary analysis, 172

genres, study of, 310–313
globalization and English language, 135–137
grammar instruction, 292–295, 303–305

Hairston, Maxine, 300–301
History of English Language (HEL): current developments, 162–165; historical background, 158–162; research needs, 165–167; teaching about, 305–307; technology impacts, 82, 84–85; traditional approach to study, 82–84
Hong Kong, English language use in, 139–141

India, English use in, 142
Irish language: development of, 217–219; dictionaries available, 220–221; difficulty in dictionary development, 224–225, 228–234; labels for, 225–226; and *OED,* 219–220; overlooked in historical dictionaries, 216–217; political aspects, 221–224, 226–228; use of, 216–218, 234–235
isogloss, 56–57, 59

Japan, English language use in, 139–142
Johnson, Samuel, 91–92, 192–194, 237

King v. Ann Arbor School Board. See Black English case, Ann Arbor (MI)
Kurath, Hans, 54–57, 59–60, 67

Labov, William, 36, 54, 57, 59–60, 67, 262, 283
LAMSAS (Linguistic Atlas of the Middle and South Atlantic States), 55
language attitudes: about usage, 318–321; about dialects, 19, 22–30; in 19th Century England, 89, 91–92, 104–106; resistance to change, 315–317; of teachers, 281–282, 295–297. *See also* African American English
language changes: back-formation, 178–181; blends, 187–189; dictionaries focusing on, 173–178; folk-etymology, 181–184; metanalysis, 185; metathesis, 185–187; reasons for, 173–174; using *Index to DARE,* 178, 189–190
Lau v. Nichols, 290
lexicography: about, 168–172; definition, 213–214; forensic analysis of, 172. *See also* dictionaries
Lin, San-Su, 259–260
Linguistic Atlas of the Middle and South Atlantic States (LAMSAS), 55
linguistic geography. *See* mapping, linguistic
linguistic insecurity, 31–33
linguistics: change of focus in, 256–258, 261; multimethod research in, 78–81; and traditional classroom settings, 249–253
Lowell, James Russell, 173–174

mapping, linguistic: deductive reasoning in, 56–57, 59–60; Eastern U.S. dialects, 56f; examples, 20f–21f, 22f, 25f, 27f; inductive approach,

60; isogloss use, 56–57, 59; LAMSAS, 55; limitations of, 14–15; Self-Organizing Maps, 60–67
MED (Middle English Dictionary), 204, 215, 239
metanalysis, 185
metathesis, 185–187
Michigan residents, language attitudes, 17, 19, 20–30
Middle English Dictionary (MED), 204, 215, 239

neural network analysis, 60
New Dictionary of the English Language, 194–195
New Oxford American Dictionary, 169
New York City residents, language attitudes, 31–33
Nichols, Lau v., 290
Nineteenth-Century English (Bailey), 175–176

online dictionaries, 239–241
Oxford English Dictionary (OED): about, 174–175; Bailey on, 169–170; complementary dictionaries to, 214–216; completion of, 213–214; forensic analysis of, 172; and Irish, 219–220; online version, 239; quotation paragraphs, 195–212

perceptual dialectology, 18, 20–21
philology, 158–162, 168
Proposition 227 (CA), 291
Pyles, Thomas, 175, 178, 181, 182

reading skills, teaching of, 263–266
received pronunciation (RP), 89, 93
relativism in science, 53–54
research methods, multiple, 78–81

science, differing views of, 53–54
Scottish National Dictionary, 215
SEP (Standard English Proficiency), 286–288
SEE (Standardized Edited English), 305, 308–310, 311
Self-Organizing Maps (SOM), 60–67
Sheridan, Thomas, 90–92, 93
signifyin as communication style, 270–271
Singapore, English language use in, 137–138, 140–141
Smart, Benjamin: on elocution, 92–94, 100–104, 106; relationship with Faraday, 89–90, 100–104; self-description, 88–89
Smitherman, Geneva, 260–261, 265
social status and language attitudes, 22–26
solidarity and language attitudes, 26–30
SOM (Self-Organizing Maps), 60–67
South Korea, English use in, 142
speech attributes, attitudes about, 28–31
Standard English Proficiency (SEP), 286–288
Standardized Edited English (SEE), 305, 308–310, 311
subjectivity in dialect study, 72–76

teachers and teaching: changes needed, 279–280, 295–297; current instruction methods, 279–282, 292–295; grammar, 292–295, 303–305; language attitudes of, 281–282, 295–297; reading, 263–266; responsibilities of, 321–324. *See also* writing, teaching of
technology and language: dictionaries, 239, 246; and History of English Language, 82, 84–85; texting, 320; and wikis, 240–241
Thailand, English use in, 142

United States, language study in: Eastern U.S. dialects, 56f; Michigan residents attitudes, 17, 19, 20–30; New York City residents attitudes, 31–33; Southern U.S. language attitudes, 26–27

Walker, John, 90–92, 93
Watts, Isaac, 91, 94–96
Webster's Third New International Dictionary of the English Language, 169
wife, etymology of: as child, 124–125; and clothing, 119–123; as compound word, 123–124; and genitals, 119–123; as neuter word, 126–127; overview, 109–112, 125–126; representing bond, 127–130; representing marriage, 127–130; and *weave,* 112–118; and *woman,* 119–123
wiki technology, 240–241
Wolfram, Walt, 11, 15, 273
writing, teaching of: African American English, 266, 271–275; dictionaries, 304; genre analysis, 313; and History of English Language, 305–307; research on, 299–301; teaching of, 300–302, 314; using Standardized Edited English, 309–310. *See also* grammar instruction